On Ideology

also by CCCS and published by Hutchinson

Resistance through Rituals
Women Take Issue

On Ideology

Centre for Contemporary Cultural Studies

Hutchinson of London

EDITORIAL CO-ORDINATOR
Bill Schwarz

EDITORIAL GROUP

Dan Coffey
Dan Finn
Neil Grant
Judy Jefferson
Richard Johnson
Roisín McDonough

Gregor McLennan
Victor Molina
Richard Nice
Roy Peters
Chris Smith
Olivia Smith

COVER
Roy Peters

Hutchinson & Co. (Publishers) Ltd
3 Fitzroy Square, London W1P 6JD

London Sydney Melbourne Auckland
Wellington Johannesburg and agencies
throughout the world

First published in 1977 by the Centre for Contemporary Cultural Studies,
University of Birmingham, as its *Working Paper in Cultural
Studies*, no. 10
Published by Hutchinson 1978

© Centre for Contemporary Cultural Studies 1977

Set by Russell Press, Nottingham

Printed in Great Britain by The Anchor Press Ltd
and bound by Wm Brendon & Son Ltd,
both of Tiptree, Essex

ISBN 0 09 134150 7 (cased)
      0 09 134151 5 (paper)

Contents

Introduction

This journal is conceived as a contribution to discussions about the nature and theory of "ideology", mainly within the marxist tradition. The questions raised by the term have been posed and apparently resolved many times: What is its connection with other notions (themselves by no means simple) such as "ideas", "consciousness", "society", etc.? How does it relate to the analysis of social formations, class composition, and political change? These questions are not the prerogative of marxism alone (see Part 1, section 1). Yet it is within a marxist framework that claims for the "scientific" or systematic character of the concept are most often made and assessed. Such contributions as there have been from other traditions, moreover, have been a response to the theoretical and political presence of socialist practice. It is with the advances made, and the problems raised, by historical materialism as the basis of a theory of ideology, that WPCS 10 is concerned.

The first part is explicitly theoretical, comprising expositions and critical readings of several important theorists of "ideology". These papers can be seen as individual pieces of work, each with their own specific object of analysis. Yet it is hoped that this part as a whole offers a relatively coherent and consistent overview of the different theoretical perspectives. The remainder of the journal consists of more particular studies. Here there is no necessary unity of approach, though the application of some of the arguments in Part 1 will be brought to bear on more delimited "cases" of ideology. Part 2 considers the theme in relation to two significant contributions to social-democratic theories and policies: education and "community studies". Part 3 suggests some approaches to the problems raised by the notions of "subjectivity" and "individuality".

In general, we make no claims to be exhaustive or definitive on every aspect or "region" of ideology. There is at present no wholly satisfactory theory of ideology: that can only emerge from a process of theoretical exchanges and, importantly, corroborative concrete analysis. Consequently there are — and must be — absences in a collection of this kind. In particular, there is no account of some of the most *politically* important ideologies of the day: racism, sexism, nationalism, etc. On a more abstract level, one problem implicit but not directly tackled is the extent to which an Althusserian approach to ideology is in conceptual opposition to the more familiar marxist distinction between "real relations" and "phenomenal forms", especially with regard to the problem of "fetishism". In addition, the general questions

5

involved in contrasting ideology with science continue to remain open.

Clearly, however, the advantages which our present theme seems to offer should be outlined. As part of a marxist problematic, a theory of ideology is both a centrally important area of study within the more general category of "cultural studies", yet has a theoretical coherence which the latter manifestly lacks. The history of cultural studies — as the work of our own Centre has made very clear — is one which encompasses not one but a range of theoretical paradigms and traditions, from Weberian *verstehen* analysis, through the various strands of the culture-in-society perspective, to more straightforwardly marxist approaches. "Cultural studies", therefore, designates descriptively a broad field of interests and not a unified body of theory.

In one sense, therefore, the natures of the two concepts — ideology and culture — are not of the kind to demand a theoretical choice between them. The latter includes diverse elements which cross different theoretical terrains only one of which is that of a theory of ideology. Yet it is possible and important to identify theoretical points of departure where they arise without dogmatically claiming that the success of the subsequent theory is guaranteed. If cultural studies as a large and progressive body of work does not preclude the development of a systematic marxism within it, then its necessary methodological generality does not always encourage it — at least *theoretically*.

Specifically, one significant tendency within cultural studies has taken as axiomatic the close, if not causal, relation between ideas, institutions, and societal context. In this conception, ideas and bodies of ideological representations are seen to be fully explained by descriptions of their social conditions of existence. Whilst readily accepting this as an important aspect in the explanation of ideology, we would contend that such an approach fails to account for qualitative — if not logical — differences between the different contents and forms of ideas and practices. A theory of ideology, as a more specific analysis of some areas of "culture", offers the possibility of a deeper knowledge than at present available from the general perspective of cultural studies. In principle at least, it can deliver a more coherent account of either pole of the culture/society couplet, and, in so doing, avoid reducing either term to the "expressive" manifestation of the other. There are, to conclude, no definitive solutions posed in a collective enterprise of this nature. If substantive suggestions arising from the articles provide material for future projects and clearer theorisation, the aim of WPCS 10 will have been achieved.

Gregor McLennan
For Editorial Group

Part I
Theories

The Hinterland of Science: Ideology and the "Sociology of Knowledge"

Stuart Hall

"Ideology" is a term which does not trip lightly off an English tongue. It has stubbornly refused to be "naturalised". English political theory sometimes refers to "ideologies", meaning simply "systematic bodies of ideas". But the concept is largely descriptive — it plays no significant analytic role. Generally, the concept of "ideology" has never been fully absorbed into Anglo-Saxon social theory. In his important collection of essays published in 1949, Robert Merton included two essays on "The Sociology of Knowledge" and on "Karl Mannheim".[1] In his introduction to this section, Merton self-consciously signalled these pieces as marking the "rediscovery" of the concept of ideology for American social science. This "rediscovery" was conducted in the context of a general *contrast* between two radically different styles of thought — the European (where the concept has played a significant role) and the American (where it had up to that point been largely absent). But Merton's opening was not followed by a flood of new studies informed by this concept. What he called "the sociology of knowledge" has, until very recently, remained a minority interest in American empirical social science.

In his labour of rediscovery, Merton openly acknowledged that " In this respect, as in others, Marxism is the storm centre of *wissensociologie* [the sociology of knowledge] . . . we can trace out its formulations primarily in the writings of Marx and Engels." The absence of an interest in the problem of ideology in American sociology thus clearly relates to the absence anywhere in this tradition of thought, until very recently, of any major open confrontation with Marxist concepts. An interesting essay could be written on what concepts did duty, in American social theory, for the absent concept of "ideology": for example, the notion of norms in structural functionalism, and of "values" and the "central value system" in Parsons. Merton's mind had undoubtedly been directed to this absence by the growing body of work in the study of mass communications and public opinion. But the concept of ideology was never rigorously applied to this promising area of work.[2]

Bacon called for a thorough-going investigation and critique of the roots of conventional wisdom — what he called a "criticism of the idols". And Helvetius — a favourite of Marx's — made much of the proposition that "Our ideas are the necessary consequence of the societies in which we live". But most of the recent "overviews" of the concept *ideology* agree that the word itself, in its modern meanings, originated with that group of *savants* in the French Revolution who were entrusted by the Convention of 1795 with the founding of a new centre of revolutionary thought — an enterprise which was located in the newly founded Institut de France.[3] It was to this group that the term "idéologues" was first applied. Their fate constitutes a salutary warning for all ideologues. For a time this group of thinkers constituted the spokesmen for revolutionary ideas — the French Revolution "in thought". Their aim was to realise in practice what they conceived as the "promise" of the Revolution — the freedom of thought and expression. But they were hoisted on the horns of a dilemma which has dogged the concept of "ideology" from its inception. As Lichtheim points out, they were concerned with "ideology" in *two* senses, which were logically incompatible. First, they saw the relation between history and thought — the tide of the Revolution and the "ideas" which expressed it. But they also wanted to advance certain "true" ideas — ideas which would be true whatever historical conjuncture they were located in. They thus compromised — "for the sake of ideas" — with that historical agent who they imagined had the power to make their ideas come true: Napoleon Bonaparte. This was an ill-judged faith. Napoleon took them up in 1799, in the "moment" of Brumaire, in order to win support in the class where the *savants* had greatest influence — the educated middle classes. He even signed his proclamations to the army during the 1798-9 period, "Général en Chef, Membre de l'Institut". But by 1803, in the "moment" of his Concordat with the Church, he abandoned them, deliberately setting out to destroy the Institut's core, the *"classe des sciences morales et politiques,* from which liberal and republican ideas radiated throughout the educational establishment". "The story of Bonaparte's degeneration", Lichtheim concludes, "can be written in terms of his relation with the *ideologues"*.

The interest in ideology did not, however, altogether disappear with the disbanding of this group. Destutt de Tracy inaugurated a "natural history of ideas", treating the history of the contents and evolution of the human mind as a species of zoology — an enterprise whose warrant he claimed to have found in such sources as Locke and Condillac. He called his study *Eléments d'Idéologie* (1801-15). But de Tracy's work was shadowed by the same contradiction as his predecessors'. He wanted to unmask the historicity of ideas — but he also wanted this unmasking to yield a true and universal knowledge of human nature. His "materialist theme" was "crossed by a normative purpose". The contradictory nature of this project revealed its true Enlightenment roots. Even Comte, the direct inheritor of this line of inquiry, did not escape its contradiction. In line with his massive evolutionary schemas, Comte also conceived of a branch of "positive science" which would be devoted to the evolution of the human mind as a "social" process. But he too thought that this study would reveal that the social was subject to "invariable natural laws". Lichtheim describes this as a "chilling thought" which, despite itself, aimed "to sustain reason's faith in itself". What these and other examples from this period suggest is that, from its modern inception, the concept of "ideology" has been shadowed by its "Other" — Truth, Reason, Science.

Whatever else it signals, the concept *ideology* makes a direct reference to the role of *ideas*. It also entails the proposition that ideas are not self-sufficient, that their roots lie elsewhere, that something central about ideas will be revealed if we can discover the nature of the determinacy which *non*-ideas exert over ideas.

The study of "ideology" thus also holds out the promise of a critique of *idealism*, as a way of explaining how ideas arise. However, the difficulty is that, once the study of ideas is placed at the centre of an investigation, an immense theoretical labour is required to prevent such a study *drifting*, willy-nilly, into idealism. This dilemma is clearly revealed in the history of one of the major philosophical currents which has informed the study of ideas and ideologies — the tradition inaugurated by Kant.

Kantianism (with its roots in both Cartesian rationalism and Lockean empiricism) took the abstract Enlightenment notion of "Reason" and subjected it to a thorough-going critique. Kant asserted the primacy of the structures and categories of "mind" over matter. It was "mind" which organized experience into intelligible wholes. Mind "constructed" reality. The trace of Kantianism is to be found in many of the subsequent theories of "ideology"; though — because it was itself a critical idealism — it did not promote a study of the *historical* roots of knowledge. The story is not so straight-forward with Kant's main rival — Hegel, even though Hegel "out-idealised" Kant's reluctant idealism. For it was Hegel's aim to heal the Kantian division of the world into the knowledge *of* things, produced by our mental categories, and "things in themselves", which were radically unknowable. Hegel's method for overcoming this discontinuity was the dialectic. The dialectic proposed a specific conception of the relation between knowledge and the world, between mind and matter, between the Idea and History: the relation of the dialectical supersession of each by the other. Once the Hegelian synthesis had been toppled from its idealist base and inverted — as it was by his radical disciples — it *did* once again produce the problem of the historical roots of knowledge as a theoretical problem. Thus for Feuerbach (who carried through the "inversion" of Hegel in its most radical form) and in the work of the Left Hegelians who followed him, a task of central importance lay in unmasking the human and sensuous roots of *religious* ideas.[4] Feuerbach's work, Marx observed, "consists in resolving the religious world into its secular basis". But

> He overlooks the fact that after completing this work the chief thing remains to be done . . . the secular basis . . . must itself therefore first be understood in its contradiction and then. . . revolutionized in practice.

Here Marx explicitly advanced to a materialist theory of ideology on the back of Feuerbach's inversion of Hegel.

For Hegel, of course, particular knowledges — one-sided knowledge, knowledge at any particular "moment" — were always partial. Analytic Reason could not overcome this limit. But in Dialectical Reason Hegel glimpsed the possibility of a truly universal knowledge. If one "moment" consisted of the objectivation of Mind in History, another "moment" represented the appropriation of History in Mind. Thorough-going idealist as he was, Hegel fixed the final apotheosis in the second of those synthetic leaps — in the disappearance of the "Real" into the "Rational". Then — just like the Revolutionary *savants* before him — he could not resist actually locating this Universal Moment in a particular historical conjuncture. The *savants* chose Napoleon — Hegel chose the Prussian State. This "concretization" served Hegel no better than Napoleon had served the *savants*.

Hegel recognized that concepts were historical: but, he argued, "historical concepts possess true generality because they relate to a universal agent that unfolds through the histories of particular peoples and civilizations". Thus, Marx argued, for Hegel, "conceptual thinking is the real human being . . . the conceptual world as such is thus the only reality, the movement of the categories appears as the real act of production."[6] But the Hegelian system, once "inverted", led to precisely the opposite conclusion: "the real" — what Feuerback called "sensuous human nature"' — is the only motor of history; ideas are simply the projections of the essential human nature and human *praxis* which they reflect. It was from this "inverted dialectic" that Marx proceeded, by a further break, to inaugurate a *historical* materialist theory of ideology. (Though, as we know, his first attempt to do so — *The German Ideology* — still contains traces of the "inversion" he was breaking from, particularly in its undifferentiated notion of "human *praxis*".) It is certainly within this general framework that we must understand Marx's famous assertion that "it is not consciousness which determines being but . . . social being determines consciousness".[7] But the materialist theory of ideology must be understood as a *break* with Hegel's system — not merely as setting Hegel's idealism on its materialist feet; since, as Althusser has shown, the inversion of a system is still the system inverted.[8] For Marx, Feuerbach simply resolved religion into its "human essence". But the point was to "rethink" human essence as "the ensemble of social relations". Thus, the Left Hegelians unmasked the "truly human roots" of religion: Marx unmasked the historical roots of the Left Hegelians. He called this his "settling of accounts" with his "erstwhile philosophic conscience".

The materialist path out of Hegel and Kant was neither the only nor indeed the most dominant residue of this theoretical encounter. In German thought, the problem of ideology is *framed*, for the rest of the century, by a double exposure: caught as Stedman Jones has argued, between the dissolution of the Kantian, and the dissolution of the Hegelian systems.[9] Each leaves its distinctive trace. This circuitous path is not without its surprising short-cuts back to Marxism. We refer here to the line which winds its tortuous way from Hegel through Dilthey, Simmel and Scheler, to Max Weber and the neo-Kantians; and thus to Lukács, Goldmann and Mannheim. The starting point for this line of descent lay in Hegel's conception that, until its final unity with Spirit, Mind was continuously, through the process of the dialectic, *objectivating itself* in palpable forms *in* the world (History). Mind was given what Hegel called "objective form". For a lengthy period, the study of ideology is nothing more nor less than a study of Objective Mind.

Though Hegel was no evolutionist, he was not so far removed from the impulse of the Enlightenment as to be incapable of conceiving this endless dialectic as arranged into distinct stages or epochs: the "age" of Religion, the "age" of Poetry, the "age" of Science — crowned, of course, by the Age of Philosophy. These epochs had a shadowy history sketched within them, though they were in no sense precisely rooted in a historical periodization. Indeed, like much Englightenment thought, they began with what *looked* like a historical moment, but was, in fact, something rather more like the essential moment of genesis of all human history: that is, with the Greeks. It was the neo-Hegelians — Dilthey above all (1833-1911) — who really seized on this notion of Mind objectivating itself through History in a sequence of distinct stages; and who set about constructing both an "objective social psychology" and an "objective history" — a history of the stages of human thought — on its foundations.[10] Ideas, Dilthey argued, could be conceived and *studied* as a series of forms, arranged progressively into stages extending through history. Each stage was characterised by its own "style of thought". The many different objectivations of each period could be studied as a *whole*, because they all reflected a particular "outlook" on the world, a world-vision, a *Weltanschauung*. Distinct *Weltanschauungen* could be identified for each period, for each society. Dilthey's notion was thus easily extended into the idea that each nation or "people" possessed its own distinctive *Weltanschauung* or "Spirit". This idea connected with earlier ideas of the *"Volk"*, stemming from German Romanticism, and fed into subsequent ideas about the peculiar historical character and destiny of each nation or national culture. A central theme in German thought could thus be plotted in terms of the complex history of this definition of "Spirit" *(Geist)*, in its successive manifestations through to its debased coinage by fascist ideology in the 1930s. Marx once accounted for the radical etherialization of this whole tradition in terms of the "over-development" of German theorizing in contrast with the backwardness of its historical and economic development. But the career of the concept of "Spirit" also reflected to a significant degree the complex and tortuous political history of German unification and the "peculiar" form in which Germany emerged as a nation state.

The transformation of the problem of "ideologies" into the study of *Weltanschauungen* constitutes something like the *dominant* tradition in German thought for most of the Nineteenth Century. It displays a complex evolution. It contributes, as we have seen, to the emergence of German nationalism. It fed into the great schools of German "historicism".[11] It nourished — through its attention to "styles of thought" — a distinguished tradition of art history.[12] Its legacy is clearly to be seen in the work of Lukács: in his translation of the Marxist notion of "ideology" as "world-vision", as well as in his use of the concept of *Weltanschauung* to analyse literary texts and periods.[13] Lukács's early works, *The Soul And Its Forms* and the *Theory of the Novel*, are directly Hegelian and Diltheyean in inspiration — especially the former, with its succession of "forms" — epic, lyric poetry, novel. In his later work, Lukács tried to relate particular "world-views" to class outlooks, but the underlying notion of *Weltanschauung* is never liquidated. The concept that each nation has its own distinctive "world-view" is transposed, in *History And Class Consciousness*, into the notion that each *class* has its "objective" world-view. The lingering presence of this concept thus accounts, in part, for the radical historicism of that text (for a fuller account, cf the following section of this journal, on Lukács).

Via the early Lukács, the tradition passes directly to Goldmann. It forms the whole theoretical basis of *The Hidden God* — Goldmann giving it a further Marxist or socio-historical gloss. But many of the same ideas are present, in a not dissimilar form, in the work of Karl Mannheim, and in what has been called Mannheim's "bourgeois Marxism". Mannheim's concern with ideology is, of course, central to his best known work *Ideology and Utopia* — a text in which Mannheim tries out his own resolution to the problem which has dogged this problematic from its inception: if ideas are "historically relative", where can "truth" be found? (Mannheim's answer is in the relatively un-relativistic thought of the detached intelligentsia). But the connections with Dilthey are even more pronounced in Mannheim's earlier studies, for example the essays "Conservative Thought" (treated as a *Weltanschauung)* and "On The Interpretation of *Weltanschauung".*[14] The history of this series of transformations of the elements of the Hegelian system therefore marks out one of the seminal points of confluence between *a certain* kind of Marxism and a *certain kind* of historicism — both deeply coloured by their Hegelian moment of inspiration.

The study of culture as Objective Mind *(Geisteswissenschaft)* and of history as the "objectivations of Spirit" *(Geistesgeschichte)* also entailed a particular *method* of studying them. Human objectivations required their own distinctive "mode of knowledge" different from the objects of the natural world. This method required an act of "understanding" *(Verstehen)* — a reconstruction of embodied meanings through imaginative projection or "empathy". This enabled the successive manifestations of Objective Mind through history, and the "world-views" they expressed, to be grasped as "wholes". Particular manifestations had meaning only in relation to the "wholes" (or totality) which they expressed. Spirit, the essence of history, could thus be seen as this larger pattern or configuration of any epoch, manifested or expressed in each of its forms. The method of studying culture through "interpretation" was called *hermeneutics;* and the procedure of relating parts to whole and whole to parts in an endless process of "double fitting" was described as "the hermeneutic circle".

The debate between hermeneutics and more positivist methods of analysis came to constitute the site of a major theoretical debate — the "struggle over method" — to which the sociologist Max Weber made a major contribution. Weber was not a Diltheyean, though the concept of the "uniqueness" of culture, exemplified in his essays in *The Methodology Of The Social Sciences,* is more than fleetingly inflected by historicist formulations. But he did engage with the hermeneutic tradition when he came to formulate his own definition of social action. The argument turned on the question of whether there were, in fact, two sets of "things" to be studied — the world of Culture (ideas, human actions, Spirit) and the world of Nature: each with its appropriate method of analysis. The cultural world would then require a "historicist hermeneutics", based on the imaginative reconstruction of the structures of past thoughts and actions; while the natural world would be subject to a positivist or causal-analytic mode of explanation. This debate divided the German intellectual world. Marburg became a centre for the stricter Kantian approach to this question. The figures associated with Marburg argued for a radical split between the two areas and the two methods, with primacy of place being given to positivist approaches, as the truly scientific one. Heidelberg was more "historicist" in orientation, and thus more receptive to the work of Dilthey and the anti-positivism of the influential sociologist, Georg Simmel. Windelband and Rickert, against whom Max Weber polemicised in his *Methodology* essays, lectured at Heidelberg. So did their distinguished pupil, the philosopher Emil Lask. The group of young European intellectuals much influenced by Lask included Georg Lukács, whose early work, as we have seen, was steeped in the *Geisteswissenschaft* tradition.

Weber, in his search for an adequate sociological method, also addressed himself to the same problems. He attempted to combine the best in each, while more radical Kantians, like Lask, presented the problem as a stark choice. Thus, in the

Methodology essays, Weber argued that Culture, the product of a historical rather than a natural process, had its own "uniqueness"; the study of it could not be expected to yield universal laws of the kind which, from a positivist perspective, would have made that study properly "scientific". On the other hand, he wanted a more empirical method than that offered by pure hermeneutics. Weber thus settled, methodologically at least, for a compromise position. The building up of heuristic models — ideal types — each of which accentuated a different aspect of a phenomenon (a position which foreshadows Mannheim's *relationism*), was one way of ensuring a more comprehensive, and at the same time more carefully prescribed, view of the phenomenon than a simple empathising with it could offer. So far as explanation was concerned, Weber argued that cultural objects and historical events required *both* hermeneutic (interpretive) *and* causal-historical understanding. The objective conditions producing an event or a cultural objectivation had to be rigorously constructed, so to speak, from the outside, showing where possible how the causal chain produced the "result" under analysis in that particular form, rather than any other. But this same path would also have to be traced "inside" — in terms of the logic of its meanings. Causal-historical explanations, Weber argued, also had to be "adequate at the level of meaning". There are many examples offered by Weber in the course of his argument for this methodological compromise in his *Methodology of the Social Sciences*. But the most important fruit of this Weberian synthesis, from our point of view, is certainly Weber's best known contribution to the substantive analysis of an ideology, *The Protestant Ethic and The Spirit of Capitalism*. Weber explicitly counterposed his attempt to reconstruct the "inner logic" of the relation of Protestantism to the rise of capitalism in Europe against what *he* defined as the one-sidedness of a materialist or Marxist explanation of ideologies. The latter he claimed to understand as a form of economic reductionism. The debate has raged ever since as to whether *The Protestant Ethic* is in fact necessarily contrary to a Marxist theory of ideology. In this study, in typical Weberean manner, both Capitalism and Protestantism are constructed as 'ideal types' — one-sided accentuations. Sometimes Weber appears to be arguing that, of course, Protestantism could be looked at from another angle — a more materialist one: and that that accentuation, too, would reveal its relative truth (though not, as he says Marxism claims, its whole truth). This is not simply a gesture on Weber's part, since his subsequent work on the world religions does examine the religions of Judaism, India and Ancient China in terms of the sociological structures which sustained them. This rather more "sociological" approach — in the traditional sense, of treating religion from the viewpoint of religious institutions — is, of course, no more "Marxist" than his method in *The Protestant Ethic*. Elsewhere, in the latter text, Weber does characterize his work as explictly "anti-Marxist"; and — so far as both method and theoretical emphasis is concerned — this characterization was undoubtedly correct.

The relation of Protestantism to capitalism was not, of itself, a non-Marxist question. Both Marx and Engels pointed to the connection.[15] It became a favourite theme of inquiry in the German historicist school. In England, the work of Tawney and Christopher Hill shows that it is possible to give this question sustained attention without falling into an idealist problematic about the necessary primacy of ideas in history. Indeed, Hill's work suggests that an attention to the crucial role of ideology and religion is a necessary feature of a Marxist analysis of the transition from feudalism to capitalism in the Seventeenth Century. It could even be argued that it was Hill's decsion to treat the religious, ideological and intellectual dimensions of the "English Revolution" seriously in their own terms — and not simply as a simple reflection of economic forces — which saved his work from its earlier tendency to economic reductionism: saved it, that is, not from but *for* Marxism (Marxism is not an economic reductionism, though, in the period of the Second International, Weber could be forgiven for sometimes thinking that it was). To say this is to say something more than that an attention to "ideas" ought to be added to an analysis of economic forces. It is to advance a proposition about the Marxist theory of ideology, properly formulated.

Marxism attempts to understand a social formation as a "complex unity", composed of different levels which exhibit their own "relative autonomy" while being determinate "in the last instance". A particular conjuncture like the Seventeenth Century Revolution is the result of the accumulation of contradictions stemming from each of those levels, and the overdetermination of effects between the relatively autonomous instances. It is precisely in giving to any social formation the full complexity of this articulation, and in not assuming a "given", simple or immediate correspondence between the levels, that Marxism *breaks* with the expressive totality central to — among other traditions of thought — the *Geisteswissenschaft* approach outlined above. The fact that the appearance of the bourgeoisie on the historical stage in the Seventeenth Century took the ideological form of a clash between religious ideologies had — to use a current phrase — *pertinent effects.* The superstructure has its own effectivity, even if Marxism requires us to think it as determined by the economic "in the last instance".[16] Ideologies are not self-sufficient; but in the Marxist theory of ideology, they are not empty and false forms, pure figments of the imagination, either. Otherwise they would not constitute an important area of analysis for Marxism. Anyone who seriously attends to the problems of a Marxist analysis of the Northern Ireland crisis would be hard put to it to say that the articulation of class struggle through religious ideologies is not a pertinent feature. In so far, then, as the study of religious ideology constitutes a real, and not merely an "epiphenomenal", problem for Marxist theory, Weber's work has something of importance on which Marxists can draw. He makes a significant contribution to the analysis of the *internal structuration* of an emergent ideological formation. His radical weakness emerges precisely at the point — a central one for all Marxist theories of ideology — where he is required to show the *articulation between* the ideological instance and other instances. His failure at this point clearly relates to his ideal-typical and nominalist way of defining "capitalism" (essentially, in terms of rationalised and regulated economic activity), and the absence of a theory of class formations in relation to an analysis conducted at the level of the capitalist mode of production.

The detailed argument of *The Protestant Ethic* — which is, by any reckoning an intellectual *tour de force* — cannot be rehearsed here. But some points which bear more generally on the theory of ideology ought nevertheless to be noted:

1. The essay works by means of what Weber calls an "elective affinity" between

16

the structure of Puritan ideas (above all, of the Calvinist variant) and the structure of the *rationalization* of capital accumulation necessary to the development of capitalism. That is, it opposes any notion that economic change *directly* provides the *content* of capitalist ideas. Instead, it suggests that what is important is the "homology" between what capitalism needed in order to become a sanctioned system of regulated economic activity, and the impulse to planned and routinized "activity" in Puritanism. It adds to this a middle, mediating term: the Puritan/capitalist "character structure". It is worth noting that the move from content to "homologies of structures" is the *key* theoretical advance represented in Goldmann's *Hidden God:* and that the attention to "character structure" is an aspect to which both the "Frankfurt School" and Reich were, later, to pay considerable attention.[17] This approach, though radically departing from a Marxist theory of ideology, does not contest Marx's proposition (in *The German Ideology*) that "the ideas of the ruling class are in every epoch the ruling ideas": it suggests, rather, one way in which, historically, this may have come about.

2. Thus, the *Protestant Ethic* suggests one approach to the question of how ideas might work to create in a class that "inner compulsion" to order its actions in certain ways: it points to the "psychological" aspect of ideologies, without falling into an individual psychologism. It also suggests how an ideology may serve to break the hold of traditional ideas and give "new" ideas a compelling force for that class in which they take root.

3. It suggests that, as well as the "logic" which connects ideologies to economic forces — Puritanism to Capitalism — ideologies have their own, complex, internal articulation whose specificity must be accounted for. In this latter respect, Weber's demonstration is startling: for it turns on the paradox that the most secular, materialist of economic systems — capitalism — emerged at the level of ideology, paradoxically, *not* through the gradual erosion and secularization of Catholicism but through the intensified *spiritualization* of Puritanism. It is only much later, when the transformation has been accomplished, that the religious component — what Jameson once called "the vanishing mediator"[18] — can disappear. Thus, though ideology and economic development exhibit, in the long term, the same tendential direction, they are articulated through the *differences,* rather than through the correspondences, in their respective logics. Europe becomes capitalist — at the ideological level — not by moving further from God, but by setting everything, including man's worldly activity, directly under His scrutiny. A theory of the "relative autonomy" of ideology *could*, therefore, be rescued from Weber's work, without doing violence to his argument. It must be added, of course, that this is certainly *not* how Weber himself put it. He did not go on to develop anything approaching a "regional" theory of ideology. In his later studies, he simply inverted the point of view. He drew no general deductions for theory from this *virtuoso* study. In general terms, Weber remained to the end a "methodological individualist". He continued to search for a resolution to the problem of knowledge within the framework of neo-Kantian, not Marxist, theory.

Three other lines of descent from the German tradition we have been examining must be briefly indicated. The first concerns what, earlier, we called certain important short-circuits in the tradition back to Marxism. The paradigm case here is that of Lukács. The most substantive contribution by Lukács to the theory of ideology — that represented by *History and Class Consciousness* — is examined more fully below. But Lukács is important to this part of the story because of his general position at the nexus of two traditions — post-Hegelian idealism and Marxism. Lukács, who is óften treated as the perpetrator of a too simple concept of ideologies — as "world-views" — sometimes also appears as its victim. He fell under the spell of *Geisteswissenschaft* as a gifted intellectual in the heady climate of the Heidelberg "school", as he has himself acknowledged. To escape the lingering strains of positivism he tried to go "further back" — to Hegel himself *(The Young Hegel)*. In order to escape from Hegel he turned to Marx — but the path from one to the other was ineradicable: the absent-presence of Hegel lay across the route Lukács took to Marx, like the sky trail of a vanished aircraft. En route, he passed by way of the German irrationalists — that final revenge which Hegelian metaphysics wreaked on European thought.

"Irrationalism" constitutes the second line of descent. The "struggle over method" had polarised into two main camps — positívism and historicism. But historicism was itself a fusion of many different strands. It included German Romanticism, which had never been fully tamed by the efforts of men like Dilthey to make the study of Objective Mind (the "beyond of Science") orderly, and in its own way, "scientific". Mannheim's study of German "Conservative Thought" brings out clearly its irrationalist roots. And at the end of the century, this impulse surfaced again in European thought — this time in the form of Vitalism. For Nietzsche, who made himself its most forceful spokesman, there was no guiding philosophy or method left at all. There was only the general *debunking* of all ideas, and their savage reduction to the sordid interests masked within their high-flown generalities. "We live", Neitzsche asserted, "only through illusions . . . the the foundations of everything great and alive rest upon illusion. The pathos of truth leads to destruction".[19] Nietzsche believed that the contradiction inside the notion of ideology had at last been dismantled: Reason *was* a ruse: all that was left was the naked power-struggle between illusions, between interests. The most successful illusion was that which evinced the greatest "will to power". We know what Hitler and the skilled masters of illusion who gathered around him in the 1930s did with that idea. They translated Nietzsche's fantasy into reality: they set about constructing a *Götzendämmerung*. When the "Frankfurt School" came, under the circumstances of fully empowered fascism, to examine the problem of "ideology", they therefore had strong reasons to treat it as requiring not much more than the analysis of the mass manipulation of administered "illusions". In their efforts to reconstruct how the Age of Reason had produced, as its result, the Destruction of Reason, Adorno and Horkheimer were forced to look back at the irrationalist element which, they argued, had always been present in the Enlightenment dream: they unearthed what they called "The Dialectic of Enlightenment".[20]

The third line of descent really followed on, not from *Geisteswissenschaft* directly, but from Max Weber's measured response to it. Though, in his *Methodo-*

logy essays, Weber had entered directly into the debate with *Geisteswissenschaft,* in his general sociology he remained, as we have said, a "methodological individualist". This does not mean that he believed all social phenomena could be reduced to the level of concrete historical individuals. He meant that sociological concepts, to be "adequate at the level of meaning", had to be constructed, *heuristically*, in terms of the *typical* actions, meanings and orientations which could be ascribed to *typical* individual actors. Hence his definition of social action was the ascription of typical motivations to an "individual" whose actions were oriented to "the other". All the sociological concepts which followed on from this were necessarily heuristic devices — second-order constructs. One of the key figures who attempted to develop a more rigorously *sociological* approach, from this Weberian synthesis, was Alfred Schutz.[21]

Schutz was a "phenomenologist" who left his native Vienna to work as an assistant to the great phenomenologist, Husserl. Schutz accepted the argument of phenomenology that all that could properly be "known" consisted of the contents and structures of *consciousness*. Whereas Marxism tended to treat consciousness as a realm of "false appearances" (Marx, of course, added *necessary* false appearances), phenomenology took the opposite position. Everything outside of consciousness had to be "bracketed out". Meaning was the product of intention, and consciousness was the domain, *par excellence*, of intentionality. What could be studied was the intentionality of individual consciousnesses — and the interaction between consciousnesses, the realm of *inter-subjectivity*. In its pure form, certainly, phenomenology was a radical retreat into mentalism. Even that "drama" in the world of social action which Weber had tentatively grasped was transposed entirely into consciousness and the interchanges between consciousnesses.

Schutz held firmly to this phenomenological perspective. But he believed that it could be developed and extended into a rigorously "phenomenological *sociology*".[22] The problem was how to account for phenomena in the "real" social world from this phenomenological starting-point. Here, Schutz once more made a stealthy return to the terrain of Objective Mind. The intentionality of consciousness was realized — *objectivated* — in the world through activity. Men then had to live in the structures of meaning which they had objectivated: the meanings inside their heads had "taken form" in the world outside. But these objective "worlds" were not the product alone of the single intentional consciousness, but of the inter-subjective exchanges *between* consciousnesses. Meaning was therefore produced through this reciprocity — the reciprocity or alignment of perspectives. This "reciprocity of perspectives" was the foundation — the common ground — for the reciprocal processes of "meaning establishment" and "meaning interpretation". Its most active basis was face-to-face exchange, where each actor is co-present to the other: where they are "consociates". They share the same perspectives, the same "history", and constantly come to "construct social reality" together. This mutually constructed space constituted the "lived" inter-subjective world. Through the medium — the store-house — of language and sign-systems, these actors could "make active" other domains of existence not actually present to them (through the construction of "typical" constructs). They could also summon up the past. Though the shared ground between "consociates" constituted, for Schutz, the most massively "present ", the most taken-for-granted, sphere of reality, the whole of social and historical life could in fact be theoretically mapped out in terms of these basic processes of meaning construction/meaning interpretation. Since everything that had ever been in the world was the product of intentional inter-subjective consciousness, everything was *meaning*. Thoughts or references to others not present "to consciousness" — whether simply absent, or deriving from the past — as well as "theories" *about* social actions were simply second- or third-order constructs.

Language enabled all the domains not actually present in face-to-face interchange to be preserved, stored, recalled. Constantly repeated or institutionalized actions had the effect of rendering the meanings active in them stable, standardized. The meanings which informed such actions no longer appeared to constitute a domain of meaning at all. Meaning, here, had become standardized, institutionalized, "backgrounded". The "typifying medium *par excellence* . . . is the vocabulary and syntax of everyday life". These constructs, once the product of intending consciousness, but now lodged "in the world", achieved a *facticity* of their own. They became objectivated meanings, capable of acting back upon the subjects who inhabited them, as if from the "outside". The activity (praxis) of meaning-construction which produced them has been lost to consciousness (alienated). They appeared now to impose their meanings, to constrain and rule men, from the outside. As Sartre, who was powerfully influenced by this general paradigm, put it:

> Thus significations come from man and from his project, but they are inscribed everywhere in things and in the order of things. Everything at every instant is always signifying, and significations reveal to us men and relations among men across the structures of our society.[23]

Though the language which Sartre employs here is far removed from the terminology of "phenomenology", and draws as much from the early Marx as it does from Husserl, it inhabits very much the same paradigm: ultimately, for the purposes of this exposition, this is a problematic rooted in what has come to be called the "Subject-Object dialectic". In whatever form it appears, the presence of the Subject-Object dialectic always testifies to the unexorcised "ghost of Hegel".

Schutz argued that the many various objectivations in the world correspond to the different levels or layers of consciousness. Reality was structured into different "regions", each with its appropriate layer of consciousness: the "multiple realities" of play, dream, trance, theatre, theory, ceremony and so on.[24] As one moved from one realm of social reality to another, so each "proposed" its own scheme of interpretation: bringing one mode of consciousness to the fore, and backgrounding the rest. The most sedimented region of reality and of consciousness was that sector of reality which men had to take most for granted, since it formed the basis of their everyday, ordinary actions. This was the realm of "everyday life": and the mode of consciousness appropriate to it was that which was the most taken-for-granted of all the modes: the domain of commonsense. When we operate "in common sense", Schutz argued, we are hardly aware at all that we are operating in a domain of constructed meanings. We simply take it for granted. Schutz proposed that sociology should concern itself, above all, with "the structure of the commonsense world of everyday life".

In the work of Schutz, we see the "sociology of knowledge" taken to its most extreme point. We are no longer concerned with the relation *between* social knowledge and social relations. Social relations are conceived *as*, essentially, structures of knowledge (provided we treat "knowledge" in its widest, everyday sense, and do not confuse it with systematic ideas; with "ideologies" in their more limited sense). Berger and Luckmann, the modern sociologists who, in *The Social Construction of Reality* (1971), have tried to advance this line to its farthest limits, put the point succinctly:

> The social reality of everyday life is thus apprehended in a continuum of typifications . . . Social structure is the sum of these typifications and the recurrent patterns of interactions established by means of them.

It is in *this* form, above all, that the "sociology of knowledge" has come to exert a powerful influence within the dominant traditions of American sociology. The later schools of "symbolic interactionism" and of "ethomethodology" are direct extrapolations from it.[25]

In general, the sociology of knowledge has a complex position in relation to the theory of ideology. Ideas are no longer treated in terms of their historical roots, the classes which subscribe to them, the specific conjunctures in which they arise, their effectivity in winning the consent of the dominated classes to the way the world is defined and understood by the dominant classes. The relation of the ideological instance to other instances in a social formation has been obliterated. Their specific practico-historical function is lost. Ideas have been given a far wider and more inclusive range: they form the background to *every* social process. Indeed, it would be more correct to say that social processes are treated essentially in terms of ideas. They are pre-eminent because *it is through ideas that we construct social reality itself.* There is no objective reality — and hence there can be no "scientific" knowledge of it. There are only the different "takes on reality", lodged in the different perspectives which social actors bring to the world. The area of everyday social interactions only *feels* like a substantial sector of reality, because it is the zone in which the vast majority of individual perspectives overlap.

Thus, whatever insights can be rescued for a Marxist theory of ideology from this tradition, it must be recognised that each is generated by a quite different problematic. Marx wrote *The German Ideology* precisely to show that the historical development of society could not be reconstructed "from what men say, imagine, conceive . . . from men narrated, thought of, imagined, conceived . . ." Phenomenology must assume that there is nothing to historical reality *but* what men say, imagine, conceive . . . (We must add that, if , for Marxism, history does not consist of what men say, imagine, conceive, it is still a problem *for* Marxism to account for why men say, imagine, conceive what they do, where these "thoughts" arise and what is their degree of effectivity. But this is a different problem.) True, for Schutz, the world is not *wholly* reduced to the thoughts in men's heads; for he was concerned with how thoughts gained an objective facticity in the world, and thus, by shaping human actions, affected how reality was constructed. But this partial dislocation of the "pure" phenomenological impulse did not take him back to Marx, nor did it point in that direction. It pointed instead to another — and quite unexpected — convergence: a *rendezvous* of phenomenology with the tradition of positive social science as represented by Durkheim and his "school".

Durkheim's position on this question was misunderstood in his day and has been much misrepresented since.[26] A major factor in this must be attributed to the selective manner in which Durkheim's work has been appropriated (expropriated might be more accurate) into mainstream American empirical social science.[27] Durkheim is regarded as the "father" of positive social science *because* he rejected all the Germanic nonsense about ideas, Mind, Spirit. He consigned "ideas" to a little black box not because they were unimportant but because they could not be analysed. Instead, he determined to treat what *could* be analysed — patterned social interaction governed by norms and channelled by institutional structures. The observable aspects of these had to be treated as if they exhibited the hardness and consistency of objects in the natural world. Hence the famous admonition — to "treat social facts as things".[28] Durkheim did believe that social phenomena had a reality of their own — a reality *sui generis*; and that they must be analysed by rigorous and objective methods of study. In all these senses, he stood four-square within the tradition of French Positivism.

What is usually left out of this account is that those famous "facts" which Durkheim wanted to treat as "things" were social actions *informed by ideas* — or to put it in more positivist language, action governed by rules and norms — rule governed behaviour. It was the constraining effects of the "rules of social life" upon individual actions which made "society" possible for Durkheim — and, at the same time, by making behaviour systematic, constituted it as the possible object of a positive science. Hence Durkheim's concern with method — with things arranged as classifications, with the discovery of "the rule", with the "type" and "rate" of social phenomena. It was because he despaired of the capacity of hermeneutics to give us an adequate knowledge of these things that he turned to the positive method. He was certainly not uninterested in how ideas informed actions. His question was: how do you discover what norms are operating? how weak or strong the norms are (and therefore what the degree of social solidarity is)? how unified or plural, obligatory or optional they are? Rather than ask what was the "intention" concealed in the mind of the individual actor, Durkheim began at the other end: from the codified legal or moral system of ideas. For these were the "collective representations" of social relations, and in them, at least, one could find, in a studiable form, those "rules" which men had thought it worthwhile to embody in the formal system of the Law. In this sense, Durkheimean positivism self-consciously closed itself off from that whole Subject-Object dialectic which Hegel had inaugurated. Positivism chose to start with *already objectivated social reality:* with the facticity which the "rules" of social life had achieved, and their constraining force over action. It treated the "knowable" world as, already, a reification. And, despite the very different routes by which they arrived at this point, it did establish a certain common terrain between Durkheimean positivism and sociological phenomenology.

Despite appearances, then, Durkheim belonged to the neo-Kantian tradition. "Noumenal" reality had to be studied through its forms of appearance — through "phenomenal" reality. Two related concerns served to inflect this neo-Kantian position in rather different directions — leading to what can only be described as "two" Durkheims. The first was a classic concern with the nature, degree and types of social solidarity. He followed earlier theorists here in believing that the bonds of social solidarity had been immensely weakened in societies of individual competition (i.e. capitalist market societies). This weakening was, precisely, to be seen in the loosening of the constraining power of "the rules" over individual behaviour. The condition, typical of such societies, in which actions were insufficiently "ruled" by norms, he called *anomic*. This is the classic terrain of positivist sociology; and to it Durkheim devoted some of his major work, including *The Division of Labour, Suicide* and the *Rules of Sociological Method*. It was *this* Durkheim which American sociology appropriated.

But Durkheim also believed that social integration depended on *normative* integration — or, as Bourdieu has recently put it, that "logical integration is the precondition of moral integration". "Normative" integration depended in turn on the strength or weakness of the norms in society — or what Durkheim called the *conscience collective*. But the source of the norms and rules was *society itself*. Thus logical categories had society as their source of origin. It was "society" — the source of the normative — which made the rules "sacred", and therefore binding: "society" which men worshipped (the central argument of *The Elementary Forms of the Religious Life*).

The seminal text in which Durkheim worked out this part of his theory was that which he wrote with his pupil, Marcel Mauss: *Primitive Classification*. In it Durkheim set out to show how the cognitive categories and mental classifications which "primitives" used to think their world were in fact modelled on social relations. Society did not — as rather crude functionalists assumed —, provide the content of social taxonomies. Rather, Durkheim believed — following Kant — that what society did was to provide the *categories* in which men "thought" their world. Of course, whereas Kant was concerned with the most abstract categories — space, time — Durkheim was concerned essentially with *social* categories. It was this line of thought which provided Durkheim's main inspiration for his French followers and collaborators, and which distinguished the group of the *Année Sociologique* which he gathered around him.[29]

It is hardly surprising, then, that when Lévi-Strauss succeeded to the Chair of Social Anthropology at the College de France, and delivered the inaugural lecture which declared that the centrepiece of Social Anthropology should be the study of "the life of signs at the heart of social life", he was able to defend this enterprise as nothing more nor or less than the resumption of the "forgotten part of the Durkheim-Mauss programme".[30] Lévi-Strauss's "structuralism" was crossed by many paths other than that of Durkheim and his followers. The influences on it included Marx and Freud, Rousseau, the schools of Prague linguistics and Russian formalism to which Jakobson introduced him, and the anthropolgical linguistics of Franz Boas, the great student of American Indian languages. The latter connected him to that strand in American cultural anthropology which had taken up what is called the "Sapir-Whorf" hypothesis — that each culture classifies the world differently, and that the principal inventory of these social taxonomies is to be found in the categories of the native language. One way or another it was *linguistics* which gave structuralism its main thrust, as well as providing it with the "promise" — at last — of a truly "scientific" study of culture. But it was the inheritance from Durkheim and Mauss which enabled Lévi-Strauss so confidently to claim this new orientation

23

for Social Anthropology. Thus Lévi-Strauss's first application of structuralism was made to two classical themes of Social Anthropology: kinship systems (where the relationship between the kin and kinship terminology is crucial) and totemism.[31] French structuralism commenced its work on this classical terrain, before (in *The Savage Mind)* it was applied to a wide range of signifying classifications and, subsequently, to the rich field of myth.

The essential difference lay in the two meanings of the key term, *structure.* By "structure" classical Social Anthropology understood the observable structures — the institutional orders — of a society. In Lévi-Strauss, the term is closer to the "deep structure": it means the underlying system of relations between terms, conceptualised on the model of a language. There was no longer any one-to-one, simple correlation between these two levels — the order of classification and meaning, and the order of "real relations". The two had to be conceived as articulated through some relation other than that of reflection or correspondence, or even simple analogy. Certainly, this approach cut decisively into any notion that in language men "named" simple functional objects in the real world. The gulf separating the two approaches is neatly caught in the following distinction: Malinowski believed that primitive peoples classified certain edibles as totems because they were good (or bad) to eat. Lévi-Strauss's response was that they were arranged within totemic systems "not because they are good to eat but because they are good to think with". In *Tristes Tropiques* Lévi-Strauss claimed geology, psychoanalysis and Marxism as his "three mistresses". Glucksmann is correct when she suggests that this is principally in a *methodolological* sense.[32] What all three had in common with Lévi-Strauss's structuralism was that "All three showed that understanding consists in the reduction of one type of reality to another; that true reality is never the most objective of realities, and that its nature is already apparent in the care which it takes to evade our detection".[33] As Marx once said of the vulgar economists, "it is only the immediate phenomenal *form* of these relations that is expressed in their brains and not their *inner connection.* Incidentally, if the latter were the case, what need would there be of *science?*"[34] The reduction of "immediate observables" to the level of structure therefore constituted for Lévi-Strauss the heart of a scientific method. But it was especially relevant to how thought, ideas, meaning related to or corresponded with the real world. Men's heads, too, were full of "ideas", notions, secondary rationalizations and "explanations" of their actions. These, too, constituted an endlessly open, variable and infinite set of cultural lexicons. Here too, it was necessary to express the variety of observable ideas in terms of the *limit* of their underlying structures, in order to make them amenable to scientific analysis. It was not fortuitous, therefore, that Lévi-Strauss declared his interest as "the savage *mind"*. It was the impulse of "mind" ceaselessly to impose forms on contents which marked the origin of thought, as well as the break between Nature and Culture. In the myriad arrangements which this produced in different cultures, Lévi-Strauss identified the trace of a universal activity, common to the primitive *bricoleur* and the modern engineer alike. This was the activity of *making things mean* the collective, unconscious activity of signification. Just to complete — and confuse — the circle, he called this universal faculty "l'esprit humain".

24

The emergence of structuralism constituted a major development in the analysis of the domain of culture and knowledge. Poole, in his admirable introduction,[35] suggests that the transformation which structuralism marked occurs at that point in the dismantling of the problem of totemism where Lévi-Strauss replaces the classic question, *"What is* totemism?" with the structuralist question, *"How* are totemic phenomena *arranged*?". This represents what some would define as the principal transformation which structuralism as a method effects. It is the shift from contents to *forms* or, as Lévi-Strauss would say, *to structure*. It is through the *arrangement* of its field of significations that the "logic of totemic classification" relates to or, better, articulates the arrangement of things and objects in the world of the Australian primitive. It is in *the forms of the arrangement* — to which the constitution of a structure gives us a privileged entry — that mental and social categories are related. Thus, discussing an important passage in Evans-Pritchard's study of *The Nuer* concerning associations in primitive thought between "birds" and "twins", Lévi-Strauss remarks that "Twins 'are birds', not because they are confused with them or because they look like them but because twins, in relation to other men, are as 'persons of the above' to 'persons of the below'; and, in relation to birds, as 'birds of below' are to 'birds of the above' ".[36] The relation between the two levels is *not* one of direct reference, function, reflection, direct correspondence, or even ressemblance or analogy. It is the internal arrangement of the field of classifications which has been made to "ressemble" the internal classification of the field of natural objects and men. "The resemblance is between these two systems of differences." It is not the "resemblances but the differences which resemble one another".

One could therefore only decipher the rules governing culture and knowledge by examining the internal relations through which these fields were produced. Structuralist linguistics (especially Saussure, but also Jakobson's seminal work on the contrastive features of the phonetic system)[37] was of critical value in helping Lévi-Strauss to develop a *method* for "decoding" their production. The arrangement was an arrangement of things — elements, terms, "bits" — into categories. These composed the classificatory sets or paradigmatic fields into which the elements of a culture were "inventoried". Then you had to know the rules by which certain terms or elements were *selected* from these cultural taxonomies and *combined* with others, to produce any specific cultural "utterance". This was the syntagmatic element of cultural articulation. The basic elementary "move" for structuralism was that which enabled the analyst to express the latter in terms of the former: to transpose a corpus of cultural significations (e.g. myths) into the classifications, the elements and the rules of selection and combination from which they were generated. This was "the structure" for a corpus of myths — many of them not yet told! The many variants of the myth could then be shown to be generated — like the surface-strings of spoken language — from variations and transformations performed *on.the deep structure*. Each variant was constituted by transforming or transposing elements in a given structure. Thus a corpus of myths was nothing but the result (at the surface level of expression) of a structure and its variants. Different "moments" of the myth, produced at different times and in different places, could therefore all be expressed as variant realizations of the structure. In these ways, what appeared as

25

articulated through time (diachronic) could only be scientifically grasped and studied when it had been re-expressed as a "structure and its variations" — that is, with time arrested (synchronically). Saussure had argued that the body of real and potential utterances (*paroles*) were not amenable to scientific study, precisely because they did not constitute a closed field. Only "the social part of language" — what Saussure called *langue* — could be the object of scientific linguistic study. In the same way, for Lévi-Strauss, the endless variety of surface productions of a culture were too amorphous to compose a scientific field of study. That field had first to be subject to the "necessary reduction" to the elements and rules of its structure to become an object of scientific investigation. Thus, in *Totemism,* Lévi-Strauss proposed

> Let us define the phenomenon under study as a relation between two or more terms, real or supposed; construct a table of possible permutations between the terms; take this table itself as the general object of analysis . . .

Culture was organized "like a language": hence it could only be studied on the analogy of structuralist linguistics. This brought structuralism directly to the terrain of classifications and codes: "the analysis of relationships and transformations within symbolic systems". These relationships were *not* those which we experienced but those which we used to "think the world with": *concus,* not *vécus.* The aim of the enterprise thus became, not deciphering the social contents locked up or somehow expressed *in* symbolic forms, or examining the relationship between *what* was conceived and *who* conceived it. Its aim was to decipher the internal articulation: to *crack the code.* This is, without any doubt, the moment of the formation, within the sphere of the study of culture and ideology, of a quite distinctive problematic, based on an altogether different notion of causal relationship between social and mental categories: the moment of inception of what has come to be called "structuralist causality".

The birth of structuralism as a general theory of culture, and of the structuralist method, constitutes something like a "Copernican" revolution in the sociology of knowledge; despite its apparently heterogeneous theoretical supports and antecedents. As intellectual fashion has tended to swing away from Lévi-Strauss's work towards other points in the structuralist field, so the seminal character of its intervention, for all that has followed, has tended to be retrospectively repressed. There are at least three "lines of descent", none of which can be traced here in anything but the most summary fashion, but which must be indicated. The first is the development of a specifically "Marxist structuralism", marked above all by the work of Louis Althusser. This is fully discussed in another contribution to this journal, and will not be further developed here. It is worth, however, noting that Althusser and his collaborator in his major theoretical work (*Reading Capital*), Etienne Balibar, go to considerable lengths in that volume to mark the distinctions between their "Marxist structuralism" and that of Lévi-Strauss. In the subsequent volume, *Essays in Self-Criticism,* Althusser acknowledges a number of theoretical debts — including, most significantly, that to Spinoza: but he continues to give little or no weight to the influence of Lévi-Strauss (the relevant section of "Elements of Self-Criticism" is only five pages). He repeats here what he has elsewhere identified as "the most important demarcation line": Lévi-Strauss tends to "the ideal production of the real as an effect of a combinatory of elements", whereas Althusser and Marx do "speak of the 'combination' of elements in the structure of a mode of production. But this combination is not a formal 'combinatory' ".[38] Althusser and Balibar made this specific point in *Reading Capital*.[39] However, since both theorists have subsequently acknowledged a tendency to "formalism" in that work, the differences between a Marxist and a non-Marxist structuralism — not as they are affirmed but as they appear in the actual exposition — is worth examining again with care.

The second important "line of descent" is constituted by the two applications of the structuralist method to the field of the semiotic: the first most clearly identified with the work of Barthes, the second with that of Lacan and Kristeva. To judge from the *Elements of Semiology* it was principally from Saussure, rather from Lévi-Strauss (that is, from linguistics rather than from anthropology) that Barthes derived the impetus for his work in semiology. Saussure saw the use of all sign-systems as part of the general science of linguistics. Barthes inverted this proposition, declaring that linguistic systems were only one element in a much wider field of sign-systems, the science of which was semiotics. Semiotics was *the* method by means of which the mental and symbolic or signifying systems of a culture could be systematically investigated. But Lévi-Strauss's concern with mapping the inventories of a culture was seminal for Barthes.[40] Unlike Lévi-Strauss, Barthes retained the concept of "ideology" as distinct from the general concept of *culture,* but it was the latter which constituted the proper object of "the science of signs". Ideologies were only the particular "uses" of particular signification systems in a culture, which the dominant classes appropriated for the perpetuation of their dominance. In the subsequent development of semiotics, Barthes is perhaps the outstanding case of the semiotician who continued to be interested in the interface between signifying systems and "fragments of ideologies". On the whole, the dominant tradition in early semiotics was more concerned with identifying the rules by which signification as such took place *at all*. Thus, though semiotics certainly placed on the agenda the possibility of a more systematic and rigorous analysis of specific cultural systems and ideologies, this promise has been largely unfulfilled. Barthes's contribution on "Myth Today"[41] — despite its tentative nature — remains one of the few seminal treatments of the relationship between signification and ideology in what might be called the first phase of Semiotics. The break with this first phase of semiology and with its directly Lévi-Straussean impetus was made by Lacan. Interestingly enough, Lacan's transformation begins with a "re-reading" of Freud from a linguistic standpoint; and the terms of structuralist linguistics continue to provide him with certain key terms in his conceptual repertoire. Lacan's Freud is the Freud of the language of dreams, and the "rules" of the dreamwork — condensation, displacement, etc. : the Freud of *The Interpretation of Dreams* rather than of *The Ego And The Id*. Lacan, too, treats the unconscious as if it were "structured like a language". Lacan's work, and more especially that of his followers, has also returned to a concern with the question of "ideology", though this is not the terrain of ideologies arising from specific historical structures and objectivated in social representations and in public languages, but the "positioning of the subject" *in* ideology, through the mechanisms

27

of the unconscious. (Lacan's work is also discussed more fully later in this volume.)

For both Lévi-Strauss and Barthes, what enables us to make a systematic study of sign systems is the fact that men never cease "to impose forms on contents" — they are constantly "classifying out the universe". But whereas, for Barthes, any particular set of significations is historically located, Lévi-Strauss was more interested in the rules of classification and combination themselves — rules which he regarded as synchronic and trans-historical. The comparison of "primitive" and "sophisticated" classification enabled Lévi-Strauss to show that every culture employs the same basic mechanisms in order to "make things signify". He prefaced *Totemism* with a quotation from Comte to the effect that "The laws of logic which ultimately govern the world of the mind are . . . essentially invariable". True, in the *Savage Mind* he described himself as making a modest contribution to "this theory of superstructures scarcely touched on by Marx".

> Without questioning the undoubted primacy of infrastructures, I believe there is always a mediator between *praxis* and practices, namely the conceptual scheme by the operation of which matter and form are realized as structures.

These are among Lévi-Strauss's most tantalizingly ambiguous formulations. However, the only characterization which Lévi-Strauss has ever accepted without demur was Ricoeur's description of him as a "Kantian without the transcendental imperative" (i.e. without God).[42]

It is difficult to know precisely why it is that this Kantian legacy, in its manifold permutations, has continued so persistently to haunt the theory of ideology. One reading suggests simply that *idealism,* in one form or another, constitutes the dominant bourgeois philosophical tradition (apart from a behavioural empiricism which has never been much concerned with the problem of ideas at all); and materialism is constantly in danger of collapsing back into it. Another reading suggests that some variant of the Kant problematic continues to exert its force over this whole field because of the unoccupied spaces, the under-developed nature, of the materialist theory of ideology. The first proposition is certainly true; but the second is not without its pertinence too.

Ideology is one of the least developed "regions" in marxist theory. And even where it is possible to construct the *site* of ideology, and the general relation of the ideological instance to other instances, the forms and processes specific to this region remain peculiarly ill-defined and underdeveloped. Semiotics has greatly contributed to our understanding of how signification systems work, of how things and relations signify. But — precisely in the hope of constituting a closed field amenable to positive scientific inquiry — it tends to halt its investigation at the frontier where the internal relations of "languages" articulate with social practices and historical structures. The materialist theory of ideology has considerably advanced our understanding of the nature of the economic and socio-historical determinations *on* ideas — but it lacks an adequate theory of *representation,* without which the specificity of the ideological region cannot be constituted.

Bourdieu has recently advanced this criticism again, in his discussion of two ·syntheses.[43] The first synthesis is that accomplished by Lévi-Strauss on ground staked out by Durkheim and others. This takes the *internal relations* of a field of classifications as the object of analysis. This completes one line of thought — the Kantian one. Marxism stresses the *political* functions of symbolic systems: it treats logical relations as relations of power and domination. Ideologies, from this standpoint, "contribute to the real integration of the dominant classes. . . to the fictitious integration of society as a whole, and hence to the demobilization . . . of the dominated classes and the legitimation of the established order by the establishment of distinctions (hierarchies) and the legitimation of these distinctions". This represents for Bourdieu a second synthesis.

Bourdieu suggests that both as they stand are inadequate. The first makes the study of the *internal* relations of a field of classifications self-sufficient — autonomous: whereas the second collapses the symbolic field of ideology *into* the social field of class relations — it is, he says, reductionist. Bourdieu wants to treat the problem in terms of the mutual articulation of two discontinuous fields. Symbolic relations are not disguised metaphors for class relations: but nor are they "merely signifying". It is *because* they do symbolic work of a certain kind, that they can function as the articulation of another field — the field of class relations: and hence also do the work of power and domination.

> It is as structured and structuring instruments of communication and knowledge that "symbolic systems" fulfil their political function as instruments of domination . . . [Thus] the field of ideological positions reproduces the field of social positions *in a transfigured form.* (our italics)[44]

We can see at once Bourdieu's own — third? — synthesis in these formulations: his concern with the "laws" which constitute many different "fields" as distinct, each reproducing other fields, by reproducing itself — reproducing them, that is to say, "in a transfigured form". And this synthesis presents its own order of problems. However there can be no doubt that Bourdieu is trying to "think" the problematic of the second synthesis (the Marxist) while holding to some of the advances made within the problematic of the first (the structuralist). For it is a first principle of structuralist linguistics that a sign cannot signify on its own (only within a field of relations to other terms): but also that it does not signify by referring directly to *an object* in the world. As Bourdieu paraphrases Saussure (and Lévi-Strauss, not to speak of Althusser), meaning arises "in the correspondence between one structure and another (ideological field and social field) or one position and another (within each of these fields) and not between one element and another". When Lévi-Strauss was discussing the relationship between totemic systems and the natural world, he insisted that we could not take any single term of a totemic classification as directly "referencing" an object or animal in Nature. It was the relation of one term to other terms within the system which ressembled — corresponded, in strucutre, to — the relation between one animal and another in the species referred to.

Whether or not we try to develop an adequate Marxist theory of ideology from this point, it seems to be the case that the problem of ideology presents us with a paradigm instance of Marxist theory *as such*: what Althusser has called the necessity — and difficulty — of holding on to "both ends of the chain" at once: the relative autonomy of a region (e.g. ideology) and its "determination in the last instance" (i.e. the determinacy of ideology by other instances, and, in the last

29

instance, by the economic). It is the necessity to hold fast to the latter protocol which has, from time to time, sanctioned a tendency to *collapse* the levels of a special formation — especially, to collapse "ideas" or ideology *into* "the base" (narrowly defined as "the economic"). On the other hand, it is the requirement to explore the difficult terrain of "relative autonomy"(of ideology) which has given the field of ideology its awkward openness. It is through this gap — to borrow a recent metaphor of Althusser's — that the "pup" of semiology continues to "slip between the legs" of a Marxist theory of ideology . . .[45]

FOOTNOTES

1. In *Social Theory and Social Structure* (1968)
2. It is not surprising that it should have been Robert Merton who reintroduced the topic to American sociology, since his own early work was concerned with the social roots of the Scientific Revolution of the Seventeenth Century England". cf "Puritanism, Pietism And Science" and "Science and Economy of Seventeenth Century England".
3. The following account is taken from G. Lichtheim's "The Concept of Ideology", in *The Concept of Ideology and other Essays.* (1974).
4. See, *inter alia, The Young Hegelians and Karl Marx* (1969), by David McLennan, and Karl Lowith's "Hegelian" discussion of these issues in *From Hegel to Nietzsche* (1967).
5. From Marx's "Theses on Feuerbach", in *The German Ideology* (1970).
6. The *1857 Introduction* to the *Grundrisse* (1973).
7. One of the best-known formulations of *The German Ideology.*
8. The metaphor of "inversion" to describe Marx's relation to Hegel is extensively debated by Althusser in *For Marx* (1969).
9. In Stedman-Jones's essay on "The Marxism of The Early Lukács", *New Left Review* 70.
10. Not much of Dilthey is available in English. But cf *Pattern and Meaning in History.* selected with an introduction by Peter Rickman, and the long, patient exposition of his ideas in *The Philosophy Of Wilhelm Dilthey*, by H.A. Hodges (1952).
11. For an outline of this development, cf Carlo Antoni's *From History to Sociology.*
12. The work of the art critic and historian, Riegl, is a good example. But the influence can be traced in both Panofsky and Gombrich. Cf, for example, Gombrich's *In Search of Cultural History* (1969).
13. Lukács re-examines his relation to Hegel in the "Preface To The New Edition" (1967) of *History And Class Consciousness* (1968).
14. Cf Mannheim's *Essays on the Sociology Of Culture* and *Essays On the Sociology of Knowledge.*
15. For example, in Engels's *Peasants War In Germany* (1956), and in "Socialism, Utopian and Scientific" and "Feuerbach and the End of Classical German Philosophy", both in *Marx-Engels Selected Works* (1951).
16. The most illuminating discussion of "determination in the last instance" remains Althusser's "Contradiction And Over-determination" in *For Marx* (op.cit.).
17. The "Frankfurt School" in their (untranslated) *Studies In Authority And The Family* and in T.Adorno *et al., The Authoritarian Personality:* Reich everywhere, but especially in *The Mass Psychology Of Fascism* (1970).
18. F.Jameson in "The Vanishing Mediator: Narrative Structure In Max Weber", *WPCS* 5 (1974).
19. For the position of Nietzsche in this constellation, cf Lichtheim, *op cit.*
20. Adorno and Horkheimer argue this case, especially, in *Dialectic of Enlightenment* (1974)
21. Cf the three volumes of the *Collected Papers* of Schutz (1966).
22. The work of Schutz's which most systematically develops a "phenomenological sociology" from the critique of Max Weber is *The Phenomenology of the Social World.*

23. From J. P. Sartre's *The Problem of Method* (1963), an essay of 1957 subsequently appended as a prefatory paper to Volume I of Sartre's *Critique of Dialectical Reason*. Sartre, who plays Existentialism off against "lazy Marxism" in that essay, sets up Kierkegaard as the "phenomenological pole" of the argument.

24. Cf Schutz's essay on "Multiple Realities", in *Collected Works,* Vol. I.

25. Schutz and Mannheim's "documentary method" are the two major supports in the volume which establishes "Ethnomethodology" as a sociological perspective — H. Garfinkel's *Studies In Ethnomethodology*.

26. Durkheim set about correcting some of the misinterpretations at once: Cf the Second Preface to the *Rules of Sociological Method*.

27. For American sociology, Durkheim's *Division of Labour* provided the basic problematic (the problems of order, social cohesion, consensus), the *Rules of Sociological Method* provided the method, and *Suicide* (read as the correlation of variables) the demonstration. A major simplifcation was involved at each stage. The actual moment of this expropriation is most clearly exemplified in the "work" which Talcott Parsons does on Weber and Durkheim to produce the Parsonian synthesis, in *The Structure of Social Action*.

28. The much-misunderstood injunction of *The Rules of Sociological Method*.

29. That work included Durkheim and Mauss's work on Australian totemism, Mauss's essays on Magic and "The Gift", Hubert and Mauss on Sacrifice, Hertz on the significance of Death and the Right Hand, Granet's seminal analysis of the "mentality" of Ancient China (one of the sources of this concept, later much expanded by the *Annales* school of French historians), Halbwachs on the categories of Memory and the social psychology of social class, Meillet's structural linguistics. Other seminal figures, less directly connected but very considerably influenced by the work of the *Année* school include Lévy Bruhl's studies of Primitive Mentality and, of course, Saussure's structuralist theory of language.

30. In *The Scope Of Anthropology* (1967).

31. The two studies are *The Elementary Structures of Kinship* and *Totemism*. But similar themes are extensively discussed in *The Structural Study of Anthropology* and *The Savage Mind*.

32. Cf Miriam Glucksmann, *Structuralist Analysis in Contemporary Social Thought* (1974).

33. From Lévi-Strauss, *Tristes Tropiques* (1965).

34. Marx to Engels, 27 June 1867. In *Marx-Engels Correspondence* (1955).

35. Roger Poole, "Introduction" to the Pelican edition of *Totemism* (1964).

36. *Totemism,* op.cit.

37. Cf Saussure, *Course In General Linguistics,* (ed. by Bally, etc) (1960), and Jakobson and Halle, *Fundamentals of Language* (1956).

38. Section 3 of "Elements of Self-Criticism" in *Essays In Self-Criticism* (1976).

39. Cf the discussion of the combination/combinatory distinction in *Reading Capital,* pp 215-6 and 226. Also, the first "reply" by Althusser to the charge of "structuralism" in his work: the "Foreword to the Italian Edition", reprinted in the English edition of *Reading Capital* (1970).

40. Cf Barthes's review of Lévi-Strauss's work, "Sociology and Socio-Logic"; English translation, CCCS.(Birmingham, 1967).

41. In *Mythologies* (1972).

42. The "Overture" to the *Raw And The Cooked* (1970).

43. For the English translation of Bourdieu's paper "Symbolic Power", cf *Two Bourdieu Texts,* trans. R. Nice, CCCS Stencilled Papers No. 46. (1977).

44. Bourdieu, *ibid.*

45. The daring metaphor occurs at the end of the "Science and Ideology" section of Althusser's "Elements of Self-Criticism", *Essays in Self-Criticism, op.cit.*

BIBLIOGRAPHY

T. Adorno and M. Horkheimer (1973) *The Dialectic of Enlightenment* Allen Lane, Harmondsworth.

L. Althusser (1969) *For Marx* Allen Lane, Harmondsworth.

L. Althusser and E. Balibar (1970) *Reading Capital* New Left Books, London.

L. Althusser (1976) *Essays In Self-Criticism* New Left Books, London.

C. Antoni (1959) *From History To Sociology* Merlin, London.

R. Barthes (1967) *Elements of Semiology* Cape, London.

R. Barthes (1972) *Mythologies* Cape, London.

P. Berger and T. Luckmann (1971) *The Social Construction of Reality* Penguin. Harmondsworth.

P. Bourdieu "Symbolic Power" CCCS Stencilled Paper No.46 Birmingham.

Destutt de Tracy (1826) *Elements d'Idéolgie* Brussels.

W. Dilthey (1962) *Pattern And Meaning In History* Harper, New York.

E. Durkheim (1964) *The Division of Labour* Routledge and Kegan Paul. London.

E. Durkheim (1964) *The Rules of Sociological Method* Free Press, New York.

E. Durkheim (1952) *Suicide* Routledge and Kegan Paul, London.

E. Durkheim (1961) *The Elementary Forms of the Religious Life* Collier, New York.

E. Durkheim and M. Mauss (1963) *Primitive Classification* Cohen and West, London.

H. Garfinkel (1967) *Studies in Ethnomethodology* Prentice Hall, New Jersey.

M. Glucksmann (1974) *Structuralist Analysis In Contemporary Social Thought* Routledge and Kegan Paul. London.

L. Goldmann (1964) *The Hidden God* Routledge and Kegan Paul, London.

E. Gombrich (1969) *In Search Of Cultural History* Clarendon Press, Oxford.

H. Hodges (1952) *The Philosophy Of Wilhelm Dilthey* Routledge and Kegan Paul, London.

R. Jakobson (1956) *Fundamentals of Language* Mouton, The Hague.

C. Lévi-Strauss (1964) *Totemism* Pelican, Harmondsworth.

C. Lévi-Strauss (1965) *Tristes Tropiques* Athenaeum, New York.

C. Lévi-Strauss (1966) *The Savage Mind* Weidenfeld and Nicholson, London

C. Lévi-Strauss (1967) *The Scope Of Anthropology* Cape, London.

C. Lévi-Strauss (1963) *Structural Anthropology* Basic Books, New York.

C. Levi-Strauss (1970) *The Raw and The Cooked* Cape, London.

G. Lichtheim (1967) *The Concept of Ideology and Other Essays* Vintage, New York.

G. Lichtheim (1970) *Lukács* Fontana, London.

K. Lowith (1967) *From Hegel To Neitzsche* Doubleday Anchor, New York.

K. Marx (1970) *The German Ideology* Lawrence and Wishart, London.

K. Marx (1973) *The Grundrisse* Penguin, Harmondsworth.

K. Mannheim (1936) *Ideology and Utopia,* Routledge and Kegan Paul, London.

K. Mannheim (1952) *Essays In the Sociology of Knowledge* Routledge, Lodon.

K. Mannheim (1954) *Essays In Sociology And Social Psychology* Routledge, London.

R. Merton (1968) *Social Theory And Social Structure* Free Press, New York.

T. Parsons (1968) *The Structure of Social Action* Free Press, New York.

R. Poole (1964) *Introduction* to C. Lévi-Strauss, *Totemism* Pelican, Harmondsworth.

J.-P. Sartre (1963) *The Problem of Method* Methuen, London.

F. de Saussure (1960) *Course in General Linguistics* Peter Owen, London.

A. Schutz (1967) *Collected Papers* Vols 1-3, Nijhoff, The Hague.

A. Schutz (1967) *The Phenomenology Of The Social World* North-Western University Press Illinois.

M. Weber (1949) *Methodology Of The Social Sciences* Free Press, New York.

M. Weber (1930) *The Protestant Ethic And The Spirit Of Capitalism,* Unwin. London.

M. Weber (1966) *The Sociology Of Religion* Methuen London.

Ideology as False Consciousness: Lukács

Roisín McDonough

History and Class Consciousness, it has often been said, owes its continuing relevance to the manner in which Lukács recaptured the Hegelian dimensions of Marx's thought. Indeed, as Lukács himself was to say in later years, the book was "an attempt to out-Hegel Hegel". Yet whatever we may think of such a project and its relevance to Marxism there can be no doubt of the importance and the significant impact of the book, both at the time of its initial publication and more recently with its English translation. It signals a systematic statement and is the *locus classicus* of many of the themes which lie at the heart of an ongoing debate about the nature of Marxism since the demise of the Second International. But the return to Hegel and the Young Marx which is evidenced in Lukács work was no *simple* rediscovery of a lost tradition currently "out of favour" within the then dominant tendency of Marxist theory, but was itself a *re-reading* of that tradition: a re-reading which was deeply imbued with many of the philosophical ideas of the Heidelberg school of thought in Germany which had exerted a strong formative influence on Lukács's own theoretical development. It is to this latter tradition with its own particular intellectual roots that we must return if we are properly to assess the import of *History and Class Consciousness* as a work within the corpus of Marxism.

Gareth Stedman Jones, in his excellent essay on the Marxism of the Early Lukács has noted the absence of a strong tradition of positivist thought in Germany, a feature which was enormously reinforced by the impact of Kantian philosophy, premised on a division of human existence into the 'phenomenal' and the 'noumenal' (man is both a physical body and a spiritual being). In the case of the natural world Kant distinguished between things as they are (in-themselves) which are unknowable and the phenomenal world of appearances subject to causal laws. Correspondingly, man's existence has a similar dual structure: man as a phenomenal being is under the sway of unalterable causal laws, while the other aspect of his existence (the noumenal sphere) is characterised by freedom and self-determination. Thus any knowledge of man as a *social* being could only be achieved through the speculative methods of philosophy. The result of Kant's distinction was radically to separate fact and value, relegating the former to the domain of nature and the latter to the social. Thus all that was specifically human about man — culture, history, philosophy, art, etc. could only be intuited *speculatively* and *holistically* as manifestations of man's human spirit: an analytic atomistic approach was deemed only to be appropriate to the natural sciences which were characterised by the discovery of partial causal laws.

The dominant intellect of the Heidelberg school was Dilthey whose work was characterised, in his later years, by a blend of unorthodox neo-Kantianism and neo-Hegelianism. He believed that genuine historical knowledge was an inward experience of its object, which in turn was comprehensible because history was essentially composed of "objectifications" of the human mind. The study of history disclosed the essential nature of man as it unfolded in the totality of human experience, and the historian entered into the life of the past generations by reliving in his own mind the thoughts and actions whereby men had previously defined themselves. The comprehension of these objectifications of the human spirit was based on a method of systematic interpretation which attempted to lay bare the innate structures of the human psyche. These objectifications of spirit, which in their totality constituted the human world werè accessible for the reason that the contemplative thinker was *himself* an actor in the process in which the universal mind differentiated itself into a multitude of individual minds. *Geisteswissenschaft* (science of spirit) as it was known, differed from *Naturwissenschaft* not only in its method but also its object. The natural sciences operated with a clear-cut distinction between subject and object, mind and matter, while the "science of spirit" was deemed necessarily reflective and introspective and ultimately a quietist philosophy, its topic being the world created by the human spirit. The latter was essentially knowable through an imaginative reconstruction of the relationship between the past as a whole and the particular individual products (of, say, an artist, a poet) which were concrete manifestations of that era. The method of this reconstruction, relating the part to the whole and the whole to the part, was that of hermeneutics.

Lukács's intellectual apprenticeship at Heidelberg, the centre *par excellence* of German anti-positivism brought him into close contact with the sociology of Simmel, who was his teacher, and of Max Weber. Simmel's philosophical beliefs owed a great deal to Dilthey's conception of culture as an objectification of the human mind but had pessimistic implications. Gareth Stedman Jones characterises Simmel's philosophy thus:

> The individual produced objects of culture to extend his life and potentialities. To do this, he had both to utilize the sum total of human products (objective spirit) and further to interiorize and re-integrate them into his own stream of life. But this re-integration of subject and object was unattainable. The objective spirit, in the shape of finished forms, became detached from the stream of life and took on its own dynamic, developing thereafter no longer as means but as ends. Thus man became progressively enslaved by his own products. (*NLR* 70, p.40)

Similar strains are to be found in Weber's sociology of the same period although his variety of neo-Kantianism had more positivistic overtones.[1] His characterisation of capitalism as the bearer of a certain mode of rationality was an important theme that Lukács was to develop later. For Weber, "rationalisation" was the inevitable destiny of Western society since its adoption of Judaeo-Christian religion which had brought in its wake the liberation from magic, tradition and affectivity. The "spirit of capitalism" meant progressive bureaucratisation and the development of instrumental rationality, calculation and control in all spheres of human life.

Lukács wrote *History and Class Consciousness* while still deeply under the influence of the intellectual impact of Weber and Simmel's sociology and Dilthey's philosophy. His key categories of rationalisation and reification, along with his hostility towards the natural sciences — something entirely foreign to all previous Marxist literature — were largely inspired by his colleagues in the Heidelberg school. Yet the book also represented a major reinterpretation of Marxism based on the use of a pre—Marxist system of thought to construct its own theoretical discourse — that of Hegel. Hegel had never been widely studied in the Second International and was in general regarded as a remote and no longer significant precursor of Marx. Lukács radically altered this appraisal of the importance of Hegel and this reassessment was to be a deep and lasting for the whole subsequent tradition of Western Marxism.

Lukács's rejection of the Marxism of the Second International is marked by a theoretical shift away from Marxist economics. More than this, it is an explicit rejection of a deterministic Marxism predicated on economic laws which forecast the collapse of capitalism and the revolutionary action of the working class. Such a mechanical determinism had resulted in political passivity as was evidenced in the political practice of the most important party of the Second International — the German Socialist Party. Lukács's stress on the autonomous, independent and willed action of the proletariat is at the centre of his political writings. Biographically the main period of his own political activity came at a time of the mass upsurge of the European working class — in the period immediately after the war when the soviets were formed in Germany and Hungary, when the Italian workers occupied the factories of Turin and, above all else, in the immediate aftermath of the Russian Revolution. This perhaps helps to account for the somewhat eschatological tone of his writings for those who read him today.

The novelty of Lukács's *History and Class Consciousness* is to be found in his treatment of two key related topics — firstly his conception of the relation between theory and practice (or knowledge and action), and secondly his assessment of science, particularly the natural sciences.

The Relation between Knowledge and Action

As Lukács's self-criticism made clear on a number of occasions, the work was written in the light and on the basis of the Hegelian theory of the identity of subject and object. In his 1967 "Preface to the New Edition" he pinpointed one of its most serious errors:

> It is in Hegel that we first encounter alienation as the fundamental problem of the place of man in the world . . . However, in the term alienation he includes every type of objectification. Thus 'alienation' when taken to its logical conclusion is identical with objectification . . . *History and Class Consciousness* follows Hegel in that it too equates alienation with objectification . . . This fundamental and crude error has certainly contributed to the success enjoyed by *History and Class Consciousness*. (1971 p.xxiii)

The error of the book consisted, therefore, in confusing two ideas: Hegel's conception in which alienation is identified with the objectivity of nature and thus with the externality of being in relation to thought; and the early Marx's conception where by contrast the object is alienated, not in that it is "external", but in that it

35

takes on the socio-historical character of a commodity which does not belong to the producer. This confusion, it has been said, completely shatters the theoretical foundations on which the whole work is based and most crucially it would seem to vanquish any claim of the book to be considered a "Marxist" text. Yet this is too simple a dismissal, for it fails to take into account the originality of Lukács's direct linking of Marxism to the proletariat through his theory of class consciousness and of the party.

The Theory of Class Consciousness

Lukács starts his essay on class consciousness by distinguishing, as Marx does in *The Holy Family,* between a class-for-itself and a class-in-itself.

> The question is not what goal is *envisaged* for the time being by this or that member of the proletariat, or even by the proletariat as a whole. The question is *what is the proletariat* and what course of action will it be forced to take in conformity with its own *nature.* (Marx, quoted in 1971, p.46)

The basis of Lukács' theory of class consciousness is not the empirically given consciousness of individuals or of the class as a whole, but rather what the class can become. Nothing happens in history without a conscious purpose or an intended aim because there is no "hidden force" that lies beyond men, but history paradoxically cannot be understood through the purposes of men. Historical understanding has to go beyond the given consciousness of the actors who participate in the process.

> The many individual wills active in history for the most part produce results quite other than intended — often quite the opposite; *their motives, therefore, in relation to the total result are likewise only of secondary importance.* (Engels, quoted in 1971, p.47)

So Lukács concludes that the essence of scientific Marxism consists in the realisation that the real forces of history are independent of man's (psychological) consciousness of them. Men do indeed make history, but in false consciousness, and in order therefore to understand history we have to understand false consciousness. First of all we have to see its rationality and subjective validity for the actors concerned and secondly we have to see how it is produced and related to the society in which it occurs. Dialectical materialism requires us to investigate this "false consciousness" as an aspect of the historical process, and as a stage in the historical process, rather than simply proclaim its "falsehood". Having achieved this analysis we are then in a position to locate the objective difference between the false consciousness of the actors concerned and the society they claim to understand, and at the same time see why they understand it in the way they do.

From this perspective class consciousness consists then in "the appropriate and rational reactions 'imputed' to a particular typical position in the process of production". (1971 p.51) In other words class consciousness (as opposed to given consciousness) is the most rational and appropriate understanding that is open to a particular class. The crucial question is, given that for a class to be ripe for hegemony it must be able to organize the whole of society in accordance with its interests, which class possesses this capacity at the decisive moment? For Lukács there is a double distinc-

36

tion here — between capitalist and pre-capitalist society and between the bourgeoisie and the proletariat within capitalist society.

In feudalism class interests are not fully articulated with the economy because there are large sectors of the economy which are much more self-sufficient and less closely interrelated than in capitalism (e.g. the semi-autonomous mediaeval village). Furthermore, in accordance with this looser economic structure, the political and legal institutions have different functions from those exercised in capitalism. Under capitalism,

> these institutions merely imply the stabilisation of purely economic forces so that . . . they frequently adapt themselves to changed economic structures without changing themselves in form or content (1971 p.57)

whereas in feudal society legal institutions intervene substantively in the interplay of economic forces: economic and legal categories are so interconnected as to be inseparable. This of course is not to deny that there is a real economic foundation to feudalism, but for Lukács the "content" of these economic relationships is obfuscated by their juridical "form", that is feudal society is largely organized on the basis of estates which have certain *legal* rights and privileges. This has important consequences for the potential development of class consciousness. Classes in feudalism can only be located by a post facto analysis based on the methods of historical materialism: they are not present in the understanding of the individual actors, because economic factors are "concealed" behind the ideological forms which overlay them in the guise of religion. Thus

> there is therefore no possible position within such a society from which the economic basis of all social relationships could be made conscious. (ibid)

In capitalism, with the abolition of the feudal estates and the creation of a society with a purely economic articulation, class consciousness has arrived at the point where it can become conscious: economic factors are no longer hidden behind the consciousness of the actors but are present *in* consciousness itself (albeit in a repressed way). This means that knowledge of history only becomes possible with the advent of capitalism because only with capitalism does the economic class interest emerge in all its starkness as the motor of history.

Yet such knowledge is not uniformly possible within capitalism either. In capitalism there are only two pure classes, strictly speaking, only two classes which are able to organise society in accordance with their own interests — the bourgeoisie and the proletariat. The petit-bourgeoisie, for example, cannot be a hegemonic class because it is impossible to see how the society could be organized in consonance with its class interests as this would entail the reorganisation of modern capitalist production into one based on small independent craft and farming methods. Such "intermediary" or transitional classes like the peasantry or the petit-bourgeoisie are doomed to ideological incoherence; from their position, the entire society can neither be understood nor organized.

The bourgeoisie, on the other hand, as the class that dominates society where for the first time the economy has penetrated the whole of society, must inevitably attempt to understand the society in which it lives. Yet the tragedy of the bourgeoisie is that its supremacy is accompanied by the development of a challenge to this supremacy, from its very incipience, in the form of the proletariat. The bourgeoisie can be said to have a class consciousness, but

> one which is cursed by its very nature with the tragic fate of developing an insoluble contradiction at the very zenith of its powers. As a result of this contradiction it must annihilate itself. (p.61)

Essentially this contradiction is a direct consequence of the bourgeoisie's position in the productive process, and not merely a reflection of its inability to grasp the contradictions inherent in its own social order. In theory the bourgeoisie should be able to possess an "imputed" class consciousness of the whole system of production given that one of the major characteristics of capitalism is its total economic penetration of society; yet it is unable to do so because of the contradictions and antagonisms inherent within that system of production, namely between the socialisation of production and its private appropriation. This is reflected within the bourgeoisie's own consciousness. On the one hand the capitalist sees himself as being subordinated to impersonal economic forces which he cannot control, and on the other he is an isolated economic actor. This dichotomy is apparent in the antimony present within bourgeois social thought, an oscillation between comprehension of society in terms of a thoroughgoing individualism and as a totality governed by powerful natural laws.

The struggle of the bourgeoisie in its attempts to achieve hegemonic domination is accompanied by its efforts to develop a coherent theory of economics, politics and society, and also to make conscious and sustain its faith in its own mission to control and organize society. Yet

> the tragic dialectics of the bourgeoisie can be seen in the fact that it is not only desirable but essential for it to clarify its own class interests on *every particular issue,* while at the same time such a clear awareness becomes fatal when it is extended to *the question of the totality.* (1971 p.65)

While the bourgeoisie dominates the whole of society, this domination is exercised by a minority in the interests of that minority, and the condition for its continued existence is that both the proletariat and the bourgeoisie should remain mystified as to such exploitation. The bourgeoisie cannot comprehend the internal, insoluble contradictions of a system based on exploitation which serves their interests, for in doing so it would necessarily have to abandon its own class position and recognise that it was a historically limited ruling class. The limits of the bourgeoisie's knowledge and consciousness, then, are ultimately constrained by the objective limits of capitalist production and for the bourgeoisie to recognise this would mean self-annihilation. Lukács commented that

> When the Communist Manifesto makes the point that the bourgeoisie produces its own gravediggers this is valid ideologically as well as economically.

The Proletariat as the Bearers of Truth

For Lukács the entry of the proletariat into history signals the potentiality of true unalienated self-conscious knowledge; for the first time man can become conscious of himself as a social being, both the subject and the object of the historical process. Such an eventuality was impossible in pre-capitalist society because social relations were interpreted as natural relations. The bourgeoisie had "socialized" society but performed this task unconsciously, since its class consciousness was incompatible with its class interests, i.e., there was a contradiction between the socialization of production and its private appropriation in the interests of the individual entrepreneur. This antinomy was reflected within bourgeois philosophy in the reified contemplative dualism of subject and object. The birth of the proletariat as a class ripe for hegemony transcends this reified dualism: thought and reality stand in a unified, harmonious relationship with each other, subject and object become one since for the proletariat to make history it must do so consciously.

> Only when a historical situation has arisen in which a class must understand society if it is to assert itself; only when the fact that a class understands itself means that it understands society as a whole and when, in consequence, the class becomes both the subject and the object of knowledge: in short, only when these conditions are all satisfied will the unity of theory and practice, the precondition of the revolutionary function of the theory, become possible. (pp.2-3)

Because the proletariat is the most totally alienated class in society, it must abolish itself in order to achieve its own liberation and doing this it necessarily liberates the rest of humanity. To understand itself, it must also understand the whole of society, and this understanding entails a move from mere contemplation to praxis.

> The unity of theory and practice is only the reverse side of the social and historical position of the proletariat . . . at one and the same time the subject and object of its own knowledge. (p.20)

Thus for Lukács understanding and knowledge per se involve a transformation of one's objective situation. Knowledge is synonymous with the possibility of taking over the leadership of society.

Of course the actual consciousness of the proletariat may not coincide with its "ascribed" consciousness. The proletariat is contaminated with elements of bourgeois reified consciousness, as is evident in its separation of the economic struggle from the political one. Unlike all other social classes that have existed historically, in which the antagonism between their class interests and those of society set an external limit to their consciousness, the proletariat's class consciousness is not constrained in the same fashion.

> For the class consciousness of the proletariat, the dialectical relationship between immediate interests and objective impact on the whole of society is located *in the consciousness of the proletariat itself.* It does not work itself out as a purely objective process quite apart from all (imputed) consciousness — as was the case with all classes hitherto. Thus the revolutionary victory of the proletariat does not imply, as with former classes, *the immediate realisation of the socially given existence of the class,* but, as the young Marx saw and defined, *its self annihilation.* (p.71)

Even in its "false" consciousness the proletariat always aspires towards truth. It cannot abdicate its mission. The only question is how much it has to suffer before it achieves ideological maturity, before it acquires a true understanding of its class situation and a true class consciousness.

The Historicist Conception of Ideology
Lukács' conception of ideology has often been termed historicist by both Althusser

and Poulantzas; indeed Lukács' particular brand of Marxism as a whole is open to such a charge, but nowhere is this more evident than in his theory of class consciousness and ideology.

Marx's thesis that the dominant ideology in any society is the ideology of the ruling class is interpreted as the saturation of the social whole by the ideological essence of a pure class-subject, which in turn is depicted as a pure reflection of the conditions of life and world conceptions of that class. Each class-subject possesses a conception of the world in which it lives and this dominates the historical epoch in which it rules. More than this, it not only dominates but also *permeates* the whole of the society, except, that is, for those untouched, hidden pockets of "ascribed" or revolutionary class consciousness which are the harbinger of a new kind of society. There are only two possible forms of consciousness for Lukács within capitalist society, that of the ruling class and "ascribed" or revolutionary class consciousness; for there are only two fundamental classes — the bourgeoisie and the proletariat — each of whom has a world view which it must express and attempt to make hegemonic. The other "intermediary" classes such as the peasantry or urban petty producers are consigned to ideological confusion and silence; theirs is a nonexistent consciousness. Thus Lukács writes of the peasantry and petit-bourgeoisie:

> We cannot really speak of class consciousness in the case of these classes (if, indeed, we can even speak of them as classes in the strict Marxist sense of the term). . . . Consciousness and self-interest . . . are *mutually compatible* in this instance. And as class consciousness was defined in terms of the problems of imputing class interests the failure of their class consciousness to develop in the immediately given historical reality becomes comprehensible philosophically. (p.61)

There is therefore no theoretical or political space in Lukács' analysis for the possibility of the proletariat making cross-class alliances with those classes that are its allies rather than its enemies — a possibility which would preclude any simple dichotomy of a consciousness which is either a ruling-class one or an "ascribed" one. Proletarian class consciousness seen in this light is not merely contaminated by bourgeois ideology or simply revolutionary, but *even* and *impure,* often deeply imbued not only with the differing ideologies of the different classes, but also shaped by the internal fracturings of these classes. Such a complex constitution of ideology is something that Gramsci tried to capture in his concept of 'corporate' and 'hegemonic' proletarian ideologies. Instead Lukács *either simply* elevates the proletariat to the achievement of a true class consciousness (the culmination of its historic mission) *or else* condemns it to remain within the confines of false consiousness, forever a prisoner of the reified structure of prevailing bourgeois thought.

What then is the underlying force that enables the proletariat to achieve this "ascribed" consciousness? For all Lukács' condemnations of the Marxism of the Second International, his answer is disconcertingly similar. The emergence of revolutionary consciousness is ultimately predicated upon a theory of the inevitability of capitalist economic crises which propel the proletariat into fulfilling its historical task.

> *The further the economic crisis of capitalism advances,* the more clearly this unity in the economic process becomes *comprehensible in practice.* It was there, of course, in so-called periods of normality, too, and was therefore visible from the class standpoint of the prole-

tariat, but the gap between appearance and reality was too great for that unity to have any practical consequences for proletarian action. (p.75; first phrase, my emphasis)

In conclusion, then, because Lukács sees ideology as essentially a manifestation or emanation of the reification of commodities (which are all-pervading in advanced capitalist society), and therefore wholly determined in a *reflectionist* manner by the economy writ large, he is unable to account for the transmission of ideology through various sets of institutions and practices each with their own specificity and internal contradictions. Ideology merely saturates. Because it is seen as an organic expression of the ideas of particular class-subjects and not as an objective systematised representation of social relations embodied in real material institutions and practices, his political solution necessarily becomes one of spontaneism. The inner logic of the proletariat's contradictory class situation will lead it inexorably to throw off the shackles of its exploitation.

Another aspect of Lukács' historicism is the conception of history implicit in his theory. It is seen as one all-embracing teleological process, in which the historical subject realises its self-positing end. This subject is no longer Hegel's Idea, but the proletariat. Since the latter is the most totally alienated class in society it must abolish itself to achieve its own liberation and in doing this it also accomplishes the liberation of the whole of humanity since the proletariat is the *universal* subject, that is, both subject and object incarnate. Thus the dualism of classical philosophy is overcome historically and politically with the birth of the proletariat — the universal subject is objectified and reification is transcended in a synthesis of subject and object History is but the progressive realisation of this hitherto unattainable unity. It is the process of the philosophical realisation of the identity between subject and object, thought and being, attained self-consciously. Finally this consciousness is itself seen as a practice which *ipso facto* alters its object: consciousness is the subjective interiorisation of its object. In other words, the proletariat's accession to true knowledge necessarily entails a change in the existing state of affairs, a modification in its class situation. Knowledge and action, theory and praxis are conflated. The identification of consciousness with class practice(s) rests on a much wider confusion of ideology with *power,* since ideology is conceived in terms of its domination or saturation of the social whole. Thus the bourgeoisie rules and organises the social totality through the permeation of it by its own reified consciousness, and the proletariat's self-consciousness challenge to bourgeois knowledge transforms society through a dialectical comprehension of the nature of the social totality.

The coercive measures taken by society . . . are often hard and brutally materialistic, but *the strength of every society is in the last resort a spiritual strength.* And from this we can only be liberated by knowledge. (p.262)

Hostility towards the Natural Sciences

The question that raises itself is why is bourgeois knowledge inevitably reified and fragmented, based on an inadequate understanding of the social totality, and why therefore is the proletariat's any less so?

Lukács' epistemological justification for such assertions are posited on a form of extreme relativism which reduces scientific knowledge to a mere ideological expression of a class who are the "bearers" of it. Thus in capitalist society science and in particular the natural sciences are regarded as the ideological weapons of the bourgeoisie. Such a conclusion is based on a particular analysis of the nature of capitalism, which goes as follows.

In capitalism the commodity form has permeated the whole of the economy and indeed the whole of society. For the first time all use values have an exchange value, that is, they are exchanged against each other on the market. This requires that labour, like all other commodities, has an exchange value. When all production occurs for the market and thus for exchange, relationships between men take on the appearance of relationships between things. Reification then is not just an illusion or unawareness of the human createdness of society, but has its own objective roots in the way in which society is organised. In capitalism labour is "abstract" in that it can be measured and compared against seemingly qualitatively different kinds of labour. Such a measurement of labour in increasing exactness involves its increasing rationalisation, its ever greater division and fragmentation into smaller tasks, since this is the only way in which the results can be predicted with exactitude and precision. This fragmentation of the work process deriving from the need for increased calculability is accompanied by a fragmentation of the product — at each stage it is a commodity which is moved around in time and space in accordance with its character as a commodity rather than a use-value. The worker too experiences this fragmentation. He finds the work process pre-existing him when he enters production: it is not a process that he is able to shape or determine in any way. "He has to conform to its laws whether he likes it or not" (p.89). This for Lukács means workers' activity in production becomes increasingly contemplative. While his human capacities are alienated from him, his labour becomes a quality which stands over and above him: time becomes space:

> Time sheds its qualitative, variable, flowing nature; it freezes into an exactly delimited, quantifiable continuum filled with quantifiable 'things' (the reified, mechanically objectified 'performance' of the worker wholly separated from his total human personality): in short, it becomes space. (p.90)

The principle of rationality and calculability thus reaches ever further into human life, yet at the same time becomes a power that stands over and above men. We thus come to the paradox that while capitalism is a mode of production that continually revolutionises itself, this production faces the producers as something fixed and beyond their control. Nowhere is this fragmentation and reification more evident than in the type of rationality exhibited by the sciences, especially those social sciences which are based on the methods employed by the natural sciences, i.e. the methods of positivism. Because a science such as economics, for example, investigates only the appearance of the economy as it presents itself to the science, and on the basis of such an appearance attempts to produce laws enabling prediction, it becomes an ever more tightly enclosed system which is unable to grasp its own subject matter. Science therefore stands in an external relationship to that which it is investigating, parallel to the contemplative attitude of the worker to his own work process. Since science takes its data as given and as a result cannot account for how *either* the science *or* its subject matter is produced, it follows that such fragmented sciences cannot be the basis for an understanding of the nature of the social totality merely by adding them all together. Thus the inability of bourgeois science to grasp bourgeois reality is not simply due to the "bias" of the bourgeoisie's standpoint, but is a result of the epistemological nature of bourgeois science itself. But alongside such a condemnation of the bourgeois sciences there exists a strong tendency in Lukács to identify *all* science with bourgeois science *tout court* and perhaps most heretically of all a denial of the claim of historical materialism to be scientific, or of the necessity of producing any partial empirical truths at all as part of its scientificity.

Thus at the beginning of the book he seriously declares

> Let us assume for the sake of argument that recent research had disproved once and for all every one of Marx's individual theses. Even if this were to be proved, every serious 'orthodox' Marxist would still be able to accept all such modern findings without reservation and hence dismiss all of Marx's theses *in toto* — without having to renounce his orthodoxy for a single moment . . . Orthodoxy refers exclusively to *method.* (p.1)

Marxism is thus reduced to a method: the method is that of the dialectic which stands in opposition to the partial, reified laws that are the outcome of the positivist method employed by bourgeois science. These are replaced by the totalizing method of the dialectic.

It must be clear therefore that any attempt to make Marxism scientific in the sense understood by positivist science is misplaced and Lukács criticizes the Marxism of the Second International for precisely this error, but in doing so he fails to distinguish between what have been termed "scientific ideologies" (based on positivistic methods), which had indeed been appropriated under the guise of Marxism when he wrote his book, and other alternative conceptions of the scientificity of historical materialism. This failure leads him to the position of condemning science as such. It also leads him to the reduction of Marxism to the theory of the self-knowledge of the proletariat.

> Historical materialism grows out of the "immediate, natural" life-principle of the proletariat; it means the acquisition of total knowledge of reality from this one viewpoint

and later,

> the essence of the method of historical materialism is inseparable from the 'practical' and 'critical' activity of the proletariat. (p.292)

It is here that the most obvious problem with Lukács' whole approach becomes evident. His argument that all knowledge is socially and historically determined is extended to include the total identification of Marxism with the theory of the proletariat (seen as its own self-knowledge which by definition results in the attainment of true revolutionary class consciousness and action). In other words his theory is essentially a speculative *tautology* which is unable to account theoretically for the empirical absence of an insurgent working class. The proletariat is seen as the revolutionary class which can transform society because its theory or understanding is based on Marxism: but how do we know that the proletariat is the revolutionary class? Because of Marxist theory . . . .

Thus it seems that the epistemological validity of Marxism and its claim to be a science are dependent upon the existence of a politically active working class. Once this is no longer identifiable the adequacy of Marxism as a science rather than as just a "philosophy of praxis" becomes inexplicable.

BIBLIOGRAPHY

Lukács, G., *History and Class Consciousness,* Merlin Press, London 1971.
Colleti, L., *Marxism and Hegel,* NLB 1973
Lichtheim, G., Lukács, Fontana Modern Masters, London 1970
Stedman Jones, G. "Marxism of the Early Lukács", NLR and 70.
Hirst, P.Q. *Social Evolution and Sociological Categories,* Allen and Unwin, 1976.

FOOTNOTE

1. See P.Q. Hirst, *Social Evolution and Sociological Categories,* where he argues that Weber's brand of neo-Kantianism had positivistic tendencies in the sense that Weber unified a "cultural scientific" conception of historical/social knowledge with a positivist conception of the nature and methods of empirical knowledge. This is particularly evident in his insistence on the separation of statements of fact and valuations and his attempt to study values "objectively" and to subject propositions made about them to criteria of empirical truth. "The Weberian object of knowledge has a dual character. It consists of phenomena given to experience ('facts') which are constituted as the coherent object of knowledge by values. 'Real' phenomena are isolated analytically as the object of a specific knowledge: the means of isolation of those phenomena from the 'infinite multiplicity' is their relevance to certain cultural values. *Values* define the analytically separate unity of the phenomena to be studied." Finally, "knowledge is constrained by values which are supposed to exist prior to it and which determine its content, and by a given field of phenomena it cannot question or alter."

Politics and Ideology: Gramsci

Stuart Hall, Bob Lumley, Gregor McLennan

1. Introduction

There is no systematic theory of ideology in the work of Antonio Gramsci, though
it is certainly true that there are many extremely suggestive passages and comments.
It is only possible to produce a reasonably coherent account of these many and
varied insights to the question providing we call to mind the densely interwoven
character of Gramsci's major concepts. The task of theoretical abstraction should
not be allowed to mask that hallmark of his thought. The first section of this
paper will therefore be an outline of the Gramscian problematic, a problematic
which, it will be argued, is geared primarily towards political perspectives and analyses
rather than general epistemological principles. Concrete, historically specific study is
of the highest importance in Gramsci's writings. With respect to our present topic,
the basis of such specificity is indicated by Gramsci's injunction that ideology should
be studied as a *superstructure.*[1] Now the latter task cannot be undertaken outside
an understanding of a Gramscian approach to the structure/superstructure complex,
the basis of which is formed by the concepts of *hegemony, civil society, the State,
the party,* and the *intellectuals.* Without these concepts, ideology as Gramsci might
have conceived it could not be "thought" at all: it occupies its extremely important
position only if subordinated to the political conceptions around which Gramsci's
thinking is oriented.

We have suggested that those who seek a "philosophy" in Gramsci will be dis-
appointed. Yet it is well known that he speaks of marxism as the "philosophy of
praxis", and devotes the last third of the *Prison Notebooks* to philosophical questions. This apparently strange juxtaposition of claims is based on an assessment of
Gramsci's so-called "historicist" tendencies, and the general problem of historicism
will be approached in later sections through a specific analysis of the way in which
Gramsci is appropriated by Louis Althusser and Nicos Poulantzas. Their "structuralist" perspective seems to offer an epistemological position in opposition to Gramsci's
more "organicist" moments, yet it is clear that they acknowledge the latter to be a
theoretical figure of a quite different stature from the much-maligned doyen of
historicism, Georg Lukács. Yet another contradiction, it seems.

We will argue that, particularly in the case of Poulantzas, these writers are less
than open about a substantive debt to Gramsci for concepts central to their own

theoretical projects. We will also suggest that the problem of historicism in Gramsci is in no sense a clear-cut issue. It is certainly true that in some of his *philosophical* generalisations Gramsci tends to reduce or imply a reduction of ideologies as "conceptions of life" to fundamental classes which are organically linked to some long-term historical goal. It is also plausible to say that Gramsci tends to relativise the criteria of theoretical validity to their historical conditions of approval.

These "fallacies" seem to fulfil the main charges levelled against historicism by Althusser and Poulantzas. Yet Gramsci's unrivalled sense of the *material* forms and production of ideology and political struggle, the anti-psychologistic stricture that ideology is an epistemological and structural matter,[2] and the lasting value of his own specific concepts (at the very least as they occur in their "practical" state): these realities ensure the complexity, the partial nature of Gramsci's historicism. If, in addition, it can be shown that Gramsci's concepts lie behind some of the main points of the Althusserians' analyses, a useful anti-reductionist task will have been achieved. In this sense we hope to help re-establish the seminal character of Gramsci's central ideas. That said, we make no claim that Gramsci offers us a rigorous theory of ideology, or indeed of anything else. In particular, the whole question of marxism as a science (or an ideology), and the delicate issue of Gramsci's relevance to communist strategy in Western Europe today, to state but two pressing theoretical and political problems, remain open and urgent.

II The Conceptual Matrix of the Prison Notebooks

In the *Prison Notebooks,* Gramsci rarely uses the term ideology itself, but rather a range of terms that serve, more or less, as equivalents — "philosophies", "conceptions of the world", "systems of thought" and forms of consciousness. He also employs notions such as "common sense", which though not equivalent to ideologies refer to their substrata. These terms have distinct applications and frames of reference, from the all-inclusive Weltanschauung to the very particular form of consciousness. Gramsci's complex conception of ideology has to be reconstructed out of these, and it has to be placed in the whole field of concepts that he uses to analyse the social formation. It is precisely here that he makes his major contribution to marxist theory through his introduction of concepts like "hegemony", and "organic intellectual", and his reconceptualisation of others, particularly "State" and "civil society". Ideology is given a new significance in his writings as a "material force" in history, far removed from the 2nd Internationalist theory of ideology as a simple reflection of the economic base, but at the same time Gramsci explores the specific forms of the organisation and propagation of ideology and culture as an aspect of the class struggle.

Structure and Superstructure

The starting point for Gramsci's exploration is given for him by the fundamental marxist model of structure and superstructure. In his writings, the structure, the "world of economy", is always present; its movements set parameters for the developments in the superstructure, but it is only the "mainspring of history in the last instance".[3] Gramsci's analyses of the relationship of structure and superstructure owe little to marxist political economy. His debt is to Marx, the historian of the *18th Brumaire,* rather than to the Marx of *Capital.* Gramsci uses terms of "historico-political analysis", such as "historical bloc" and "organic" and "conjunctural" movements. However, they do not refer simply to the superstructural level. The "historical bloc", for example, refers both to the structure in which classes are constituted at the economic level (on this basis Gramsci distinguishes between "fundamental" classes and class fractions), and to the political level in which classes and class fractions combine.[4] Similarly Gramsci uses "organic" and "conjunctural" to distinguish movements in the superstructure according to the degree to which they have a basis in the transformation and reorganisation of the mode of production.[5]

It is often said that Gramsci inquires into the formation of the superstructures alone, and gives entirely politico-cultural analyses of history.[6] Whilst it is true in terms of emphasis, Gramsci's project is to break with both the culturalist/idealist tradition represented by Croce, and with the economic determinism of the 2nd International. A series of concepts employed in the *Prison Notebooks* cut across the simple topographical model of base and superstructure (e.g. historical bloc, hegemony), and open the way to an understanding of the complex articulations of the social formation. One of the key concepts is "civil society".

Civil society is a difficult concept to pin down, and Gramsci is more than usually elusive in his use of it. For example, in a section on intellectuals, civil society is called a "level of superstructure",[7] whilst in a number of other instances the term refers also to the structure.[8] The English translators of the *Notebooks* admit to some bewilderment over Gramsci's diverse usages.[9] A useful way of understanding civil society is as a concept that designates the intermediary sphere that includes aspects of the structure and the superstructure. It is the area of the "ensemble of organisms that are commonly called 'private'"; hence it includes not only associations and organisations like political parties and the press, but also the family, which combines ideological and economic functions. Civil society, then, in Gramsci's words "stands between the economic structure and the State". It is the sphere of "private" interests in general. But this notion of civil society cannot be assimilated to that of 18th century political theorists, who thought of it as entirely separate from the State. When Gramsci uses the formula "State = political society + civil society" he is indicating the real relation between the formally 'public' and 'private'. This leads him to break down the abstract ideas of Politics and Law. In the case of the latter, Gramsci writes that the ruling bloc has to subordinate the other classes to the requirements of the productive process not just by issuing decrees, but through an ongoing transformation of moral values and customs in civil society.[10] Hence civil society is the terrain in which classes contest for power (economic, political and ideological). It is here that hegemony is exercised, and where the terms of the relations of the structure and superstructure are fought out.

Politics, itself described by Gramsci as a "level of the superstructure", is the key moment in the relations of structure and superstructure. It is the "purely political moment" that "marks the passage from the structure to the sphere of the complex superstructures",[11] and where the nature of class relations is ultimately constituted and contested in a continuously shifting relation of forces. Gramsci's project in writing the *Notebooks* is a theorisation of the political level through reflection on

47

his own experience and on Italian history. For him, the political level has its own laws, distinct from the economic, and its own "incandescent atmosphere",[12] and it is through an analysis of the political that he conceives of ideology.

In this context, ideologies are not judged according to a criterion of truth and falsehood, but according to their function and efficacy in binding together classes and class fractions in positions of dominance and subordination. Ideology serves to "cement and unify" the social bloc.[13] Gramsci makes two related distinctions concerning ideology. The first distinction is between systematic ways of thinking ("philosophy" and "ideology", in his usage) and aggregated and internally contradictory forms of thought ("common sense" and "folklore"). The second distinction is between organic, semi-organic and non-organic ideologies; that is, according to the degree to which ideologies correspond to the potentialities and movement of fundamental classes in history, and to their capacity for concrete analyses of situations. The "truth" of an ideology, for Gramsci, lies in its power to mobilise politically, and finally in its historical actualisation.[14]

The theoretical inadequacy of this conception which tends to pragmatically assimilate historical materialism to other ideologies will be dealt with in the next section. But here it should be noted that Gramsci is breaking new ground vis-à-vis marxist understanding of ideology, which had stood still with the famous formulation of *The German Ideology*: "The ideas of the ruling class are in every epoch the ruling ideas; i.e., the class which is the ruling material force of society is at the same time the ruling ideological force."[15] Gramsci maintains Marx's important conception that the dominant bourgeois ideology presents itself as universal. Any stains of "rank and station" that presuppose any inherent inequality between men are washed away; the ruling bloc's power to speak in the name of the "people", the "nation", "humanity" and so on is a precondition of the founding of its own state and the guarantee of its survival.[16] However, Gramsci breaks with the conception of ideology as a simple reflection of relations at the economic level, and as the uniform expression of the ruling class. Whilst the dominant ideology is necessarily systematised and presents itself as universal, it does not spring automatically from the ruling class, but is usually the result of the relation of forces between the fractions of the ruling bloc.[17] Hence Gramsci conceives of the differential appropriation of the dominant ideas within the ruling bloc itself and within the dominated class. The first has its basis in the fractioning of the ruling bloc and in a division of labour between broadly intellectual and more practical functions; the second, in the complex process of assimilation, transformation and rejection of the dominant ideas by the subordinate classes.

Hegemony

This leads us to Gramsci's concept of hegemony. Recent usages of the concept have tended to assimilate it to "ideological domination" and to instrumentalise it by suggesting a simple mirror relation of domination and subordination;[18] it should therefore be made clear that hegemony, for Gramsci, includes the ideological but cannot be reduced to that level, and that it refers to the dialectical relation of class forces. Ideological dominance and subordination are not understood in isolation, but always as one, though crucially important, aspect of the relations of the classes and class fractions at all levels — economic and political, as well as ideological/cultural. The concept of hegemony is produced by Gramsci to analyse these relations within classes and between classes. It involves the organisation of "spontaneous" consent which can be won, for example, by the ruling bloc making economic concessions that "yet do not touch its essential interests", combined with other measures that foster forms of consciousness which accept a position of subordination (what Gramsci refers to as sectional and corporate consciousness).[19] The concept allows an·analysis that keeps the levels of the social formation distinct and held in combination; hence Gramsci uses "political hegemony"[20] or "hegemony in philosophy"[21] to indicate the dominant instance of that hegemony. This more specified use of the concept is not theorised by Gramsci, though he opens the way for a more complex and articulated notion of hegemony.

Gramsci acknowledges Lenin to be the originator of the concept of hegemony,[22] but the latter's idea of it is far more restricted to the political level. Lenin defined it in terms of the leadership of the proletariat in its alliance with the poor peasantry. Gramsci maintains this usage, as can be seen in his Leninist approval of the Jacobins, but broadened its scope because for him hegemony had to be fought for on the terrain of civil society. Gramsci's frequent reference to "ethico-political hegemony" indicates its breadth; the hegemony of the ruling bloc is seen not simply at the political level, but as affecting every aspect of social life and thought.

Gramsci has neither a theory of ideology as imposed by the ruling class, nor a spontaneous, immanentist one, like Lukács. He combines elements of both, but does so by working in a different problematic from that of the simple totality. Where the majority of theorists of ideology think only of systematic thought, or do their best to systematise forms of ideology to bring out their coherence, Gramsci is acutely aware of the way in which ideology is a "lived relation". His own experience of the peasant culture of Sardinia[23] and as a revolutionary organiser in the 1920s taught him the importance of grappling with the problem of how ideas are appropriated and the relation between those ideas and forms of action and behaviour. He is perhaps the first marxist to seriously examine ideology at its "lower levels" as the accumulation of popular "knowledges" and the means of dealing with everyday life — what he calls "common sense".

Common Sense, Intellectuals and the Party

Common-sense thinking for Gramsci is both a historical formation and specific to each class. This is evident in his account of the development of the concept from a term of the 17th and 18th century empiricist philosophers battling against theology, to its subsequent usage as a confirmation of accepted opinion rather than its subversion.[24] However, Gramsci's brief notes on common sense consist largely of general observations on a way of thinking. He characterises it as inherently eclectic and disjointed. Because common sense is not systematic and does not make explicit its own mode of reasoning, it can combine ideas that are contradictory without being aware of that fact. As a consequence, it builds up a storehouse of "knowledges" that are drawn from earlier ideologies and from a variety of social classes:

"(Common sense) . . . is strangely composite; it contains elements from the Stone Age and principles of a more advanced science, prejudices from all past phases of history at the local level and intuitions of a future philosophy which will be that of the human race united the world over."[25]

Gramsci identifies the absence of a "consciousness of historicity" and hence of self-knowledge as the principal feature that condemns common-sense thinking to a position of dependence and subordination. Popular notions such as "human nature" effectively discount the possibility of change and "naturalise" the social order.[26] The "naturalisation" process, which for Marx was central to bourgeois Political Economy, is regarded by Gramsci as a key mechanism of common-sense thought. It is precisely in the "materiality" and the matter-of-factness that has gathered around the notion of "human nature" that we can see the intimate articulation of the "structure in dominance" of the "higher" and "lower" realms of ideology.

The relation between the dominant ideology and common sense is not, however, hierarchically fixed, but driven by the class contradictions within it. The former can intervene in popular thinking "positively" in order to recompose its elements and add new ones, or "negatively" by setting boundaries on its development, whilst leaving it the restricted freedom of internal elaboration.[27] The terms of these relations are often affected by other factors such as language, which can itself become a means of self-defence and proud self-assertion on the part of the masses. Thus a dialect functions both as the infrastructure for folklore and parochialism, and as a means of resistance, which can be called the negative and positive poles of corporativism.[28] Nevertheless, the contradictions between the modes of thinking remain and are manifested within common sense itself between ideas borrowed from ruling ideologies and those spontaneously generated through the experience of class solidarity. In moments of open conflict those contradictions open up a gap between "the superficial, explicit or verbal consciousness" and the consciousness "implicit in activity".[29] These moments often signal a crisis in the hegemony of the ruling bloc.

Whilst the dynamic of ideologies is affirmed by Gramsci through its positioning as a level of the superstructures, it is never free-floating. He introduces the category of "intellectual" to designate those with the task of organising, disseminating and conserving skills and ideas associated with mental rather than manual labour. To analyse the formation of ideology and culture in relation to classes, he distinguishes between "organic intellectuals", who have functions firmly based on the interests of a fundamental class, and "traditional intellectuals", who belong to classes and strata remaining as remnants of a previous social formation.[30] The two categories do have a different conceptual value in that the "organic intellectual" refers to a definite class affiliation, whilst the "traditional intellectual" suggests a lack of that affiliation. The key issue is one of function in the system, but Gramsci is sensitive to the differential relation of levels of the superstructure to the structure, and hence to the significance of sub-ideologies that he sees as particularly important among "traditional intellectuals". It accounts for a degree of affiliation to a group or organisation that can come into conflict with allegiance owed to a fundamental class. Referring to the Church (the locus classicus of the "traditional intellectual"), he writes of the "internal necessities of an organisational character" and that

50

"if for every ideological struggle one wanted to find an immediate primary explanation in the structure, one would really be caught napping."[31]

The category of the "intellectual" in Gramsci enables him to analyse the organisation and production of ideology as a specific practice that is not reducible to the classes to which the intellectuals are linked. Hence ideas are not expressive of classes, but comprise a field in which class conflict takes place in particular forms. Through organisations like the Church, the press and political parties (organs of civil society) and through the State (for the ruling bloc) the intellectuals play a leading role in the battle to gain spontaneous support for one of the fundamental classes.[32]

In the organisation of hegemony in capitalist society, the ruling bloc mobilises the organs both of civil society and of the State. Gramsci drew attention to the aspects of class rule that are non-coercive, whereas previous marxists, including Marx himself and Lenin, regarded the State largely as the organised violence of the ruling class. Gramsci writes of the "positive educative" influence of the schools and the "repressive and negative educative" influence of the courts.[33] The vital relation, however, for Gramsci, is between the State and civil society; that is, to what extent the ruling bloc can keep civil society under its hegemony. Ultimately the ruling bloc retains power because of its control of the repressive apparatuses (police and army), which enable it to keep other classes in subjection even when it has lost hegemony over them.[34] Hence the "war of movement" the seizure of State power, is an imperative corollary to the "war of position" in which classes move to take the vantage points in civil society. However, the central position of the State in the maintenance of class rule is radically reconceived by Gramsci. The crucial development of civil society in the West, for him, changes the relation of the State to the rest of the superstructure so that it becomes merely the "outer ditch" of the defences. This is because civil society makes up the "system of fortresses and outworks" that provide the long term guarantee of stability for the ruling bloc.[35] This leads Gramsci to reconceptualise a strategy for the revolutionary party based on winning political hegemony prior to the seizure of power.[36] Since the ruling bloc determines the political terrain and organises its hegemony increasingly in civil society, the party has to explore the terrain and construct a strategy accordingly. Central to this is the development of organic intellectuals by the party and the detachment of traditional intellectuals from the ruling bloc.

Hegemony is based on voluntary and spontaneous "consent", but takes different forms according to the relationship of classes which it embodies. For example, the Church maintains its hold over the masses through external impositions — by clamping down on the freedom of thought of its intellectuals, and by the masses themselves from rising out of the mish-mash of common-sense thinking to more systematic forms of thought. In contrast, the revolutionary party's struggle for hegemony marks a break with previous forms of hegemony. Marxists seek to raise cultural levels, and to break down the cultural oppression institutionalised in the rigid division of mental and manual labour in capitalist society. Gramsci proposes that the party does not act mechanically on popular thinking from outside, but enters the mind of common-sense thinking in order to open up its contradictions:

It is not a question of introducing from scratch a scientific form of thought into everyone's lives, but of renovating and making 'critical' an already existing activity.[37]

The relationship of the party to the masses is not that of a one-way relay mechanism, but a dialectic between leadership and spontaneity. Because Gramsci does not work with a true/false consciousness or science/ideology model his thinking is directed towards the contradictory possibilities within spontaneous, non-systematised forms of thinking and action. (And here he makes a positive evaluation of appeals to emotional and moral attitudes, and rejects a rationalist notion of persuasion by pure logic[38].) In itself, he sees spontaneity as doomed because riven by internal contradictions and incapable of producing a systematic account of the world, but when "educated and purged of extraneous contradictions" that spontaneity is, for Gramsci, the motor of revolution.[39]

Ideology as conceived in the *Prison Notebooks* is bound to the political; it is through politics that the "relation between common sense and the upper level of philosophy is assured",[40] and politics is essentially concerned with conceptions of the State. Gramsci's analyses of sectional/corporate consciousness and common-sense thinking are aimed at revealing their inability to understand the role of the capitalist State, and hence their failure to grasp the political as the crucial level of the social formation. Corporate consciousness and common sense share a ground of thought which is specifically non-theoretical, and often anti-theoretical. Here 'feeling", "personal experience" and immediate empirical perception are dominant. Gramsci's comments on peasant "subversivism" highlight these features as a "negative" class response:

> Not only does that people have no precise consciousness of its own historical identity, it is not even conscious of the . . . exact limits of its adversary. There is a dislike of officialdom — the only form in which the State is perceived.[41]

There are, nevertheless, "positive" aspects to corporate consciousness and common sense (Gramsci refers to the element of class solidarity, and to the "earthy suspicion" involved in popular anti-clericalism). However, they remain necessarily subordinate and defensive.

The whole force of Gramsci's work is to insist on the importance of theory for the analysis of social formations, precisely because the non-theoretical cannot go beyond immediate appearances, and therefore cannot identify the "enemy" except in a vague way. Marxism is, for Gramsci, in an important sense unlike any other ideology because it enables an understanding of the terrain on which class struggles take place. The *Prison Notebooks* are remarkable as a work of theory which polemically engages with the persistent hold of the dominant ideology on parts of the workers' movement; in so doing, he re-poses the whole question of ideology in relation to the political level.

III Ideology and the Problem of Historicism

Gramsci's conceptions of politics and the social formation in general, we have tried to indicate, are attempts to explain *complex* objects. It is important to keep in mind that his work is directed against a mechanistic or economistic marxism, and ideology, correspondingly, can for Gramsci in no sense be reduced to an irrelevant epiphenomenon. Nor can it be interpreted in a psychologistic fashion as a search for the "dirty-Jewish" interests of individuals of particular (ruling) classes.[42] Fatalism and conspiracy theses play no part whatever in his work. Correspondingly, for Gramsci, there are no pregiven "interests" for the working class either. While acknowledging the moral comfort which a fatalistic economism can offer to the masses in politically adverse periods, he constantly points to the need for a general political perspective — one which necessarily involves a recognition of the importance of ideology. His specific concern with common sense as the substratum of ideologies, reveals an analysis quite opposed to any simple dichotomy between "ideas" and the economy. The repeated stress on the complex unity of structure and superstructure makes clear that Gramsci (correctly in our view) rejects any simple unilinear causal hierarchy. The economistic standpoint itself has its roots in practical experience, is a material consequence of the daily struggle of wage labour with and under capital, and it is a paramount task of the marxist party to overcome the dualities and sectionalisms of what Gramsci terms "corporate" consciousness. Ideology is not a "trick" imposed by a ruling class in order eternally to deceive the workers, and thus prevent the class from achieving its (supposedly) predetermined historic role. Ideologies have their ground in material realities and are themselves material forces. Nevertheless, materially based working-class outlooks are not inevitably condemned to remain corporate. Common sense and practical experience can and must be worked on. They contain elements of "good sense" and class instinct[43] which can be transformed into a coherent socialist perspective because that day-to-day corporate struggle, however characterised by relations of domination and subordination, is itself a contradictory phenomenon.

Ideology, then, for Gramsci, has, like the social formation of which it is a necessary part, a complex and contradictory identity. Unlike Althusser, for example, Gramsci does not offer an epistemological definition in addition to an explanation of ideology's material social role. Ideologies *qua* ideologies, for Gramsci, are neither true nor false, though they can certainly be coherent to a greater or lesser degree. Ideology is principally regarded as the "cement" which holds together the *structure* (in which economic class struggle takes place) and the realm of the complex superstructures. Yet whether and to what extent ideologies succeed in performing this role is never pre-given. There is, it follows, always a certain openness in the ground of ideology, and, in particular, with regard to common sense. This openness constitutes the space in which the communist party works: to break with the theoretical limitations of corporate consciousness (under which the masses necessarily "borrow" their conceptions of the world from the dominant class),[44] in order to achieve the required level of coherence and political-cultural breadth for the exercise of hegemony. Only when this is obtained — and it can only be the product of the differential unity of political, economic, and intellectual practices — can the conception of life concerned be said to be genuinely "organic". Ultimately, therefore, mass adhesion is the "validation" of an ideology. But Gramsci's argument about the objective intellectual function of certain "technical" strata organic to modern capitalism, and his repeated suggestion that these must be won over by the political party, are significant. They militate against any explanation of mass adhesion by recourse either to spontaneism or to the *a priori* notion of a privileged class-subject. It is interesting to note that whenever Gramsci refers to the "psychological validity" which mass adhesion confers upon an ideology, his account is couched in metaphorical rather than literal terms.[45] The recognition that the party itself must function analogously to a "collective intellectual"[46] in order to become adequate to the complexity of the structure/superstructure bloc sharpens his keen sense that history is never made other than in concrete historico-political situations.

It is relevant at this point to raise again the problem of Gramsci's "historicism", for the above formulation of "mass adhesion" suggests the kind of concessions to relativism which Althusser and Poulantzas, amongst others, see as characteristics of the historicist tendency. Briefly, to recapitulate, historicists are accused of reducing the complexity of a social totality to a simple, uniform essence, and of reducing the validity of theoretical positions to the historical conditions of the period which the ideas are said to "express". Now this concept entails an *a priori* collapse of base and superstructure (or levels of a social formation) into an "expressive unity" which can be either economically, culturally or spiritually defined. For example, the "essence" of a period or process might be taken to be the *level of the productive forces,* which according to a teleologically defined schema, sets the pace for a series of "progressive" historical stages. And we have seen in the previous section how a "culturalist" appropriation of Gramsci — in contrast to the "economistic" position — is achieved. However, being diametrically opposed to that of economism, the culturalist appropriation is excessive in just the opposite way. Alternatively, history might be seen as a movement in which the most progressive class is that which is potentially capable of the greatest degree of self-realisation in history. Thus, for, say, Lukács, the proletariat is the first class capable (in socialism/communism) of total *self-consciousness* and thus self-realisation in history, for history is nothing other than the expressive unity of consciousness and practice. Formally opposed to economism, this conception self-evidently shares with the other two an essentialism which defies rational verification. It is the fundamentally abstract, and even mystical, nature of these ideas of processes, essences, ends, and class subjects which troubles the theoretically "rigorous" French schools of marxism. There is no room in a science for irrationalist conceptions, however politically or morally "progressive".

Now, undoubtedly, Gramsci tends at times to express himself in historicist terms. In the next section of this paper, that problem is given greater textual elaboration in response to certain structuralist constructions of Gramsci's positions. It should suffice here to indicate the existence of that problem and to suggest the basis or elements of an assessment of it.

Ideologies are, we have seen, "conceptions of life". This is a concept, it could be argued, which is close to Lukács' notion of "world-view" or "class consciousness" Furthermore, Gramsci argues that organic ideologies are those linked to "fundamental classes" and mediated by (another example of a "bloc") a political party.[47] Indeed at one point Gramsci suggests that there is a party for every class: something which allows the political level little autonomy. Now clearly there is a position here which might be interpreted as involving self-moving class "subjects" each having their own historically sequential organic ideas. The necessity of ideologies is then justified by their expression of and *as* the essence of the historical process itself. We have said that Gramsci's main reflections are premissed upon the idea that the social totality is complex, but doubt appears to be thrown on that assertion when the above thesis is accompanied by a selection from Gramsci's philosophical comments. For example, Gramsci asserts that the activities of economics, politics, and philosophy "form a homogenous circle".[48] This could be taken to imply a pregiven harmony between social levels, and seems to undermine the claim for any real or theoretical complexity. The notion of an essential unity between history and human praxis is taken further in arguments of which the following are representative examples:

> It might seem that there can exist an extra-historical and extra-human objectivity. But who is the judge of such objectivity? . . . Objectivity always means 'humanly objective' which can be held to exactly correspond to 'historically subjective': in other words objectivity would mean 'universal subjective'.

> We know reality only in relation to man, and since man is historical becoming, knowledge and reality are also a becoming and so is objectivity.[49]

Clearly, in the light of these Hegelian and somewhat mystifying remarks, marxism itself could not be expected to escape relativistic criteria:

> But even the philosophy of praxis is an expression of historical contradictions.[50]

> Hegelian immanentism becomes historicism, but it is absolute historicism only with the philosophy of praxis — absolute historicism and absolute humanism.[51]

The problem, then, of whether marxism is a science or an ideology is one of the thorniest in Gramsci. The difference between (social) science and ideology seems not to be a qualitiative one. (The case of the natural sciences is more problematic.) Thus there is no explicit sense in which marxism as a conception of life is any different from, say, Calvinism. Indeed, genuinely organic ideologies (and marxism seems to be numbered amongst them) appear to differ only in the historical circumstances upon which their mass adhesion rests.

We can begin to throw doubt on the "historicist" accusations by first of all calling to mind other of Gramsci's general pronouncements, and, more importantly, by arguing that his major concepts are unintelligible if those accusations are correct.

> The claim, presented as an essential postulate of historical materialism, that every fluctuation of politics and ideology can be presented and expounded as an immediate expression of the structure must be contested in theory as primitive infantilism.[52]

Even Gramsci's philosophical comments are not theoretically uniform. For example, there is no doubt that he allows considerable autonomy to the sciences,[53] and his argument against Bukharin is not, as is sometimes claimed, a rejection of scientificity. Rather, in denouncing the latter's mechanicism, Gramsci argues that each science is specific and that it is therefore impossible to generate a general, normative, model of scientific practice. A positivist criterion such as Bukharin adopts in fact hinders that which it is meant to facilitate: an account of the intrinsic "method" of science. Gramsci concludes that what in later discourse has become known as "science-in-general" is a metaphysical or *philosophical* notion, and that it can no more cover differences *within* the individual natural sciences than it can those *between* natural and social sciences. Gramsci maintains that an irreducible difference in method and and object separates the latter. Those familiar with Louis Althusser's recent self-criticism (for more of which see the conclusion to this article and the separate paper on Althusser in this journal), will be struck by its intriguing resemblance to these ideas of Gramsci.

However, it is above all to Gramsci's substantive concepts of historical materialism that we should turn for a less simplistic picture of his historicism. This argument will be elaborated in a moment. Similarly, Gramsci's stress on the material forms of ideology, its lack of uniform content, and, above all, its social *production* (the intellectuals) directs us once more away from simple (general) philosophical positions.

It is the insistence on historical specificity (and *not* historical relativism) which militates against any blanket categorisation. This is not to dispute — especially with regard to his philosophical remarks — that Gramsci adopts at times positions akin to humanism and even pragmatism.[54] Yet in fairness it should be pointed out that the best examples of this tendency occur in a polemic against positivism and theoretical economism within marxism. To speak of the unity of the levels of a social formation in this context is entirely justifiable, though Gramsci's own term of "homogenous circle"[55] is certainly an overstatement. In general, Gramsci never questions the complexity of unified social levels.

The perspective which the identification of hegemonic classes, parties, and ideas offers has absolutely no implications of a prior teleology. Rather, those conceptions facilitate a material and theoretically consistent analysis of what is specific about historical conjunctures, and therefore the relation of a marxist party to that practical situation. It is crucial here to point out that an account of factors "relative" to a conjuncture implies no necessary relativisation of the concepts used in such an analysis. The concepts, of course, are *general* ones, but they do not refer to general *entities.* For Gramsci, ideology-in-general does not exist. There are only conceptions whose political roles depend on the material effect they carry in specific situations.

He is not interested in the "arbitrary elucubrations of individuals"[56] but in the social and political role which ideas play. If this is the case, it would seem more accurate to claim that Gramsci deals with the practico-social function of ideologies at the expense of philosophical theses, rather than to somewhat misleadingly seek a unity between his philosophical speculation and his contribution to the substantive work of historical materialism. This concern with specific analysis of ideologies — their relation to economic class formation and the existence and degree of hegemony exercised in a conjuncture — is considered by Gramsci to be a theoretical precondition for practical interventions by marxists. Such a position cannot be reduced to the fallacies of historicism (humanism, and especially economism), for it explicitly and convincingly advances upon them.

IV The Structuralist Appropriation of Gramsci: — Althusser

We have already referred to the complex nature of Gramsci's "historicism". This question is further compounded when we come to examine the relation to Gramsci of the "structuralist marxists" (referring here specifically to Althusser and Poulantzas). Structuralist marxism is diametrically opposed to — indeed, is constructed on the back of a systematic dismantling of — "historicism". Gramsci's relation to "historicism" is exceedingly complex: as we have suggested, in many important ways, he is not a "historicist" at all, if we have someone like Lukács in mind as a representative figure of that tendency. Hence, the relationship of Althusser and Poulantzas to Gramsci must be anything but straightforward.

Gramsci frequently referred to historical materialism as a "philosophy of praxis". He clearly took this designation seriously — the reference cannot be wholly explained as a euphemism for "marxism" adopted by Gramsci to evade the prison censor's eye. Thus, when the structuralists come to deal with Gramsci at this general philosophical level, he is the object of their sharp criticism. However, even here Althusser draws some criticial distinctions. He is always at pains to "except" Gramsci from the *general* critique of historicism such as he levels at Lukács, Korsch and Sartre. He also takes great care to distinguish Gramsci's position on the status of "historical materialism" as a "philosophy of praxis", from the latter's substantive concepts, which are singled out for favourable and positive attention. These distinctions are of great importance in defining some of the parameters within which the structuralist encounter with Gramsci has been conducted. But, over and above any specific references to Gramsci or direct acknowledgements of his contribution, it can be plainly seen that Gramsci has played a *generative* role and occupies a pivotal position in relation to the work of structuralist marxism as a whole.

The relationship between Gramsci and the structuralists reveals, however, a significant unevenness. A sort of "graph" could be drawn, which would not only plot this relationship more accurately, but would go some way to explaining *when* and *why* Gramsci's work has a particular pertinence for the structuralists, and when it does not. Plotting the relationship in this way also helps to establish the main points of convergence and divergence between the two positions. In his early, seminal, essay on "Contradiction and Over-determination" (in *For Marx,* 1969), Althusser is concerned with defining the nature of "contradictions" within a social formation. His argument is that a social formation is not a simple "expressive totality": contradictions do not necessarily arise at all levels of the social formation at the same time, or flood all the levels simultaneously from some "principal contradiction" lodged in some simple way "in the (economic) base". Contradictions have their own specificity. The point of importance is how contradictions which arise from "absolutely dissimilar currents", to use Lenin's phrase, can effectively "merge" or fuse into a major ruptural unity, and thus constitute the site of a decisive political conjuncture. This question is "thought" by Althusser principally with reference to Lenin and 1917.[57] But the terrain of concerns is not at all foreign to that which Gramsci explored in his writings in the *Prison Notebooks* — for example, his discussion of how to distinguish between "organic" and "conjunctural" features of a crisis in the relations of class forces in "The Modern Prince".[58]

As Althusser advanced into the period of *Reading Capital*, he became preoccupied by a different set of questions — not unrelated, but posed with a significantly different theoretical emphasis. Here he was concerned with identifying the nature of "Marx's immense theoretical revolution" in *Capital.* This question is "thought" with the aid of a distinctive set of concepts: the distinction between ideology and science; the nature of "theoretical practice"; the role of philosophy in providing the epistemological guarantee of the "scientificity" of marxism; the theory of "structuralist

57

causality". Many of these concepts are developed in direct contestation with the conceptual terrain of "historicism". At this point, Althusser is at his farthest distance from Gramsci. Though there is, as we shall see in a little more detail in a moment, no blanket condemnation, the critique of Gramsci's "historicism" constitutes a central strand in the long and important essay in *Reading Capital* devoted to the proposition that "Marxism Is Not A Historicism".[59]

There have been two significant developments in Althusser's work since that point. The first is the important "ISAs essay", in which Althusser turned his attention once more to the concrete analysis of the ideological instance, and to the function of the "ideological state apparatuses" in reproducing the hegemony of a dominant ideology in particular social formations.[60] The second is that remarkable labour of self-clarification and modification represented by the essays in *Essays In Self-Criticism* (1974). Full justice cannot be done to the latter volume here. But it is important to note the following: Althusser has much modified the simple ideology/science distinction established in his earlier work; he has admitted the "theoreticism" of some of the positions adopted; he has abandoned the idea of a self-sufficient "theoretical practice"; philosophy is now defined, not as an "epistemological guarantee" but as an intervention in "the class struggle in theory". Whilst the scientific status of Marx's theoretical breakthroughs cannot be reduced to the historical conditions which made them possible, those conditions are no longer considered irrelevant to when and how such "breaks" are made. Althusser has continued to insist that these modifications — not all of them securely founded — have not touched the essential points in his critique of humanism and historicism. But the shift of emphases and the substantial reassessments *have* had the effect of, once again, lowering some of the barriers between "structuralist marxism" and Gramsci's work. For example, they have made it possible for the structuralist theorists to acknowledge what those critics who were critical of Althusser's "theoreticism" have always argued: that in Gramsci's attention to the specificity of "the political", his attack on all forms of economic reductionism, and his insistence on the necessary complexity of the structure-superstructure complex, we *already find traversed* — albeit in terminology very different from that of the structuralists — precisely those questions about "relative autonomy" and the "ever pre-given complex unity of a social formation" which are, rightly, believed to constitute *Althusser*'s "immense theoretical revolution". Thus, whether Gramsci is a "historicist" or not, *something* led him, in the *Prison Notebooks,* to register, with remarkable force, clarity and consistency, his necessary break with a Marxism conceived *either* as an economic reductionism *or* as a theory of social formations as "expressive totalities". And this was a break with what Althusser defined as the essence of "historicism" — as well as of its mirror-image, economism.

To put the matter summarily, then. If Gramsci remains a "historicist", then his is a historicism which *broke* with what the structuralists have defined as the essence of the problematic of historicism. It is therefore a "historicism" with which the structuralists are obliged to come to terms — to reckon with, not simply to dismiss. Gramsci constitutes *the limit case* of "historicism" for structuralist marxism.[61] Far from this being now a closed matter, it remains an open and unconcluded encounter one of the most important encounters in the field of contemporary marxist theory. Objectively, this is the *position* in which the problematic of Gramsci and that of Althusser and Poulantzas stand to one another. How Althusser and Poulantzas have actually negotiated their own particular positions within this theoretical conjuncture at different points in their work is a matter for more detailed tracing.

There are only scattered references to Gramsci in Althusser's early essays (*For Marx*). They all signal his importance, often in direct contrast with Lukács, the arch-historicist. Gramsci is "of another stature" (p.114). This is acknowledged specifically in relation to Gramsci's awareness of the need for an "elaboration of the particular essence of the specific elements of the superstructure". "Hegemony" is also specifically cited as a new concept, a "remarkable solution". In the later essays in this collection, Althusser begins to develop a theory of ideology — first through the ideology/science distinction, then in terms of "the way men 'live' the real relations of their conditions of existence", or as an "imaginary relation to the real relations of existence": here 'ideology' is being "thought" by Althusser largely without benefit of Gramsci's work.[62] Gramsci's "great theses on Marxist philosophy" are, again, identified in *Reading Capital* as of considerable significance. He is, of course, identified with those marxist theoreticians — Lukács, Luxembourg, Korsch — who contributed to the development of marxism as a "revolutionary humanism and historicism", affirming that it is "advancing 'men' . . . who always triumph in the end" (p.120). Althusser acknowledges that some support for this reading can be discovered in Marx's own work. But he insists that Marx must be read "symptomatically" — attending to the changing problematics which inform different periods of his work, and the "epistemological ruptures" which mark one period off from another. However, as we might predict, it is just here that the major critique of Gramsci is launched. Althusser's tread is a cautious one — lest his "necessarily schematic remarks may disfigure the spirit of this enormously delicate and subtle work of genius" (p.126). He distinguished Gramsci's "historicist" view of dialectical materialism and of the role of philosophy in marxism, from his "discoveries" in the field of historical materialism. The distinction leads Althusser to call for a "symptomatic reading' of Gramsci *too*. His humanist statements are "primarily critical and polemical" (p.127). The work on ideology is positively exempted. The aspect commented on here — Gramsci's attention to the role of ideology in "cementing and unifying" a whole social bloc, preserving its "ideological unity", and his rooting of ideology in the superstructures — points forward to the ISAs essay, and to Poulantzas's *Political Power and Social Classes* (1973). But still, Gramsci's stress on the *historical* side of "historical materialism" is unfavourably compared with Marx's stress on the *materialist*. This is the *nub* of the critique of a philosophy of praxis: that it conflates knowledge and "the real" — thus Marxism becomes, not scientific knowledge but simply another of the great, organic ideologies.[63] Gramsci's problematic is crossed by more than one path: but when historicism crosses it, everything else in the argument "submits to its law".

There is one additional point about the treatment of Gramsci in *Reading Capital* which requires further comment. In a criticial footnote, Althusser attacks Gramsci's use of the concept "civil society", and declares that it should be struck from the Marxist theoretical vocabulary (p.162). Later, Poulantzas is to be even fiercer about it. But, as we have seen, the concept "civil society" is of central importance to

Gramsci — a matter made more difficult because of the ambiguity of some of his formulations of it, and the difficulty of locating it precisely in Gramsci's structure/ superstructure topography. More than a mere disagreement is signalled here; hence it is worth pursuing somewhat further, not only for the light it might throw on Gramsci but for what it reveals about Althusser and Poulantzas.

There is no mystery to the hostility with which the Althussereans regard the concept of "civil society".[64] It played a prominent role in both classical Political Economy and 18th-century political theory, but more significantly in Hegel. All three use it to refer to the sphere of bourgeois "individualism" *par excellence* — the terrain of possessive individualism, of market relations of contract between "bare individuals", of individual bourgeois "rights and freedoms", above all, the terrain of economic needs and of economic man *per se (homo economicus)*. The Political Economists regard it as the arena of economic life as such: Hegel regarded it as that "egoistic" sphere of particularity which had to be raised to a wider univer- sality — that of political citizenship — by the State. Marx frequently engaged with *all* the themes posed by this problematic. His frequent critique of Political Economy is that it treats market relations as the sum of capitalist economic relations, ignoring the *production* of surplus altogether: it is *this* concept which confined classical Political Economy, in Marx's eyes, to its "bourgeois skin". The "naturalization" of the market is dismantled in some of Marx's most ironic remarks in *Capital* about an economic theory based on the model of Robinson Crusoe. He directly confronted Hegel's use of the concept in, *inter alia,* the *Critique of Hegel's Philosophy of Right.* He assailed the notion that the dismantling of capitalism could be regarded as a struggle for "bourgeois political rights" alone — in *On the Jewish Question.* In the *German Ideology* we still find Marx using the concept, but now with a more inclusive meaning of his own:

> This conception of society depends on our ability to expound the real process of production, starting out from the material production of life itself, and to comprehend the form of intercourse connected with this and created by this mode of production (i.e. civil society in all its various stages, as the basis of all history).[65]

The structuralists want to insist — it seems to us correctly — that the Marx of *Capital* had left this problematic behind. They want to expunge it from the marxist theoretical vocabulary because to preserve it is to sustain, inside the marxist dis- course, the "humanist" echoes of a reference to the sphere of "the needs of human subjects".[66] Marxism, they argue, is a "theory without a subject". The presence of "civil society" in Gramsci's work is therefore taken as an implicit index of his lingering "humanism" (though this attribution is not, in our view, sustained by any of the *uses* of this concept which Gramsci actually makes). But if it no longer preserves its 18-century meaning in Gramsci, what is it referencing? We tried, earlier, to say how the concept appears to us to function in Gramsci's discourse. Here we want to indicate why we would also want to say that this is not incompa- tible with Marx's problematic in *Capital,* even if Gramsci does not use the concept in exactly the same way.

Explicitly, in *Capital I,* Marx advances on classical Political Economy by insist- ing on going behind the exchange relations of the market to the "hidden abode" of capitalist production, where surplus value is generated and labour power exploited. He does not, of course, totally excise the moment of market relations and of "exchange". In the *Grundrisse* and again in *Capital I* he demonstrates how capital reproduces itself at an expanding rate and realizes itself through the long circuit of capital accumulation — one which requires the articulation between different "moments", between different *forms* of capital, including the "dependent" sphere of circulation and exchange. Having established the primacy of the determination of production over the whole circuit of capital, he takes up again in *Capital II* the key questions of circulation and reproduction. Relations of circulation and exchange are capitalist relations too — necessary, though not determining. The sphere of exchange is articulated with the sphere of production, not loosely and fortuitously, but by specific mechanisms. It is in the sphere of circulation that commodities become "exchangeable" through the "passage of forms" into the most abstract and universal of commodities — the commodity which has the ability to mediate all commodity exchanges — money. It is through this "metamorphosis" — C — M — C' — that commodities find their "equivalent" expression in money terms — prices. But is it also in this sphere that capital hires "free labour", through the mechanism of the labour market (i.e. where it purchases that valuable commodity which it must set to work in production — labour power). And it is also in in this sphere that capital pays the individual labourer the means of his subsistence, the cost of the reproduction of his labour power. Both these absolutely vital functions for capital are paid out of capital — they are the "variable part" of capital, produced by labour power, which capital *advances* for the reproduction of labour power. But this "variable part" appears in the sphere of exchange (again through the mediation of money) in the form of a particular economic relation — the wage relation — capital in the "wage form". In so far as capitalism is a mode of production founded on "free labour", distributable to the branches of production only through the means of the market, and is a mode of economic production in which the labourer is separated from the means of existence, it *requires* a sphere of exchange, even though that sphere is dependent on capitalist production relations. The relations of exchange are, thus, the "phenomenal forms" of the "real relations" of production. Marx goes through this argument time and again in *Capital,* but the reference we have specifically in mind here is the Chapter on "The Buying and Selling of Labour Power" *Capital* I, (Part II, Ch.6). Marx may no longer use the term, "civil society" to designate this phase of the circuit of capital: but he certainly thinks its relation as a part of the economic relations of capitalism, and he retains, if not the term, then the conceptual space which it designated.[67]

But Marx says several other important things about the relations characteristic of this sphere of circulation and exchange. He suggests that it has the *ideological* function of concealing its real foundations — the generation and expropriation of the surplus in production. The "noisy sphere" of exchange disguises the "hidden abode" of capitalist production. You have to abandon the former and penetrate the latter in order to "force the secret of profit making" (p.176). This is not simply because the former suspends over the latter the forbidding sign, "No admittance here except on business". A specific ideological mechanism is involved. This is the mechanism of representation or re-presentation. For the exchanges of the market

61

appear to the agents involved as "free and equivalent" exchanges. They appear to exchange "equivalent to equivalent". Thus if, both in economic theory and in "experience", the labourer "lives" his relation to capitalism exclusively in the terms and categories with which he is presented in the sphere of the market, the source of his exploitation (in production) will be rendered invisible. He will "live" — experience — the exploitative relations of capitalist production *as if* they were "exchanges between equivalents". If and when these "free exchanges" become the object of class struggle, they will, of course, be confined to attempting to "restore to their proper equivalence" relations which, in reality, are non-equivalent, exploitative in their very foundations. Such struggles Lenin called "economist" and Gramsci called "corporatist" — they do not, Gramsci said, "touch the essentials".

But Marx says something more about this sphere. From it, he says, there arise the principal relations of the political and juridical superstructures of bourgeois society, as well as the key ideological themes and discourses. This sphere "is in fact a very Eden of the innate rights of men. There alone rule Freedom, Equality, Property and Bentham". This arises precisely from the fact that this "noisy sphere" *is* the (dependent) sphere of individual exchange — and hence the seat and origin of the "possessive individualist" political and juridical freedoms of bourgeois society (all of them predicated on the individual subject) and of those ideologies of individualism which characterise bourgeois "common sense". Thus, "Freedom, because both buyer and seller of a commodity, say, labour power are constrained [i.e. *appear* to be constrained] only by their own free will ... the agreement they come to is but the form in which they give expression to their common will. Equality, because each enters into relation with the other, as with a simple owner of commodities, and they exchange equivalent for equivalent. Property because each disposes only of what is his own. And Bentham because each looks only to himself." (p.176). In short, to adopt a phrase from Althusser himself, this "noisy sphere" provides the basis for those superstructural practices and ideological forms in which men are forced to "live an imaginary relation" of equivalence and individualism to their real (non-equivalent, collective) conditions of existence. This is not only the site of one of the very few passages in *Capital* where Marx explicitly marks the articulation between the economic, politico-juridcal and ideological levels of a social formation. It is also the place where, far from simply *abandoning* all that Hegel, Locke and Adam Smith referenced in the term "civil society", he takes it up, and by thinking it through again, now on the transformed conceptual terrain of capital and its circuit, *produces a new concept of it*. It is no longer the seat and source of individualism. It is simply the individualizing sphere of the circuit of capital's path to expanded reproduction. "Individualism" is thus not the origin of the system — either in fact (Robisonades) or in theory. It is what capital produces as one of its necessary "phenomenal forms" — one of its necessary but dependent effects. What most distinguishes Marx's designation of this new theoretical space is his use of it as a concept with which to reference some of the complex relations between base and superstructures. To identify the "immediate forms" of capital at this point in its circuit, is to begin to trace what Gramsci called the "passage" from base to the "complex sphere of the superstructures".

Althusser sometimes appears to be on the threshold of grasping this, but pulls back at a critical point. If we retain the concept "civil society" he says, we must recognize that it has no economic existence, but is only a "combined effect of law and legal-political ideology on the economic". This reading cannot be squared with Marx's in the chapter quoted above. Poulantzas follows Althusser in this — again by identifying it with the level of the juridico-political and the ideological only. But Marx is clearly demonstrating the accumulation of effects — economic, politico-juridical, ideological — in this single instance.

Gramsci, as we have already seen, makes a quite distinctive use of the concept "civil society". First, without its being precisely the same as Marx's just outlined, he *does* appear to hold quite closely to Marx's provisional formulation: at least in the sense of regarding "civil society" as a concept which marks the *coupling* effect of base and superstructure. But Gramsci also employs it in a second sense, which is broader in conception, less directly attributable to Marx's formulation in *Capital,* and belonging more unambiguously to the concepts developed by Gramsci to "think" the specificity of the political instance, and to articulate the concept of hegemony. Gramsci makes a critical distinction between the "domination" of a ruling class alliance over a social formation, by force and coercion; and the "direction" or leadership of such an alliance, by consent. The latter moment is that for which he reserves the term "hegemony". It is characterised by the capacity of a dominant bloc to extend its sphere of leadership and authority over society as a whole, and actively to *conform* economic, civil and cultural life, educational, religious and other institutions, to its sway. Many of these spheres are apparently far removed from the direct authority of the State, political society and the economy. In his second usage, these are some of the areas Gramsci includes under the loose designation, "civil society".

Now the function of the dominant ideology and of the ideological state apparatuses in "cementing and unifying" a social formation under the hegemony of a particular class alliance *is* a question to which Althusser directed his attention in the ISAs article. But his dislike of the civil society/State distinction leads him to jettison it, declaring the distinction to be a purely legalistic one under capitalism, not of substantive importance. This obliges him to designate all the "ideological apparatuses" as *state* apparatuses: he calls them "ideological state apparatuses". He argues that it is of no consequence that some of these are directly organized by the State, and others are privately organized, since all of them function "beneath the ruling ideology".[68] This definition is tautologous. It also serves to mask certain critical distinctions. There *are* differences between apparatuses directly coordinated by the State and those which are not. These differences matter — they affect how such apparatuses function, how they are articulated *with* the State; they can also provide the basis of significant internal contradictions between different apparatuses within the complex of the State and the ruling bloc. For example, in the British case, the functions of the press (privately owned) and of television (indirectly coordinated with the State) are different because of their different modes of insertion; and these differences have *pertinent effects* — for example, in the manner in which different aspects of the class struggle are ideologically inflected in each. The ideological role of the Church, for example, differs depending on whether or not it is the organizational basis of a 'state religion' — as Gramsci's concern with Catholicism in Italy clearly revealed. The complex position of the trade unions is also not resolved by simply designating them, for all practical purposes, as 'state apparatuses'. For this masks the 'work' which the State has to do, and do ceaselessly, actively, to *hegemonise* the corporate, defensive institutions of the working class. Thus, too swift a designation of the trade unions to the sphere of the State blurs the critical question of the articulation between modern capitalism and Social Democracy. The same, from a different angle, could be said about the family. Those moments when functions for the reproduction of capital and of labour power, hitherto performed by the family as a "private" institution, are taken over for the State are pivotal moments of transition, and require careful analysis. Althusser has always insisted on the need for specificity as part of the "necessary complexity" of the Marxist concept of totality. But the opposition to the concept of "civil society" has the theoretical effect, here, precisely of leading us to abandon specificity for a rather too convenient generalization. Again, Althusser insists on the primacy of "the concrete analysis of a concrete situation". But it is Gramsci's use of the distinction between State and civil society, and between different moments and types of combination within the different forms of hegemony, which has the real pay-off for the analysis of specific conjunctures.

We have identified one of the problems which beset Althusser's ISAs essay — the dissolving of the public/private distinction, the too swift absorption of all apparatuses onto the terrain of the state, and the tendency then to see the "reproduction" functions of the State for Capital as too unproblematic. (A problem of a rather similar kind can also be identified in Poulantzas's *Political Power and Social Classes,* which follows on closely from Althusser and which also shows a tendency to absorb everything under the umbrella of the capitalist state.) Yet, at a more general level, the seminal ISAs essay seems to us unthinkable without benefit of Gramsci's work. Here, the whole problem of ideology appears to have been re-thought with Gramsci's categories very much in mind. Althusser's list of ISAs is a direct borrowing from Gramsci's *Notebooks*. Ideology is thought, less in terms of its contrast with science, more in terms of its practico-social effect in cementing a ruling bloc beneath a dominant ideology. This is a very Gramscian conception. Althusser defines the whole. terrain introduced in this essay as that of "reproduction" — the apparatuses which serve to "reproduce the relations of production". But this is not far from Gramsci's notion that the superstructures serve to "conform" society to the long-term needs of Capital. The centrality given by Althusser to the educational system as an ISA — with the family, the *key* ISA couple, replacing the Church-family couple — corresponds to Gramsci's discussion of the role of the school and the educational system in elaborating the various categories of intellectuals.[69] Both give education a central place in the complex nature of the superstructures in modern capitalism — and, later, Poulantzas relies centrally on the education system as an ISA in reproducing the pivotal distinction between mental and manual labour.[70] "Gramsci," Althusser acknowledges, "is the only one who went any distance in the road-I am taking . . . " Unfortunately, "he did not systematise his institutions . . . " The first half of the ISAs essay could be represented as an attempt to carry through that "absent systematization" of Gramsci. Althusser undertakes this, not by directly extrapolating from Gramsci's "intuitions", so much as by *relocating* Gramsci's concepts on the firmer structuralist terrain of "reproduction". This relocation of Gramsci undoubtedly lends systematization and rigour to Gramsci. It also, sometimes, tends to make the work of the ISAs on behalf of Capital more unproblematic than it is in Gramsci, more of a necessary, functional, effect. And, in general, it centres the argument more in a "general theory" of ideology, and less in the analysis of particular historical conjunctures. In this work of transformation and transposition which Althusser undertakes, there are both gains and losses. Perhaps the single, most significant point of convergence between the Althusser of the ISAs essay and Gramsci is the rooting of the concept of "ideology" firmly in the practices and structures of the superstructures. Gramsci appears always to think the problem of ideology in this way. For Althusser, it represents a shift of emphasis — and a commendable one — in comparison with some of his earlier positions. The argument here is not undertaken so as to prove or disprove a direct theoretical line of descent, or to plot overt "influences". The point is to demonstrate the close convergence of the two problematics. To put the point metaphorically, when the shift of emphasis with respect to "ideology" takes place in Althusser's work, Gramsci is clearly, theoretically, "close at hand".

In sum, then, we would say that if the Althusser of *Reading Capital* and *For Marx* is always respectful and positive in his appreciation of Gramsci's "brilliant insights", the Althusser of "Ideological State Apparatuses" is working on terrain very much first staked out by Gramsci's concepts; even though his treatment of the problem differs from Gramsci's in the manner of theoretical formulation and in the direction (very much towards Lacan and "the constitution of the subject in ideology" — the subject of the second half of the ISAs essay) towards which one element of Althusser's discourse points.

V The Structuralist Appropriation of Gramsci — Poulantzas

Poulantzas is dealt with at length at another point in this review. Hence his relation to Gramsci is more summarily treated here — principally in terms of the text where this relation is of central importance, Poulantzas's *Political Power and Social Classes*. This work aims to apply a general marxist-structuralist framework derived from Althusser to the development of a "regional" theory of the political instance and the capitalist State. Its central preoccupation, therefore, is with the "relative autonomy" of the political, types of political regime, the relation between classes and the State, questions concerning hegemony and the dominant ideology. These are, of course, the matrix of problems to which Gramsci's work is also addressed. Moreover, the ways they are formulated by Poulantzas reveal the seminal impact of Gramsci. Thus, for example, Poulantzas draws on the distinction between the "fundamental classes" and the different class alliances which dominate the State — one which Gramsci also elaborates.[71] Both do so by drawing heavily from Marx's analysis of Britain and from the *18th Brumaire* and *Class Struggles in France* (some of the very few Marx texts Gramsci seemed able to quote from and remember in detail in prison). Poulantzas is the first marxist theorist after Lenin and Gramsci to give the concept "hegemony" a central position in his theory of the State. He also shares with Gramsci (and, we have argued, with the later Althusser) a preoccupation with the "cementing" function of the dominant ideology in a social formation.

The many overlaps and convergences, then, are clear. Of course, as Poulantzas notes, Gramsci's theorising is far less systematic than his. Gramsci never makes what Poulantzas calls the full advance to the theory of "structuralist causality". (For Althusser, this means abandoning the notion of a causal chain, and trying to "think" the relation between the different levels of a social formation in terms of "a cause immanent in its effects, in the Spinozist sense of the term . . . the whole existence of a structure consists of its effects" (*Reading Capital,* p.189). Poulantzas defines it as the necessity to theorize "the specific autonomy of instances of the capitalist mode of production". (*Political Power and Social Classes,* p.139) Gramsci certainly never uses this "structuralist" language. He does not think a social formation in the formal terms of relations between "specifically autonomous instances". Therefore he has no developed theory of the different *regions* of a social formation, and thus of the theories appropriate to each as constituting "regional" theories.[72] But he does, throughout his writings, insist on the "relative autonomy", the specific effectivity, of the political and the ideological; and he rigorously opposes all forms of reductionism of superstructures to base, whether of the expressive, economist or spontaneist kind. He also, in the *Prison Notebooks* — like Poulantzas in *Political Power* — gives extensive attention to politics and the State. Thus it is difficult to think of the theoretical structure of Poulantzas's book except in relation to terrain which Gramsci was instrumental in opening up, even when we acknowledge that Poulantzas's mode of theorising this space is not Gramscian but rigorously Althusserean in character, and his tone is rigorously Leninist in inspiration. The problem, then, is that Poulantzas is, throughout, far less sympathetic to Gramsci than Althusser is: far less generous in acknowledging his theoretical debt. His attack on Gramsci's "historicism" is far more *purist* than Althusser's.[73] And he goes to far greater lengths to distinguish his work from any Gramscian taint.

Some of these distinctions are real and fruitful. Others appear to be distinctions without real theoretical differences. An example of the first is the debate about "Caesarism" and "Bonapartism" (it is even more fully developed in Poulantzas's subsequent study, *Fascism and Dictatorship*). These are terms which Gramsci employs when he is discussing different types of political resolution to moments of crisis and rupture — non-hegemonic resolutions, or "exceptional" forms of the capitalist State. Gramsci defines them rather loosely: Poulantzas, correctly, subjects them to a more systematic scrutiny. Poulantzas argues that Gramsci's concept of "Caesarism" refers to that exceptional moment when neither of the fundamental classes can rule — when there is an equilibrium of power, a stalemate. Fascism, however, is *not* the result of a stalemate between the classes, even though, under Fascism, the capitalist State does exhibit certain features of "autonomy" which Gramsci identified with a "Caesarist solution".[74] This allows Poulantzas to distinguish between different types of the exceptional State more carefully than Gramsci does. It is, therefore, a useful and generative distinction.

The case is rather different with "hegemony".[75] Poulantzas claims to use "hegemony" to refer to "how a power bloc composed of several politically dominant classes or fractions can function". And he distinguishes it from Gramsci's usage. The distinction seems a false one: surely this *is* one of the ways in which Gramsci employs the concept? Poulantzas objects to the fact that Gramsci also uses "hegemony" to apply to the strategies of the *dominated* classes. Now this problem of whether a class which does not possess State power can be "hegemonic" has presented problems for the use of Gramsci's work before. In his famous exchange with Anderson, E.P. Thompson *also* questioned this usage of the concept — paradoxically adopting there Poulantzas's position. But the question has been posed in a more urgent and practical form by the whole strategy of the Italian Communist Party, and its aim to achieve a social "hegemony" — for example through the "Historic Compromise" with Christian Democracy — *before* it grasps State power: a strategy in the construction of which, moreover, Gramsci's name has been constantly invoked. Whether any of these applications can really be sanctioned by reference to Gramsci's work is open to question. But certainly, in his delicate distinction between a "war of manoeuvre" (a frontal assault on State power) and a "war of position" (occupying and infiltrating the outer trenches and fortifications of civil society) Gramsci does envisage the party of the working class as, at least, requiring a "hegemonic strategy".[76] Poulantzas, however, argues, with Lenin, that the dominated classes "cannot win ideological domination before conquering political power" (p.204). Now the difficulty is that Poulantzas is not content with reaffirming this more classical Leninist position. He goes on to ascribe what he sees as Gramsci's error to Gramsci's historicism. Though, he says, Gramsci's problematic "is on the face of it opposed to the Lukácsean thesis" — the rising proletariat as a class subject, the bearer of a universal "world view". This appears to collapse the many real, substantive *differences* between Gramsci and Lukács. As Poulantzas himself elsewhere acknowledges, Gramsci does deal theoretically with the "dislocation between a dominant ideology . . . and the politically dominant class".[77] Indeed, this attention to "dislocations" is what grounds, theoretically, Gramsci's attention to the specificity of the political, and his refusal to tolerate any collapse or simple identity between base and superstructure. This is the site of a *major and irreversible theoretical difference* between Gramsci and Lukács. Poulantzas has been driven in his urgency to attack "historicism" in all its guises, to reduce this difference — and thus to give a distorted impression of Gramsci's distinctive theoretical contribution.

It is *not* a Lukácsian view of class subjects and ascribed world views which is at issue here. It is an enlarged concept of *hegemony.* Gramsci *does,* as we have tried to show, use "hegemony" in an enlarged and encompassing sense. He uses it — albeit "untheoretically" — to deal with a major issue in marxist theory: the question of the complex and often indirect means by which the whole fabric of capitalist society is drawn — often by means of what Althusser has called a "teeth gritting harmony"[78] — into conformity with the long-term needs of Capital. As we have already argued, this is Gramsci's way of opening up the question which Althusser has posed in terms of "reproduction". As we have also noted, the moment Althusser advances to this question, he is obliged to give Gramsci his full measure. Poulantzas uses a more restricted definition of "hegemony". He tends to limit it to the terrain of *the political,* and to the ideological in so far as it flows from the political and from the State. It is this more restricted treatment, coupled with the compulsion to attack "historicism", which produces Poulantzas's "misrecognition" of Gramsci's problematic.[77]

This then ties in with certain other features of Poulantzas's work in general. His tendency to "over-politicize" the problems concerned leads him to neglect Gramsci's use of the concept "civil society" (also dismissed here as "historicist": see the earlier discussions of this point). And that, in turn, tends to lead Poulantzas (as we have argued it also led Althusser) to draw everything on to the terrain of *the State*. (We say this while fully recognizing the major contribution which Poulantzas has made to our conceptualization of the capitalist State.) It may also have something to do with another feature of Poulantzas's work in this book: a certain "functionalism" in his treatment of the State and of ideology. When Althusser exposed himself to the same problem, he tried to remedy it by invoking the "class struggle": but in the ISAs essay, this is primarily in footnotes, asides and in the Postscript: it is not centrally woven into the problematic of his text. The appeal to the "class struggle" plays a far more central role in Poulantzas's work — it is everywhere and generally invoked. But there remains a sense in which it is — to use an Althusserean metaphor — gesturally, rather than theoretically present in Poulantzas's discourse. Now, though the term itself is not always present in Gramsci's writing, the concept of it is never absent. For Gramsci there is *no* state or moment of "hegemony" which is not contested; none which is not the result of the ruling class alliances *mastering* the class struggle; no "hegemony" which does not have to be won, secured, constantly defended. And this is so even when the site of that class struggle is apparently far removed from the terrain of the economic and the direct confrontation between the fundamental classes. It is something of this kind which leads Gramsci to speak of the need for a hegemonic practice even by the political organizations of the dominated classes; which leads him to identify the continuing struggle for "hegemony" even when the proletariat can only struggle on unfavourable terrain — in the "war of position". He may, then, be wrong to speak of the "hegemony" of the dominated classes — strictly speaking, in his own terms, it is a contradictory concept. But he is *not* wrong to employ the concept "hegemony" in this enlarged sense, or to see it as a struggle to win over the dominated classes in which any "resolution" involves both *limits* (compromises) and *systematic contradictions.* Poulantzas does tend to treat "hegemony" as a "functional effectivity" of the domination of the class alliance in power — i.e. to treat it unproblematically. This Gramsci is never guilty of.

Hence, whereas for Poulantzas "hegemony" appears as a more or less guaranteed feature of the domination of the capitalist state by a ruling class alliance, Gramsci tends to treat the concept in a more contested, more conjuncturally located manner. For Gramsci classes *can* "rule" for long periods without being "hegemonic": the example of Italy was paramount in his mind here. There can be "crises of hegemony" which do not result in a breakdown of the system. There can be shifts within the mode of hegemony — moments when "coercion" outdistances "consent", or vice versa. Indeed, this further distinction which Gramsci draws between "hegemonic" and "non-hegemonic" forms of domination enables us more precisely to *periodize concretely* different moments and forms of the capitalist state, and different phases within any one form. This leads us directly to what Gramsci conceived of as constituting, *par excellence,* the specificity of the marxist theory of *politics*: the analysis of particular conjunctures, of particular moments of "hegemony", and of the relations of class forces which sustain one kind of "unstable equilibrium" or provoke a rupture in it. It also led him to consider what was the nature of the "compromises"

68

which enable a ruling bloc to consolidate its rule by winning subaltern classes to its side; and to examine not only any particular "equilibrium of forces" but what the prevailing *tendency* in such an equilibrium consisted of — whether producing favourable or unfavourable terrain for the conduct of class struggle, and thus defining the strategy for the Party of the proletariat. Far from this constituting, for all practical purposes, a Lukácsian approach, with its ascription of a particular form of "class consciousness" to an undifferentiated class-subject, Gramsci's concepts here seem to point us *directly* to the terrain of Lenin: the "concrete analysis of concrete situations". Their application to the analysis of a whole variety of political conjunctures appears to us to hold a rich promise — and to have hardly been begun.

It is not surprising, however — given what we have argued — to find that Poulantzas *also* disagrees with Gramsci's distinction between "hegemony" and "domination" and attacks Gramsci for reserving the term "hegemony" for those moments when consent prevails over coercion. Poulantzas objects to this distinction — a central one for Gramsci (caught in the couplets coercion/consent, domination/direction, etc.). He criticizes Gramsci for saying that there is always a "complementarity" between those two elements of political or state power. The state, he argues — in addition — cannot be "hegemonic"; only the dominant classes can be "hegemonic". With respect to the first objection, we can only say that there *is* a complementarity between coercion and consent, and the distinction is a fruitful one. And we note how useful Althusser himself found it, when, in the ISAs article, he demonstrated how apparatuses of consent also work by coercion (e.g. censorship in the media) and apparatuses of coercion require consent (the concern of the police for their public image). With respect to the second objection, it seems true that the State, as such, cannot be "hegemonic". But the State plays a pivotal role in raising the domination of a particular class alliance over a social formation *to the level of consent.* This captures precisely the concept of how the State functions to maintain "hegemony" by winning, securing and cementing the "consent" of the dominated classes. This is also Marx's concept of the State as the site of "universalization" — the legitimation, the rendering invisible, of class rule, through the giving of the form of the "general interest" to what are in fact the interests of particular class fractions. Poulantzas himself has fruitfully explored and developed just this argument.[80] But by collapsing the two "poles" of State power — coercion and consent — and by restricting "hegemony" to the dominant classes only, Poulantzas appears to neglect what at other points he is at pains to underscore: namely, why the capitalist State, based on universal suffrage, is *par excellence* the necessary site for the generalization of class domination. Thus, in his haste to distinguish himself from Gramsci, Poulantzas appears to neglect arguments, implicit in Gramsci and often quite well developed, which actually support his own theoretical position. Poulantzas certainly recognizes the importance of "consent" for the normalization of domination in the capitalist state, but he sometimes seems to take it for granted. Gramsci's treatment of the problem of the capitalist State as, above all, an exercise in winning and keeping the consent of the dominated to their own domination, does not allow us for a moment to neglect this central feature of class struggle *and* state power.

It is certainly true that, as Poulantzas argues, Gramsci's "insights" are provisional and unsystematic. (Althusser calls them "brilliant" — echoing a term which Marx

69

used of an early essay by Engels which had greatly influenced him; Althusser's reference can be seen as an implicit acknowledgement of a theoretical debt. [81] Poulantzas and Gramsci here exhibit opposite strengths — and weaknesses. What Gramsci lacks at the level of systematic theorisation, he gains at the level of conjunctural analysis. What Poulantzas gains by his theoretical rigour, he lacks at the level of the specific and the concrete — the source of his residual functionalism. Gramsci's references to class struggles and to specific conjunctures — and the movement between conjunctures — are always detailed, illuminating particular social formations. Poulantzas tends to draw on particular conjunctures "illustratively" (at least in this book) and to be better at dealing with systematic features and functions, less attuned to "moments in the relations of forces". We might want to say that Gramsci's concepts are *always conjunctural* — there are no "general" concepts or "general" functions. This is both a strength and a weakness. Poulantzas has a more developed theory of regions — of regional instances, and of the specific autonomy of levels of a social formation. Gramsci works with a more fused or *coupled* concept of structure-superstructure. The former is certainly clearer, more rigorous. The latter is more dynamic, less fixed in the form of a combinatory of instances.

It is not, then, a straightforward matter of a theoretical choice *between* Gramsci and Poulantzas. If, as we have argued, Gramsci constitutes something like the *limit case* for the structuralist marxists, this is an uncompleted theoretical encounter, as Althusser's *Essays in Self-Criticism* all too clearly reveals. The problem is rather that Poulantzas tends to *foreclose* on this theoretical debate. And he does this by means of the mechanism — one is almost tempted to call it a complusion — not only of attacking "historicism", but of eliding all "historicisms" into the figure of one, general, theoretical Enemy; to reduce them all to their "historicist" elements, their logic; and then to attack the historicist problematic whenever and wherever it raises its head. It is this which leads Poulantzas to *over-exaggerate* his differences with Gramsci, and to simplify the nature of Gramsci's marxism in the process.

The consequence of this reductionist procedure, and the theoretical "purism" which informs it, is that it leaves Poulantzas is a position where he is not free to acknowledge his intellectual and theoretical debt to Gramsci. He presents Gramsci as a more reduced figure than does his great mentor, Althusser. In this sense, he out-Althusser Althusser. This tendency is discernible elsewhere — for example, in the rather mechanical "Althusserian orthodoxy" of the opening section of *Political Power and Social Classes.* Such orthodoxy is particularly difficult to sustain since Althusser himself insists on constantly re-examining and redefining his own position — always, of course, with its own kind of polemical certitude. Generally, there is a striking contrast between Poulantzas and Althusser in the manner in which they have "appropriated" Gramsci. In this exercise, it is Althusser who has come closer to giving due recognition to the *necessary complexity* of Gramsci's work. The fact that Gramsci has survived this appropriation, and retains his independent position, is a testimony to his continuing stature as a marxist theorist and militant.

VI Conclusion

This paper has undertaken two tasks which, we hope, will contribute to the current

70

and widespread discussion about Gramsci. First, an account was given of how the concept "ideology" relates to and is taken up in the theoretical matrix of the *Prison Notebooks.* Secondly, the idea that Gramsci was a historicist in a strong and simple sense was rejected. Whether and to what extent he was a historicist in any sense is a question which raises as many problems about the scope of the concept of historicism as it does about Gramsci.

It was argued, with respect to the first task, that there is no "obvious" theory of ideology in Gramsci's writings. Although such a theory can be constructed from its "practical state" in the *Notebooks,* the concept only becomes meaningful insofar as it is subordinated to Gramsci's general, and politically-inspired, corpus of concepts. At the centre of that corpus are the notions of "hegemony", "common sense" and the "intellectuals". Now, these concepts exist for Gramsci in order to examine specific, historical conjunctures; or, to put it more politically, to analyse the balance of forces within specific conjunctures. They are therefore concepts of historical materialism. Consequently, it is not surprising that Gramsci is more concerned with specific ideologies than with the question of ideology-in-general. This is not to say that the concepts of ideology or hegemony are not general concepts which can be defined at a general level (if — for Gramsci — they are of limited value at that level). It is, however, to insist that they do not refer to general entities. Ideology-in-general is not, for Gramsci, a legitimate object of inquiry. And since he does not accept a division between marxism as historical science and as philosophy (dialectical materialism),[82] it could not be recognised as a legitimate object for marxism. Therefore, although he cannot be regarded as a relativist over the status of theory (concepts are not wholly reducible to the historical situations to which they refer), it is certainly true that marxism, for Gramsci, is *at one and the same time* a philosophical and historical theory of specific, and only specific, phenomena. Ideology is no exception.

It has also been argued in this paper that Althusser and Poulantzas, despite their critique of historicist forms of marxism (and Gramsci's is numbered amongst them), owe a greater theoretical debt to Gramsci than they (and particularly Poulantzas) are prepared to admit. This is especially so with regard to questions concerning the role and relative autonomy of politics and the State. The relation of theorists such as Althusser to the complex "historicism" of Gramsci becomes compounded when we consider the propositions put forward in Althusser's recent *Self Criticism.* We therefore conclude this article with an outline of that position. We have said that Gramsci does not comfortably "fit" the historicist criterion. If, in the light of *Self-Criticism,* that criterion itself appears less sound than was once believed, then not only does Gramsci's work escape blanket condemnation from the anti-historicist quarter; it can be restored to a central place in serious discussions of those theoretical questions of marxism which remain inadequately dealt with.

The critique of historicism was largely based on the arguments of *Reading Capital.*[83] For our purposes, the most important of these is the claim that marxism provides a scientific and unique epistemology; one which definitively separates marxism from any form of empiricism or idealism. Historicism of course, contains elements of both. If the scientificity of marxism can be shown in general theoretical terms, it would follow that all forms or elements of historicism have nothing whatever to do with marxism. It should be made explicit here that such an argument relies on the notion that marxist philosophy is alone capable of such distinctions of scientificity. Historical materialism, in contrast has a quite different object: the analysis of concrete conjunctures. (Some of the other problems of *Reading Capital* are indicated elsewhere in this journal and are therefore omitted here.)

Althusser's self-criticism rejects the idea of a scientific philosophy. He reasserts the proposition, implicit in more "orthodox" marxism and explicit in Gramsci, that there can be no such thing as science-in-general, and no such discipline as philosophy insofar as the latter claims to be the logical guarantor of "Science". Despite the claims in *Reading Capital* to the contrary, Althusser argues, a procedure of this kind cannot escape the (bourgeois) "problems of knowledge". Now in the earlier text, ideology (in general) is defined in logical opposition to science (in general). Against this "speculative" position, Althusser now maintains that science should be understood as "the *minimum of generality* necessary to be able to grasp a concrete object".[84] This conceptual generality, moreover, is to be placed *within* historical materialism.[85] If Althusser's self-criticism is correct, then the generalised divorce between science and ideology as an *epistemological* proposition ceases to be a tenet of marxism, and with its demise fall arguments which depend on it. At least a part of the argument against historicism comes under this category. For historicism involves opposition to the separation of dialectical from historical materialism, and concentrates purely on reducing the contents of theories and ideologies to the "expression" of their historical conditions and effects — features which would certainly have come under the axe of philosophical marxism. Is it then the case that the historicists are, after all correct?

Fortunately, things are seldom quite so simple, and theoretical debates are no exception. In defending what we see as the central concepts of Gramsci, we do *not* imply that the critique of historicism is mistaken. Neither do we suggest that there can be a return to an "innocent" reading of Gramsci in the light of the structuralist intervention. Rather, we have argued that it involves a danger of bringing genuine concepts of historical materialism under that generalised category. There is thus a need to re-examine, for example, the idea that there is a theoretical equivalence between *reducing* theories and ideologies to their historical conditions of existence, and *relating* theories and ideologies to such conditions. The latter, it seems to us, is a proposition of marxism; the former is not. Similarly, Althusser himself remains intransigently opposed to historicism, empiricism, and idealism, and to that extent the problem is not easily resolvable. Specifically, the *Self-Criticism* involves a rejection of only *some* of the features of the problematic generated in *Reading Capital.* Indeed, it could be plausibly argued that the latest position is internally inconsistent (or at least is a "transitional" work awaiting fuller treatment), and that consequently a uniquely marxist theory of knowledge and ideology-in-general is still required. Philosophy, certainly, continues to play, for Althusser, a special (if demoted) theoretical role in relation to the sciences.

These important issues cannot be appraised here. What can be asserted is that advances are still to be made in the domain of the self-definition of marxism. Whatever the problems in Althusser's shifting theoretical perspective, his claim that the concepts of science and ideology must be subsumed under historical materialism and not philosophy cannot easily be dismissed. It is a claim that was put forward consistently and persuasively by Gramsci in the elaboration of his scientific (as opposed to philosophical) concepts. It is a contribution which should be openly acknowledged.

This essay went to press before the appearance of Perry Anderson's lengthy study of Gramsci in New Left Review *100. There has therefore been no opportunity to include any discussion of Anderson's interpretation of Gramsci in this essay.*

Notes
1. Gramsci, 1971, p.376.
2. 1971, p.164-5.
3. 1971, p.164.
4. 1971, p.60.
5. 1971, p.177.
6. According to Norbeto Bobbio (*Gramsci e la Concezione della Società 'Civile'*, Feltrinelli, 1976), Gramsci's usage of "civil society" marks a radical break with the Marxist tradition. Whereas Marx uses the term to designate the "whole complex of the material conditions of life" (i.e. as an aspect of the base), Gramsci lifts "civil society" into the superstructure. On the basis of this interpretation, Bobbio makes a reading of the Prison Notebooks in which the determination of the base on the supestructure is reversed, and "objective" conditions are turned into the potential instruments of class subjectivity. The poverty of the reading becomes apparent when he comes to identify Gramsci's analytic usage of "civil society" in his historical work as simply a means of identifying "progressive" and "reactionary" blocs. Bobbio is trying to fit Gramsci back into the historicist mould, and succeeds in making his writings very similar to those of Lukács.
7. Gramsci, 1971, p.12.
8. 1971, p.52.
9. 1971, p.208.
10. 1971, p.265.
11. 1971, p.181.
12. 1971, p.139.
13. 1971, p.328.
14. 1971, p.376-7.
15. Marx, 1970, p.64.
16. 1971, p.78.
17. 1971, p.83.
18. Carl Boggs (Boggs, 1976) tends to do both these things. In his attempt to refute the economism of the 2nd International, he reproduces the other side of that same problematic, namely "historicism". For example, his explanation of hegemony is in terms of "permeation" of value systems: "Hegemony in this sense might be defined as an 'organising principle' or 'world-view' . . . that is diffused by agencies of ideological control and socialisation in every area of life." Gramsci's concept of hegemony is thereby collapsed into a Marcusean model of social control. Charles Woolfson (Woolfson, 1976) in his article on the "Semiotics of Working-Class Speech" is clear that "any hegemony in a class society is necessarily limited and incomplete, and exists in tension"; however, he conflates hegemony with ideological domination and subordination.
19. 1971, p.161.
20. 1971, p.57.
21. 1971, p.442.
22. 1971, p.357.
23. This becomes particularly evident when reading Gramsci's *Letters from Prison* (New Edinburgh Review Special Editions, 1974).
24. 1971, p.348.
25. 1971, p.324.
26. 1971, p.355.
27. 1971, p.420.
28. 1971, p.325.
29. 1971, p.333.
30. 1971, pp.14-15.

31. 1971, p.408.
32. 1971, p.12.
33. 1971, p.258.
34. 1971, p.275-6.
35. 1971, p.238.
36. 1971, p.57.
37. 1971, p.331.
38. 1971, p.339.
39. 1971, p.198.
40. 1971, p.331.
41. 1971, pp.272-3.
42. 1971, p.165.
43. 1971, p.197, p.331.
44. 1971, p.328.
45. 1971, p.377.
46. 1971, p.152.
47. 1971, p.152-3.
48. 1971, p.403.
49. 1971, pp.445-6.
50. 1971, p.405.
51. 1971, p.417.
52. 1971, p.407.
53. 1971, pp.432-40.
54. 1971, pp.446-7.
55. 1971, p.403.
56. 1971, p.376.
57. The whole of Althusser's essay "Contradiction And Over-determination" is relevant here, but especially pp.98-101.
58. See, especially, the section entitled "Analysis of Situations, Relations of Force", in "The Modern Prince" essay, *Prison Notebooks,* pp.175-185.
59. Chapter 5 of *Reading Capital.*
60. "Ideology And Ideological State Apparatuses: Notes Towards An Investigation" in *Lenin and Philosophy and Other Essays,* New Left Books, 1971. Hereafter referred to as "the ISAs essay".
61. Althusser calls Gramsci's case a "limit-situation", in "Marxism is Not a Historicism", p.131.
62. The first formulations of ideology as "imaginary lived relations" is in Section IV of Althusser's essay on "Marxism and Humanism", in *For Marx.* These are subsequently developed in *Reading Capital,* but especially in the ISAs essay.
63. "Finally, as well as his polemical and practical use of the concept, Gramsci also has a truly 'historicist' conception of Marx: a 'historicist' conception of the *relationship between Marx's theory and real history*". Althusser in "Marxism is Not a Historicism", p.130.
64. The first critical assault by Althusser on the concept of 'civil society' is launched in the context of a discussion on "the ghost of the Hegelian model again" and Marx's so-called 'inversion' of Hegel. See the "Contradiction and Over-determination" essay, pp.108-11; and *Reading Capital,* pp.162 ff.
65. Since the term "civil society" appears here in what, for this text, must be considered a seminal formulation, Althusser's reading of it appears forced: "Of course, Marx still talks of 'civil society' (especially in the *German Ideology . . .*) but as an allusion to the past, to denote the site of his discoveries, not to re-utilize the concept". It is more accurate to say that, here, Marx *does* "utilize" the concept, in a *transformed* way, *thereby* indicating the site of his discoveries . . .
66. Althusser's argument is that the reference to "the society of needs" disappears from Marx's discourse: *hence* he did not merely invert, but broke with, Hegel. However, theoretical discoveries cannot be limited to "making old concepts disappear", but must

also include retaining them, but in a transformed position within the discourse: or designating the theoretical space which they referenced differently. Althusser knows this well — for both Marx and Hegel use "the dialectic", though, as he shows, they mean different things by it. Whenever Althusser deals with the question of the "inversion", he seems compelled to force distinctions, which are correct and necessary, to an absolute point. This stems from too fixed a use of "epistemological rupture" — a point now acknowledged by Althusser himself in *Essays in Self-Criticism.*

67. Cf: Marx to Engels, April 2nd, 1858: "Simple circulation, considered by itself — and it is the surface of bourgeois society, obliterating the deeper operations from which it arises — reveals no difference between the objects of exchange, except formal and temporary ones. This is the *realm of freedom, equality and of property based on 'labour'* . . . The absurdity, on the one hand, of the preachers of economic harmony, the modern free traders . . . to maintain this most superficial and abstract relation as *their* truth in contrast to the more developed relations of production and their antagonism. (On the other hand) the absurdity of the Proudhonists . . . to oppose the ideas of equality, etc. corresponding to this exchange of equivalents (or things assumed to be equivalents) to the inequalities etc. which result from this exchange and which are its origin." For a much developed exposition of the same argument, see Chs. 48, 49, 50 of *Capital III,* Part VIII.

68. Unexpectedly, Althusser finds a warrant for this collapse in *Gramsci:* "As a conscious Marxist, Gramsci already forestalled this objection in one sentence. The distinction between the public and the private is a distinction internal to bourgeois law, and valid in the (subordinate) domains in which bourgeois law exercises its 'authority'." ("Ideological State Apparatuses", p.253.) Althusser is, of course, correct to see that the public/private distinction is principally one enforced by bourgeois law, and that therefore the boundary between them *is constantly being shifted.* But he is wrong if he is arguing that where, at any specific historical moment, this boundary was drawn was regarded by Gramsci as irrelevant. As Althusser notes, without comment, in a previous footnote (footnote 5), when Gramsci had the "remarkable idea" of adding "Church, the Schools, trade unions, etc." to the Repressive State apparatuses, "he included . . . a certain number of institutions from *civil society*". Thus for Gramsci, the public/private distinction remained significant, though not determining "in the last instance".

69. See Gramsci's essays on "The Intellectuals", "On Schools" and "Americanism and Fordism", in the *Prison Notebooks.*

70. This argument is most fully developed in Poulantzas, *Classes in Contemporary Capitalism,* 1974.

71. See, especially, *Political Power and Social Classes,* pp.227-252.

72. On a "regional structure as an *object of science*", see *Political Power,* pp.16-18.

73. For example, *Political Power,* pp.137-9.

74. The passages concerned with "Caesarism", "Bonapartism" and "Fascism" are mainly to be found in *Political Power,* pp.258-62.

75. The concept of "hegemony", and the differences between his and Gramsci's use of the concept are most fully discussed by Poulantzas, in *Political Power,* pp.137-9, 204-5.

76. Gramsci elaborates on the distinctions between 'war of position', and 'war of manoeuvre' in "Notes on Italian History", pp.108-110, and in "State and Civil Society", pp.229-235. Both in *Prison Notebooks.*

77. *Political Power,* p.204.

78. The phrase is from the ISAs essay, p.257.

79. The following passage is a good example of what we mean by "reduction"; "To grasp the relation between these two 'moments' ['force' and 'consent'] he [Gramsci] uses the significant term 'complementarity'. From this stems a confusion of the areas in which hegemony is exercised . . . according to which, force is exercised by the state in 'political' society, hegemony in 'civil society' by means of the organization usually considered to be private . . . This distinction is the key to the model with which historicism apprehended the relations between the economic and the political: it saw the political (the class struggle) as the motor, the force, of the 'economic laws' conceived in a mechanistic fashion;

75

in other words, politics is conceived as the motor of economic 'autonomism'." (*Political Power* p.26).

The 'complementarity' between the moments for force and consent is, certainly, Gramsci. He does not, however, assign the former to political society and the latter to civil society in that simple way. Hence it does not follow that Gramsci thinks the relation of the political to the economic in a historicist way. It would certainly be difficult to reconcile any reading of Gramsci as regarding politics as the motor of automatic economic laws "conceived in a mechanistic fashion". The final move in this reductionism, moreover, appears to operate on the back of a pun — on the word "force" — which cannot be supported from a reading of Gramsci (i.e. he nowhere uses the "moment of force" to refer to politics as "the force" of automatic economic laws). In short, the more the argument advances, the more clearly "historicism" emerges as a theoretical deviation — but the farther we get from a reading which refers in any recognizable way to Gramsci's work.

80. Particularly in *Political Power,* pp.210-28 ("Bourgeois Political Ideology and the Class Struggle"), and pp.274-207 ("The Capitalist State and the Field of the Class Struggle").
81. See *Pour Marx,* Maspero 1965, p.78 n. and p.114 n. *Génial* in French, but "brilliant" in English, rather than the "genial" of *For Marx,* p.81 n. and p.114 n.
82. 1971, pp.38, 434-5.
83. See the Althusser article in this journal.
84. Althusser, 1976, p.112 n., emphasis original.
85. Ibid., p.124 n.

BIBLIOGRAPHY

A. Gramsci, *Selections from the Prison Notebooks,* ed. Hoare and Nowell Smith, Lawrence and Wishart: London 1971.

L. Althusser, *For Marx,* Allen Lane: London 1969. *Reading Capital,* New Left Books: London 1970. *Essays in Self-Criticism,* New Left Books: London 1976.

N. Bobbio, *Gramsci e la Concezione della Società 'Civile',* Feltrinelli 1976.

C. Boggs, *Gramsci's Marxism,* Pluto: London 1976.

G. Lukács: *History and Class Consciousness,* Merlin: London 1971.

K. Marx: *Capital,* Vol.I, Moscow, 1966. *The German Ideology,* Lawrence and Wishart, 1970

N. Poulantzas, *Political Power and Social Classes,* New Left Books: London 1973. *Fascism and Dictatorship,* New Left Books: London 1974.

C. Woolfson, "The Semiotics of Working-Class Speech" in *Working Papers in Cultural Studies 9,* Birmingham 1976.

Althusser's Theory of Ideology

Gregor McLennan, Victor Molina,
Roy Peters

I. General Introduction to Althusser

The work of Louis Althusser has been the most significant contribution to marxist theory in many years. No other figure has generated such thought-provoking discussion, and controversy. The fact that his work has encountered heavy criticism should not disguise the overall beneficial effects which his seminal texts have had on the re-statement and clarification of those ideas which in today's theoretical and political context are taken to be the 'basic' concepts of historical materialism. Not all of his conceptions, however, can be accepted. Indeed, in this paper, we shall throw doubt on a few. Yet there can be no question of the importance of Althusser's contribution In particular, he has rightly insisted that a critique of Stalinism, economism, and an over-humanist interpretation of Marx must be *theoretically* grounded, and that such an elaboration can reveal many submerged interconnections between apparently opposed schools of socialist thought. In Althusserian language, they share the same 'problematic', or sets of questions and presuppositions. By means of such a theoretical clarification, Althusser aims to leave marxism the better equipped to confront the principal anti-marxist philosophies.

Against both the mechanistic interpretation of the "base-superstructure" metaphor, and the essentialist or Hegelian view of the social totality, Althusser proposes a quite distinct concept of the social whole (social formation). This will be outlined briefly below. Althusser exposes the fundamentally irrational nature of conceptions of society which justify either an "economistic" or "technicist" view of history; or the assertion of the centrality of human agents, or classes of agents, as self-constituted subjects of history. Both these conceptions and their consequent politics, Althusser argues, share an essentialist, and metaphysically derived, conception of history as an unfolding process which has no place in scientific marxism.

Through his concern for rationality and scientificity — and some would argue that this is his primary achievement — Althusser reintroduces basic epistemological questions into the sphere of marxist theory. Thus, for example, the idea that history unfolds towards a goal (be that technically or spiritually defined) entails that the analytic concepts used to describe such a process can only receive such justifications as they have from their realisation *in* that process. In conceptions of this kind, thought and "reality" form a single, undifferentiated unity derived from a teleologically defined process. Yet they exhibit a failure to make crucial analytical distinctions between different categories, and between categories and reality (they merely 'express' one another). Althusser accuses humanism and economism of sharing this same 'historicist' conception. His intervention arises as much from a concern for rationality and a relatively autonomous *theoretical* mode of conceptual validity as it is a political polemic. He argues throughout his work that these 'suspect' notions (teleology, causality, process, undifferentiated "praxis", the 'correspondence' of concepts with 'reality') must be totally eradicated in the name of a scientific rationality capable of assigning to marxism its rightful, and quite distinct, 'continent' of knowledge.

We have posed these points briefly and provocatively. They are raised not as definitive outlines of Althusser's thought, but for a number of less ambitious reasons. First, they form the indispensable context of Althusser's theory of ideology. Secondly, they set the question of the extent to which his contribution to marxism is primarily an epistemological one. Thirdly, they show that whatever clarity is achieved in our exposition of 'ideology', many points of debate will have to be referred to the kind of thorough reading of all aspects of Althusser's texts which is obviously not possible here, but which must be performed if a rigorous critique and serious evaluation of his work — political, epistemological, and genuinely marxist — is to replace over-hasty gut reactions. For he more than most has shown how to criticise "problematics" rigorously — including his own.

II.   Social Formation and Superstructure

Our account aims to follow closely the overall theme of the current journal, namely, ideology. It is not intended to be a systematic engagement with the many other major theoretical problems generated by Althusser's work. In attempting to analyse Althusser's concept of ideology, however, it has been necessary to locate the various formulations within the context of his theoretical "system" as a whole. In Althusser, probably more so than in other marxist writers, "ideology" is integrally related to a number of other important concepts, in particular those of "science" and "social formation". In some texts, especially *For Marx,* ideology is conceived as a *level* which, together with the economic and political 'levels' , comprises a social formation. Elsewhere, in *Reading Capital* for example, the status of the concept is principally epistemological. This distinction, however, should not be taken as final. In the sections which follow we try to unravel their combination and separation in a series of texts or 'phases'.
Indeed, there is a further aspect to the concept which runs throughout Althusser's writings, namely, that ideology constitutes the fabric of society (e.g. "Marxism and Humanism" and "Ideology and Ideological State Apparatuses") insofar as it is the medium in which all history occurs, and the relay by means of which men "live" their relation to their real conditions of existence. The single term "ideology" is often invoked to specify any one of these meanings, but may also condense a plurality of usages. It is important, therefore, to avoid any unnecessary overgeneralisation from particular usages of the term by relating it to, and rooting it in, Althusser's concept of the social formation . For it is this latter concept which stands at the heart of his theoretical enterprise. As a preface to a more detailed discussion of ideology, we accordingly propose a necessarily schematic evaluation of the social formation first.

Historical materialism is the science of the history of social formations. A central point of Althusser's contribution to marxism is his account of the nature of this social formation which is based upon a particular reformulation of the classic structure/superstructure unity. By this reformulation Althusser transforms the whole problematic of the marxist dialectic, submitting it to the primacy of materialism.[1] The specificity of the marxist dialectic (of its structure and forms) consists in its being the dialectic of a particular kind of materialism which has to be rooted in an adequate concept of the social formation.

The distinguishing feature of every social formation is to be found in the particular unity of *levels* or *instances:* the economic structure (the base) and the political and ideological superstructures. These levels are different not only because they refer to distinct practices or objects but also because each of them differs in its capacity to determine the others (their degree or index of "effectivity"). The unity which they form is based on a hierarchical relationship between the levels in which we find that the economic determines, *in the last instance,* the political and the ideological levels but at the same time is *overdetermined* by each of them.

The relation between structure and superstructure is not one of 'expression' where the superstructures are reflexes or "phenomena" emanating from the economic structure or essence. Rather, the superstructures could be seen as the *necessary* conditions of existence of the economic base. The relation is one of reciprocal determination, although there is an *unevenness* in the determination because it is governed by the determination *in the last instance* by the economic. In this sense, the superstructure has a *relative autonomy* with respect to the base : it has a relative independence, the parameters of which are nevertheless fixed by its ultimate dependence on "determination in the last instance".

As opposed to a simple, expressive totality, a social formation always exists as a *structured complex whole.* Its elements and contradictions are maintained in determinate relations of domination and subordination. Althusser distinguishes between the element in a social formation which is determinant (which is always the economic) and that which is dominant. That is, that the most important conditions of existence of a social formation need not necessarily be economic. In Ancient social formations, for example, politics was the dominant level. The economic, however, remains determinant in the sense that the dominant (and other) levels are conditions of existence of a specific mode of *economic* production. There is, then, no simple, unilinear primacy of the economic level. This implies the possibility of the *displacement* of domination from one element to another, a type of metonymic causality. The social formation, then, is always structured *in dominance.* This uneven complexity represents the necessary concreteness of the determinations of a social whole. It is in this sense that Althusser refers to the "ever pre-giveness" of a complex social whole which is structured in dominance. For Althusser, there is never an original essence or single cause; there is only and always a complex articulation of determinations and levels, which is ever pre-given in the real concrete whole. To summarise, the superstructures exist as the essential conditions of existence of the social formation. The specific effectivities of the political and ideological are thus present in the complex and structural determination of any of the elements in the structure of the social formation.

We have outlined some of Althusser's basic concepts: the necessary relative auto-nomy of the superstructures, their overdetermining effect on the principal contra-diction (the economic), yet, nevertheless, the continuing determination by the economic "in the last instance", even though, in real, historical terms, that "lonely hour of the last instance never comes". By this expression, Althusser again refers to the fact that, for him, the economic level is never the sole determinant, and conse-quently that the real causal efficacy of other levels must be taken seriously. There is never a single, original cause of a state of affairs, or "conjuncture". Certainly, the relative autonomy of other levels is only gauged in terms of what is or is not compatible with the principal mode of production: but such a proposition entails the possibility of an indirect causal relation so that "His Majesty the economy" does not and cannot appear "in person". The political and ideological levels do not trans-parently reveal the presence of the economic lurking behind them. In *Reading Capital,* Althusser often refers to this "absent determination" as the presence of a "structure immanent in its effects", or "structural causality" ("metonymic causality").[2] Now, it is the terms *structure* and *structural causality* which sometimes give rise to criticism. We shall briefly indicate here some of the major problems in what is an otherwise complex and ongoing debate.

Generally speaking, *structure* refers, as indicated above, to a complexly structured social formation : complex because it is a combination of elements 'structured in dominance', because the various levels cannot be collapsed into one single contra-diction. One 'level' predominates over the others, yet whether that level coincides with the economic (as in capitalism, for example) or not, the two are theoretically distinct, and the dominant level is itself specified by the derterminant, i.e. the economic level.

The main difficulty revolves around whether the concept *structural causality* in *Reading Capital* entails an important shift from the concepts of *overdetermination* and *structure* in *For Marx.* In the latter text, the term *structure* mostly designates the social formation, as in the conceptualisation of a *structure in dominance,* where no room for ambiguity is afforded.[2] In *Reading Capital,* structural causality or *Darstellung* appears to be the same concept. And in one sense in which Althusser uses the notion, no problem of continuity arises; for it represents a rigorous re-examination of those mechanisms of the *economic* region of the capitalist mode of production (hereafter CMP) sometimes referred to by marxists as the relation between real rela-tions and phenomenal forms. Althusser proposes "Darstellung" as a means of analysing the real effectivity of seemingly 'surface' forms, such as wages, while retaining the notion that production (as opposed to exchange) is, so to speak, determinant in the last instance. The phenomenal forms/real relations couplet is, in Althusser's view, in-capable of an adequate account of this double articulation, for it rests on a Hegelian notion which reduces given phenomena to the emanations of a supposedly unprob-lematic "essence".

In the following extract, Althusser links *Darstellung* to the concept of *overdeter-mination.* He quotes the passage from the *1857 Introduction* in which Marx refers to the influence, and assignment of rank and influence, of a predominant structure of production upon other structures of production within the social formation.[4] "This text", Althusser argues, is discussing the determination of certain structures of production which are subordinate to a dominant structure of production, i.e. the determination of one structure by another and of the elements of a subordinate structure by the dominant, and therefore determinant structure. I have previously attempted to account for this phenomenon with the concept of *overdetermination,* which I borrowed from psycho-analysis. . . With what concept are we to think the determination of either an element or a structure by a structure ?. . . *'Darstellung',* the key epistemological concept of the whole of Marxist theory of value, the concept whose object is precisely to designate the mode of presence of the structure in its *effects,* and therefore to designate structural causality itself. (1970 p.188)

As well as referring to the concept of overdetermination, *Darstellung's* resemblance to a *structure articulated in dominance* cannot be overlooked. A structure in dominance refers to the various levels in the social formation along with their respective contradictions, each with principal and secondary aspects, As the contradictions admit of principal and secondary aspects, so too, the structure or particular concatenation of contradictions and levels is articulated in terms of a hierarchy of significant instances. This articulation is the social formation and constitutes an "ever pre-given complexly structured whole". But it is the economic which assigns the principal contradiction its role, and so overdetermination, *and* relative autonomy, *and* determination in the last instance, are all preserved in this formula.[5]

However, there can be little doubt that Althusser has adopted a *specific episte-mological concept* (taken, in fact, from Spinoza) by means of which he tries to recast his earlier notions. The concept of structural causality as the presence of a cause (structure) in and as its effects, has, it could be argued, logical consequences which cannot be simply reduced to "another way of saying the same thing". If the structure specifies its effects, yet is nothing outside its effects, the material or multiple causality of overdetermination appears to have given way to an "essentialist" and self-sustaining totality. This "eternity" (as it has been called)[6] of the structure logically prevents the kind of marxist analysis of change and complex historical processes that "overdetermination" seemed to offer.

We cannot enter into an assessment of this counter-argument, though it is certainly one to which Balibar is vulnerable. We would want, rather, to point out that it is not entirely clear in *Reading Capital* what exactly, for *Althusser* at least, the "structure" refers to. Does it designate the mode of production, for example? Or the social formation? It is possible, in fact that it applies to *both,* since Althusser speaks of a "global" mode of production in addition to a "regional" theory of the (economic) mode of production, thus suggesting that the concept "mode of production" refers to something larger than simply the economic level. Now, it is reasonable to suggest that if the term "structure" refers to a *social formation,* then the formula of structural causality, where "effects" are conceived as constituent parts or levels of a "global" structure, is intelligible, and — it seems to us — substantially correct.

On the other hand, it is certainly true that if this is interpreted as a global structure of regional structures where in both instances a "cause" (structure) is logically and literally present in and as its effects, at the very least the formal universality of the concept raises doubts: is the specificity of different objects of analysis not being sacrificed to the logical demands of the organising philosophical principle? A strict application of the Spinozist model hinders rather than aids the clarification of the "basic" concepts in question.

81

A final point of distinction arises if we consider that a "regional" theory of the mode of production is often referred to by Althusser as an abstract *concept*. Yet it is plausible to assert that this is none other than the analysis of relationships within the economic level of social formations characterised by the CMP. The analysis of the "global mode of production" would then be the relationship of the economic to the other levels : a structural relationship which constitutes social formations. It is on the basis of this *difference* in the use of the term "mode of production" that we can posit Althusser's ambiguity as to the specific rules of application of "structural causality". This may not be an ideal defence — it is not intended as such — but it allows the possibility of a number of "readings" only one of which commits Althusser to the structural eternities of Balibar's "elements of a combination".[7]

We raise these problems because they seem to us both important and often easily oversimplified, yet they are central to current debates within marxism. On the whole — and this would require several qualifications — we would assert that Althusser's *structure,* without necessarily implying structural causality, is best seen as a specific social formation: the particular combination of three hierarchical levels — the economic (defined primarily, but not exclusively, by the appropriate and dominant mode of production), the political, and the ideological. We would also defend, as a legitimate reading of Althusser, the notion that "structural causality" is a concept that, in spite of its damaging logical consequences, Althusser uses to elaborate the mechanisms of overdetermination. At least, in his application of structural causality to the critique of Political Economy's conception of the economic mode of production, the positions are compatible and usefully elaborated. Now, since a mode of production does not exist except in its concrete and various forms in specific social formations, the economic level of a social formation would constitute the principal variant form of the dominant mode of production. The political and ideological levels have a relative autonomy with respect to the economic, and an over-determining capacity : they enter directly into the *reproduction* or non-reproduction of a mode of production. Yet insofar as the degree of autonomy is gauged only in relation to the economic "contradiction", these "superstructural levels" are ultimately determined by the economic level, as the social formation is articulated as a hierarchic complexity of dominant and subordinate instances. To summarise, it seems to us that whatever the limitations of Althusser's various positions, an Althusserian conception of a social formation constitutes an engaging and genuinely innovating intervention in the "base/superstructure" debate.

III   Ideology in *For Marx*

The essays gathered together and published in the volume *For Marx* (1969) contain formulations about ideology which do indeed cover the whole range of definitions we mentioned earlier. In "Contradiction and Overdetermination", Ideology is a *level* or an instance of the special formation. In "On the Materialist Dialectic", ideology is regarded epistemologically, as a theoretical problematic which is "broken" by science via the operations of the Generalities (see the section below on *Reading Capital*). Here, Generality I designates (mainly) ideology — the practico-social realm of everyday experience, Generality II refers to the body of concepts which constitute the tools which operate upon Generality I (the raw material of a science) to produce Generality III which is a "knowledge" or science. The movement through the Generalities defines the specificity of theoretical practice, which is posed as a fourth level of the social formation [8]. In "Marxism and Humanism", too, there is the notion that ideology is quite distinct from science. Althusser's intervention in this essay is framed in the context of an increasing influence of humanist positions within the socialist movement grounded in certain texts of Marx which, Althusser argues, precede Marx's "epistemological break" (see below).

In this essay there is also the conception of ideology as the fabric and medium of all societies — a formulation which has much in common with the ISAs essay. (1971).

However, the principal elaboration of ideology in these texts is concerned with ideology as a *level* or an *instance,* of the social formation. This is first proposed in "Contradiction and Overdetermination" and picked up again in the ISAs essay in the form of a topographical metaphor of a three-storey building.[9] While the other formulations are important, their importance is largely conferred upon them as an index to the problem of ideology. In theorising the social whole, especially in relation to their own levels and in relation to the power these levels have to *overdetermine* one another — Althusser refers to the levels of the social formation as being equally material:

> In constituting this unity, they [i.e. the instances] *reconstitute* and complete their basic animating unity, but at the same time they also bring out its *nature:* the contradiction is inseparable from the total structure of the social body in which it is found, inseparable from its formal *conditions* of existence, and even from the instances it governs; it is radically *affected by them,* determining but also determined in one and the same movement, and determined by the various *levels* and *instances* of the social formation it animates; it might be called *overdetermined in its principle.* (1969 pp.100-101)

That ideology is material is confirmed in "On the Materialist Dialectic", where the definition of a *practice* involves a labour of transformation, which is none other than a determinate mode of production (referring to the political, ideological, theoretical as well as the economic, levels):

> every transformation (every practice) presupposes the transformation of a raw material into products by setting in motion determinate means of production. (1969, p.184)

Ideology is not a single, homogeneous substance. Yet it has properties which are specific to it and which define it as distinct from the other levels or instances. It must not be forgotten, too, that Althusser's pronouncements are posed as an attack on vulgar, economistic and technologistic tendencies within marxism. These varieties of marxism all suffer from a basic reductionism, which Althusser argues has its roots in Hegelianism : the superstructures are reduced to epiphenomena of the base; or they are the phenomenal forms of a simple, essential contradiction — the economic. Ideology is thus relegated to the surface of appearances, occulting an inner essence. Ideology is reified and excluded from material existence, always mentioned last among the superstructures. Althusser's vital reconceptualising of this metaphor transforms these relations into ones of *equivalence* between the levels, doing away with the crass determinism of the base on the superstructures — for, if that were the case,

83

a revolution in the infrastructure would automatically modify the superstructures, especially ideologies, "at one blow" (1969 p.115). The levels have their own (specific) power, or *effectivity*, to determine one another including the economic. That the economic is determinant in the last instance, is not a late addition, nor an afterthought, to the Althusserian problematic; it is a crucial moment throughout marxist determination. That it is the last instance implies that there are other instances with effective determinisations: the economic is not the first, nor the only instance[10]. It is this primacy which Althusser reaffirms for the levels other than, but including in a very particular way, the economic, which marks his intervention as significant and singular in the history of marxism.

In spite of the different formulations, what is clear throughout *For Marx,* is that ideology is necessarily concomitant with the social formation, any social formation. .. There is a necessary relationship between ideology and historical transformations. This is the conception put forward in "Marxism and Humanism".

> Human societies secrete ideology as the very element and atmosphere indispensable to their historical respiration and life.
> So ideology is not an aberration or a contingent excrescence of History: it is a structure essential to the historical life of societies. Further, only the existence and the recognition of its necessity enable us to act on ideology and transform ideology into an instrument of deliberate action on history. (1969 p.232)

In each determinate historical society, ideology has a specific role to play. As ideology, for Althusser, is firmly entrenched in the practico-social function, socialist humanism is ideological because it wholly reduces theoretical categories to their practico-social effects. The practico-social refers to the realm of experience and cannot be confused with scientific knowledge which is the specific product of theoretical practice. The latter is marked by the openness of its problematic compared to the closed system of an ideology – even if it is internally consistent and coherent, like theology, for example. The distinction between science and ideology arises out of the distinction Althusser discerns between certain of Marx's texts. The idea of an epistemological break is derived from Bachelard. Applied to Marx, the break refers to the discontinuity between the early ("humanist") problematic in the *1844 Manuscripts* and the mature work of the *1857 Introduction* and *Capital. The German Ideology* is a text of the break because it historicises the Hegelian dialectic and points to a radically new way of conceptualising the dialectic and history. Socialist humanist ideology has its roots in the *1884 Mss,* which are concerned with the indeterminate themes and general categories of "man", alienation", and the restoration of man to man. Whereas in the *1857 Introduction,* for example, these categories, Marx says, are too general to get us very far – we must produce specific concepts which are grounded historically in determinate ways if we are to know anything of a particular social formation. Science is not the truth of ideology in the sense that if only ideology gave you a bit more, it would render a 'full' or 'true' picture. It is radically different from it, in that ideological relations hide, or misrepresent, real relations, yet at the same time, they designate a *lived* and therefore *real* relation. This relation is not illusory, nor does it comprise the phenomenal forms of an inner essence. It is *material* and *necessary*. The qualifier

84

is that it is an *imaginary* relation, though it has little to do with consciousness as such:

Ideology is indeed a system of representations, but in the majority of cases these representations have nothing to do with "consciousness": they are usually images and occasionally concepts, but it is above all as *structures* that they impose on the vast majority of men, not via their "consciousness".

and

So ideology is a matter of the *lived* relation between men and their world. This relation, that only appears as "conscious" on condition that is *unconscious,* in the same way it only seems to be simple on condition that it is complex, that it is not a simple relation but a relation between relations, a second-degree relation. In ideology men do indeed express, not the relation between them and their conditions of existence, but *the way* they live the relation between them and their conditions of existence: this pre-supposes both a real relation and an *"imaginary", "lived"* relation. Ideology, then is the expression of the relation between men and their "world", that is the (overdetermined) unity of the real relation and the imaginary relation between them and their real conditions of existence. (1969 pp.233-234)

Ideology in this sense is very close to ideology in the ISAs essay.[11] Here, ideology is seen as a system of representations[12] indispensable to any given social formation but endowed with a particular historical existence and role within that given social formation, whose practico-social function is more important than the theoretical function (as knowledge).

In a class society ideology is the relay whereby, and the element in which, the relations between men and their conditions of existence is settled to the profit of the ruling class. In a classless society ideology is the relay/whereby, and the element in which, the relation between men and their conditions of existence is lived to the profit of all men. (1969 p.236)

This latter formulation falls somewhere between *The German Ideology* and Gramsci's concept of hegemony. Althusser moves somewhat closer to the latter in the ISAs essay. It is also interesting to note that there is no notion of the "end of ideology". For this notion entails a collapse of, and at some point, a qualitative fusion between, two levels which for Althusser remain entirely distinct.

IV Reading Capital

For this section, we must be aware of the overall argument of *Reading Capital,* namely, that Marx's *Capital* explicitly provides the concepts of analysis of the CMP, and implicitly (from a "symptomatic reading"[13]) provides an epistemology which is capable of theoretically isolating or specifying the scientificity of well-founded knowledge *as such.* If *Capital* is to be the unique opening of a scientific "continent of history", then it must conform to scientificity in general: the construction (production) of a unique object of knowledge, quite removed from all forms of ideology. So the question of ideology arises on general grounds in *Reading Capital* as *what knowledge is not.* The *necessity* of the distinction is also general: if all ideas are qualitatively the same, structurally similar, one's choice is determined by non-knowledge factors. These factors (ideologies, "interests", social practices) are themselves equally "valid", because no "practice" is *a priori* more important than any other except on metaphysical or moral, i.e. subjective, grounds. So irrationalism is the logical result of not making the distinction between science and ideology. Having assumed this, Althusser wants to argue that we can in fact establish structural differences in the character of knowledge from that of other conceptions. We should note that his procedure is only really concerned with ideologies which *consciously* pose themselves as well-founded knowledge, although it is true that such a notion, again, is central to a definition of *all ideology:* as necessarily setting itself up to be what it is not, namely science.

What, then are the main formulations on ideology?

In the mode of production of ideology (which is quite different from the mode of production of science in this respect), the formulation of a *problem* is merely the theoretical expression of the conditions which allow a *solution* already produced outside the process of knowledge because imposed by extra-theoretical instances and exigencies (by religious, political, ethical "interests") to *recognise itself* in an artificial problem manufactured to serve it both as a theoretical mirror and as a practical justification. (1970, p.52, emphasis original)

This formulation contains much of what, in different places, Althusser has to say about ideology. First, on the positive side, it grants ideology the status of a separate practice: it has a distinct identity. But in the construction of its "problem" and in the mode of production of the end "product" (ideological "knowledge"), ideological practice "poses" as scientific. It is this peculiarity which entails that in an analysis of ideological practice, it it crucial to separate it from genuine scientific practice.

Ideology's more specific characteristics are (i) that its conceptions are motivated by extra-theoretical "exigencies"; (ii) that the 'problems' which ideology sets itself are *false* problems, in that their solutions have been prefigured in the 'questions' asked by extra-theoretical interests. It must then be the case that (iii) the mode of analysis, of, or mediations between, aspects (i) and (ii) is a kind of relatively autonomous "mirror" or structure of recognition, however technically sophisticated. We should note here that although the paradigms of ideology are *theoretical* ideologies, this sort of analysis could be fairly easily reproduced to account for other kinds of ideology. For example, reference to "common sense" can be seen as the justification of most people's beliefs about practical matters: you believe what you want to believe, or whatever suits your interests.

This "problem" of ideology is not that of science. Science poses genuine problems of a theoretical nature for which there is absolutely not a pregiven solution. When Althusser uses this anti-dogmatic idea to excuse his own very partial identification of the 'knowledge effect' peculiar to science (we will return to this), he provides another useful and typical formulation.

This circle is not the closed circle of ideology but the circle perpetually open by its closures themselves, the circle of well founded knowledge. (1970 p.69)

Here it is clear that ideology theoretically "closes" arguments, because of the limited problems it sets itself:

Unlike a science, ideology is both theoretically closed and politically supple and adaptable. (1970 p.142).

By way of example, we will try to outline another way in which Althusser defines this same characteristic. Indispensible to ideology are the "theoretical characters" Subject and Object (1970 p.55). Generally, Althusser equates *empiricism* with *idealism* because although they differ in the emphasis which they place on the subject-object relationship (empiricism: object; idealism: subject), just about all classical *philosophy* adheres to the so-called "problem of knowledge" with a schema of a conscious-knowing-perceiving Subject and a to-be-known, "out there", Object of knowledge. Spinoza is one

86

very important exception for Althusser, since for him Spinoza is Marx's only philosophical predecessor, who, like Marx, has been buried by the ideological significances imposed by the dominant empiricist/idealist history of ideas. For empiricism, crudely speaking, knowledge is obtained by a process of "abstraction" by the subject of the essential aspects of the objects from the inessential. So that knowledge is regarded, by means of a projection of those essential aspects onto the object, and, we must presume, unconsciously, as a *part* of the object itself, and since that is all that can be meaningfully said (known) of the object, this abstracted essence *is* or becomes the object itself. Subject (concept) and Object become the same thing. In strict (sensualist or positivist) empiricism, the process of abstraction is little more than that which is perceivable by the senses of you or me (ie. the intersubjective empirical individual). Explained in this way, we can see the relation between Althusser's somewhat obscure identifications and the now familiar criticisms made by Marx himself of the "errors of classical Political Economy".

For Idealism, despite inner differences (eg. Kant vs Hegel), the process outlined above is reversed: the abstraction is acknowledged to be impossible without the conceptual framework of the Subject, so "reality" is no more than the properties of the Subject, or in the extreme notion, its very creation. According to Althusser, however, the one conception (empiricism) is but the inversion of the other (idealism), and inversions, for him, in simply reversing the terms of a problem, retain their validity and thus share the same "problematic". The problematic here is what he calls the "empiricist temptation" — the temptation to fill the gap between concept and reality. In doing so, the absolutely crucial distinction between the logical order and the "real" order (natural, and historical, or social) is glossed over. Such a confusion, again, is a hallmark of ideology as opposed to science. The filling of the gap is the elaboration of the mirror recognition structure which Althusser sees as necessary to ideological mechanisms.

Now, it is important to see that Althusser wants to claim that Marx himself, given the initial proposition of *Reading Capital* that contained in the latter's work is an epistemology, consciously held this position — at least implicity! Accordingly, we find a lengthy rejection both of Engels' view in *Anti-Dühring* (where Engels appears to insist that the movement of the real order dictates changes in the logical order), and some of Marx's own more "ambiguous" formulations, in mainly, the *German Ideology*. In opposition to those texts, Althusser calls Marx to his side (primarily the *1857 Introduction* to the *Grundrisse), claiming that Marx himself insisted upon just that necessary distinction between the conceptual and the real orders which Althusser has "rescued". In fact, the dictum in Marx to the effect that "if appearances were no different from reality, there would be no need for science" is in many respects the touchstone of Althusser's whole project (though undoubtedly he would want to argue against the "Hegelian" connotations of the "appearance/real" metaphor).

One major consequence of this interpretation is the wholesale rejection of the so-called marxist notion that 'practice' is the criterion of theoretical validity. That would be an appropriately easy way out of what is in fact a false (ideological) problem of knowledge, while retaining the terms of the problem. For what is a practice? Which ones are materially effective and when? What precisely is the relation of theory to practice? These questions, in order to make any sense at all, require a well-founded theoretical criterion which claims for "practice" attempt to replace. Althusser insists, therefore, that marxism is not true because it works; it works because it is true. Depending as it does on an undifferentiated pre-theoretical substratum, the criterion of practice is as open to empiricism and arbitrariness as the philosophic speculation it confusedly attempts to supersede. Consequently, one of Althusser's innovative reformulations has been to propose his own distinct notion of a practice (see Section III).

Empiricism, therefore, involves ideological conceptions, and not those of science. The major theoretical breakthroughs, for Althusser, are premised on (i) the distinction between the real object and the object of knowledge. This distinction can best be grasped in the illustration which he borrows from Spinoza: the concept "dog" cannot bark. (ii) The fact that they have all, without exception, removed the Subject from the centre of knowledge: Galileo in physics, Lavoisier in Chemistry, Copernicus in astronomy, Marx in history, and Freud in psychoanalysis. Knowledge becomes *de-centred,* while ideology depends on fictitious central subjects, be they empirical or transcendental.

Ideology is, however, the *prehistory* of science. Science effects an epistemological *break* with its ideological background. Their proximity up to that point of rupture always suggests that there is a continuity, as if science were the high spot or goal of ideology. This false sense of continuity is itself an ideological conception (it is no more than a historicism based on the inner movement of a history of ideas). Science is, for Althusser, the "surprise" of ideology, not its goal. In other words, there is a radical discontinuity because the same object is no longer shared, nor are the same questions being asked: in the case of a science, the mirror reflection structure has been replaced. A new problematic has been opened up, and the old shown to be false/closed/incapable of generating *knowledge.*

We have indicated the main formulations of ideology in *Reading Capital.* Ideologies are taken to entail, consciously or unconsciously, "false" problems. They depend on the centrality of a fictitious philosophical subject of knowledge and ethics. Non-theoretical "interests" necessitate a mirror recognition structure from which science must irrevocably break. There are no "givens" for science, however.

> The *concept* of a history of knowledge must be constructed before "collections" of empirical "givens" about the science can be made. (1970 p.44, emphasis original)

There are no guarantees of the answer to a scientific problem; only ideological philosophy involves the search for guarantees. The structure of science is therefore *open.* It discovers its own weaknesses or absences on the basis of its own theoretical problematic or terrain. It follows that only the systematicity of the theoretical concepts constitutes a science. Further, as might be expected from Althusser's views on the social formation, science is not to be regarded as a part of the superstructure (nor is language). Marxism is *not* (nor is any science), as historicists and even Gramsci would have it,[14] an organic ideology. A final consequence of Althusser's concept of science is to throw doubt on the clarity of the marxist couplet real relations/phenomenal forms. This formula risks the empiricist/idealist temptation to reduce the specific effectivity of an element to its metaphysically postulated "essence". The relation of interiority, Althusser insists, should be taken, rather as the relation between a phenomenon and the concept or knowledge *of* the object: a move which prevents us reducing the metaphor to a historicism. On the other hand, since such a danger is inherent in the Hegelian connotations objectively belonging to the expression, the terms themselves must be replaced by more adequate ones.

The epistemological task, as Althusser sees it, is to identify and elaborate the mechanisms by which the object of knowledge cognitively appropriates the real-concrete. Now, this is not, he claims, the old "problem of knowledge,"[15] since it has been arrived at by the rejection of the Subject-Object schema. There is no one-to-one correspondence between concept and reality, because the two orders are not directly comparable. Also, it is not a question of examining the conditions necessary for the emergence of specific knowledges, because the latter task accepts the knowledges as already-given *products* whereas Althusser's concern is to find out what is specific about knowledges *as knowledges:* what the "knowledge-effect" is and how it works, as opposed to, say, the ideological-effect or the aesthetic-effect. In a polemic against thinkers such as Sartre, he rejects any schema of "mediations" as an answer, since these are merely more or less complex versions of a simple (expressive) formula of subject/object. He ends his introduction by saying "the knowledge effect is therefore only possible given the systematicity of the system which is the foundation of the concepts and their order of appearance in scientific discourses" (1970 p.68). He would, it seems, justify the cryptic or partial nature of this solution by invoking the openness of crucial scientific questions.

At this point it might be useful for both clarification and criticism to outline some counter-arguments.

1. The first and ever-present problem concerns the epistemological status of marxism itself. *If* marxist philosophy is the epistemological clarification and justification of the propositions of historical materialism, is this philosophy not simply another theoretical ideology? Science, we should remember, does not *exist* in general for Althusser: each science has a *specific* object and practice within its own internal criterion of validity. So the elaboration of the reasons why any particular theory might be classified as a science cannot be the province of science itself. Yet this theoretical justification for sciences, the search for their epistemological guarantee, is precisely how Althusser defines *ideological* philosophy. Within the terms of *Reading Capital,* though probably not in his later texts, this paradox cannot be dealt with.

2. In the identification of ideology, too much is made to hang on the "empiricist temptation". It is a paradigm enlarged enough to include both classical idealism and the many contending schools of logical empiricism. As many academic philosophers would no doubt rejoice in pointing out, this blanket category reduces the precision of Althusser's critique. But more importantly, the generality of his conception cannot sufficiently account for different ideologies, and in particular, those associated with "everyday common sense". It is at this point that we would prefer a more detailed and detached confrontation with the "descriptivist" kind of marxism which retains value in the idea that ideology is mediated by the social position of the agents. To put it another way, however "valid" Althusser's account of the logic of ideology may be, after a certain point — and this is perhaps a material consequence of an over-formal approach — there is not a great deal more to say.

3. If, as is assumed by *For Marx* and *Reading Capital*, the social level "ideology" will persist under communism, will it necessarily take the forms of the "empiricist temptation"? If so — and the centrality of his equation of ideology with subjective experience suggests as much — the concept "ideology" seems unnecessarily restricted to those kinds of outlook that Marx for one would specifically ascribe to capitalist forms of ideology.
4. There is a tension between the idea that ideology is a level of the social formation, yet is to be *defined* by its epistemological antithesis to, and function as prehistory of, science. The general point can be raised, therefore, as to whether the analysis of ideology belongs to dialectical materialism or historical materialism. In *Reading Capital,* of all Althusser's texts, the overall tendency is towards the former, but as we have seen, the unresolved problems concerning the status of marxist philosophy itself in the text prevent the possibility of an independent "extraction" of its theory of ideology.
5. And finally, one of the central sources of all the difficulties and silences in *Reading Capital* hangs around the following question. Does Althusser's position on the specificity of the "knowledge-effects" do away altogether with the "problem of knowledge"? or even "correspondence" with reality? For Althusser the real object still remains outside the head, to be somehow "cognitively appropriated" by the concrete-in-thought (thought-object). It would be a severe empiricist who would insist that the *general* problem of correspondence is not raised by this formulation! That problem, of course, is not new, nor is it absent in Marx himself, but it seems to us that Althusser's claim to have abolished an ideological problem is far from wholly the case. Whether or not such a problem is constitutive of knowledge *however conceived,* and whether, therefore, this kind of epistemological perspective is fraught with problems about which Marxism has little to say, are complex questions which we must be content to merely raise for discussion in a paper of this kind.

V.   The "ISAs" Essay

The "ISAs" article carries with it some novelties with respect to early formulations about ideology. These novelties relate to the propositions contained in the so-called *self-criticism* made by Althusser about some arguments in *For Marx* and *Reading Capital.*

This self-criticism implies a radical reformulation of his conception of marxist philosophy. After *Reading Capital* philosophy has no longer the status of a science (which in *For Marx* was "Theory of theoretical practice"), has no object, and has no history. From now on philosophy is conceived as being *in the last instance, class struggle in the field of theory.* The philosophical purpose is not to give the knowledge of science but to represent philosophical tendencies informed by class struggle and to intervene in this class struggle by producing specific *theses* and philosophical *categories.*

By means of his self-criticism Althusser makes explicit what he thinks is a *theoreticist deviation* present in *For Marx* and *Reading Capital,* primarily concerning his interpretation of the "epistemological break" which marks the beginning of marxist science. The theoreticism consisted in the reduction of the philosophical revolution made by Marx to the limited theoretical fact of the epistemological *break,* and in the rationalist-speculative interpretation of this break in terms of an opposition between *science in general* and *ideology in general.* In this speculative opposition, ideology is reduced to a mere philosophical category (error or illusion) in which ideology seems to be only "the marxist name for error". What was forgotten in this formulation is that there is in Marx a break with *bourgeois* ideology, but that the marxist concept of ideology is a *scientific* concept concerning the existence of the superstructure, and that the class struggle is present from the very beginning (in the philosophical revolution which made possible the epistemological break).

Briefly, there is a rejection of the speculative formulation of a difference between science/ideology in general. There is instead the recognition that what is needed is something other than a theory of the difference between science and ideology. What is needed is (1) a *theory of the superstructure,* and (2) a theory of the *conditions* (material, social, ideological and philosophical conditions) of the process of production of knowledges.

The "ISAs" article is a clear attempt to elaborate that theory of the superstructure *as such,* free from the old epistemological problematic. The problematic is here clearly one belonging to "historical materialism". This explains the appearance of two new theoretical problems: that of *reproduction* and that of *state* apparatuses.

The formulations concerning a theory of the superstructure (the state and ideologies) shed new light on the nature of ideology, but for the purpose of analysis a distinction must prudently be made between the problems of the superstructure and the problem of ideology. It seems that not all the formulations correspond to the same theoretical level or have the same theoretical weight. For instance, the problem of reproduction does not easily coexist with a problem of "ideology in general" or with the problem of "subjects". It must, however, be borne in mind throughout, as Althusser declares at the head of the essay, that these *are* "notes towards an investigation". These *notes* are a significant opening onto several *aspects* of a problematic; they are not organized as coherent chapters of a theory already developed. Above all these notes are relatively *independent* from each other and the theoretical weight of the different theses as components of a theory of the ideological superstructure cannot be seen directly from this essay.

A real discussion of the implications of Althusser's propositions can be made only by going beyond this article (for instance, by reviewing the problem of reproduction in *Capital,* and by discussing Poulantzas' formulations etc). Within the purpose of our article we shall take the "ISAs" essay only to clarify some points about Althusser himself and the ongoing process of his contribution to the problematic of ideology.

The main propositions in the "ISAs" essay concern three aspects of the problematic.

1. The point of view of reproduction.

Althusser's proposal is "to think what characterizes the essential of the existence and nature of the superstructure *on the basis of reproduction"* (1971 p.131), with the addendum that this problem cannot be posted *except* from this point of view, every theoretical approach other than that of reproduction remaining abstract (i.e. distorted). This point of view having the character of Marx's own *global* procedure in his analysis of capitalist reproduction.

He takes as his immediate problem that of the reproduction of the relations of production. And he formulates his central question: how is the reproduction of the relations of production secured?

The reason for this question and for the answer he later proposes is clear:

> The capitalist social formation, indeed, cannot be reduced to the capitalist production relation alone, therefore to its infrastructure. Class exploitation cannot continue, that is, reproduce the conditions of its existence, without the legal-political and ideological relations, which in the last instance are determined by the productive relation. (1976 p.203)

It must be noted that Althusser offers merely a *contribution* to the analysis of the reproduction of the relations of production and how it is secured. He is well aware that the relations of production "are first reproduced by the materiality of the processes of production and circulation" (1971 p.141), ie, by the structure of production itself (that self-expanding process of accumulation of capital). But he is aware that this is not an automatic process of formal reproduction, and also not a simple problem of reproduction of the form of those relations of production. The process of reproduction is a *process* which has at its centre the class struggle; it is a process of class exploitation, and the flux of this process implies the specific intervention of the whole superstructure.

In this respect he is very clear:

> the bourgeoisie can only secure the stability and the continuity of exploitation (that it imposes in *production*) on condition that it wages a permanent class struggle against the working class. This class struggle is fought by perpetuating or reproducing the material, ideological, and political conditions of exploitation. It is carried out *within production* (cuts in the wages intended for the reproduction of labour power, repression, sanctions, redundancies, anti-union struggle, etc.). At the same time, it is conducted outside *production*. It is here that the role of the state — of the RSA and of the ISAs (the political system, school, churches, channels of information) — intervenes in order to subject the working class by both repression and ideology. ("Marxisme et lutte des classes" 1976 p.65 - our translation)

This is an important clarification of the problem of reproduction as seen in *Reading Capital,* in which it is the specificity of the relations of production as types of connection (modes of liaison) between agents/means of production and agents/agents that entails the necessity of *imposing* and *maintaining* those connections by means of material force (state) *and of moral power (ideologies).* [16]

Here this maintenance is linked to the problem of the reproduction of the elements of production (means of production, labour force) and to the class struggle. The need for specific superstructural conditions of existence comes then from the specific combination which gives to the capitalist relations of production their character of *relations of exploitation* which must be reproduced as such.

That is why Althusser tells us that to adopt the point of view of reproduction is therefore, in the last instance, to adopt the point of view of the class struggle[17]: because this reproduction (stability, duration, security) is obtained by a permanent class struggle which must be *fought.* The role of the ISAs, therefore, is to attempt to force the working class to submit to the relations and conditions of exploitation through ideology. The problem of reproduction goes beyond a mere repetition and maintenance of the "form" of the combination, to imply a continuous re-production of the conditions (economic, political, ideological) necessary for this combination to *work.*

2. The Ideological State Apparatuses

The problematic of reproduction, which implies the intervention of the whole super-structure, leads Althusser to a reformulation of the classic theory about the nature of the superstructure and of the state.

He confronts and resolves two problems:

i. First, the classic base/superstructure metaphor has theoretical limits which must be surpassed. Its descriptive character (it is a spatial metaphor of an edifice) serves to reveal the theoretical problem of *determination* (the index of effectivity) within the structure of the social whole, ie, it shows the complex and hierarchical char-acter of the marxist social whole. It demonstrates the problems of "determination in the last instance" by the economic, the "relative autonomy" of the superstructures, etc. But it says nothing about the nature of the superstructure itself. The only way to think the existence and nature of the superstructure is from the point of view of reproduction.

ii. The classic marxist theory of the state also remains descriptive and must be expanded. The reality of the state has been restricted, theoretically, only to its reality as a re-pressive apparatus around which is resolved the problem of political power (as state power). This is the essential point for a definition (which is an identification) of the state as a class state, but the state is a more complex reality. The state involves not only the classic repressive apparatus (RSA) but also other kinds of apparatuses with their own specificity: the ideological state apparatuses (ISAs). This addition is es-sential for a complete theoretical account of the *mechanisms of the state in its func-tioning.*

This distinction between the RSA and the ISAs is at the centre of Althusser's conception of ideology. The ISAs are different from the RSA precisely in their function-ing: they function massively and predominantly by *ideology.* This functioning is also what unifies the diversity of institutions because the ideology by which they function is already unified beneath the ruling ideology.

This implies that the problematic of ideology is closely linked to the problem of state power and class domination. It is the theoretical recognition that "no class can hold state power over a long period without at the same time exercising its hegemony over and in the ISAs" (1971 p.139). More precisely, it is the recognition that for the reproduction of capitalist relations of production the *ideological hegemony* exercised through the ISAs is indispensable.

What is realized through the ISAs is, in the last instance, the ideology of the rul-ing class, the class that holds state power. Moreover the ISAs "represent the *form* in which the ideology of the ruling class must *necessarily* be realized" (1971 p.172). In fact, the ideology of the ruling class *becomes* the ruling ideology only through the installation and the development of the specific ISAs in which it is realized (the church in feudalism, the school in capitalism, etc.), and this installation is the result of a class struggle.

It is interesting to note that this problematic of the ISAs can only be referred to in talking about the reality of class societies, social formations with class dictatorship organized through the state. This is an important restriction with respect to *For Marx* and *Reading Capital,* in which ideology is an "indispensable atmosphere" (1969 p.232) representing the "moral power" necessary for the maintenance of the relations of production even in classless societies. It is also a restriction with respect to the treatment of ideology in the second part of the article, concerning ideology in general and its necessary material existence in "ideological apparatuses" (without being *state* apparatuses). These shifts are important if we are discussing the functioning of the superstructures from the point of view of reproduction. The problem is, what is the relation between the *nature* of ideology and *class* domination? In *For Marx* and *Reading Capital* there is no relation; our problem is to see whether in the "ISAs" article the same holds true. Briefly, with the problematic of the ISAs, are we facing a theory of the state and/or a theory of ideology?

The role of the ISAs is a role in the re-production of the relations of production. The main thesis is that this reproduction is *secured,* for the most part, by the exercise of state power in the state apparatuses: in both the RSA and the ISAs, where the ISAs are the main contributors. Each ISA contributes in its own way to the same result: the reproduction of relations of production.[18]

All the functioning of the ruling ideology is *concentrated* in the ISAs and their result, securing the *ideological conditions* for that reproduction (the RSA securing the *political* conditions).

The dominant ISA in capitalist social formations according to Althusser is the *educational* ideological apparatus, because the reproduction of the capitalist relations of exploitation is obtained mainly by "an apprenticeship of know-how wrapped up in the massive inculcation of the ideology of the ruling class" (1971 p.148). The educational ISA inculcates ideology in relation to the roles of the socio-technical division of labour, with all the advantages of an educational apparatus: an obligatory audience of the totality of the children in the years in which they are most "vulnerable" etc. In capitalism the school-family couplet has replaced the feudal church-family couplet.

The ideological hegemony necessary for the reproduction of relations of production which is organized through the ISAs, is based on state power exercised in them, but the specific security for this reproduction provided by the functioning of the ISAs is rooted in the nature of ideology as such, which seems to be independent from its particular existence in *state* apparatuses.

In fact, the ISAs seem to be merely the place where a particular "subjection to the dominant ideology" is organized, in which the practico-social function of the dominant ideology is accomplished. But the effectivity of the dominant ideology on reproduction arises from the nature of ideology itself, from the fact that the dominant ideology assures individuals a specific "lived relation" to the relations of production. In this sense the assurance for the reproduction of the relations of production is a process which occurs *"in the consciousness,* ie. in the attitudes of the individual-subjects" (1971 p.170).

3. The nature of ideology

What Althusser tries to elaborate in the second part of his article is a very precise problematic, which must not be confused with that of the ISAs: it is a theory of *ideology in general.* This project is, for him, a pertinent one because the structure and functioning of ideology are always the same. The problem is that of the *mechanism* of ideology, which is a non-historical reality, i.e. it is immutable in form throughout the extent of the history of *class* societies.[19]

His explicit restriction to the history of "class societies" is, once more, an important distinction from his formulations in *For Marx*, but there is no explicit argument about the reason for this restriction or about the importance which it has for his theory of ideology. However, this restriction is a logical one if the link with the problematic of reproduction and the ISAs is to be maintained, and if the problem of "ideology in communist society" is to be avoided.

There is another restriction. The mechanism of ideology "in general" is *abstract* with respect to the real ideolog*ies* (regional and class ideologies) existing in a social formation. He explicitly recognizes that the conceptualization around that "mechanism" is as poor as the category of "production in general" criticized by Marx (see the 1857 *Introduction*). If this comparison is taken seriously, then his "ideology in general" represents only the abstraction of the common elements of any concrete ideology, the theoretical fixation of the general mechanism of every ideology.

A last consideration is that a theory of ideolog*ies* depends on this theory of ideology in general which must be developed.

All this implies that we are now in a different conceptual terrain from that of the ISA. If the problematic of the ISAs and of reproduction is directly related to the problematic around what might be called the "dominant ideology", the conceptualization around ideology in general applies to every ideology, even to those "class" ideologies not engaged in a process of reproduction or in the functioning of the ISAs. Whether the thesis about ideology in general also applies directly to a revolutionary ideology is now an open problem.

There are three main theses in which Althusser explains the nature of ideology, its general mechanism.

a) *Ideology is a representation of the imaginary relationship of individuals to their real conditions of existence.*

This thesis, which comes from *For Marx* (see the section above on *For Marx*) implies a definite break with all conceptualisations of ideology as "false consciousness". In opposition to the current conception about ideology, for Althusser ideology is not a representation of reality. It is a very different thing: a representation of an (individual) relationship to reality. What is represented in ideology is men's *lived relation* with reality: a relation to real conditions of existence, i.e. a relation of the second degree.[20] Briefly, ideology is not a representation of the real conditions of existence (i.e. the existing relations of production and other relations that derive from them) but a representation of an (imaginary) *relationship of individuals to these* real conditions of existence.

What is at the centre of this formulation is that if there is an imaginary distortion in an ideology it is only because of the necessarily *imaginary* character of the relationship which is represented in ideology. The old problematic of ideology as a "distorted representation" is replaced by one of ideology as a representation of an "imaginary relationship".

In this respect, ideology does not refer to distorted "ideas" about reality but to real "relationships" to reality. Among other things, this implies that the reality of ideology is not on the same terrain as that of science. Ideology is on the terrain of the practico-social and it is a specific instance of a social formation.

b) *Ideology has a material existence*

The existence of ideology is material because ideology *always* exists within an *apparatus* and its practices. The "lived relations" represented in ideology involve individual participation in determined practices and rituals within concrete ideological apparatuses. The material existence of ideology involves a complete system which is resumed by Althusser as follows: ideology exists in a material ideological apparatus, prescribing material practices governed by a material ritual, practices which exist in the material actions of a subject. Given this particular existence of ideology, an important thesis arises: there is no practice except by and in an ideology.

c) *Ideology interpellates individuals as subjects*

Ideology represents *individual* relationships to reality and exists in material apparatuses and their system of rituals and practices. This particular functioning of ideology implies that it is addressed to individuals.

The practico-social function specific to ideology is to constitute concrete individuals as subjects, to transform individuals into subjects. Indeed, it is by its concrete functioning in the material rituals of everyday life that every individual recognizes himself as a *subject*. This recognition of being a subject (with such characteristics as uniqueness, freedom etc.), this recognition of what appears to be an obvious and natural fact, is in fact an ideological recognition of an obviousness *imposed* by ideology. One recognizes oneself as a subject only in the practice of concrete ideological rituals inscribed in ideological apparatuses.

This implies that to be a subject (in the first place to recognize oneself as a "free subjectivity") is an effect of subjection to ideology, is an effect of the permanent insertion of individuals and their actions in practices governed by ideological apparatuses. The subject recognizes that he or she is "working by him/herself" in the very moment when he or she is working by and in ideology. In this sense, it appears that the subject *acts* insofar as he or she is *acted* upon by the material system of ideology.[21]

This constitution of individuals as subjects is the result of the functioning of the *category of the subject* which is the constitutive category of all ideology and which operates through the mechanism of interpellation. Ideology interpellates individuals as subjects in the name of the Subject.

Some Conclusions

The ISAs essay represents advance in Althusser's theorisation born of a greater precision and an expanding account of the terrain of "ideology". First, the specificity of the structures of ideology (materiality, apparatuses, constitution of subjects, etc.) is fleshed out to a greater degree than previously. Secondly, there is a fuller account of the interrelation of the ideological levels to the social formation as a whole: to the economy (reproduction of the relations of production) and to the state. These developments allow the possibility of more concrete analysis of ideologies, since they signal an advance beyond the treatment of ideology as mere "theoretical formations", and towards an understanding of its specific effectivity *in* and *by* the class struggle.

This latter claim seems paradoxical, since the most widespread criticism of the essay is to reduce it to a static or "functionalist" account in which class struggle is almost entirely absent. The argument in the present section has attempted to show the possibility of a reading of the essay in the light of which Althusser's rhetorical invocation of the class struggle in the Afterword — so often taken as an ill-disguised apology for absences in the text — is not simply artifice. Nevertheless, having mentioned both the defence and the criticism, the latter should be outlined in more detail: for it indicates a *tendency* in the essay which does not directly support what we see as its central achievements.

Briefly, the critical argument[23] runs as follows: in *defining* the role of the ISAs as the crucial mechanism of reproduction, Althusser has insufficiently recognised the relative autonomy of the political level from the economic. Further, in defining all those institutions of — in Gramsci's terms — "civil society" (trade unions, family, political parties, etc.) as necessarily *ideological* and as ideological *state* apparatuses, the collapse from the economic, through politics, to the definition of ideological functions, is entailed. Thus ideology becomes a "one-dimensional" concept, and Althusser's much-acclaimed "complexity" with regard to the social formation, correspondingly weakened. The role of the state, is illegitimately extended — and, importantly, by assertion rather than by argument. Rather than being seen as the product of a complex multi-levelled struggle, the reproduction of the CMP has become unproblematically secured.

Now there is some substance to this view, but it should not be taken wholly to undermine the important advances which we have been concerned principally to emphasise. It seems to us that taken as a model of how a concrete dominant ideology works, when working well, even the "functionalism" of the essay is not entirely wrong. Of course, as a general proposition about the CMP, it is liable to produce some distortions. But these "notes" are characterised by unevenness both between and within the two parts of the essay, and the direction in which the various aspects point need not be ultimately compatible. It seems rational, then, to try to think the continuities as well as the points of departure between these elements. Unilaterally to denounce the essay as functionalist cannot permit that approach. Our reading for the purposes of this paper has been one which attempts to locate the advances rather than the acknowledged discrepancies in the text.

We have seen, then, that the essay embodies a differentiated problematic: that of the *dominant ideology* (state apparatuses, reproduction), and that of the necessary *mechanisms* of every ideology ("ideology in general"). The latter has also given rise to some immense problems: is it merely different from, or in contradiction to, the conclusions of the first part? It is important with respect to this debate to maintain that the "general" character of ideology refers only to the common and general mechanisms of every concrete ideology. It is neither an "abstract" as opposed to a "concrete" ideology, nor an abstract schema looking for or awaiting "realisation". This mechanism of ideology is investigated in detail in the third part of this journal. It is crucially to be located at the level of *individuality* (individual "imaginary-lived" relations), and cannot be regarded, therefore, as simply false or "distorted" *ideas*. It is possible, therefore, in spite of the remaining difficulties, to display the coherence of a precise but complex thesis: ideologies, for Althusser, are

bodies of representations existing in institutions and practices: they feature in the superstructure and are based in the class struggle. (1972 p.7)

97

We saw in *For Marx* that ideology was principally located as a level of the social formation. Now, while an epistemological definition was also used (particularly to indicate the pre-history of a science), we would argue that in *For Marx,* unlike *Reading Capital,* this definition functions in order to define the place of ideology in the social formation, and not simply to clarify an epistemological position. Because science is not the "truth" of ideology, we should not be misled by the fact that ideology *poses* as a theoretical truth in varying degrees. Rather, we should see that its function is not mainly theoretical, but practico-social. The analysis must begin by a reformulation of the question of the superstructures, and therefore it arises as part of historical materialism rather than dialectical materialism, or philosophy. In *For Marx,* ideology is a system of representations which is unconscious and rooted in the practices of everyday life. It is not therefore necessarily illusory, yet it does pose as truth or common sense. The extra-theoretical interests of agents which ideological formations represent, themselves "reflect", in relatively autonomous ways, the (economic, political, and ideological) structured social formation in which they arise. Ideology as part of the social formation, any social formation, remains a constant proposition throughout Althusser's work. Although it is simultaneous with the history of any social formation, its content and functions will depend on the nature of each given social formation.

A problem arises, however, in relation to the definition of science; this is raised but not fully tackled in *For Marx.* In *Reading Capital,* the question of social location (historical materialism) remains, but takes second place in the discussion of ideology to a philosophical elaboration of the concepts. As Althusser continually remarks, in his *Essays in Self Criticism,* this "theoreticism" consists in asserting the primacy of the question of science-in-general,[24] so that marxism (which seems to give rise to the very concept of ideology) becomes merely a special case of the general epistemological thesis: the absolute theoretical separation and differences between Science and Ideology.

The question of science (theoretical practice) was raised in *For Marx.* It seemed to constitute a distinct, fourth level of the social formation. Yet marxist philosophy, or the Theory of theoretical practice, was even more adrift from social determinations, operating precisely as the *guarantor* of the scientificity of science — something for which Althusser relentlessly reproves "bourgeois" philosophy. This aspect of *For Marx,* especially in "On the Materialist Dialectic", is taken further in *Reading Capital.* There, ideology is defined as what is not scientific, not so much by virtue of its socio-practical function as in the theoretical organisation which that function requires. Similar attributes to those found in *For Marx* are reiterated: especially the feature of ideological circularity, self-recognition, or closure. His main targets, as exemplars of this unchanging structure of ideological argument, are the "temptations" and tendencies of idealism/empiricism. The primary Althusserian concepts generated in *Reading Capital* (separation of the concrete-in-thought from the real-concrete, structural causality) are attempts at avoiding an ideological closure in the name of science and Marx. And this is based on a particular reading of the *1857 Introduction.*

Throughout Althusser's work, including the *Self-Criticism,* the notion that a science has to break with its ideological preconditions is fundamental to his thought. Despite his claim to the contrary, however, this has entailed at least the risk of defining science as the truth of ideology; what ideology is not. Science, by definition, is not ideological, therefore it is not thoretically closed, empiricist, or idealist. It is subject to internal criteria of validity (which cannot be specified *in general*). It does not confuse the object of knowledge with the real concrete, and its knowledge is not "given" but *produced.*

From *Lenin and Philosophy* onwards, and especially in the ISAs essay, Althusser returns to the social location of ideology, and in effect, fills out that proposition as it occurred in *For Marx* (especially "Marxism and Humanism"). Its crucial feature here is that ideology directly intervenes in the reproduction of the conditions of production (the relations and forces of production) in a class society, and, therefore, reproduces the conditions of exploitation. We should note that this signals a problem about the "eternity" of ideology as a level: it is a partial return to the concept of superstructures; the superstructural conditions of existence of the relations of production. The state, in the ISAs essay, is the crucial mechanism for the unity of the ideological level. Despite the tendency to over-emphasise the all-powerful and theoretically equivalent role of ideology and the state — unifying what in Gramsci remain distinct categories of state and 'civil society' — the point of view of reproduction allows and requires not simply the possibility, but the actuality of class struggle. This dimension is notably lacking in *Reading Capital*. It is also commensurate with other important later texts ("Lenin and Philosophy", "Philosophy as a Revolutionary Weapon", and the *Self-Criticism*), where philosophy is seen as a political intervention (class struggle) in the field of theory.

Far from being the guarantor of (marxist) science, philosophy, like ideology, is a battleground upon which class positions arising from scientific discoveries are fought out. Ideology, then, in the later texts, becomes an elaboration of the "society-effect" indicated in *For Marx* but displaced somewhat in the explanation of the "knowledge-effect" in *Reading Capital*. The *function* of ideology gives it its peculiar nature (allusion/illusion) — that is not conferred simply because ideology is taken to be a theoretical structure in contradistinction to science-in-general.

We have tried to indicate that the two ways of beginning to explain "ideology" in Althusser persist in uneasy partnership throughout his work. Despite his current tendency to move away from the epistemological angle, there is still no complete break with it. This is not just Althusser's problem: we can study in concrete detail as many ideologies as we like, but unless we have a clear conceptual idea of what, theoretically, separates ideology from other realities (and concepts) — including science — we will not know what it is that we are studying.

The analysis of ideologies within a specific social formation (the articulation between ISAs of domination-subordination) still depends upon there being a structural feature common to *all* ideology. At least, this is a position held by Althusser in the ISAs essay. In *For Marx* and *Reading Capital,* this was formulated in terms of the peculiarity (amongst others) which ideology has of placing a constitutive and constituted Subject at the centre of history, theory, ethics, individuality, etc. This idea received more specific attention in the ISAs essay in the shape of the thesis that ideology constitutes individual agents as subjects. We have indicated the order of problems which this gives rise to, problems which remain unresolved in Althusser, and perhaps even more intractable in the light of his more recent *Self-Criticism.*

VII Conclusion/Critique

The purpose of this paper has been mainly expository, yet at several places we have indicated some problems in "reading" Althusserian concepts such as "social formation" and "ideology", while incorporating some points of criticism. In this section, we try to sketch out a number of influential arguments which have been formulated against Althusser, and staying as closely as possible to the question of ideology, to expand the basis of our own appraisal.

Perhaps the most common charge against Althusser's work as a whole is that in spite of his important category of "relative autonomy", the theoretical consequence (particularly in the earlier texts) has been to allow to the "levels" of science and philosophy a wholly autonomous status. Autonomous, in this sense, means without social determinants. Althusser, it is claimed, is inconsistent when he refuses to allow to science *and* to the *philosophy* of science (as the theory of theoretical practice) the *necessary* determinateness which is constitutive of relations between levels of the social formation. Over several years, from the criticisms of A. Glucksmann and Geras to the more recent ones of Callinicos,[25] it has been argued that this privileged status of theory in Althusser commits him to "idealism", and "Kantianism", and even to a reactionary elitism, one which Ranciere sees as typical of the PCF.

Such a criticism can be linked to some earlier comments on *Reading Capital.* Althusser's insistence on a definitive separation between science and ideology, and on the permanency of the social level "ideology", takes no account of, indeed necessarily relegates, the importance of differences between distinct ideologies. It could be argued that the level of generality *analytically* prevents a "concrete analysis of a concrete situation", and *politically,* the possibility of changing people's views towards a socialist perspective. Indeed a key question for militants (which sections of the people are, given their present situation and ideas, more likely to be won over to the cause of the working class?) plays little part in Althusser's scheme of things. There is also the point that whatever the changes in the direction of "class struggle" which the ISAs essay brings, the all-encompassing and "static" and therefore, inevitably *conservative* role of ideology in that paper affords little more encouragement. Parallel to this problem, it has been equally intransigently insisted that Althusser's idea that science is ideology-free is simply nonsense: finance for research programmes, the relation between "pure" science and technology, and even the outlooks of scientists themselves — these factors undermine such a naive assumption. Althusser, therefore, is to be rejected on the basis that his positions are a retreat from marxism itself: conceived not as pure knowledge, but as critical science, a revolutionary weapon asserting the primacy of class *practice.*

We have said that this is a generalisation of often more subtle arguments. But there seems to us no reason to doubt that it is nevertheless the essence of the majority of published criticisms. Callinicos, for example, insists that the arguments be examined in terms of internal coherence rather than from the point of view of practice.[26] Yet it is the latter conception which ultimately informs the critique: ideology is the site of class struggle, and though it might extend into the period of transition to socialism, it cannot by definition continue indefinitely (it is the product of class societies). If ideology is the way we live our relations to our real conditions of existence, it is therefore changeable and capable of being ended altogether. Callinicos undoubtedly distances himself from Ranciere's more extreme pronouncements, but they share — with many others — substantially the same position.

It is interesting to note that both Althusser and Balibar have recanted on the infamous question of *theoreticism,* though they still refuse to be called structuralists. While acknowledging that it is not implausible to find, as M. Glucksman[27] has done, similiarities between Althusser and, say Lévi-Strauss, we have indicated that, for *Althusser* at least, this latter charge cannot be satisfactorily established. We therefore do not discuss it.

The effect of his self-criticism, however, is certainly not an unproblematic return to the kind of "orthodox" position outlined above: a position, however qualified, resting on the idea that ideologies are organically related to historically specific forms of class struggle, defined primarily by the economic level. If Althusser accepted such a line of argument, not only his theoreticism, but his attacks on economism and historicism would have been brought into question. But they have not been so questioned, and the problem of the self-criticism cannot therefore be reduced to a mature rectification of early academicism.

Without denying that there has been a change in position, it is worth pointing out that certain basics have not altered. The effect of the self-criticism is to reject the position alloted to philosophy in *For Marx* and *Reading Capital,* but *not* that of science. The fundamentally differential nature of genuine sciences or "continents of knowledge" does not change in Althusser. Nor does the *status* of ideology. Now, it is not often made clear that there is nothing in Althusser's "system" to deny that scientific research is socially determined. But *epistemologically,* we must be aware that the validity of scientific knowledge can in no sense be reduced to its social conditions of existence. The content of ideologies, for Althusser, can be so reduced. Here we have the reason for his twin characterisation of science as being close to, yet the "surprise" of, ideology. To argue, then, that the claim for an epistemological differentiation of science and ideology contradicts Althusser's conception of the social formation is simply misdirected. There remains, however, the problem of philosophy. In the later texts, it is clear that philosophy is no longer the guarantor of science, so while it is not exactly to be subsumed under the category "ideology", it nevertheless plays a crucial role "in the neighbourhood of the sciences" as "class struggle in the field of theory" (1976 p.37 n). He has *ipso facto* allowed that field a certain internal differentiation and malleability. In principle, the study of ideolo-*gies* is not ruled out, though it could fairly be said that Althusser displays no theoretical commitment to such conjunctural studies.

The genuine points of criticism, then, have — to some extent — been answered. Yet the status of science and ideology (not to be confused with their qualitatively identical conditions of existence) remains in one sense the same as before. Why is this? In a useful and readable pamphlet, Paul Hirst[28] has outlined some of the reasons. Althusser's marxism is the first to break theoretically with economism and historicism. If in rejecting "theoreticism" Althusser also rejected the formal specifications of *knowledge,* then his theory of ideology — even in the ISAs essay — simply would not stand. Yet the elements of that theory do remain the same, and are directed against those consequences which many of his critics favouring anti-theoreticism are committed to — economism and humanism (historicism). Ideas, for Althusser, do not derive from the "real" world, for this involves an unacceptable reductionism. They do not (more or less) *reflect* their conditions of existence. Neither do they "belong" to economically defined classes which are mysteriously linked to the long-term fate of the globe. Any of these denials entails an intransigent theoretical effort to break with economism and empiricism. When he counterposes science to ideology, in spite of appearances, he is not saying that science is the "truth" of "false" ideology. On the contrary, their respective objects of analysis are not comparable. Ideology is every bit as "real" as science; its role is far from unimportant. His argument that in fact ideology has as much to do with material, everyday practices as ideas-in-the-head, should guard against such an "idealist" construction of this position. The ideas of ideology, therefore, are as true as they are false, and have real, identifiable conditions of existence. What then is the qualitative or logical difference between science and ideology? Ideology is the way men live their relation to their real conditions of existence, and this relation is a *necessarily imaginary* one. That is to say, that ideology rests on subjective experiences which present themselves *as if* they represented the deeper, unseen and unfelt conditions of social existence. It follows then, argues Hirst, that for Althusser *experience* is not the sort of thing which can achieve knowledge of the subject's circumstances. Knowledge rests on neither experience nor subjects.

Before going into this line of thought any further, mention should be made of Hirst's more developed position,[29] for it represents an approach to Althusser which is both original and diametrically opposed to the first series of critics. Briefly, Hirst applauds Althusser's attempt to break with economism in the theory of ideology. It is, however, only an attempt, because Althusser himself, far from advocating "autonomism", is the victim of certain persistent economistic deviations. In the ISAs essay, for example, ideology and the state are simple pre-given functions; mechanisms derived by a transparent causality from elsewhere, ie, the economy. In his remarks on the nature of the "subject" of ideology, Althusser is prevented from a genuine dialogue with disciplines in the area of subjectivity — psychoanalysis and semiotics — because he retains a concept of the human individual which is pre-Freudian. That particular notion is retained to preserve the logic of "representation". That is, that the imaginary *means* of ideological representation (images, language, emotions, symbols, rituals etc.) are derived from, or subordinated to, *that which is represented.* And, for Althusser, ultimately, the latter is an economically defined goal or function (the perpetuation of class rule), the place of which is filled by human agents. In this sense, the coherence of his remarks is compromised by economistic hangovers. Hirst further argues that the concept of representation itself — a version of relative autonomy — is, like the latter concept, inherently unstable. The necessary means of ideological representation (like the superstructures) are said to have a relative autonomy with respect to their "objective" social function. Nevertheless, it appears in Althusser's theory that those means can only be coherently situated in terms of that function. Relative autonomy, Hirst contends, whether it refers to "levels" of the social formation, political practices, or to ideological mechanisms, is a concept which, in attempting to effect a unified synthesis, simply juxtaposes two notions (autonomy and determination) which are logically opposed to one another. Hirst insists, rather, that we have to take the distinctiveness of ideological practices seriously or revert openly and honestly to simple economism: there is no other way. Althusser's middle ground has not wholly broken with the legacy of economism, though he, more than anyone, has produced the concepts for doing so.

Clearly, our account of prevalent attitudes to Althusser's texts on the theory of ideology is no more than a guide to critical discussion. We will conclude the paper with a short assessment of their rationality. The first point to make in this context is to render problematic the centrality of philosophy in Althusser's work. Obviously, there have been excesses, or as he prefers to say, "deviations". In particular, the Theory of theoretical practice as the guarantor of marxist (or indeed any) science, as Althusser and other have since acknowledged, is an untenable thesis. It falls into precisely those errors of classical philosophy against which Althusser initially directed his theoretical project. On the other hand, we have tried to show that "theoreticism" apart, there is an ongoing coexistence of — and perhaps an irresolvable tension between — ideology conceived as the epistemological antithesis to science-in-general and conceived as an intrinsic element of the structure or fabric of social formations. Whatever else is to be said of Althusser, we have tried to show that his account of the social formation and its concomitant concepts — for example, conjuncture, overdetermination — is a lasting contribution to historical materialism. The "philosophy" however, is not an irrelevant side-show. Althusser has consistently argued that the necessity of anti-essentialism within historical materialism must be (politically and conceptually) dependent on a clarification of the positions arrived at within marxist philosophy, or dialectical materialism.

It is at this point that Hirst's clear exposition of the Althusserian theory of ideology is rewarding. To reject theoreticism does not entail a return to the relatively orthodox marxist positions advocated by the first of the critical tendencies discussed above. For these latter do require a fairly unproblematic or transparent generation of ideology (and politics) from an economically defined class struggle. And this in turn depends on a certain untheorised but necessary philosophical materialism which regards class struggle and "practice" as both "given" pre-theoretical substrata, and therefore as "more real". It is these (supressed) philosophical presuppositions which Althusser has brought into question. The problem of an adequate theory must include the analysis of such premises: in that sense *a* marxist philosophy cannot be wished away under essentialist slogans such as "back to practice". For to do so obstructs an adequate theory of ideology. In accepting the rationality of this line of argument, we would thereby distance ourselves from the conclusions of the first critical tendency. Wholly to agree would be to reduce Althusser's theoretically coherent position to one or two *ad hoc* '"insights", and would thus fail to grasp the novelty and seriousness of his contribution.

In drawing such a conclusion, we therefore interpret Althusser's conception of ideology in much the same manner as Hirst. On the other hand, our insistence that *whatever* its reliance on philosophic categories, the idea that ideology's position as a relatively autonomous social level is something to be valued, would not be accepted by the latter. This is because Hirst sees the concept of relative autonomy as a logical obstruction to the scientific analysis of both politics and ideology. The means of political and ideological (signifying) practices, he argues, must be given a self-determined status, free from essentialist taints. This conclusion — perhaps over-schematically presented here — nevertheless follows from Hirst's latest contribution. Its internal cogency cannot be properly examined here. Yet it does appear that in the drive against economism and essentialism begun by Althusser, Hirst has extended the terms of reference of those two concepts to include the very concept of marxism as a science of the social formation based on determination in the last instance by the economic level. Despite the often arbitrary character of interpretations which appear to be justified by "relative autonomy", Althusser's so-called unstable concept at least reserves a central place for determination in the last instance. To that extent, we would claim that to reject Althusser's "economism" (as opposed to his "functionalist tendencies"), is also to reject the idea that marxism, whatever else it might be (revolutionary politics alone, for example), at least provides a scientific (ie. determinate) analysis of social formations.

The alternative criticisms outlined, while being intrinsically in opposition, appear to share that notion of a dilemma facing marxists which Hirst has posed: economism or autonomism? It has been our contention that the seemingly mythical ground of "relative autonomy" — whatever its problems — remains an inhabitable position with respect to Althusser's intervention, and, indeed, to marxism itself conceived as a scientific analysis of social formations.

NOTES

1. 1976 p.179
2. 1970 pp.182-193
3. 1969 p.254
4. Marx, 1973, pp.106-107
5. See 1969 pp.193-214
6. Hindess and Hirst, 1975 pp.272-278
7. See 1970 Part III "The Basic Concepts of Historical Materialism."
8. See 1969 pp.183-193
9. 1971 pp.134-135
10. See 1976 pp.175-187
11. The notion of the Imaginary, here, is very close to that of Lacan. See, for example *New Left Review*, 51.
12. 1969 p.231
13. 1970 p.28
14. But see the article on Gramsci in this journal.
15. 1970 pp.52-53
16. 1970 p.177
17. 1971 p.171
18. See 1971 p.146
19. 1971 p.152
20. 1969 p.233
21. See 1971 p.159
22. 1971 pp.170-173
23. For the most advanced example of this argument, see Hirst 1976.
24. 1976 p.68

25. See bibliography
26. Callinicos 1976 pp.7-9
27. M. Glucksmann 1974
28. Hirst 1975
29. Hirst 1976

BIBLIOGRAPHY

Works by Althusser

For Marx : especially "Contradiction and Overdetermination", "On the Materialist Dialectic",
    "Marxism and Humanism" 1969, Allen Lane, London.
Reading Capital with Etienne Balibar, 1970 New Left Books, London.
Lenin and Philosophy and Other Essays especially "Ideology and Ideological State Apparatuses",
    "Freud and Lacan," " Lenin and Philosophy", "Philosophy as a Revolutionary Weapon" 1971
    New Left Books, London.
Politics and History 1972 New Left Books, London.
    "The Conditions of Marx's Scientific Discovery", in *Theoretical Practice* 7/8 Jan. 1973.
Essays in Self-Criticism 1976 New Left Books, London.
Positions, 1976 Hachette, Paris.

Critical Texts

A. Callinicos, *Althusser's Marxism* Pluto, 1976, London.
N. Geras, "Althusser's Marxism: An Assessment and an Account", *New Left Review, 71.*
A. Glucksmann, "A Ventriloquist's Structuralism", *New Left Review, No. 72.*
M. Glucksmann, *Structuralist Analysis in Contemporary Social Thought,* RKP, 1974, London.
B. Hindess and P. Hirst, *Pre-Capitalist Modes of Production,* RKP, 1975, London.
P.Q.Hirst, *Problems and Advances in the Theory of Ideology,* Communist University of
    Cambridge Pamphlet, 1975.
P.Q.Hirst, "Althusser's Theory of Ideology", in *Economy and Society, vol.5.* no. 4, Nov. 1976

References

K. Marx, 1857 Introduction to the *Grundrisse,* Pelican, 1973. London.
J.Lacan "The Mirror Phase," *New Left Review,* no. 51.

MISRECOGNISING IDEOLOGY: Ideology in Political Power and Social Classes

John Clarke, Ian Connell, Roisín McDonough

This paper offers a consideration and a critique of the formulations of a Marxist theory of ideology presented by Nicos Poulantzas in *Political Power and Social Classes* (NLB 1975). Thus it is neither an attempt to review the whole of that text* nor to assess the conceptions of ideology present in Poulantzas' subsequent work. The major reason for concentrating solely on this particular text is that it signals the most systematic and elaborated treatment of ideology by the author concerned, although it is not the prime object of his enquiry. Before dealing with his conceptualisation of the nature of ideology, it is therefore necessary to see how it is connected with the political level (the main focus of the book) and the way in which it is situated within an overall theoretical framework generally known as 'structuralist'.†

The General Concepts

Poulantzas' elaboration of a regional theory of the political is posited on an exposition of the necessary concepts of historical materialism, the two most important of which are those of a *mode of production* and *social formation*. A mode of production, for Poulantzas, is not just what is usually designated as the relations of production but is a specific combination of structures and practices (economic, political, ideological and theoretical), in which the economic is 'determinant in the last instance'. A mode of production is characterised by a *complex* unity in which the relations between the structures/instances is one where the 'structure in dominance' governs the very nature of the other levels by "assigning them their place and distributing functions to them". (1975 p.14)

This formulation involves a rejection of the economic reductionism attributed to base/superstructure models with their assumption that there is one primary contradiction expressed or reflected at each level, and the inversion of these formulations, the historicist conception of an 'expressive totality' premised on a pre-given teleological purpose which history strives to realise. Therefore what distinguishes

---

*See a forthcoming Stencilled Paper by the authors which is an attempt to assess the theorisation of the nature of the state in contemporary capitalism.

†For a more detailed discussion of the structuralist framework see the first section of the article on Althusser in this journal.

one mode of production from another and consequently specifies its nature is the form of articulation maintained by its levels.

The economic level (which is determinant) is itself composed of three invariant elements, which in particular modes of production are combined in specific relations. These invariant elements are:

1. The labourer, the 'direct producer', i.e. labour power.
2. The means of production, i.e. the *object* and the *means* of labour.
3. The non-labourer who appropriates to himself the surplus labour, i.e. the product.

These elements exist in a specific combination in a particular mode of production, a combination which is composed of two relations: first a *relation of real appropriation* which refers to the relation of the labourer to the means of labour (that is, the labour process) and secondly a *relation of property* which allows the non-labourer to intervene as owner of the means of production or of labour power or both. and hence of the product. It is this latter relation which defines the relations of production, in the strict sense. Taken together these elements and instances constitute the 'ensemble of structures' of a mode of production. The concept of social classes as the *effect* of the 'ensemble of structures' (the economic, political and ideological) flows from this fundamental principle: classes are not seen as constituted solely at the economic level (in relations of production); they are produced via the combination of *all* the instances, and are manifested in particular practices — economic, political, ideological practices. There is, in other words, a firm distinction made between the *structures* and *social relations* which are the effects of the structures: classes do not appear as structures but as social relations (of production, of politics, of ideology). At the economic level, these two distinct areas are covered respectively by the terms 'relation of production' and 'social relations of production'. The former refers to the relation between capital and wage-labour (in the capitalist mode of production — CMP), while the latter designates the distribution of agents/supports into social classes as capitalists and wage-labourers: that is, relation of production corresponds to what has earlier been termed the combination of labourers/non-labourers/means of production, of the structure.

From this standpoint the functions or categories of labourer and non-labourer at the economic level of the CMP can be respectively designated as capital and wage-labour, and they are combined in a specific form (in terms of the two relations we noted earlier). These two relations occur in what Poulantzas calls a *homology* in the CMP. That is, in all class societies, the relation of property always results in a separation of the labourer from the means of labour, which are the property of the non-labourer, who, as owner, appropriates the surplus labour: but the relation of real appropriation can set up *either* a union of the labourer with the means of production (as in pre-capitalist modes of production), *or* a separation of the labourer from the means (as in the stage of heavy industry in the CMP).

> In the combination characteristic of the CMP, the two relations are *homologous*. The separation in the relation of property coincides with the separation in the relation of real appropriation. (p.27)

This is the first and determining characteristic of the CMP — it is this economic combination which determines the relation/articulation of the ensemble of levels, and ascribes functions and positions to each. Crucially it produces the relative autonomy of the political from the economic. That is, the separation of the direct producer from the means of production and the consequent breaking of the 'ties of personal dependence' characteristic of the feudal mode of production produces this separation of the political from the economic. It is this 'relative autonomy' of the political which, for Poulantzas, makes possible the construction of a 'regional theory' of this level in the CMP. However, modes of production do not exist in their pure states — all that 'really' exists are historically determined social formations which are composed of several overlapping modes of production, in which one is dominant. Thus it is only possible to analyse a social formation concretely at one particular historical moment e.g. France under Louis Bonaparte, Britain under Macmillan etc.

These, then, are the general set of concepts in which the analysis of ideology is located — both in terms of its general characteristics as a particular level of *all* modes of production and of the specific forms which it takes in the *capitalist* mode of production.

Errors in Marxist Conceptions of Ideology

Poulantzas begins his discussion of ideology with a criticism of 'historicist' conceptions. This criticism is directed at the position of the 'young' Marx in which ideology is contained within the model: "The subject/the real/alienation" (p.195), within which "Ideology is a projection in an imaginary world of the subject's mystified essence". This problematic leads to the reduction of ideology to consciousness — or rather false consciousness. However, the main object of criticism is Lukács' conception of "class consciousness" and "world view", in which the "world view" of the particular "class subject" of history appears as the central principle in establishing the unity of a social formation. He traces this conception through its transfiguration and uses in a variety of hands — Weber, Parsons, *New Left Review*, and Gramsci, though allowing that Gramsci's work also involves "scientific and original features" — the most significant elements of which are: "the ambiguous metaphor" of the "cement" of a society; and the break "with the conception of ideology as a conceptual system". He returns to both of these themes in his own analysis.

There are, however, further objections to the historicist conception, which focus around its "genetic" connection with the particular class subject. This conception is seen to lead to two major errors. First, the "over-politicisation" of ideology (p.202), in which ideologies are treated "as if they were political number plates worn by social classes on their backs", makes it impossible to decipher the concrete relation between the dominant ideology and the politically dominant class or fraction. By contrast Poulantzas argues that

> in reality, the dominant ideology does not simply reflect the conditions of existence of the dominant class, the 'pure and simple' subject, but rather the concrete political relation between the dominant and dominated classes in a social formation. It is often permeated by elements stemming from the 'way of life' of classes or fractions other than the dominant class or fraction. (p.203)

Secondly, the identification of ideologies with specific class subjects makes it impossible to establish the existence within the dominant ideology of elements belonging to the ideologies of classes other than the politically dominant class and to account for the permanent possibility of the contamination of working-class ideology by the dominant and petit-bourgeois ideologies, because in a historicist conception each class ideology "functions, as it were, in a vacuum" (p.205).

These observations constitute an important opening in the reformulation of the question of ideology. Above all else, by removing ideology from its construction by a single historical class subject, they raise the possibility of thinking ideologies as complex unities, produced under specific conditions and shaped and reconstituted in the process of class struggle. This is the task to which he addresses himself in the subsequent sections.

The Marxist Conception of Ideology

Poulantzas proposes a definition of ideology as both a "relatively coherent ensemble of representations, values and beliefs" and as a specific objective level within the social formation. Its raw material is the world in which men live, their relations to nature, to society, to other men and to their own political and economic activity, and finally ideology reflects the way in which the agents of a formation 'live' their conditions of existence.

> The status of the ideological derives from the fact that it reflects the manner in which the agents of a formation, the bearers of its structures, live their conditions of existence; i.e. it reflects their relation to these conditions as it is 'lived' by them. Ideology is present to such an extent in all agents' activities that it becomes indistinguishable from their *lived experience*. (pp.206-7)

While Poulantzas rejects the equation of ideology with false consciousness, his own formulation is made problematic by the introduction of the concept of "lived experience". From the above quotation it can be seen that "lived experience" is considered, in some way, to provide the "raw material" of ideology, that is, ideology "*reflects* the manner in which the agents of a formation, the bearers of its structures, *live* their conditions of existence". So, it appears, in analytic principle at least, that "lived experience" is separable from ideology. However, having made this distinction Poulantzas does not then specify what it is that distinguishes "lived experience" from ideology, either in terms of their contents, or in terms of the processes by which the former acts upon the latter to produce "a relatively coherent universe" of "representations, values and beliefs". Indeed, he then proceeds to abolish this distinction, practically rather than theoretically, with the claim that "ideology is present to such an extent in all the agents' activities that it becomes indistinguishable from their lived experience". Thus, from being distinct, "lived experience" and ideology now appear to be inseparably one and the same.

With the "practical" abolition of the category "lived experience" the discussion of ideology is relocated in terms of its functional relation to the structure as a whole. The social function of ideology "is not to give agents a *true knowledge* of the social structure but simply to insert them as it were into their practical activities supporting this structure"; indeed, ideology is "therefore *necessarily* false" (p.207). This falseness may include "elements of knowledge", but always in a relation of "adequation/inadequation vis-a-vis the real", "which Marx grasped under the term 'inversion'" (ibid). This falseness has the character of "hiding the real contradictions" and "of reconstituting on an imaginary level a relatively coherent discourse which serves as the horizon of agents' experience: it does this by moulding their representations of their real relations and inserting these in the overall unity of the relations of a formation" (ibid).

The function of ideology, then, is 'cohesion' (the "fundamental meaning of the ambiguous metaphor of 'cement' used by Gramsci") — and, like cement, ideology "slides into every level of the social structure". Cohesion designates the production, at the "level of experience", of relations which are "obvious but false", which permit the agents' practical activities to go on. Cohesion is its consequence because of the form in which ideology reflects the *unity* of a social formation;

> From this point of view, its specific, real role as unifier is not that of constituting the unity of a social formation (as the historicist conception would have it) but that of reflecting that unity by *reconstituting* it on an imaginary plane. (pp.208-9)

This imaginary reconstitution — which ideology accomplishes through "those biases of *inversion* and *mystification* which are specific to it" — is "imaginary" in the sense that the *real contradictory* unity of the formation is reconstituted in a non-contradictory form.

It is from this general analysis of ideology that the nature of the relation of the *dominant ideology* to the dominant class or fraction can be posed. Contrary to the historicist conception, which reduces this relation to the dominant ideology being the direct product of the dominant class, Poulantzas proposes that the *correspondence* between the dominant ideology and the dominant class comes about because

> the ideological (i.e. a given ideology) is constituted as a regional instance within the unity of the structure; and this structure has the domination of a given class as its effect in the field of the class struggle. The dominant ideology, by assuring the practical insertion of agents in the social structure, aims at the maintenance (the cohesion) of this structure, and this means above all class domination and exploitation. (p.209)

Thus, he proposes a distinction within the ideology of a social formation between the "dominant ideology" and what he terms "ideological sub-ensembles" (e.g. feudal and petit-bourgeois sub-ensembles). There are complex relations involved in this formulation because these sub-ensembles are dominated by the ideologies of the corresponding classes — feudal, petit-bourgeois — but only to the extent that the ideologies which dominate the sub-ensembles *are themselves dominated* by the ideology.

What Poulantzas presents then is a set of ideologies, each of which *corresponds* (though the theoretical weight of this concept is not clear) to a specific class or class fraction within the social formation. Each of these specific ideologies forms the dominant element within a particular ideological ensemble or sub-ensemble; but that ensemble also contains elements of other ideologies — they are "contaminated". Further, each of these specific ideologies is *itself* dominated by the dominant ideology — that which corresponds to the dominant class — to the extent that the dominated classes "often . . . live even their revolt against the domination of the system within the frame of reference of the dominant ideology" (p.223).

However, this "dominant ideology" is itself not "pure"; it is an ensemble whose structure (unity) . . . cannot be deciphered from its relations with a class consciousness/ world view, considered in a vacuum, *but from the starting point in the field of the class struggle,* i.e., from the concrete relations between the various classes in struggle, the relation within which class domination functions. (p.209)

This conception of the relation between the dominant ideology and the dominant class, we would contend, sits uneasily with his earlier formulations of this relation in terms of a *structurally* generated correspondence. We shall return to this later.

Bourgeois Political Ideology

Poulantzas' focus on bourgeois political ideology is given considerable weight not simply because it is empirically connected with the main object of his enquiries, namely the capitalist state, but because it has a specific and significant role within the structure of bourgeois social formations. In social formations dominated by the CMP, it is possible not only to identify a variety of ideological regions within the dominant ideology, but also to decipher the dominance of one region of ideology over others. This region is the "juridico-political region", and its most crucial aspect is what is termed "the isolation effect". The latter, contrary to the historicist supposition, is not an inherent feature of the structure of capitalist relations of production which historicists see as engendering agents of production as individuals, but rather it is the result of the operations of the juridical and ideological structures which have the effect on socio-economic relations of concealing from the agents the fact that their relations are class relations.

> This effect of isolation is terrifyingly real: it has a name: competition between the wage earning workers and between the capitalist owners of private property. In fact it is only an ideological conception of the capitalist relations of production which conceives them as commercial encounters between individuals/agents of production on the market. But competition is far from designating the structure of capitalist relations of production; it consists precisely in the effect of the juridical and the ideological on socio-economic relations. (pp. 130-1)

The point for Poulantzas is that this isolation results from the state's juridico-political structure and its corresponding juridico-political ideology which defines agents of production as individual agents rather than classes, and that therefore this isolation forms the *real substratum* of the *appearance* of the state as 'nation'.

> In this way the capitalist state constantly appears as the political *unity* of an economic struggle which is in itself a sign of this isolation. It presents itself as the representative of the 'general interest' of competing and divergent economic interests which conceal their class character from the agents who experience them . . . the capitalist state systematically conceals its political class character at the level of its political institutions: it is a popular-national-class state, in the truest sense. (p.133)

One further aspect of bourgeois juridico-political ideology through which the capitalist state presents itself as a popular state standing above all classes, is that "all traces of class domination are absent from its language". This is in marked contrast to the pre-capitalist state where distinctions were ideologically 'justified' as 'natural' or 'sacred'.

This distinguishing feature of the capitalist state leads to the question of its relation to ideology: a relation which Poulantzas acknowledges is captured in

111

Gramsci's formulation of the 'ethico-political' role of the state. He reformulates this relation as "organizational" : it "is merely the result of inserting the capitalist state's specific unifying role into the discourse which is itself constructed according to the particular role of the dominant bourgeois ideology". A number of elements are identified in the functioning of ideology in relation to the state. First the representation of the state as the embodiment of the 'general interest', in which the domination of a specific class is absent from its institutions and practices: this is contained in the notions of representativeness and representation. Here the role of ideology is to intervene

> in the functioning of the state in order to provide the class-actors with the veneer of representation by means of which they can insinuate themselves into the institutions of the general popular-class state and under cover of which they can mask the divergences inevitable in the capitalist state between the actions of these actors and the classes which they represent. (p.216)

Secondly, the political significance of these ideologies is concealed "in a very specific manner:" the concealment is achieved by the fact that they explicitly present themselves as science.

> Political ideology, in the form of public opinion, presents itself as a body of practical rules, as technical knowledge, as the citizens' 'enlightened consciousness' of a specific practice, as the 'Reason' of this practice. This is the underlying conception of the whole series of political liberties: of the freedom of speech, of the freedom of the press, etc. Public opinion, which is a necessary factor in the functioning of the capitalist state and which is the modern form of political consent (consensus), cannot in fact function unless it manages to present itself and to be accepted in terms of 'rational' scientific technique, *i.e. in so far as it sets itself up in opposition to that which it designates and marks out as utopian.* It thus designates as utopian any representation in which the class struggle is present in any form whatsoever. (p.218)

Here Poulantzas attempts to indicate the means by which the dominant political ideology tries to appropriate the domain of political debate to itself by using its own constitutive elements as designating the limits of "debate" — or, as Marx and Engels put it, presenting its ideas as the only rational ones.

Finally we must note that at the end of the chapter on ideology, Poulantzas once again returns us to the complex task of understanding ideological formations in his discussion of the problem of legitimacy.

The type of legitimacy which predominates in a social formation depends upon the complexity of the relations between the dominant ideology and the form in which it dominates the ideological sub-ensembles, that is,

> Political domination corresponds to a *mode* of acceptance and consent from the unity of a formation, including the dominated classes. (p.223, our emphasis)

This is not to posit the absence of class struggle or to see these relations of struggle as having been incorporated or integrated into the social formation through the mechanism of consent, but merely to point to the complexity of ideological relations of domination and subordination. Thus the dominated classes may live "even their revolt" against the domination of the system *within the frame of reference* of the dominant ideology — for example in the case of "classical reformist ideology" or even in the case of the "coexistence of a strongly articulated revolutionary ideology with an ideology subject to the basic framework of the dominant legitimacy".

This warning of the complexity of ideological relations of domination and subordination is further impressed through the noting of different types of legitimacy which may coexist in a concrete situation, including class alliances (in ideological terms) with other classes and fractions. For example, feudal legitimacy has not only often characterized feudal structures coexisting in capitalist states but even structures typical of capitalist states: this is the case in contemporary Britain with a modern executive body which exists alongside and gives support to monarchical legitimacy. In dealing with such an example we should not underestimate the existence of such a form of legitimacy which depends on a particular class ideology — that of an almost non-existent aristocracy.

This return to and emphasis upon the *necessary* complexity of ideological relations of domination and subordination concludes Poulantzas' treatment of ideology. In subsequent sections, we shall advance some criticisms of this treatment and try to make explicit the basis which informs our criticisms, while noting those aspects of his work which are both useful and illuminating and which therefore we would wish to retain.

PROBLEMS WITH THE THEORY OF IDEOLOGY

For us, the most immediately striking feature of Poulantzas' formulations on ideology is the degree of theoretical confusion which they exhibit. We have been unable to identify one single organising theoretical principle which dominates these formulations. In what follows we shall take up what seem to be the most significant of these errors and confusions, but begin by pointing to some general aspects of this confusion.

In the course of the exposition we remarked on the peculiar role which the concept of "lived experience" played in the initial formulation of ideology, and on Poulantzas' prevarication as to whether this term is separate from or constituted by ideology. The former would appear to imply a problematic which distinguished ideology and lived experience, in which ideology had the force of an external presence impinging on agents' experiences and moulding "their representations of their real relations". Whereas the latter is more recognisably derived from the Althusserian conception of agents being constituted by and living in ideology. Poulantzas, however, elides this disjuncture by merely *collapsing* lived experience into ideology.

A similar prevarication is evident in his attempt to define the connection of ideology to the real: first, its function is not to give "true knowledge", so, it is claimed, it is therefore "necessarily false". But he immediately withdraws from the strictness of this position to allow that ideology may include "elements of knowledge". This confusion does indeed take place around a vital question in the analysis of ideology — that of the form of the relation between ideology and the real — but the proliferation of conflicting definitions hardly leads us towards a decisive answer.

In addition, we would argue that the use of an empiricist vocabulary of truth and falsity involves Poulantzas in an excessively over-simplified conception of the nature of the "real relations" — a point to which we shall return. Finally, all these propositions are set alongside a conception of ideology again derived from Althusser, of ideology as an "imaginary relation to the real relations". The force of 'imaginary' for Althusser does not imply empirical falsification, but a specific form of the *relation*. Poulantzas' attempts to grasp this relation in terms of its truth/falsity are also manifested in his surprisingly uncritical appropriation of the terms "inversion" and "mystification" to define the "biases" of ideology. There is here, amidst all the complexity of the propositions, more than a residual presence of the much denigrated 'camera obscura' metaphor of ideology to be found in *The German Ideology.*

Finally, in this context, we must note the unacknowledged difficulties raised by the proposition that ideology establishes relations "which are obvious but false". The problem is how to think this "obviousness". Are we to grasp it within what we termed above the first problematic — that agents experience their conditions of existence, and that ideology connects with this experience (obvious) but mystifies it (false)? Or is it that ideology itself constitutes the agents' 'experience', it produces these relations as if they were experience? If it is the latter, ideology cannot be *other* than obvious, since it forms all experience — there is nothing against which agents can recognise these ideological relations as obvious.

We cannot do more than raise these as profound and unresolved theoretical ambiguities in the text; Poulantzas himself offers us no guidelines to their resolution, and we do not have the capacity to claim to do this on his behalf. However, there are other problems within the account of ideology which are more demanding of attention, in part because they are located within the broader theoretical tendency of the text as a whole. In what follows we focus upon two of these.

One of the central and recurring difficulties is the tension between the theoretical weight attached to the notion of structural causality and the important role that class struggle is accorded in Poulantzas' analysis. At the most abstract level, this relation is unproblematically given — class struggle is the effect (manifested in the social relations of production, ideology, politics) of the 'ensemble of the structures'. The basic theoretical position then is one of structural effectivity. However, at more detailed points in the argument the structures are restricted to their role in determining a field of possible variations within which the *class struggle* determines the particular outcomes within this field of variations. (cf.p. 188)

This ambiguity is again reflected at crucial stages of his argument where he frequently "doubles up" his causal explanations. On the one hand, a particular characteristic is identified as the consequence of the function or role performed by a particular instance, while on the other hand, it is attributed to the specific balance of forces in the class struggle. Thus in his analysis of the question of the dominant ideology he moves (on the same page) from an approach to the dominant ideology which identifies its correspondence with the dominant classes as being a consequence of its status as a level of the structure which has the dominance of a given class as its effect, to proposing that the unity of the dominant ideology can only be deciphered from "the starting point of the field of the class struggle".

The first formulation implies an automatic transference of dominance, formally established in the structures, onto the terrain of class ideological formation, while the second implies that there is something to be struggled over and that struggle has particular effectivity. We would want to argue that it is this second formulation which is the more valuable in the discussion of ideology. Rather than *formally* attribute the function of "unifier" to ideology, we would suggest that an emphasis on

114

ideological class struggle directs attention to its function of unification as the contingent outcome of struggle in which one class attempts to "universalize itself", to transform economic dominance into a hegemonic ideological domination. The structural correspondence of ideological domination to class domination has the effect of reducing the weight to be given to what Gramsci called the "passage to the superstructures"; it smooths out the unevenness and disjunctures between the different forms of class domination and the specificity of the various struggles into a structurally 'expressive' correspondence of class domination at all levels of the social formation.

This formal structural causality also has the consequence of producing outcomes which are more *closed* than is warranted theoretically, empirically or politically. The attribution of the role of unifier to ideology is accompanied by an assumption of its effectiveness: unification is accomplished unproblematically. Similarly, the proposition that "ideology refuses to allow a contradiction within it" (p.208) would seem to deny the possibility of class struggle at this level — if an uncontradictory unity is established, with what materials and in what form does ideological class struggle take place? These propositions seem to us to involve a second error, which is the transposition of tendencies characteristic of the dominant ideology to ideology in general, e.g. ideology's 'ability' to unify and to exclude contradictions. This can also be seen in his argument that both the dominant ideology and the ideological level have the "function" of "inserting agents into their practical activities".

This conflation of the ideological level and the dominant ideology in terms of their 'function' is symptomatic of a much wider confusion and elision in Poulantzas' whole chapter on ideology, in which it often becomes impossible to distinguish whether he is referring to ideology in general, ideology in the capitalist mode of production, ideology in particular capitalist social formations, or the dominant ideology per se. This we would argue occurs as a consequence of his attempt to specify a set of general, formal propositions about the nature of ideology at the most abstract level (which we see as a necessary corollary of his effort to appropriate "the general concepts of historical materialism" — see the introduction). It is the generality of this analysis which inevitably leads him to reduce the conception of ideology to a functional imperative. However there can be *no* analysis of ideology at this general level. The posing of the question of ideology in this abstract functionalist manner is theoretically incompatible with a concrete understanding of the forms and conditions under which ideology operates. This latter type of analysis is something which Poulantzas himself addresses in those passages concerning the nature of the ideological class struggle. Nevertheless he is unable to accomplish any *theoretical* unity between these two forms of analysis *precisely* because the sets of concepts are generated at different levels of abstraction.

Poulantzas' most substantial contribution to the analysis of ideology seems to us to be made in his attempt to demarcate the field of ideological class struggle. His denial of a relation of simple expressivity between a class subject and its pure ideological representation leads him to the more complex and satisfactory formulations involving such concepts as "ideological ensembles and sub-ensembles" which constitute the ideological field. Thus for example, the petit-bourgeoisie does not live in an ideological world which is purely and simply petit-bourgeois, but in relation to an

115

ideological sub-ensemble within which the petit-bourgeois ideology is contaminated by elements of other ideologies, and which exists within an ideological field which is itself in turn dominated by the dominant ideology.

Our second major area of criticism concerns the statement about bourgeois juridico-political ideology — more specifically his thesis on the nature of the "isolation effect". As we have noted earlier the production of "bare individuals" is not an inherent feature of the structure of capitalist relations of production but rather is an effect of the juridical structure, the juridico-political ideology and the ideological in general. Crucially, Poulantzas is unable to specify *how* the separation of the direct producer from the means of production, which he correctly states brings about the socialisation of the labour process, at the same time establishes agents of production as juridical and political "individual-subjects" without positing a *real* objective basis for this "individualisation" at the level of the economic, something to which he is resolutely opposed. Thus when he states the following,

> The juridico-political superstructure of the capitalist state is related to the structure of the relations of production. This becomes clear as soon as we refer to capitalist law. The separation of the direct producer from the means of production is *reflected* there by the institutionalised fixing of agents of production as juridical subjects, i.e. political individuals-persons (p.128, our emphasis)

he would seem to contradict his earlier argument that the agents of production actually appear as individuals only in those superstructural relations which are juridical relations and not within the structure of the relations of production. The question then is what is the mechanism of this reflection and more importantly what is the basis of this "reflection"? Our point is that the individualisation of agents *really* occurs in the process of the exchange of commodities. Marx puts it this way:

> Out of the act of exchange itself, the individual, each one of them, is reflected in himself as its exclusive and dominant (determinant) subject. With that, then, the complete freedom of the individual is posited . . . The general interest is precisely the generality of self-seeking interests. Therefore when the economic form, exchange, posits the all-sided equality of its subjects, then the content, the individual as well as the objective material which drives towards the exchange, is *freedom*. (*Grundrisse,* Penguin 1973, pp.244-5)

Marx's analysis of the exchange relation demonstrates the necessary equality between the two exchanging parties as its constitutive basis: and notes that minor variations (i.e. contingent factors such as the particular cunning of one of the contractors) do not interfere with this fundamental basis of equality between the exchangers. This is crucial, for it touches one of the central problems of Marx's "economics" — the creation of surplus value. He emphatically denies that surplus value can be created through the medium of exchange in any regular and systematic way. Not even the most central exchange relation of capitalism — that between the wage labourer and capitalist — is exempt from this "equality".

Clearly, then, the missing term in the equation which is the mediating link between the sphere of exchange and that of production is that of labour power, or, more precisely, the transformation of the value and price of *labour power* into the wage form, the value and price of *labour,* of which Marx says:

> This phenomenal form, which makes the actual relation invisible, and, indeed, shows the

direct opposite of that relation, forms the basis of all the juridical notions of both labourer and capitalist, of all the mystifications of the capitalist mode of production, of all its illusions as to liberty, of all the apologetic shifts of the vulgar economists.

Though Marx terms the wage, the exchange relation and so on, phenomenal forms, or forms of appearance, they are not, and cannot be reduced to mere illusions or errors on the part of the "subjects" of these processes, whether we see these subjects as constitutive of these processes or merely performing the function of "supports". What we are dealing with are *real processes, real forms of relationship.* Agents do exchange, buy and sell, the wage labourer does indeed sell his labour and receive a wage in (equal) exchange. It is these relations themselves which are "false", but false in a very specific sense — not, as we have said, in the sense that they are not real, but false because they hide other sets of relations and processes of a very different quality and nature.

Nor, we must emphasise, solely because Marx uses the terminology of "appearances", "phenomenal forms", "forms of appearance" and so on, can the distinction which he is making between these forms and the real relations be understood as being an idealist couplet of essence and appearance. This would be to reduce the appearances to mere epiphenomenal irrelevancies, in which only the "essence" is of any serious concern. Marx's efforts, on the contrary, run in completely the opposite direction — not only are the "appearances" real sets of relations but they are also *absolutely necessary* for capitalist production. The sphere of exchange is both the starting and the finishing point of the process of capitalist production — the starting point, because it is here that capital in the form of money is exchanged for labour power and the means of production to initiate production itself; and the finishing point because it is only with the exchange of the commodities created in the process of production for money that surplus value is realised. Exchange, then, and specifically the exchange of equivalences, is an absolutely necessary element of the circuit of capital as analysed by Marx. It cannot be treated as a merely epiphenomenal appendage of the "real" process ot production.

We must now take this argument further. More complexly the relationship between the phenomenal form and the real process involves a *necessary contradiction* which the surface appearances occlude. Thus the freedom of atomised and isolated individuals is a corollary of the increasing socialization of the process of production in capitalism, a corollary, that is, of the increasing *interdependence* of individuals. Similarly, the equality of exchange between wage-labour and capital is posited upon the pre-existing and more fundamental relation of inequality in the distribution of the means of production. What we have then is an analysis of a process — the circuit of capital — which is posited on a fundamental set of relations (those of capital and wage-labour), but which is divisible into a number of particular processes and corresponding sets of relations (production, exchange, distribution, etc.). Certain of these subordinate processes (those of circulation and exchange) involve relations and processes of a qualitatively different order from the fundamental relations on which they rest and which they serve to mask.

We are not claiming here that what is provided by Marx's analysis of the circuit of capital is a theory of ideology. It is not. We are not told how ideology works, how agents are inserted into ideological relations, how ideological class struggle operates etc. What we are told is that in capitalism the "error" of thinking men as "free", individuated and equal subjects is not an "error" produced by and in ideology, but is fundamentally located in the real processes of capitalist accumulation. It provides us with a necessary *starting point* for thinking the processes and content of bourgeois ideology and it is here that Marx founds his analysis of one particular ideology — that of bourgeois political economy, whose errors he locates in its inability to penetrate the surface forms and processes of capitalism.

But we cannot be seduced into collapsing the specificity of ideological processes into this analysis of the economic. We have focussed considerable attention on the question of the isolation effect, but this is not simply as an excuse for a lengthy exposition of its errors and their correction. The isolation effect is a crucial part of Poulantzas' overall argument; it connects his analysis of the political level, and specifically here, the nature of bourgeois juridico-political ideology and its effects both on economic class struggle and on the mode of functioning of the capitalist state. It is thus a central theoretical mechanism for the work as a whole.

Similarly, what for Marx is an aspect of capitalist *production* (in the broad sense of the circuit of capital) is misappropriated by Poulantzas to being a characteristic of capitalist state and ideology. This is not merely confined to his thesis on the "isolation effect". It is symptomatic of a tendency within the work as a whole, which is incorrectly and systematically to overestimate the significance of the political vis-a-vis the economic. This tendency to "over-politicisation" has been noted by others in different ways.

To be clear, however, we are not saying that Poulantzas is incorrect when he states that the juridical, juridico-political ideology and ideology in general have the effect of masking from the agents the fact that their relations are class relations; nor are we denying that the economic is over-determined by the political and the ideological. What is at issue here is the way this over-determination is thought; we have argued that this "isolation effect" is the appropriation within the political and ideological of real economic processes and relations which thus form the basis of the content of the political and the ideological's over-determination of the economic. This isolation — the production of "bare" individuals — occurs primarily within the economic at one and the same time as the socialisation of the productive forces and the creation of the "collective labourer", but within different aspects of the circuit of capital, the former in exchange, the latter in production itself. Both socialised production and the creation of free and equal subjects in the process of exchange are absolutely necessary elements of the process of capital accumulation.

We would argue that this tendency to "over-politicisation" noted in Poulantzas owes much to the conception of the mode of production within which he locates his more specific analysis, and that the errors originating here have profound effects on his analysis of the relations between the economic, the political and the ideological.

The Concept of Mode of Production

We are introduced to a concept of mode of production which is seen as consisting of a combination of instances (the economic, ideological, political, etc.). This seems to us to be an erroneous conception for which there is, in Marx, no warrant. Marx constantly designates by "mode of production" the *economic* level only, or, as he puts it, the "economic structure on which arises a legal and political superstructure and to which correspond definite forms of social consciousness" (1859 *Preface*). Rather than attempt to reproduce the occasions on which Marx uses this formulation or its variants, we shall merely refer to one quotation which Poulantzas himself uses in this connection, to indicate how even with selective quotation the concept of mode of production cannot be generalised to include the ideological and economic instances:

> My view that each special mode of production and the social relations corresponding to it, in short that the economic structure of society is the real basis on which the juridical and political superstructure is raised and to which definite social forms of thought correspond . . . (quoted in Poulantzas, p.28)

To prevent the charge of merely "quoting the classics" in the furtherance of this argument, we may arrive at the inadequacies of the theorisation of the mode of production as a combination in a different way. In the analysis of the economic instance, Poulantzas elaborates what the elements which constitute this instance are (labourer, non-labourer, means of production), but is unable to specify the elements which make up the other two remaining levels — the ideological and the political — with which he is concerned. We would argue that this theoretical absence arises because the other two levels are of a fundamentally different order from that of the economic. They are in fact levels which enter the analysis of concrete societies, social formations dominated by a particular mode of production — they are *super-structural*.

This question is crucial for understanding the constitution of social classes. Poulantzas insists that they are the "global effect" of the combination of the structures, but we would argue that the *constitution* of classes must be thought at the economic level. This does not mean that we envisage "His Majesty the Economy" striding forth across the plain of history as naked as if he were wearing the Emperor's new clothes. In the same way that the Althusserian mode of production always exists in a concrete social formation, so Marx's formulations always stress each "special" mode of production, together with its particular social relations, its corresponding superstructures and forms of thought as constituting particular societies. Classes do indeed appear and struggle on the terrains of ideology and the state, but these cannot be understood as forming the constitution of classes. Rather they are the re-constitution of economically produced classes on the different levels of a social formation — they are "the ideological forms in which men become conscious of this conflict and fight it out" (1859 *Preface*).

The Constitution of Social Classes

Any analysis of the constitution of classes in social formations dominated by the capitalist mode of production must begin by locating itself within an understanding of the complexity of the economic constitution of classes within this mode. Schematically, there are four major points here.

First, the fundamental social classes are designated by their relation to the means of production.

Secondly, and more complexly, this means following Marx's analysis of the circuit of capital — grasped as a process with specific moments (production, distribu-

119

tion, exchange and consumption) which are necessary and irreducible elements of the capitalist mode of production, and in which production is determinant. It is within this process that classes are *complexly constituted* — they never appear as a homogeneous entity; thus, for example, it is possible to distinguish between landed, industrial and finance capitalists, etc. This fractioning of the bourgeoisie necessarily produces a fractioned proletariat — created by their subsumption under the different types of capital. In addition to this, Marx's analysis of the circuit of capital indicates another form of internal differentiation of the proletariat, in that human labour in the abstract is only manifested in specific concrete forms: the production of each specific commodity necessitates labour power of a particular type because it involves the transference of value from one specific set of raw materials and instruments of production to one particular finished commodity (cf. Capital I:200).

Thirdly, it is within the economic structure that we find the basis of what Marx describes in *The 18th Brumaire* as the bourgeoisie's "narrowest and most sordid private interests" — for private, competitive self-interest is the fundamental structure of capital, it is the necessary form taken by the inherent tendency of capital to self-expansion. It is, together with the fractioning of capital already noted, that which constitutes the basis of the relative autonomy of the state from the dominant classes; there is *no* economic general interest of the bourgeoisie at *this* level.

Fourthly, production is also for Marx reproduction — of both the forces and relations of production; wage labour and capital, wage labourers and capitalists, and proletariat and bourgeoisie are reproduced. What is significant though, is that this reproduction is inherently *contradictory* — it is the reproduction of a constantly antagonistic class relation, and indeed, as constantly expanded reproduction, it is the constant development of that antagonism to higher levels. Thus, although reproduction takes place at the economic level, its consequences (as contradictory reproduction) cannot be *contained* there — they must be organised and managed at the level of the state. The state, then, as Althusser correctly recognises, secures (or, rather, attempts to secure) the reproduction of the social relations of production.

What we have attempted to do here is to schematically return the debate to its fundamentals, to begin with the determinacy of the economic (and with a conception of its complexity, which we find lacking in Poulantzas) from which the specificity of other levels must be thought. Without this, we would argue, attempts to think determinacy (in the last or any other instance) are likely to be reduced to an abstract functionalist schema.

These criticisms are those which we would level at Poulantzas' attempt to give an account of ideology. It is these tendencies which undercut those aspects of his analysis which we take to be of positive value, and make them of more peripheral import than they might have been in a sustained attempt to come to terms with these problems. To redress the balance of our criticisms, we must finally note where these points of value lie, and to what they direct us. Firstly, we accept that there is an irreducible advance provided by the criticisms of the historicist schema of ideology as the product of the couplet subject/consciousness, and by the connected insistence that ideologies cannot be thought as existing "in a vacuum". Class ideologies are then never the transparent product of a pure thinking class subject, but are only to be found within the terrain of class struggle, with their (abstract) purity always overdetermined by the effects of this class struggle.

Secondly, we would point to the analysis of the role of ideology in the functioning of the capitalist state, particularly to the vital role of ideology in connecting (and disconnecting) the individual and general interests via the processes of representation, within which the political arena constructs this "general interest". This seems to us to identify crucial areas and mechanisms of the state's operations, and also to identify the vital importance of the state and its associated ideologies in the functioning and maintenance of capitalist social formations through its persistent transposition of class interests into the form of the general interest.

Conclusion

We have argued at some length in the previous section about the necessity of grasping the connection between ideology and the economic. This is not solely because we believe that the analysis of the economic which we have offered is one whose importance has been reduced within the Althusserian canon, but because it is this connection — the economic and ideology — which we believe to be the vital nodal point of any Marxist theorising upon ideology. Poulantzas has rightly criticised the errors of historicist conceptions of ideology — its reduction to the consciousness of simply economically defined class subjects — but has failed to provide a rigorous and substantial alternative to this position.

The construction of ideology via its *function* is not an adequate foundation for this alternative theory. It assumes, incorrectly, we would argue, that the problems of a Marxist analysis of the economic structure are resolved and closed, and the retreat to the function of ideology comes about precisely because Poulantzas cannot specify the relation between the real relations in which agents are located, and the ideological forms in which they are thought, understood and represented. The "function" of ideology is inserted directly into this theoretical space.

We do not claim to have resolved the nature of the relationship between these fundamental relations and their ideological forms. What we have attempted to do is to present one way of thinking one half of the relation. We have begun from the economic and attempted to show how Marx identifies the *basis* of central aspects of bourgeois ideology within the different aspects of the economic structure of capitalism. These glimpses, however, are not marginal to Marx's analysis of the workings of capitalism, they recur *throughout* his critique of bourgeois political economy; indeed, they form a crucial element of that critique in his insistence that the errors of political economy derive from the fact that it cannot and does not penetrate the surface movements of capitalism.

These observations, however, do not constitute a theory of ideology. They approach it by specifying how it is to be grasped from one side of the relation of the economic and the ideological. They do not provide us with a way of thinking ideology itself. They do, however, insist that the "primacy" of the economic in Marxist theory must be thought in a more persistent and active way than its reduction to the "matrix" of the structures by Poulantzas would seem to allow. The difficulty of thinking ideology adequately is the task of holding this extended conception of the economic without allowing further analysis to lapse back into vulgar economism in which ideology and politics are treated as mere reflective epiphenomena. Here we would accept the definitive advances made within the Althusserian paradigm (though not necessarily their prescribed solutions) around the irreducibility of ideology, the decentredness of the agents with respect to the relations and processes within which they are inserted.

The task for a Marxist theory of ideology, we would suggest, is to grasp this double-sided connection — of the economic and its own effects and the ideological forms in which the agents live these relations — without abolishing the specific effectivity of either side of this connection. It is precisely this connection which is *identified* by Althusser as a relation to the real relations; the nature of the connection is, however, not resolved by its definition as an *imaginary* relation. This does not allow us to think the determinacy of the economic over the ideological, nor the specific processes involved in ideological representation.

Finally, and by way of a return to Poulantzas, it is absolutely necessary that these relations be grasped as class relations, and as a process of class struggle, at each level, both at the economic and in the "ideological forms in which men become conscious of the struggle and fight it out". This is the theoretical issue which is at stake here, and its political significance cannot be underestimated.

BIBLIOGRAPHY

K. Marx Capital Vol. I (Lawrence and Wishart 1974)
K. Marx 1859 Preface, Contribution to the Critique of Political Economy (Lawrence and Wishart 1971)
K.Marx Grundrisse (Penguin 1973)
N. Poulantzas Political Power and Social Classes (NLB 1973)
N. Poulantzas Classes in Contemporary Capitalisms (NLB 1975)

Part II
Problems of
Social Democracy

Working Class Images of Society and Community Studies

Eve Brook, Dan Finn

One of the defining characteristics of sociology, and its sub-disciplines, has been its overwhelming concern with questions of social class, particularly in relation to the working class. Its major encounter with the located experiences of working-class people has been conducted through the medium of community studies and in this article we want to evaluate the impact and development of these studies as a genre. This evaluation is particularly important because the findings of this body of work have provided material, both directly and indirectly, which has been used in the analysis of class imagery and class-based meaning systems. The focus of this article then, is on the way in which working-class imagery has been typified by certain sociologists, and the arguments they have advanced to justify these typifications.

We would argue that the introduction of the term 'ideology' into a discussion of working-class imagery is essential. The main problem seems to be arriving at an operationalised definition of what ideology actually is. For many Marxists it is seen as a systematised form of false consciousness (yet another elastic concept), and here it would be the ideas of the ruling class in their best clothes — formalised theoretical constructions epitomised, for example, in religion. On the other hand, ideologies are seen to arise from the working class itself — trade unionism as a purely defensive force is an instance.

Both of these examples are of national, and even international significance, and perhaps for this reason are often seen as existing 'up there', as ahistorical and controlling forces. Similarly, this is why they are often seen abstractly, as 'general value systems', imposing constraints on human conduct. However, we cannot accept any definition of ideology as existing outside material life. This means that ideologies are not only expressed and based in material life, but that they are also under constant pressure to change, as the conditions of material life change. It follows then, that the first part of our definition would be that it is material life which determines ideology.

The next question, inevitably, is how? We would not disagree that certain aspects of working-class ideology are representations of the interests of the ruling class, though we would take issue with any suggestion that this is done conspiratorily. But even here, the ideas of the ruling class are endorsed, modified, or rejected according to certain material conditions.

These material conditions, of course, exist at the level of everyday class experiences and class practices. These experiences and practices differ, not only between classes, but also within them — generating occupational or local class fractions. Thus, it is not only ruling-class ideas that are put to the test in working-class experience, but just as importantly, we would suggest, class practice generates its own kind of consciousness and culture. Thus, the contradictory nature of working-class consciousness reflects the difference between the real experience of capitalist production and the phenomenal forms of the market, reflected in the superstructure. The collective, lived experience of capitalist production gives alternative sets of practices and organisations embodied in working-class culture. The consciousness generated is ideologically 'commonsense': learning through experience what can and cannot be done in *given* conditions. This is ideological, therefore, because the conditions are *given,* they are not questioned — only the best way of manipulating them to advantage is considered.

Here locality and workplace become extremely important. The material base of sectionalism resides in a labour market differentiated by industry, by variations among firms within industries, and by the division of labour within particular workplaces. While in general terms geographically distinct groups of workers have similar sorts of problems, the problems of any specific group are particular and unique. They are bound in time, revolve around particular people, and are confined to a particular workplace or section within it.

Thus, TV assembly workers do not see their ultimate dependence on the coal miner, and there is no 'commonsense' reason why they should. In these situations class activity is industry- and locality-based. Loyalties are formed across a region, a factory or an occupation, *and in some circumstances these loyalties can become so exclusive as to cover up the ultimate reality of being working class.* The best thing that can happen here is indifference to the struggles of other workers. The worst is outright conflict between sections of the working class, for example, the recent struggle between dockers and transport workers, carefully orchestrated by industrial interests, but displaying that inability to transcend sectional interests. Besides the 'particular' ideologies existing on an occupational basis, they can also exist where the occupation is identical, but the locality is different. Cousins and Brown, in a paper on shipbuilding workers, give an example:

> Favouritism based on localism and residence is a factor in employment in an industry and area where unemployment is a major problem. The 'market' or daily callstand encourage localism. A chargehand from the former Blyth shipyard a little farther up the coast and now closed told us 'with us it was always keep the Tynies out'. (1975 p.58)

The material conditions underlying this sectionalism are not hard to spot — long-term unemployment in a depressed industry. But a parochial ideology is the mode of responding to it — attacks are directed at other workers, rather than the owners.

It is the relationship between these local, fractional ideologies and the theoretically developed ideologies generated by national institutions, which has been at the heart of sociology's attempt to understand working-class images of society. In this paper, it is the understanding of these 'images' developed by two central theorists that we wish to consider. Both address themselves to the question of how diverse 'images' are created/determined within those sections of the working class characterised, on the one hand, as privatised and traditional, and on the other hand, as accommodative. They are Lockwood (1975) stressing the primacy of immediate work and community relationships, and Parkin (1971) stressing the ideological dominance of national meaning-systems.

Lockwood's typology distinguishes three different working-class images of society, spontaneously generated through work experience and the values held by the local community. Firstly the traditional proletarian, typified by miners, dockers and shipyard workers. Secondly, the traditional deferentialist, whose defining characteristic is that he is likely to work in rural, or craft-based industry, and have face-to-face relationships with a paternalistic employer. Thirdly, the privatised worker who is 'instrumental' in his attitude to work and 'privatised' in his home life.

Before going on to evaluate the theoretical adequacy of these typificiations, we want to pursue a line of investigation suggested by Lockwood, in that it should be possible to examine these types and 'flesh them out' or reject them in terms of the data from community studies. However, as we hope to demonstrate, it is not quite so simple, and to outline our reservations it is necessary to say something about the historical, ideological and methodological development of community studies as a genre — particularly in its social democratic forms. The outline and critique of community studies is lengthy, but we feel this is justified because of its position as the major accredited source of 'qualitative' accounts of working-class culture.

Post-War Community Studies

Post-war community studies can be seen as a reaction against certain developments in sociology, coupled with apprehensions about the direction of social democracy. As with many other developments in the sociology of the fifties, they can be seen against the background of the proliferation of 'post-capitalist society' and 'embourgeoisement' theories, which, however unwittingly, added a new dimension to the discussion of class. To summarise a familiar argument, during the 1950s it was commonly asserted that capitalism as such had ceased to exist and had been superceded by 'post-industrial' society. All the theorists with something in common with this thesis held that the old sources of class conflict were being progressively eliminated, or rendered irrelevant, and that Western society was being recast in a middle-class style.

These interpretations rested on three basic assumptions. Firstly, that the liberal and social democracies were pluralistic, power being held by a number of social groups. Secondly, that the substantive inequalities of early capitalism were diminishing and losing their former significance: differentials in income were being eroded and other inequalities were being dealt with by an economy stabilised through the application of Keynesian economic policies; due to nationalisation there was now a mixed economy; and most importantly, the post-1945 implementation of the 1942 Beveridge Report had, through the Welfare State, bridged any remaining inequalities — a process expressed in Britain through social security, council housing, the National Health Service, and State-funded secondary education. Thirdly, for

127

the above and other reasons, radical dissent had been progressively eliminated or weakened as new patterns of living and aspirations cut across older class-bound horizons: amongst manual workers a faith in collective action was being replaced by reliance on individual achievement; the old loyalties of class were being replaced with preoccupations of status — the ethos of the middle class.

The major ideological impact of these developments was the widely held and potent belief that class was 'withering away' or had disappeared. This utopianism was not just complacency but a diagnosis of something real and important in the 1950s: working-class apathy and lack of enthusiasm for collective ends. In fact, the sheer number of writers who espoused the thesis was some sort of evidence that the political apathy of the time was not an illusion — a fact not always recognised by some of its opponents.

The fallacies underlying these conceptions went unchallenged, at least ideologically, until the development of the 'New Left' — arising from disillusionment both with the effectiveness of Labour's social reforms and with the sterility of organised left-wing thought. The thrust of this changing ideological stance was characterised in certain key books — Hoggart's *Uses of Literacy* (1957), Williams' *Culture and Society* (1958). Despite the difference of scope, subject and emphasis, these works stood in one way or another for a favourable evaluation of the meanings of working class culture. As Hoggart makes clear:

> I think such an impression is wrong if it leads us to construct an image of working class people only from adding together the variety of statistics given in some of these sociological works . . . clearly we have to try to see beyond the habits to what the habits stand for, to see through the statements to see what the statements mean . . . , to detect the differing pressures of emotion behind idiomatic phrases and ritualistic observances. (1957 p.17)

In the New Left's interpretation of working-class culture, the idea of 'community' plays a pivotal role. 'Community' is important because it allows the Culture/Society question to be thought through in a number of dimensions. Twenty years on, it is difficult to appreciate the radical implications of this — but what more than anything else distinguished these literary/cultural studies at this time was their attention to 'meaning': how separate texts/rituals/institutions interrelated in a 'whole way of life'. The idea of community necessarily pre-supposed an intellectual commitment to go beyond immediate empiricism, the 'obvious', the isolated text, to interpret cultural phenomena in terms of structural relationships or parts of a whole.

The critical developments of Williams and Hoggart were closely linked with a movement in social administration, in which Titmuss (1958) was the leading figure, which stressed the gaps and inadequacies in welfare services, the extent to which working-class material standards remained below those of the middle class, and argued that political policy rather than individual competence was responsible for these differences.

The theme linking the two areas was the realisation that working-class people had characteristics that were not explicable simply in terms of their financial position; that proposals for change needed to be grounded in a more complex theoretical understanding of working-class life. It is within this context that we find the development of those community studies with which we are centrally concerned (see Appendix). These publications, such as the work of the Institute of Community Studies, were conducted at a time when more than superficial social research was rare, and when sociology as an academic subject had gained footholds in only a few universities.

These community studies in fact very largely ignored the assumptions of the 'post-capitalist' society/'embourgeoisement' thesis; or at most they conceded that higher wages had meant a rise in the standard of living of the working class, but asserted that this had made no real difference to working-class culture. Importantly, then, class was understood primarily as a cultural formation, and not as a phenomenon generated by production. Community studies set out to 'rediscover' class, and in this sense 'community' carried connotations which can only be described as political. There was a kind of smuggling process, whereby the idea of 'community' was identified with the central socialist/social democratic preoccupation with class cultures. Not accidentally, we might add, for it was based in part on real anxieties about Labour's electoral base. It is noteworthy in this context that many of the studies researched in the late 1950s had authors with some formal connection with the Labour Party (e.g. Jackson [1968], Young and Wilmott [1962], Dennis, Henriques and Slaughter [1969], Townsend [1957]). The notion of 'community' with its overtones of tradition and oppositional culture had an obvious attraction.

So, whilst we can see that the development of community studies was, in part, a reaction to the more vulgar embourgeoisement thesis and a reflection of the concern generated by the apparent erosion of Labour's electoral base, it is also clear that many of the community studies were specifically aimed at the practice of social policy, or directed towards an illumination of those consensually defined 'social problems'. Thus, for Young and Willmott:

> The assumption was that the policy-makers were . . . insufficiently aware of the needs and views of the working class people who form the bulk of the users of the social services, and we hoped that social research might help to provide a more realistic basis for policy. (1961 p.2)

Whereas, with Jackson: "The communal urge could then have been harnessed for a common good". He took ". . . the illustration of productivity to show the practical help that can flow from an understanding of the otherness of working class life". (1969 p.156)

It is important at this point to step back and attempt to understand the position that sociology occupies within bourgeois ideology, and to explain the phenomenal growth of sociology, both as an academic discipline and an applied science, during the late 1950s and 1960s. Sociology, as Gouldner (1971) attempts to point out, arises and assumes that 'social problems' cannot be solved within the framework of bourgeois economics:

> Sociology focuses upon the non-economic sources of social order. Academic sociology polemically denies that economic change is a sufficient or necessary condition for maintaining or increasing social order. (1971 p.4)

That is to say, when the social character of capitalist production has become apparent in the oppositional life-style and activities of the chief force of production, the working class, sociology arises as a theory of how to respond to this opposition without abolishing the capitalist mode of production.

Sociology recognises the social character of production — but denies that it has to do with production, which is, after all, the concern of economics. 'Social problems', that is, those activities or phenomena which impinge on the interests of capital, are seen to be the result of 'social' life — not economic contradictions. It is no longer the individual 'problem family' that is at fault, it is a lot of 'problem families' living in a 'problem area'. Thus, for example, in regard to education, we can now see that it is the community which largely determines educational success:

> What is unchallenged, however, is that the concept of community provides us with an illuminating guide to the expectations and requirements of the population of the school catchment areas, as well as the prevailing factors in the behaviour of its pupils and teachers. (Eggleston 1967 p.36)

This ideological role is clearly exemplified in the notion of a 'culture of poverty'. This argues that the poor constitute a distinctive culture or community within society; that the experiences, attitudes and values generated in poor communities are passed on from one generation to the next in a never-ending cycle. Thus, this culture is able:

> . . . to perpetuate itself from generation to generation because of its effect on the children. By the time slum children are aged six to seven they have usually absorbed the basic attitudes and values of their subculture, and are not psychologically geared to take full advantage of changing conditions, or increased opportunities which may occur in their life-time. (Lewis 1968 p.60)

So it is not unskilled, meaningless, irregular employment, or bad housing, or an irrelevant education that is at fault — its their basic attitudes that are wrong.

Thus, within the total context of bourgeois ideology, sociology provides important methodological and empirical data for the social-policy makers. Because it has no understanding of contradications within a total structure it is conceptually limited to understanding class conflict in terms of either cultural or individual deprivation, and its policy formulations boil down to 'tinkering with the machine' — never mind the engine. At one and the same time, sociology is both reformist and repressive. By providing palliatives to real material problems, conceived of in terms of 'social problems', it also, by definition, secures means of social control.

This inability to understand society as a total structure has meant that sociology in general, and community studies in particular, have automatically limited themselves to the appearance of things, never trying to analyse the relationships latent in the things themselves. It is in this area, and for this reason, that community studies have drawn on functionalism, particularly as manifested in the work of social anthropologists. A practice, custom or belief is interpreted in terms of its present and ongoing functions in the surrounding society. But whereas anthropologists within small-scale societies are able to study social life at first hand, sociologists have adopted the same model as if their 'communities' were excused participation in national structures of class or politics.

In practice this approach leads to a concentration on 'normative' facts (to treat social facts as things), so that social structure refers to relations between actual, empirically given social phenomena. These relationships are either given in the facts as directly observed, or arrived at by simple abstraction from the facts. Thus, social structure when used in functional analysis refers to no more than the actual organisation of a given social system.

From within this perspective social behaviour is seen as determined by 'norms', enforced by implicit or explicit sanctions. These structure, in a regular and predictable fashion, the social life and relationships of individuals. Thus, to Young and Willmott, the mother/daughter relationship is one where: "Though they both derive benefit from the relationship, it is far more than a mere arrangement for mutual convenience. The attachment between them is supported by a powerful moral code." (1962 p.193)

Thus, many community studies erect a social reality which is taken as given and giving of itself in immediate appearance. We are presented with a single-levelled social totality consisting of attitudes, behaviour, activities and institutions and the relationships between these things. There is little awareness of *process,* or dynamic relations between different forces and groupings; there is no sense of *levels* within the social whole, and in particular no notion of the relations and mediations between the subjective level of experience, ideology and determining material conditions. In general, people are seen as passive, with things happening to them, rather than as showing some attempt to create their lives: there is no dialectic between objective and subjective factors.

The ideological construction of a world which is self-evident, single-layered and functionally interrelated, in which ideas are just there as they have always been, delivers a specific kind of methodological unconsciousness. Since *one* reality is there for the seeing, there is no more than one way in which to see it — why therefore give the groundings or detail of your observations? It is not a reflexive world so why should your methodology be reflexive? The techniques are 'naturalist', direct and unproblematic and usually unrecorded.

With no clear statement of the paradigms in this work; without any information about research techniques, or how respondents see investigators; with no information independently presented both concerning the relationship of the researched to the researcher, and concerning the raw data untreated by theories of the writers — it is impossible for us to *triangulate,* to read back along the lines of the prior theoretic predisposition, to deconstruct and reconstruct, to come to our own principled interpretation of the evidence.

Community studies form the single most massive encounter with the located experience of working-class people, and are the major accredited source of 'qualitative' accounts of working-class culture. As such, they should be demystified and also salvaged as sources for our own, hopefully more reflexive, research procedures. As it is, 'reading back' from community studies is an uncertain exercise. We are dealing with a peculiarly untheorised, naturalised, impacted problematic which methodologically conceals its own tracks.

Thus, if we take it as axiomatic that people are not simply on the 'receiving end' of their objective class position, then it is apparent that their actions are partly projected in terms of creative expectations and definitions. Unfortunately, as we have shown, most of the examination of this semi-autonomous layer of working class experience has been carried out via the medium of community studies, and it is with this imperfect material that the argument about typifications of working class imagery and the changes occuring within it have been carried out.

131

In returning to Lockwood's typology we find that he argues that there are two crucial variables in the formation of working-class images of society — work and the local community. He then draws a distinction between two basic models of class imagery: a model based on power, conflict and a dichotomy between classes; and a model based on prestige, status and hierarchy. Lockwood argues that it is the proletarian traditionalist who is likely to endorse a dichotomous model, and thereby he implies that it is this type of worker who is the most class conscious. Consequently, it is on this aspect of Lockwood's analysis that we shall be concentrating in this section.

The proletarian traditionalist is the archetypal subject of community studies, and he is certainly the most colourful, romantic and inaccessible representative of his class. He is inevitably male and usually works in a situation of physical discomfort and danger. Nevertheless, he retains a high degree of job involvement and a strong attachment to his primary work-group. His occupational culture spills over into his leisure, facilitated by the fact that most of this kind of work requires an 'occupational community'.

The classic community study in this field is undoubtedly *Coal is Our Life* (1956). This study has shaped a whole generation of academics' perceptions of the miner. The data for this study was collected in the 1950s and it is avowedly a community study influenced by anthropology. The note of caution this strikes in us seems to be shared by a least one of the authors: Henriques in particular is very sensitive to the implications of his approach and method. In the introduction to the second edition he writes: "By its focus upon the 'community framework' as such, this technique will tend to abstract from the societal framework at every level of social life" (1969 p.7). His example is that whereas relationships between husband and wife and the nature of leisure activity is:

> Viewed primarily from the standpoint of grasping their *interrelationships* with the forms of activity and social relations *imposed* by the coal mining work upon which the community is based, this emphasis will tend to obscure the fact that each of these particular sets of relationships is extended beyond the community, in both space and time. By itself the community study technique provides no way of measuring the significance of its findings against 'external' factors. (1969 p.7)

Ashton miners certainly display a dichotomous class imagery; but whether this conforms to Lockwood's model or not will be discussed subsequently. The question of whether this is spontaneously generated through the social relationships of work is highly debatable. The above extract suggests that Henriques would recognise that miners could be drawing on extra-local factors for their class imagery.

The central features of the community life described by Dennis *et al.* are the recurring conflict and attitudes of the miners to their cultural poverty and isolation, and the oppression of their wives. These are seen as the outgrowth of actual economic relationships and working conditions. From the peculiar class situation and from the work situation (to use Lockwood's terms) of the miner, much else follows. There is certainly a logical connection between the common work experience of the miner and a dichotomous social imagery, but logic never made a fact. One objection is the totally different life experience of women in mining areas. Whilst men have been

132

thrown together by coal, it has exerted the opposite or 'centifrugal' influence on women. There is no paid work for them unless they go outside the area. Nor can they identify very easily through the family: marriage and the family is a battle arena, and seems completely devoid of affection. Men and women are as effectively separated as Eskimos and Africans. In fact, the experience of the sexes is so totally different that one has to make the effort to remember that they live *together* in the same town. Since Lockwood is contending that the work and community experience is crucial in the formation of perceptions of class, it is reasonable to expect that the men's and women's images would be different.

However, voting returns from mining areas (admittedly very partial evidence) tend to show that the women vote the same way as the men, at least partly suggesting they share the same type of class imagery. This interpretation would tend to suggest that far from this imagery being spontaneously generated, people are recognising some kind of national ideology and their acceptance or rejection of it is mediated through their local experience and work.

According to Lockwood, however, the old working-class traditions of community and collective culture are undergoing a major change. The modern tendency is to break up traditional working class communities — whether 'occupational' or not — and to throw people into low-cost private or council housing estates — the living conditions of the 'privatised worker'. This change, he argues, has been an evolution towards a new 'narrower' kind of collectivism — no longer 'instinctual', based on the kinship ties so beloved of social anthropologists, but 'instrumental', based on a rational calculation of self-interest. But despite its Durkheimian connnotations, we see no reason why the second form should be judged as 'narrower' than the first. On the contrary, a 'solidarity' based on kinship, community and locality is itself a 'narrow' form of social consciousness, because of its exclusiveness.

So there are several problems with Lockwood's formulation of the traditional worker. In the first place, since Lockwood's typology is heuristic, it is inappropriate to criticise it on the grounds that in every case it does not coincide with empirical reality. We have tried to avoid this by criticising aspects of the type, rather than whether or not particular groups of workers fit the category. Furthermore, 'traditional' and 'proletariat' seem to us to be contradictory terms when applied to working class consciousness. We would suggest that some of the factors Lockwood associates with traditional community — the existence of face-to-face emotional interactions at work, the localised labour market, and the high degree of job involvement — inhibit the development of proletarian consciousness rather than support it. Again, as Westergaard points out (1970), the economic developments underlying the cultural response of privatisation are leading to an increasing transparency in the cash nexus — a development not unproblematic for capitalism.

Finally, another problem is the determinist/positivistic idea of consciousness displayed by Lockwood in this particular paper. Consciousness is seen merely as a *reflection* of activity at the base. This is surprising in view of Lockwood's (earlier) Affluent Worker monographs when, in the discussion of embourgeoisement, he insisted that three aspects of working-class activity must be taken into account: the economic, the relational and the normative, all of which had relative autonomy, with the relational acting as a mediation between the other two. In this sense, consciousness could never be just a reflection of what people *do,* since the mediations of *how* they did it, and *with whom,* were crucial. In *Sources of Variation in Working Class Images of Society,* Lockwood seems to collapse the levels of economic and relational, giving us instead a crude base-superstructure formulation with mechanistic determinations. An example of this mechanism is displayed in Lockwood's identification of the pro-letarian traditionalist as the most class-conscious worker. Here is Lockwood's account of their image of the social structure:

> Shaped by occupational solidarities and communal sociability, proletarian social consciousness, is centred on an awareness of 'us' and 'them'. 'Them' are bosses, managers, white collar workers and ultimately the public authorities of the wider society. (1975 p.18)

This characterisation displays a crude simplification of a dichotomous imagery of 'us' and 'them'. Shaped by work and the local community, the proletarian traditionalist sees 'them' as a hierarchy impinging on the activities of work and community, an imputed characteristic of the privatised worker. Fundamentally, a dichotomous con-ception of 'them' and 'us' reflects a power and class relationship with wider ramifi-cations than those within the local community. This point reflects Westergaard's criticism that Lockwood's schema does not allow for a 'radical class consciousness' that is, one which transcends occupations and localities and becomes generalised to other sections of the working class. Since they are both hierarchical, neither of Lock-wood's models displays radical overtones and neither represent a dichotomous *class* imagery.

Lockwood is subsequently reduced to arguing that only when a sense of 'relative deprivation' permeates working-class consciousness, will radical alternatives appear as viable objectives — almost suggesting that mass unemployment is the pre-requisite of revolutionary activity. His inability to draw a distinction between the experience of the labour process, and the experience of the capital relation, compounds his reifi-cation of the difference between the privatised worker and the traditional worker.

In political terms the consciousness of Lockwood's traditional proletarian is an 'accommodation' to capitalism — a cultural transcendence rather than a material trans-formation. Far from engendering a radical class consciousness, the type of community relationships experienced by the traditional proletarian tend to bring about the opposite result — a parochial self-interest. And, as Westergaard has pointed out in numerous articles, localism and parochialism are endemic in the working class and this factor in-hibits them in the pursuit of their interests.

Whilst we do agree with Westergaard on the importance of locality-and community-based ideologies, we do find his formulation of this rather bizarre:

> Victorian reformers and critics. . . often explicitly recognised the clash (either actual or poten-tial) between the conservative restraints of localism, on the one hand, and the radical and therefore frightening implications of any breach of those restraints, on the other. I am always reminded on this point of Thomas Chalmers who in his book *The Civic and Christian Economy of Large Towns* in the 1820 advocated a system of 'localism' to break down working class districts of the big cities into small units. . . to stifle any rebellious tendency. His argument was precisely that if working class interests could be turned inward to the locality, then workers would be prevented from forming alliances and loyalties across the restraining boun-daries of the locality; and social order would be safeguarded. Divide and rule. (1975 p.252)

We find Westergaard's thesis untenable insofar as it suffers from the weakness of all

134

conspiracy theories, in that it attributes far too much power and intelligence to the conspirators. We do find that there is something piquant about Westergaard's intellectual career, mainly built on castigating the ruling class for its stupidity, yet in this article pointing to the fiendishly clever plots they manage to devise to keep the worker in a state of 'false consciousness'.

One thing seems very clear. Workers may not view the class structure in one way, but in different and contradictory ways. This is more understandable in view of the effects on class consciousness and imagery of the educational system and the mass media. Given all the different influences working on the consciousness of workers we would suggest that any kind of coherent 'images of society' would be the exception rather than the rule. If neither the social situation of a particular group of workers, nor the interpretations of these situations are as homogeneous as Lockwood suggests, the way is opened for apparent contradictions between attitude and conduct and also for a considerable variation in the attitudes themselves.

Parkin: National Meaning Systems and the Accomodative Worker

In turning to Parkin's categories we find significant differences in the way working-class imagery is typified. Primarily they do not refer to spontaneously generated ideologies, but to national ideologies imposed by some means or another and to which different sections of the working class give allegiance. Firstly, there is the dominant value system, the social source of which is the ruling class. Typically it is accepted by the 'deferential' or 'aspirational' working class. Secondly, the subordinate value system, the social source of which is trade unionism, and into which is collapsed the 'traditional proletarian' and the 'privatised worker' which Lockwood distinguishes. Thirdly the radical value system, which is not the property of the working class, since it is incapable of autonomously generating its own *systematic* critique of capitalism: 'the working class on its own can only develop trade union consciousness'. One is left with the interpretation that individuals rather than whole social groups subscribe to this value system since its only institutional bearer is the 'mass political party', and no conditions are suggested for its social acceptance.

Linked to these categories is a specific political thesis about the nature of trade unionism and the working-class political party, in this case the Labour Party. In the case of the former: "Collective bargaining does not call into question the values underlying the existing reward structure. Trade unionism could in fact be said to stabilise the modern capitalist order by legitimising further the rules and procedures which govern the allocation of resources." (1972 p.91). Thus, trade unions are viewed as an accommodative response to inequality.

Furthermore, in the case of the Labour Party, the only source of the radical value system, he points to its post-war revisionism, and argues:

> It seems plausible to suggest that if socialist parties ceased to present a radical, class-oriented meaning system to their supporters, then such an outlook would not persist of its own accord among the subordinate class. Once the mass party of the underclass comes to endorse fully the values and institutions of the dominant class, there remains no major source of political knowledge and information which would enable the subordinate class to make sense of their situation in radical terms. (1971 p.98)

Now the basic error that Parkin makes in his analysis of both the trade unions and

135

the Labour Party is to generalise into atemporal categories characteristics peculiar to a particular historical period. In the first place his description of economism, despite his quote from Lenin, is a simple characterisation of the labour movement at a particular juncture. Lenin was describing the limitations of trade unionism as a political and revolutionary force — its relation to political activity. Fundamentally, whatever the degree of reformism of trade union leaders, the very existence of a trade union *ipso facto* asserts the unbridgeable difference between capital and labour in a market society; it embodies the refusal of the working class to become integrated into capitalism on capital's own terms. Trade unionism always has been a direct response to economic forces — a response to a system where workers are forced to sell their labour power as a commodity in the market. As Benyon (1973) points out, this situation has generated a factory class consciousness which understands class relationships in terms of their direct manifestation in conflict between employers and workers within a factory. This consciousness is rooted in the workplace where struggles are fought over the control of the job and the 'rights' of management and workers. Whilst it may be a a 'politics of the factory', the fact that it concerns itself with exploitation and power indicates that it contains definite political elements. Trade unions, therefore, reflect and express a 'working-class consciousness': a consciousness which recognises the validity of the proletariat as a distinct social force, with its own corporate interests in society. This may not be the same thing as a socialist consciousness, but it must be recognised as a necessary precondition for its development.

Furthermore, whilst the 'instrumental collectivism' of workers expresses itself in aggressive economism and defensive shop-floor control, Parkin's articulation of this as purely 'accommodative' is one dimensional. He assumes that economistic demands will consistently be met and that shop floor control is something which only has to be defended from time to time. Both these implicit assumptions are contentious. Crucially, the delicate balance of bargaining power in modern industry is not determined by any abstract standards of 'fairness'. It is an unstable equilibrium of forces. If one of the forces is weakened, the balance will shift. At the moment it is shifting against the unions. Against a hostile press, which is itself an integral arm of the power structure, unions find themselves constantly under attack. At the same time, under the pressure of a State which is equally subordinated to monopoly power, they find themselves responding to a series of carefully imposed pseudo-choices such as 'either you accept a restrictive incomes policy or high unemployment will result' — in the event, the unions have had to accept both options. At the same time, industry by industry, attempts are made to push back and whittle down the areas of control which local union initiatives have already established over management prerogatives (the most recently publicised example being the case of the 'door-hangers' at Fords in Dagenham). The motive behind all such pressures, of course, is the appreciation of the competitive weakness of British industry, and the need to cut costs accordingly.

Similarly, both economistic demands and the system's ability to concede them are subject to change and fluctuations, and this defines limits to the logic of business unionism. Thus, whilst Parkin describes working-class consciousness to an extent, the understanding is superficial, in that there is no appreciation of the tensions and contradictions within the aggressive economism/defensive shop-floor control formula. The cash-nexus of instrumentalism is a 'brittle bond' with shifting and problematic implications for industrial conflict and class consciousness.

Similarly, the development of oligarchy and/or conservatism in unions, with the resulting control of rank and file militancy, must be seen within a particular economic and political context rather than as a result of the dynamics of organisation *per se*. For example, as Lane (1974) has argued, the conciliatory policies of the craft unions in the 1880s have to be seen within the context of the real concessions being made by the State in a particularly favourable economic climate; whereas the more militant tendencies of the 1910s in part represented reactions to real economic and legal threats. And again, within the unions there are counter-tendencies, which confront oligarchic trends, and they must not be lost sight of. Thus, whilst in most unions there is continual opposition to reformist leaderships, more importantly, local groups, through a parochial bargaining leverage, are able to take their own initiatives and   act as sources of opposition (see Benyon 1973). Thus, in the 1960s sustained unofficial action generated a radicalisation of sections of the trade union bureaucracy and saw the revival of the 'official' strike.

We are not arguing that trade unions constitute a revolutionary base from which an effective assault on capitalist society can be made. Indeed, we recognise that at their core trade unions are defensive organisations built and supported by workers who need protection in the labour market. However, unlike Parkin, we would argue that they involve more than this. Crucially, they are working-class organisations and con- sequently the numerous conflicts experienced by workers find their expression within the union. As Benyon points out:

> The disjuncture between what has been termed a 'trade union consciousness' and a political consciousness' is not a clear one. Politics and a political understanding can be contained implicitly in the way in which workers and activists deal with and come to understand their union and their employers. What is clear though is that while politics is contained within trade unionism, trade unions restrain rather than develop this political awareness. . .Tradi- tionally the British trade union movement has coped with the contradiction of opposing the employer while at the same time recognising him through a dichotomy of the 'indus- trial' and 'political' wings of the Labour movement. Anything to do with changing society has been hived off to the Labour Party. (1973 p.231)

Turning to Parkin's treatment of the Labour Party, we see that, initially, he defines it as the major historical source of the radical value system. He then argues that in the post-war period the Party has been characterised by its acceptance of the status quo, and its consequent abandonment of any policies directed towards a radical alternative. The first point we would make is that to characterise the pre-war Labour Party as 'radical' is misleading — if by it he means a class-conscious radicalism. Labour's funda- mental characteristic since its inception has been its overriding commitment to the parliamentary route and to reformism.

Whilst we would accept that the transition from a party of opposition to a party of government has increasingly seen the Labour Party adopt the revisionist role of 'manager' of a mixed economy we would reject Parkin's assertion that this has not only led to a de-radicalisation of the working-class, but effectively precludes the working class from developing a radical perspective.

Just as the 1950s can be seen as a period of 'consensus', characterised by working class quietism, so the 1960s has to be seen as a period of economic conflict, charac- terised by a developing working-class militancy. It was a period in which capital became concentrated in the hands of fewer and larger corporations. This, combined with the declining rate of profit on domestic capital and an inflationary economy, produced an economic situation against which the notions of 'one country', so prevalent in the 1950s, were beginning to crumble. "The 1960s brought home the existence of social classes and the class struggle" (Benyon p.148).

The upsurge in industrial militancy was paralleled by a growing tendency for direct action to spill over into other areas. This was especially marked in housing where there was a rapid growth of associations among corporation tenants. These developments, and others, generated an intense period of extra-parliamentary radical political struggles - in housing and community politics, in women's politics, both personal and economic, in the shop stewards' movement, and so on (for examples, see Bailey 1973; *The Body Politic* (Feminist Books) 1972; Blackburn and Cockburn 1967). Surely not soley reducible to the activities of disaffected students and intellectuals?

Our argument, then is that in Parkin's treatment of trade union activity and radical politics he abstracts particular historical developments from their economic and political context. In this process important contradictions and tensions are submerged and hidden within a one dimensional presentation of a superficially coherent analysis. The suggestion is that the Labour Party, and consequently the working class, is now embarked on an irreversible process of deradicalisation and that the radical value system will now only "influence small parties on the political fringe" (1971 p.101). Do we not detect a note of determinism? Furthermore, class struggle is not a figment of the 'intellectual's' imagination. It is a real dynamic process arising from the contradictory interests of capital and labour. Whilst we accept that in a particular historical period — where an 'orchestrated' consensus excludes the articulation of any socialist options — the traditional parties of the left can become agencies of the status quo, this process is not without contradictions, and this juncture is not fixed for all time.

Having consigned the radical value system to the 'ivory towers', Parkin is left with two meaning systems that characterise working-class imagery — the dominant and subordinate. The subordinate value system he identifies as being generated in the local working-class community:

> Subordinate class communities throw up their distinctive value systems more or less independently of one another: there is no 'national' subordinate value system in the way there is a truly national dominant value system. The similarity in the normative patterns of working-class communities derives largely from the similarity of the conditions they are exposed to. They generate a meaning system which is of purely parochial significance, representing a design for living based upon localised social knowledge and face-to-face relationships. (1971 p.90)

One of the major conditions to which they are exposed is the dominant value system by way of the educational apparatus, the media and so on. The working class are unable to negate these values, as they lack other sources of knowledge and information, there being no radical party, so their reaction is not to reject these values ". . .and thus create an entirely different normative system, but to negotiate or modify them in the light of their own existential conditions" (1974 p.92). "On these grounds it is useful to regard subordinate values as a negotiated form of dominant values" (1971, p.95).

Within this conception is collapsed both the proletarian traditionalist and the privatised worker. Although we criticised Lockwood's typification, it at least made some reference to history, whereas Parkin has subsumed the whole development of working class culture within the category 'subordinate value system', its defining characteristic being an accommodative response to inequality. Yet even this value system is merely a negotiation of dominant values, and once again we seem to be in the realm of determinism. For working-class meaning systems are merely a negotiation of dominant values, to fit the prevailing exigencies of the working class community. We are given no sense of the creative aspect of working-class response to material conditions, nor of the accumulated reservoir of cultural practices and meanings embodied in working-class culture which act as determinants of and tools for the transformation of culture in response both to changing material conditions and to evolving ideological assaults from the bourgeoisie, in the form of education, social security, housing, and so on.

Thus in effect, Parkin has only one value system, and a residual category. The former has a dominant and a negotiated version, whereas the latter is confined to 'free-floating' intellectuals and the 'looney left'.

Conclusion

In the preceding discussion, we have outlined a critique of two conceptual typologies and what we saw as their empirical base. In the case of Lockwood we have argued that almost all workers within capitalism are placed in such a contradictory real situation that it is unlikely that they can develop insulated and cohesive sub-cultures, of the kind he posits. Consequently, we argued that 'images of society' are likely to be contradictory rather than homogeneous, displaying ambiguities in attitudes and behaviour and even contradictory attitudes. Methodologically, we would also argue that the heuristic typologies within which Lockwood's argument is couched are too static to aid the understanding of the essentially dialectical relationship between capital and labour.

Parkin tries to account for these contradictions by arguing that in abstract situations workers will answer in terms of the dominant value system, but in situations involving choice and action they will call upon the negotiated subordinate value system. However, the monolithic and determinist nature of these value systems provides no explanatory power. Reified, abstract value-systems, which blanket the cultural complexity and divergencies of working-class imagery, coupled with a de-historicised political thesis, serve to smother the potential oppositional elements displayed in the contradictory nature of working-class consciousness.

Within both these sociological attempts to understand working-class imagery a homologous relationship betwen ideas and experience is posited, the difference consisting in the emphasis placed on the different levels — Parkin emphasising ideas, and Lockwood work and community experience. Both typifications, we would argue, degenerate into a crude single-levelled determinism because they collapse both consciousness and ideology into a uniform 'image of society'.

Our basic argument is that in analysing working-class 'images of society', what must be placed at the heart of the analysis is their historical nature. The historical development of the relationship between capital and labour has thrown up specific

139

forms of resistance peculiar to the material conditions and strategies of particular conjunctures. These specific forms can be analysed in terms of the uneven development of capitalism, not just on an international, but also on a intra-national level, thus leading to differences in regional industrial development or even differences within a region. John Foster's book *Class Struggle and the Industrial Revolution* is a useful starting point for this kind of analysis, dealing as it does with the development of different degrees of class consciousness in three towns, ultimately based on different relations between capital and labour and different forms of the labour process. Also methodologically useful are the analyses of Lenin (1960) and Gramsci (1971) on the development of capitalism within Russia and Italy.

Once established, particular forms of resistance achieve institutional expression in, for example, trade unions, working men's clubs, etc. Within these institutions, which are in a constant process of struggle, ideologies are constructed — about the job, about the area, and specific local social relationships — which come to have a great influence on the people they serve and are addressed to.

However, these ideologies are not simply determining; they not only influence but change in accordance with developments in material life. This process is examined sociologically in Stacey's Banbury (1960), which at the time of the study was a small market town with handicraft industry. Stacey's book explores the changes in class composition and class consciousness due to the introduction of modern machinofactures in the shape of a plastics factory. In the book, the author almost sees the inherent contradiction between class and community, but the analysis ultimately fails because there is no examination of the relationship between these ideologies and the real experience of wage labour as mediated through consciousness. It is also this contradictory level which Parkin and Lockwood subsume under 'imagery', and it is this semi-automomous layer of working-class experience which throws up new 'forms' of resistance and defends and adapts old 'forms' to meet new conditions.

Thus, the quest for working class 'images of society' collapses contradictions in its search for coherence. The coherence established is achieved 'one dimensionally' at a verbal level, at the expense of de-historicising the complex phenomen in question. Crucially, an analysis of the uneven development of capitalism and the labour process with their attendant ideologies — local, occupational and national — is necessary to understand the relations and mediations between the subjective level of experience, ideology and determining material conditions.

REFERENCES

Bailey, R. (1973) *The Squatters* Penguin
Benyon, H. (1973) *Working for Ford* Penguin
Blackburn, R. and **Cockburn, A.** (eds) (1967) *The Incompatibles: Trade Union Militancy and the Consensus* Penguin
Cousins and **Brown** (1975) "Patterns of Paradox: Shipbuilding Workers' Images of Society" in Bulmer (ed) *Working Class Images of Society* RKP
Dennis, Henriques and **Slaughter** (1956) *Coal is our Life,* 2nd edn 1969 Tavistock
Eggleston, S.J. (1967) *The Social Context of the School* RKP
Foster. J, (1974) *Class Struggle and the Industrial Revolution* Weidenfeld & Nicolson

Gouldner, A.W. (1971) *The Coming Crisis of Western Sociology* Heinemann

Gramsci, A. (1971) "Notes on Italian History" in *Prison Notebooks* Lawrence and Wishart

Hoggart, R. (1957) *The Uses of Literacy* Penguin

Jackson, B. (1968) *Working Class Community* Penguin

Lane, T. (1974) *The Union Makes Us Strong* Arrow

Lenin, V.I. (1960) "The Development of Capitalism in Russia" in *Collected Works* Moscow

Lewis, O. (1951) *Life in a Mexican Village: Tepoztlan Revisited* University of Chicago Press (1968) *La Vida* Panther

Lockwood, D. (1975) "Sources of Variation in Working Class Images of Society" in Bulmer *op.cit.*

Parkin, F. (1971) *Class Inequality and the Political Order* Paladin

Stacey, M. (1960) *Tradition and Change: A Study of Banbury* OUP

Titmuss, R. (1958) *Essays on the Welfare State* Unwin

Townsend, P. (1957) *Family Life of Old People* RKP

Westergaard, J.H. (1970) "The Rediscovery of the Cash Nexus" *Socialist Register* 1970, (1975) "Radical Class Consciousness" in Bulmer *op.cit.*

Williams, R. (1958) *Culture and Society* Penguin

Young and Wilmott (1961) "Research Report No. 3: Institute of Community Studies: Bethnal Green" *Sociological Review* July 1961,
1962 *Family and Kinship in East London* Penguin

APPENDIX

We include this appendix to illustrate how interest among sociologists focussed both on 'community' as an ideology and on community studies themselves in the 1950s. We have included American material as a comparison, since a similar development occurred there in the 1930s.

Allcorn, D.H. (1954) *The Social Life of Young Men in London*/Manchester

Arensberg & Kimball (1940) *Family and Community in Ireland* Peter Smith, London.

Baltzell, D. (1958) *Philadelphia Gentlemen* Free Press, Glencoe

Bell & Newby (1971) *Community Studies* Allen & Unwin

Bell & Newby (1972) *The Sociology of Local Communities* Allen & Unwin

Birch, A.H. (1959) *Small Town Politics* OUP

Boal, J.W. (1969) "Territoriality on the Shankhill-Falls Divide, Belfast", in *Irish Geography,*

Bonjean & Olsen (1964) "Community Leadership: Directions of Research" in Zollschen & Hirsh, *Exploration in Social Change* RKP

Bott, E. (1957) *Family & Social Network* Tavistock

Brennan, Cooney & Pollins (1954) *Social Change in S.W. Wales* Watts

Coates & Silburn (1970) *Poverty: The Forgotten Englishman* Penguin

Coleman, J., (1957) *Community Conflict* Free Press, Glencoe

Collinson, P. (1963) *The Cutteslowe Wells* Faber

Dahl, R. (1961) *Who Governs* Yale U.P.

Davies & Gardner (1944) *Deep South* Chicago U.P.

Davies & Rees (1960) *Welsh Rural Communities* University of Wales Press

Dennis, N. (1970) *People & Planning: The Sociology of Housing in Sunderland*

Dennis N. *Public Participation & Planning Blight*

Dennis, Henriques & Slaughter (1957) *Coal is Our Life* Eyre & Spottiswood

Doherty, M. (1955) *A Miner's Son* Lawrence & Wishart

Dollard, J. (1937) *Caste & Class in a Southern Town* Yale U.P.

Durrant, R. *(1959) Watling: A Survey of Social Life on a New Housing Estate* P.S. King

Engels, F. (1969) *The Condition of the Working Class in England* Panther (first English edn. 1892).

Firth & Djamour. (1956) *Kinship in South Borough: Two Studies of Kinship in London* Athlone Press

Frankenberg (1957) *Village on the Border* Cohen & West

Frankenberg (1966) *Communities in Britain* Penguin

Gamson, W. (1966) *Rancorous Conflict in Community Politics* A.S R. 31

Gans H. (1952) "Urbanism & Surburbanism as a Way of Life" in Rose (ed) *Human Behaviour and Social Processes* RKP

Gans, H. (1962) *The Urban Villagers* N.Y. Free Press

Gans, H. (1967) *The Levittowners* Allen Lane

Glass R. (1948) *The Social Background to a Plan: Middlesborough* RKP

Glass R. (1955) "Urban Sociology" in *Current Sociology Vol IV No. 4* UNESCO

Glass, R. (1966) "Conflict in Cities" in *Conflict in Society* Churchill

Glass & Frenknel (1946) "How they lived at Bethnal Green" in *Britain East and West* Contact Books, London

Goldthorpe & Lockwood (1963) "Affluence & the British Class Structure" in *Sociological Review*

Green, B.S.R. (1968) *Community Decision Making in Georgian City* unpb. Phd. University of Bath

Hatt & Reiss (1957) *Cities & Society* Free Press, Glencoe.

Havinghurst & Jansen (1967) Community Research, *Current Sociology*

Hawley, A. (1950) *Human Ecology: A Theory of Community Structure,* Ronald, New York

Hillery, G.A. Jnr. (1955) "Definitions of Community: Areas of Agreement" in *Rural Sociology* 20

Hodges & Smith (1954) "The Sheffield Estate" in *Neighbourhood & Community* Liverpool U.P.

Homans G.C. (1953) "The Rural Sociology of Medieval England" in *Past & Present.* No.4

Hunter, F. (1953) *Community Power Structure* University of N. Carolina Press

Jackson, B. (1968) *Working Class Community* Penguin

Jeffrys M. (1964) "Londoners in Hertfordshire" in *London: Aspects of Change,* Urban Studies Report No. 3

Kerr, M. (1958) *The People of Ship Street*

Konig, R. (1968) *The Community* RKP

Kuper, (1953) *Living in Towns* Cresset Press

Lewis, O. (1965) *Life in a Mexican Village: Tepoztlan Revisited* University of Chicago Press

Lewis, O. (1965) *Children of Sanchez* Penguin

Lloyd, A.L. (1952) *Come All Ye Bold Miners,* Lawrence & Wishart

Loudon J.B. (1961) "Kinship & Crisis in S. Wales" BJS Vol X11 No.4

Lupton & Mitchell (1954) "The Liverpool Estate" in *Neighbourhood & Community op.cit.*

Lynd, R & H. (1929) *Middletown: A Study in Contemporary American Culture* Harcourt Brace, N.Y.

Lynd, R & M. (1937) *Middletown: A Study in Transition* Harcourt Brace

Martindale, D. (1964) "The Formation and Destruction of Communities". Zollschan & Hirsch: *Exploration in Social Change* RKP

Maud Report on Local Government (1967)

McKinney & Loomis (1957) "The Application of Gemeinschaft & Gesellschaft to Other Typologies" in intro. to American ed. Tonnies, *Community & Society* Harper Torch Books.

Mitchell, G.D. (1951) "The Parish Council and the Rural Community" in *Rural Administration* Winter 1951

Mitchell, *et al.* (1954) *Neighbourhood and Community op.cit.*

Mitchell, J.C. (1969) *Social Networks in an Urban Situation* Manchester U.P.

Mogey, J.M. (1956) *Family and Neighbourhood: Two Studies in Oxford,* OUP

Nisbet, R. (1966) *The Sociological Tradition* Heinemann

Pahl, R. (1966) "The Rural Urban Continuum" in Sociologia Ruralis V

Pahl, R. (1968) *Readings in Urban Sociology* OUP

Peterson, W. (1968) "The Ideological Origins of Britain's New Towns" in *American Inst. of Planners Journal* Vol. XXXIV.

Plowman, Minchington & Stacey (1962) "Local Social Systems in England & Wales" in *Sociological Review*

Polsby N., (1963) *Community Power and Political Theory* Vol. X no.2. Yale U.P.

Redfield, R. (1947) "The Folk Society" AJS 52

Rees, A.D. (1950) *Life in the Welsh Countryside,* University of Wales Press

Rex, J. (1968) "The Sociology of the Zone of Transition" in Pahl, *op.cit.*

Rex, J. (1972) *Race, Community & Conflict* OUP

Robinson W. S. (1950) "Ecological Correlations and the Behaviour of Individuals" ASR 50

Rosser & Harris (1961) "Relationships through Marriage in an Welsh Urban Area" in *Sociological Review* Vol X.

Schnore (1967) "Community" in Smelser (ed) *Sociology* Wiley, N.Y.

Seabrook, J. (1971) *City Close Up* Penguin

Seeley *et al.* (1956) *Crestwood Heights* Basic Books

Sjoberg, G. (1965) "Community" in Gould & Klob, *Dictionary of Sociology* Tavistock

Skeffington Report (1969) *People & Planning*

Spencer (1964) *Stress and Release in an Urban Estate* Tavistock

Stacey, M (1960) *Tradition and Change: A Study of Banbury* OUP

Stacey M (1969) "The Myth of Community Studies", in *BJS*

Stein, M. (1960) *The Eclipse of Community* Princeton U.P.

Sussman, M.B. (1959) *Community Structure and Analysis* Cromwell

Sutton & Kojola (1960) "The Concept of Community in *Rural Sociology* 25

Theodorson, G.A. (1961) *Studies in Human Ecology*

Thrasher, F.M. (1963) *One Thousand Boys' Gangs in Chicago* Chicago U.P.

Townsend, P. (1957) *The Family Life of Old People* RKP

Viditch & Bensman (1958) *Small Town in Mass Society* Princeton U.P.

Viditch et. al. (1964) *Reflections of Community Studies* Wiley

Walton, J. (1966) "Substance and Artifact: The Current Status of Research on Community Power Structure" AJS

Warner & Lunt (1941) *The Social Life of Modern Community* (Yankee City)

Warner & Lunt (1942) *The Status System of Modern Community* (YC) Yale U.P.

Warner & Srole (1945) *The Social System of American Ethnic Groups* (YC) Yale U.P

Warner & Low (1947) *The Social System of a Modern Factory* (YC) Yale U.P.

Warner (1949) *Democracy in Jonesville* (YC) Yale U.P.

Warner (1959) *The Living and the Dead* (YC) Yale U.P.

Warner (1963) *Yankee City* (as one abridged volume) Yale U.P.

Warren, R. (1963) *The Community in America* Rand McNally

Warren, R.L. (1966) *Perspectives on the American Community* Rand McNally

Watson, W. (1964) "Social Mobility and Social Class in Industrial Communities" in *Closed Systems and Open Minds* Oliver Boyd

Webber, M.L. (1963) "Order in Diversity: Community without Propinquity" in *Cities and Space* Johns Hopkins Press

Williams (1956) *The Sociology of an English Village: Gosforth* RKP

Williams (1958) *The Country Craftsman* RKP

Williams (1963) *A West Country Village: Ashworthy* RKP

Willmott & Young *(1957) Family and Kinship in East London* RKP

Willmott & Young (1960) *Family & Class in a London Suburb* RKP

Wilson, R. (1963) *Difficult Housing Estates* Tavistock

Wirth, L. (1938) "Urbanism as a Way of Life" AJS 44

Wolfinger, R. (1960) "Reputation and Reality in the Study of Community Power" ASR

Wood, R.C. (1958) *Suburbia: Its People and Their Politics* Boston

Zorbough H.W. (1929) *The Gold Coast and the Slum* Chicago U.P.

Social Democracy, Education and the Crisis

Dan Finn, Neil Grant, Richard Johnson

Introduction

There is a challenge to us all in these days and a challenge in education is to examine its priorities and to secure as high efficiency as you can by the skilful use of the £6 billion of existing resources.

Let me repeat some of the fields that need study because they cause concern. There are the methods and aims of informal instruction. The strong case for the so-called core curriculum of basic knowledge. What is the proper way of monitoring the use of resources in order to maintain a proper national standard of performance? What is the role of the inspectorate in relation to national standards and their maintenance? And there is a need to improve relations between industry and education, (James Callaghan, Ruskin College, October 1976)

The leading questions of Labour's Prime Minister marked a fundamental shift in the field of the debate about educational means and ends. They marked, at the "highest" political level, the end of the long post-war phase of educational expansion which had been largely promoted by Callaghan's own party. His speech, banal enough in content, was nonetheless a well prepared media event, delivered in an appropriate place, important more in the anticipation than in the speaking. Intended, then, to be a signal event — a public re-definition of educational objectives — the speech was also a response to more immediate events: the history of economic crisis and of cuts in public expenditure and, Callaghan's own real challenge, the polemical weight of the Tory critique of Labour's educational past. If we understand it correctly, Callaghan's speech crystallized many aspects of the current situation.

We wish in what follows, as a political-intellectual project, to contribute to an understanding of this conjuncture. We write especially for people, like ourselves, who work in an educational system under siege or who are blocked from entering it. For all of us the awareness of educational crisis is enforced by daily experience of insecurity or the loss of apparent autonomies. But our contribution is of a particular and limited kind: we take as our object *ideologies about education*; we approach them historically; we see them as having determinate (or "material") social bases and effects.[1] It is important to say a little, at the outset, to characterize this approach.

In analyses of educational systems (or of the ideological work of the State in general) it is useful to distinguish two aspects. In the existing literature these are often divorced but ought in fact to be viewed together. The first aspect is the work of schools and colleges themselves; their institutional structures, their disposition of knowledge, their pedagogic relationships, their informal cultures and organisation. We designate this the ideological work of school itself. But secondly these primary processes are the object too of broader definitions and practices. This debate *about* education is often constructed at some distance from the processes it purports to describe. It has, however, through *policies,* a real effect upon the educational system itself. It also forms part of a general political discourse. In developed forms of the democratic State (which pre-suppose an equal citizenry) debates about education are part of a history of hegemony; they are a regional instance of the process of bidding for the consent of the governed. The educational sphere has, in other words, its own ideologies, designated by Althusser (somewhat monolithically) as "a universally reigning ideology of the school" (Althusser 1971). Such ideologies (and we shall continue to insist on the plural) express particular versions of what schools are for, of how they work and of what it is possible for them to achieve. These ideologies are properly so-called where they can be shown to mis-recognise, mask, or incompletely grasp the primary workings of the institutions they have most closely in focus.

This essay is mainly concerned, then, with the second aspect. We will refer occasio-nally to our own understanding of primary educational processes mainly to highlight the inadequancies of ideologies *about* schools. Our position is best sketched where it is relevant and where it enters our critique of other positions. But there are two main features which we see as essential to an adequate theory. First theory must grasp the relations between school and other sites of social relations. The most important of these can be specified: family, work and the formal political sphere. But these sites themselves will be inadequately grasped unless viewed in *their* relations within a particular social formation. These are some of the reasons why we choose to work within the Marxist problematic of reproduction while recognising that there are more or less adequate variants of it. This takes us to our second principal point. One of the weaknesses of some versions of this theory, Althusser's for instance, is that they appear to have little place for that capacity for resistance which may be exercised by children and teachers in schools, (Althusser 1971, Willis 1977).

Further features of our approach — a concern to define our object historically and relate it to a particular social base — are best introduced more concretely. The ideology of the education system which is our principal object has a particular history. It was constructed by particular agencies and produced by a particular social coalition. All of the elements in this coalition had their provenance in the years before the Second World War; two of the three, indeed, have a considerably longer history. But it was only in the post-war world, and especially in the 1960s, that these combined elements acquired hegemony over educational policy as a whole. The educational crisis of the 1970s is, in part, a crisis of this formation and of the social coalition that underpinned it.

Each party in the alliance made its own contribution, but the effective nucleus was the Labour Party. The ideology of progress through education was a regional expression of what critics to the left of the party have dubbed "Labourism", and which we see as a variant of the general category "social democracy". As we show in more detail later, Labour's education programmes bear the stamp of the internal formation of the party and of its relations within British society. Its politicians and intellectuals have been the main bearers of these ideologies. Before the professio-nalisation of educational report and inquiry it was intellectuals of a Fabian or British Socialist persusasion who supplied the main source of the party's policies. The absence of a more than passive contribution from working-people is a matter which will concern us later.

The party, itself a complex social alliance, was joined by other agencies. These do not constitute, in any useful sense, organic classes or even fractions of classes; rather, specialised intellectuals of a particular tendency and the organised professional interests of the educational sphere. The emergence of a specialist, academic sociology of education was, in our view, one of the most significant developments in post-war education. The sociologists of education replaced or at least supplemented the intellectuals of an older kind. They worked in a more technical manner within an intellectual field which specified quite narrow problems. It was this alliance with sociological expertise which gave to Labour's post-war programme much of its tone and shape.

The third component in the alliance was the teaching profession itself, or, more specifically, the tendency to teacher professionalism. If the Labour Party supplied the general political-ideological context and the sociology of education specified some short and medium term objectives, teacher-educationalists supplied much of education's content. They supplied the obvious absence in the more politicised contributions. They cultivated "the secret garden of the curriculum".

In what follows we develop the sketch outlined above, considering each of the agencies in the post-war coalition in turn, examining their particular contributions. In Part IV we show how these elements were articulated in the policies and reports of the 1960s. Although it is impossible to divorce exposition from critique in earlier sections, we then show, in Part V, some of the intrinsic inadequacies of the social-democratic position. Finally we analyse the crisis itself from this perspective — as a crisis of social democratic ideology and as a splintering of its social base.

The Labour Party

We do not intend, in this section, to recount the familiar history of the Labour Party, nor in detail its educational policies. The general history of the party has been much studied. (Pelling 1965, Nairn 1964, Anderson 1964, Coates 1975, McKibbin 1974, Howell 1976, Miliband 1972). There are useful accounts too of its contribution to State educational policies especially for the period up to 1951. (Barker 1972, Simon 1974) The aim is rather to examine, more "structurally", certain key features of the party which seem to have determined its educational stance. We are less concerned with shifts of policy than with their continuities — the pattern of emphases and absences which was the party's particular contribution to post-war educational ideologies. Our account is not intended to be "original" except in so far as it may render problematic a pattern of assumptions normally taken as self-evident. This pattern of assumptions was initially formed in the early years of the party and reinforced during its inter-war history. This is why, in this section of our paper, we choose to concentrate on the period before World War II.

The Parliamentary Route

One of the crucial determinants of Labourism has been the party's relationship to the working class. Despite appearances to the contrary and especially the post-war attempts of "democratic socialists" to "broaden the base" of the party's electoral support, it has remained dependent upon a working class vote and an historical alliance with trade unionism. The growth of its support from World War I to the early 1930s rested in part on the enfranchisement of new sections of the class and in part on a shift of popular allegiances away from the Liberal Party, the traditional, nineteenth-century focus of the politics of organised labour (McKibbin 1974 p. 236-47). Even the post-war strategies of the party aimed at other class fractions have still retained the older identifications, and in the case of trade unionism has even developed them.

The second crucial determinant of the party's ideologies has been its acceptance of those concepts of legality and political-constitutional conventions which Miliband (1972) has termed "parliamentarism". These assumptions were materialised in British political practices long before the emergence of the Labour Party itself, though they were only completed or realised in the full, late achievement of universal adult suffrage and the emergence of the party as a "legitimate" representative of the working class. Notions like the sovereignty of parliament, and especially of the House of Commons, derive in fact from the days of a propertied parliamentary system, representative of different fractions of capital. Other elements - formal equality before the law for example — have a still longer history. The insertion of working-class politics into this structure also pre-dated the emergence of separate labour representation. The party's parliamentarism was pre-figured in the mid-nineteenth century alliance of radical popular liberalism with the bulk of organised labour. The formation of the Labour Party, however, consolidated this relationship rather than challenged it. As Miliband puts it, characteristically over-emphasising the enigma of Labour's leadership:

Of political parties claiming socialism to be their aim, the Labour Party has always been one of the most dogmatic — not about socialism, but about the parliamentary system. Empirical and flexible about all else, its leaders have always made devotion to that system their fixed point of reference and the conditioning factor of their political behaviour. This is not simply to say that the Labour Party has never been a party of revolution: such parties have normally been quite willing to use the opportunities the parliamentary system offered as one means of furthering their aims. It is rather that the leaders of the Labour Party have always rejected any kind of political action (such as industrial action for political purposes) which fell, or which appeared to them to fall, outside the framework and conventions of the parliamentary system. The Labour Party has not only been a parliamentary party; it has been a party deeply imbued by parliamentarism. (1972 p.13)

It is worth digging behind the term "parliamentarism" and considering what it entails. It involves, firstly, a belief in the neutrality or the potential neutrality of the State apparatus: there is nothing in this "machinery" which prevents it from being used for the benefit of all. It also involves a faith in legislative-administrative procedures as the main route to the solution of "social problems" or the equalisation of conditions. This in turn gives a primacy to formal political processes — basically the marshalling of a popular vote at elections as the means to a Labour hegemony. Accordingly less mediated forms of class power are regarded with distrust: at best they are an embarrassment to parliamentary proprieties, at worst they constitute a really undemocratic threat. The only clear exception to this inhibition are working-class actions which are held to be industrial. These are the proper concern of the party's *alter ego* — the trade union movement.

147

The force of this analysis may be seen if we review the party's relation to other tendencies in working-class politics in the period 1910-26. Throughout this period, forms of working-class politics arose that differed markedly from what became the dominant Labourist adaptation: a trade unionism which united industrial action and political aims; rank and file movements, suspicious of officialdom and challenging the war-time State; the evolution of British communism and a tradition of industrial direct action and mass sympathy strikes. Without these legacies the General Strike would not have taken place; its defeat was one of the ways in which tendencies like these were educated out of the class's repertoire. This pattern cannot be explained here in full, but it is important to place the Labour Party within it. We may note that the party's policies were not directly related to these struggles, although they necessarily affected them. From 1910 the State increasingly intervened in major industrial conflicts, workers themselves demanded the State re-organisation of their industries, and the class as a whole was involved in bitter fights to defend existing wage levels and hours of work. In practice if not in theory, this opposition involved a repudiation of the economic policies that made wage-cutting "necessary". One role for a political party in these circumstances would have been to back and organise such demands, re-think economic orthodoxies and combine agitation with the (necessarily) political strike. Labour, rather, began the long haul to parliamentary respectability, avoiding "unconstitutional" action. Its marginality during the General Strike was only a signal instance of a general situation. All this was skilfully played upon by bourgeois politicians for short-term tactical advantage, the appeal to the "constitutional" against the "revolutionary" being the key propaganda theme. There was no full hegemony in these years; rather there were successive crises and partial stabilisations heavily backed by force. The high points of conservative strategy were those periods of Labour minority government when it was permitted to "rule", but remained too weak, irresolute and baffled by underlying economic problems to pursue its own policies of reform with any force. In 1931 a section of the party's leadership was actually recruited to the side of a bourgeois coalition to help perform tasks which Conservatives could not have performed on their own. Hence for the Labour Party, the political debacle of the early 1930s, the loss of electoral support and the need for a major recuperation thereafter. The result, by the 1940s, was a form of Labourism more self-confident than at any time since 1918, but it is clear that the main long-term consequences of the inter-war years was an education into "legitimate" trade unionism and the necessities of the parliamentary road.

These relations, to the working class and to the State, underlay the party's educational stance. Educational tendencies within the class were neglected and a form of educational politics was constructed within the State. To grasp the particularity of this adaptation, we need to compare it with other historical experiences and another way of thinking the role of a working-class party. It is useful to compare what Marx satirised as "parliamentary cretinism" with Gramsci's theory of "the new Machiavelli". The choice of Gramsci and the Italian Communist Party at a contemporaneous moment is especially apt since the relation of a party to its class was Gramsci's central problematic. It specified most of his major concerns: the role of the party itself, its relation to the State, the problem of the intellectuals and the master category 'hegemony'.

148

Parties, Politics and Education

According to Gramsci parties arise on the basis of particular social classes. He himself was especially concerned with the working-class parties of the era of the transition to monopoly capitalism and their appropriate strategies. Parties always control and direct their class, always have a "policing" function. Yet this function can be performed in different ways. In "regressive" modes of the relation, an external control of the class by the party is uppermost. The party's "educative" function is negative. Accepting existing definitions of legality, possessed of only a partial analysis of the place of its class within the social formation, pursuing immediate, limited reforms, the party acts to hold the class within the existing order. Gramsci's alternative was a working-class party whose role was positively educative. Such a party directs, educates and "civilises" its class, raising its activities to a new level of legality. It works within the grain of common-sense conceptions of the world held by worker or peasant but raises them to a higher power of critical self-awareness and coherence. It teaches the classes their place within the social formation and within "history" as a whole. It adopts "global" functions, beyond the "economic—corporate", embraces in its programmes the whole range of social issues and develops a particular vision of the future. Such a party forms a state within the state, a state in preparation. Since the state is an "ethical" as well as a coercive agency, the party must possess a "philosophy" of its own, capable of becoming the cement of a new social order. Such a philosophy should be rooted not only in Marxism ("the philosophy of praxis") but also in the conditions of existence of workers and peasants. It can only be developed ("developed" because not given in existing forms of Marxism) and propagated by "organic intellectuals" who share the conditions of existence of the popular classes. Their production and their articulation with other groups (notably with intellectuals of an older more "traditional" kind) are, pre-eminently, the work of the party. Such a party-class will already have developed an effective cultural and political control or "hegemony" over "civil society" especially over intermediate or subaltern classes before it acquires State power. The main aim of the party may be defined, indeed, as the construction of such a counter-hegemony or hegemony-from-below. This strategy is very different from the forms of class activity specified by economistic forms of Marxism, or the anarcho-syndicalism of early Italian trade unionism or the Fabianism of the English Labour Party. Many of the differences are summed up in Gramsci's common (and commonly misunderstood) duo: "economic-corporate" and "hegemonic". It is important to stress too Gramsci's distance from the common language of the revolutionary political left — "trade union consciousness" versus "revolutionary class consciousness" or the "reformist" party versus the revolutionary one. Gramsci was, of course, a revolutionary, but he had an unusually complete and subtle sense of what such a transformation required.

The value of his formulations for our purposes lies in his stress on "education" as a necessary aspect of political transformation. This use of "education" is of course a very expanded one. Education happens not only in schools but also through law and other State practices and through all those agencies of civil society — including the cultural apparatuses of different classes — which, in their different ways, cultivate consent. It happens, pre-eminently, in the political parties of all classes. In this way Gramsci refuses the restricted notion of education which has actually been

149

constructed around State schooling as part of the ideology of the region. (In some ways, indeed, his actual discussions of schooling are disappointing — see Gramsci 1971 pp.26-47.) Yet if we follow him in rejecting the identification education = school, or college or university, the expanded definition gives us a real analytical purchase on the "educational" strategies adopted by any party.

We can see, for instance, through this set of categories that the British Labour Party's educational object was not, and never has been, its own class, or classes. It is interesting to find Labour intellectuals, later in the tradition, actually disavowing what they regard as a 1920s 'continental' and Marxist model — the model of the PCI and early SPD (Crosland 1962 pp.210-11). As a national party (as opposed to an agglomerate of groups and tencencies) it never was an educational-agitational movement. It did not have a starting-point in some conception of socialist education. Nor did it set out from the cultural and educational resources of existing working-class communities. Its educational policies, like its general politics, were posited instead on a pre-existing machinery — in this case a structure of State schools and a particular distribution of formal "educational" opportunities. It was these that the party set out to reform. Thus the party began as and remained an educational *provider for* the popular classes, not an educational *agency of* and *within* them.

This displacement has been reproduced throughout the party's history and has had major consequences to which we shall return in Part VI. We can understand it more concretely if we note the main absences and presences in the party's inter-war educational strategy. The major absence was the party's inability to connect, as an organised whole, with a revived tradition of collective working-class self-education which was a marked feature of the period 1880-1926. The major presence was the first full elaboration of a policy for state schooling in the shape of *Secondary Schools for All,* R.H. Tawney's book, published under the party's auspices in 1922.

The Labour Party and "Counter-Education"

According to some views of the British working class which threaten to become an orthodoxy, British working-class politics and culture were formed in an undyingly corporate mode and have never shifted out of it since. (Nairn 1964, Anderson 1964, Stedman Jones 1974 — but there is more than a hint of this interpretation in most "Marxist" accounts of the Labour Party and Trade Unionism). The formative moment has been variously identified: the defensive tendency of "Labour Representation" (a response of trade unionists to the employers' 1890s counter-offensive and the Taff Vale judgement); the "re-making" of the class under imperialist ideologies at the turn of the century, or even the original defeat of the "first" working class in the Chartist crisis of the early 1940s. *One* of the problems with such interpretations is that they overlook the "education" (in something like Gramsci's sense) that accompanies the trade union expansion and the formation of the Labour Party.

From the 1890s there was a marked revival of a radical or socialist educational and cultural politics. It resembled, in many ways, the radical counter-educational impulse of the early nineteenth-century in which the popular classes had developed their own conceptions of knowledge, their own educational forms and a critique of "provided" schooling (Johnson 1976). The late nineteenth-century upsurge had no single organisational focus, was organised by a plethora of groups to the left of

150

Labour's ideological centre of gravity, but was massive and diffuse and is still under-recorded. It included the educational work of socialists who led the pre-war "new unionist" and "syndicalist" insurgencies. It included the Marxist study groups promoted by the Social Democratic Federation, the socialist league, the socialist Labour Party, the British Socialist Party and the early CPGB.

It included the tendency to a self-governing education for working-class adults re-presented by the Plebs League and the Labour Colleges and, finally, the more diffused, "brotherly" cultural politics of the Socialist Sunday Schools, Labour Churches, and Clarion Movement. We still lack as full and as integrated a picture of all this as we have for the Chartist-Owenite phase (but see E.P.Thompson 1960 and 1976; Simon 1974; P. Thompson 1967) though some features are clear enough. Once more a radical and socialist press was very important; once more critiques were launched of orthodox educational forms. Anti-imperialists and radicals and the Labour Colleges contested the liberal humanism of "university extension" and the Workers' Educational Association.

This process of education must have played a part in winning working people, "converting them" in the contemporary phrase, from Liberal and Conservative allegiances. It certainly, in the early days supplied the leadership of trade unionism, and many later labour stalwarts have recalled their early conversions. Without the whole movement it would be difficult to understand the Labour Party's greater sense of assurance immediately after the war and its break with the Liberal Party. Yet once fully formed on the political scene, the party's relation to a continuing education-agitational work was indirect and even, where rivals were involved, hostile. This followed the logic of the political adaptation we have already examined but the party's educational inertia, outside moments of electoral mobilisation, also rested on the trade union alliance. Increasingly after 1918 it was the large trade unions, themselves increasingly bureaucratic and stabilised, that supplied the party with its local and national organisers. As McKibbin has shown (1974) the party increasingly depended on this alliance and modelled its organisation on the trade union pattern. The party rested, then, not upon an active ideological recruitment but upon a type of class support similar to the loyalties of a fully formed trade unionism. This essentially passive relationship to its class can be seen in the fate of its more agita-tional elements: the decline of the ILP, the subordination of the *Daily Herald* to party and union officialdom, the expulsion of the Labour Research Department, the suspicion of "socialist intellectuals" and their marginality in the party's organi-sation. Such a party was hardly adapted to the production of Gramsci's organic working-class intellectuals. Significantly, continued working-class education owed more to the Communist Party and to certain Trade Unions than it did to Labour.

All this is not to suggest that "independent" working-class education could have *substituted* for an educational provision through the State. Even if adapted to that purpose, the Labour Party would hardly have been wise to adopt a free-schooling strategy with schools under working-class control. Chartists and Owenites had explored that route almost a hundred years earlier. What had sustained them then, in the face of pitifully few material resources, had been an expectation of imminent political success. Within its own logic the Labour Party's emphasis on increasing opportunities within the State system was quite rational and a position already

151

reached by later Chartists and popular Liberals. The gross unfairness of the system and the opposition of Conservatives, economising governments and many fractions of capital made the struggle necessary and compelling. Yet, as we shall see, the party's relation to the educational system was similar in form to its relation to Parliament. It accepted State Education *in toto,* including many of the ideologies of the region. This involved the disseverance of a whole number of relations essential to a successful socialist strategy. It divorced (as State Education itself does) the education of children from the education of adults. Any connection between the *content* of schooling and the conditions of existence of the popular classes disappeared. This made it impossible to draw on the "independent" tradition in order to wage struggles in the schools. But all these points, consequences of a fundamental orientation, will only really become clear at the end of this essay.

Secondary Schools for All

There are several reasons why Tawney's text is exemplary. First, Tawney himself was the most important "philosopher" of British Social Democracy in the interwar period. Gaitskell called him "the Democratic Socialist *par excellence*", though he ought to have added that Tawney often found himself on an anti-Fabian end of what he himself liked to call "British Socialism". He was the author of two socialist classics, *The Acquisitive Society (1921)* and *Equality (1931).* As an intellectual he was typical of his time and the movement he served. His most enduring intellectual work was in history and not "theory". His attitude to Marx, though occasionally appreciative of the latter's "genius", was more distant than his relation to Weber. He is properly placed by Raymond Williams in the English culture-and-society tradition (1968). An intellectual of a "traditional" kind, an idealist and a moralist, he was recruited to the side of labour as an external educator of it, first as a WEA tutor, then as a party adviser. *Secondary Schools for All* was also in itself a significant text. It was produced by a Labour Advisory Committee which Tawney himself seems to have dominated and, as one recent commentator has put it, is "a perfect illustration of the character of the Labour Party." It expressed sentiments that were to remain typical of its educational policy long after Tawney's direct influence had ceased. (Barker 1972 p.37).

Finally, it arose at a significant conjuncture. It was very much the product of the Labour Party's formative phase in the immediate post-war period. At the same time, it was written in the aftermath of a more widespread working-class mobilisation. As we have seen, this was manifested in part by independent educational movements, but it also took the form of demands for full educational rights by working-class organisations and the growth of popular pressure on existing secondary school places. There is no doubt that Tawney's document mediated and shaped this pressure from working-class organisations and a section of working-class parents.

We wish to stress five main features of the text: Tawney's critique of English education in terms of the persistence of a Victorian inheritance; his identification of a progressive educational consensus opposed to this "fatal legacy"; the overwhelmingly mechanical nature of Tawney's solutions — his stress on the means of access to education or "the material scaffolding of policy, administration, organisation and finance"; the text's main absence — Tawney's inveterate lack of

152

clarity on the content and purposes of secondary education; finally, the general character of Tawney's arguments on such things as selection compared with other positions within the Labour Party.

Tawney's analysis was phrased, characteristically, as a history. Education had developed along class lines in the nineteenth century, as a system of social apartheid. There were two separate sectors: elementary education was the training of "a special class", of workmen and servants; secondary education was the preserve of their masters. The systems ran parallel; no progression was possible between them, even for the individual child. The assumptions of this system — "the doctrines of 1870" — had been somewhat undermined since 1902. Despite the recent mangling of Fisher's inadequate proposals, some bridges had been built between the two systems. But the elementary/secondary division remained substantially intact: "exclusive" forms of selection, building bridges for the exceptionally able, were a compromise that served to perpetuate it. So too did piecemeal schemes like day continuation or the extension of education within the *elementary* system. For most children "elementary education" was all that could be expected; secondary education remained "an exceptional educational privilege".

The task then, was to secure "a living and organic connection" between elementary and secondary schooling, re-classifying them as successive, age-defined stages through which each child should go. Only thus would the illegitimate intrusion of "class" into "educational" matters be ended.

It is worth stressing at this point that though "class" is one of Tawney's key words, he uses it very loosely. In *Secondary Schools for All* it is most commonly used to denote assumptions and prejudices, especially where these are seen as archaic or otherwise irrelevant to the question in hand. Thus, though Tawney sometimes refers to "class stratification" in the sociological manner, his typical use is idealist and moralist. Class is an invariably pejorative term: "the vulgar irrelevances of class inequality and economic pressure", "the odious doctrine of class domination", "the vulgarities of the class system". Sometimes class is counterposed to "community", division against a social harmony: "Its (Labour's) policy is ·not for the advantage of any *single class,* but to develop the human resources of the *whole community"* (p.64, underlining supplied and cf the section on "class" in *Equality).*

Against the residue of the class-bound doctrines of the past, Tawney discerned (and helped to marshal) an increasing movement of opposition. Sometimes this was presented as but another aspect of "community" — "our common sense and our humanity", a vehicle for values assumed to be agreed on, outside certain vested interests. But the supporters (and the opponents) of educational progress were also identified more precisely:

> Both in the criticisms passed upon the present system and in proposals for improving it there are signs of a fundamental agreement which did not exist ten, or even five, years ago. In England it is not ungentlemanly to steal halfpennies from children, and industrial interests, it may be assumed, will oppose any reform which interferes with the supply of cheap juvenile labour. But among educationalists and teachers, economists and social workers, administrators and, not least, the parents themselves, there is not a wide diversity as to the main weaknesses of the existing system. (p.18)

Throughout the text, this dual identification is maintained: the progressive consensus includes on the one hand parents and the Labour Movement and on the other all those who are professionally concerned with the educational system: "Nearly all enlightened educationalists" (among whom Tawney manages to enlist the *Times* and the early intelligence testers); teachers and social administrators. The arguments of each are duly presented. Parents, having, with a Biblical vagueness, "tasted of the tree of knowledge", will not now be fobbed off with "educational shoddy". The Labour Movement should fight class domination in the class room, just as it fights it in Parliament and the factory. Educationalists mostly favour major extensions of secondary education. Educational psychologists have revealed the random distribution of ability and argue that "a great deal of educable capacity misses education". Social inquiry has shown the disastrous results of educational neglect, especially for the adolescent. "Common sense" and "humanity" do indeed support reform.

We should note two main things about Tawney's progressive alliance. First, it prefigures in an oppositional form, precisely the type of dominant coalition we have discerned in the period since World War II. Especially significant is the way he treats the teachers. He spends a whole chapter on their position and prospects. Labour supports their legitimate demands including professional aims like the defence of the Burnham scale, the search for secure tenure, the opposition to "secret reports" on practising teachers, and the strengthening of teacher autonomy. The uniting of the profession is seen as the natural corollary to breaking down barriers in school organisation. Tawney ends this section with a peroration that pointed significantly to future relations between Labour and the teachers:

> The aim should be to make our educational system an organic unity, alive in every part, served by teachers united, *self governing* and *free.* (p.123, our emphasis)

Secondly, we should note the conspicuous absence of any industrial interests from the alliance. Industry indeed, especially the Federation of British Industries (the inter-war CBI) was the main butt of Tawney's satire. The progressive consensus was articulated *against* industry and those who were held to represent it in the government and the Conservative party. As we shall see, it is precisely Tawney's purpose to rescue the children from the clutches of employers, and to define an education *against* the demands of employment.

The actual proposals of *Secondary Schools for All* focus exclusively on questions of access. Such essential if mechanical matters are distinguished by Tawney from "imponderables of personality, spirit, and atmosphere" which are still more important but impossible to legislate for. His writing is similarly chock full of metaphors of access and exclusion, somewhat more homely than later cliches: secondary schools are "a landing without a staircase"; primary schools "a staircase without a landing"; education in general is a "cul-de-sac"; scholarship systems are "bridges", "frail handrails" or even "greasy poles". Primary schools are, again, "like a rope which the Indian juggler throws in the air to end in vacancy".

How, then, to end this segregation? The aim should be to secure the transfer of all (or most?) children from the primary to the secondary stages as part of a continuous full-time education to the age of 16. All the proposals flowed from this: regrading of all schools into secondary or primary; the abolition of secondary school fees; the increase of maintenance allowances; the increase of secondary school places. Despite his title, Tawney remained vague about the universality of secondary schooling. Sometimes he seemed to accept that only 75 per cent of children were likely to benefit, a figure drawn from some psychologists. Sometimes he presented this as an interim target to be achieved as an "instalment of reform", and then surpassed. We shall return to consider this ambivalence.

Most of the book was taken up in discussing the feasibility of these proposals. They were presented in a careful, pragmatic way, with a weight of argumentation and under the slogan "idealistic but not visionary". Yet the discussion of what the schools were to be for, of the content and purposes of the education was, by contrast, cursory and vague. Tawney's own assumptions on these matters have often to be inferred from his treatment of other themes. His direct attempts at definition were formalistic, tautological and rather feeble:

> Defined by the stage of life for which it provides, it is the education of the adolescent. Defined by its curriculum, it assumes that the preparatory work of developing the simpler processes of thought and expression has been accomplished, and that its pupils are ready to be introduced, at least in outline and by degrees, to the subjects which will interest them as adults, and an acquaintance with which may reasonably be expected from educated men and women. Defined by its purpose, its main aim is not to impart the specialised technique or trade of any particular trade or profession but to develop the faculties which, because they are an attribute of man, are not peculiar to any particular class or profession of men, and to build up the interests which, while they may become the basis of specialisation at a later stage, have a value extending beyond their utility for any particular vocation, because they are the condition of a rational and responsible life in society. (p.29)

At first sight this and other passages seem contentless, and in a sense they are. Their meaning is almost entirely negative. What is significant is what is denied. In particular Tawney opposes definitions of secondary education that are derived from the children's future employment. Labour must reject, he later writes, "the vulgar commercialism which conceives of the manufacture of efficient typists and mechanics as the primary object of adolescent education" (p.111), in other words the legacy of Central and Junior Technical Schools. The doctrine of the determinacy of occupation is "fundamentally vicious", robbing children of their chances for a fuller human development in the interests of producing "cannon fodder" for industry.

Tawney's anti-industrialism produces a particular tangle of arguments. On the one hand education is seen as a sphere whose autonomy from economic and social (ie. "class") considerations must be defended. This pushes him into defining certain criteria as purely "educational", so that, for instance, psychological notions of "natural development" are appealed to against considerations of economic utility. The "experts" of the region are also proportionately exalted along with "the progress of educational science". The tendency of this part of the argument is radically to separate the social formation and a principal means of its reproduction, an odd position for a socialist who seeks to change the world! On the other hand, education *is* seen as having some pertinent effects at a more than individual level. It does (if of the right kind) develop and improve the social order. Tawney is quite as capable as any economist of coining the ringing phrase about education and human capital:

> It is possible for the *personnel* as well as the material equipment of industry to be under-capitalised, and a nation which has the courage to invest generously in its children "saves", in the strictest economic sense, more "capital" than the most parsimonious community which ever lived with its eyes on the Stock Exchange. (p.144)

In this sense, education is seen as increasing the productiveness of labour power — "it adds to that particular type of productive power on which the ability to use all other natural advantages... ultimately depends " (p.145). Yet these contradictions in Tawney's version of the relations of school to economy were never fully explored, neither by Tawney himself, or any other intellectual in the tradition he helped to found.

Tawney's failure to specify, positively, an educational content can be explained in a number of ways. He refused, on principle, to specify any precise curriculum in the interests of variety. He insisted on the importance of trusting the teachers. It is also clear that he was heavily influenced by the developmental psychology of the period, hence the definition of secondary education as "adolescent education", appropriate to a stage in the child's maturation. But if "nature" in very general terms specified what should be learnt, there is little need to worry about what "society" (or class interests and experiences) might demand unless indeed it conflicts with "nature". The argument from nature seems to have been reinforced by one from "culture". For Tawney undoubtedly conceived of culture in a thoroughly Arnoldian manner: it was a potentially classless inheritance which schools (or the WEA) could bring to everybody. Unlike "utilitarian efficiency" it had an unproblematic content. Thus, in the last resort, he was quite happy to endorse the Board of Education's list of secondary school subjects without further comment. Finally, we should note the complementarity of all this to the notion of "rights" informing Tawney's whole position and that especially of more working-class egalitarians. What was claimed as a right was evidently what some privileged children already possessed. Secondary education after all, already existed; the problem was to generalise it.

But the consequences of this absence were very important. In this phase and thereafter, social democracy possessed no conception of the nature and purposes of education which could be said to be its *own*. It was reliant on the liberal humanism of sympathetic intellectuals like Tawney or on the educational professionals themselves or on altogether more subterranean social processes by which the real meaning of school was fixed. It lacked therefore the one really essential component; a conception of *really* useful knowledge to set against both capitalist utility and the attractive but impossible idea of a classless "culture".

It is important, finally, to set *Secondary Schools for All* within a wider context of Labour Party thinking on education. We may start by recalling the fact that Labourism in general is a complex of ideologies. As several commentators have noted, much of the character of the party itself can be understood in terms of a persistent duality. On the one hand Labour has embraced a broad, ethical anti-capitalism, concerned, above all with social justice and egalitarian in temper. This tendency has been represented by the radical ILP-ish tendencies in the party and by more or less independent English intellectuals like Tawney, G.D.H. Cole or George Orwell. On the other hand, Labour's repertoire has included the tradition of Fabian social engineering, best understood as a drive for "national efficiency" and scarcely incompatible either with a corporate liberalism or a State capitalism. This dichotomy has certainly been visible in education and we shall analyse it in much more detail later in this essay. For the moment we may follow Rodney Barker (1972) in noting the opposition between an educational egalitarianism and the more elitist or merito-

156

cratic emphasis of Sidney Webb and the early LCC.

Tawney was well aware of this opposition, wrote eloquently of the differences between "equality" and mere "equality of opportunity" and stigmatised the LCC's policies as inegalitarian. Yet his treatment of the crucial matter of selection was very curious. He identified two kinds: "exclusive selection" which was a way of building bridges which individual children might cross and "inclusive selection" that would almost amount to universal provision. (The 75 per cent target for children in secondary schools was presumably a case in point). The peculiarity of these formulations is that although they are clearly egalitarian in spirit, they fall short of explicitly advocating universal provision. The whole tendency of Tawney's argument and rhetoric and moral stance was egalitarian, yet at the level of practicalities even his work seems to illustrate the power of the categories of the intelligence testers and their construction of broad types of children. As Tawney's own acceptance, later, of tri-partitism suggests, even Social Democracy's leading "philosopher" did not quite escape the duality of Labour's educational thinking. It is perhaps a measure of his status, however, that the tensions and contradictions appear more honestly here than at other moments in the tradition.

Post War "Affluence" and Revisionism

Some fundamental features of the policies of the 1960s were already present in *Secondary Schools for All*. Post-war development was, in many ways, an elaboration, in radically changed conditions, of that basic stance towards the State and the educational system. The party's subsequent history constitutes a prolonged testing of the adequacy of social democratic politics. It is important to emphasise, however, if only in outline, the changes of context in the post-war period. If more powerful determinations are ignored, there is a risk of overestimating the contributions of teachers or educational "experts".

First, and most obviously, the war-time coalition, the victory of 1945, and the period of the third Labour Government, transformed the party's place on the political scene. In the inter-war years, despite the periods of minority government, it had been a party of opposition, subject to ridiculous charges of Bolshevism and identified with the poor and oppressed. Political success and governmental responsibility strengthened the liberal, "progressive" elements in the party, at the expense of its socialism. Labour made a crucial contribution to the post-war consensual hegemony, accepting the "mixed economy" and building "the Welfare State". A fuller incorporation within the forms of the capitalist State and the achievements of many social democratic goals meant, among other things, that the tendency to identify working-class with "National Interests" was all the stronger.

War, recovery and the post-war boom also transformed the character of the "economic problems" with which the capitalist State had to deal, whichever party was in power. Keynesian solutions mitigated the main source of inter-war discontent — massive and structural unemployment. The problem pushed to the front was now that of "growth", or a rate of accumulation comparable to that of other capitalist economies and free from inflation or from monetary crises. Despite the 1930s shift into monopoly, the War, and the long boom, British industry and perhaps the social formation as a whole, seemed to remain "archaic". Even Marxist commentators accepted this diagnosis in the mid-1960s. (Anderson 1964). Labour policy was in-

157

creasingly framed by this analysis. What was needed was a massive social, economic and educational "modernisation".

The whole cast of Labour's ideologies was similarly affected by the party's fortunes after 1951. The party helped to construct the post-war hegemony, but it was Macmillan's conservatism that completed the edifice and presided over it. In what has been called: "one of the few privileged phases of hegemony by consent in recent British history" (Hall 1975 pp.21-22), that is 1951 to 1960, Conservative success, under the banners of "affluence", "embourgeoisement" and "political consensus" precipitated Labour's "revisionism". The most significant Labour theorists of the 1950s, like Crosland, accepted much of the affluence myth and sought to provide political programmes acceptable in "present-day, as opposed to capitalist, society". (Crosland 1962). The programme that resulted has been very adequately summarised as "an attack on the ascriptive elements of British society which were presented as causes of economic inefficiency and offensive social distinctions." (Howell 1976 p.193).

Finally, it is important to note that Labour's own legislation of the 1940s eroded much of the ground of its traditional ideologies. Working-class support in the inter-war period had depended in large part upon the very open and conspicuous exclusion of working people from anything like a full citizenship. The War, the removal of the "Old Gang", Labour's reforms and post-war prosperity undoubtedly produced a real amelioration in some of the more contingent and phenomenal aspects of class relations, giving a greater appearance of equality. In this sense "revisionism" was a sensible enough adaptation, more convincing than anything the "left" could offer, and perfectly consistent with the party's fundamental reformism (Howell 1976). In so far as the old egalitarianism was to be retained, it had to take somewhat finer and more discriminating forms — either that, or the nature of class had to be grasped more completely.

These changes had three main effects on the party's educational thinking. First, they tended to change the balance of emphases within the social democratic repertoire. The assumption of economic responsibilities (or their prospect) together with the whole modernisation argument, laid an overwhelming emphasis on the economic reasons for educational expansion. Economic considerations, however, were not seen as in any way incompatible with educational goals. Crosland, while invoking Tawney's general argument, did not share his suspicion of industry. On the contrary, there was assumed to be a quite unproblematic harmony between the equalisation of educational opportunities and the necessities of "growth". The first was a necessary condition of the second.

Secondly, education had, by the later 1950s, assumed a very prominent place in the party's total strategy and it became, in its way, the success story of the years that followed. In general, "revisionism" presented Labour as a party of "social reform" and gave education a priority within that definition. Education did in fact become a site of policy innovations that spilled over into other fields, "positive discrimination" and "priority areas" for instance. Education was designated the key area of remaining class inequalities, "the greatest divisive influence" (Crosland 1962). Moreover there is no doubt of the substantial success, at an ideological level, of this part of the party's programme. From the early 1960s to the appearance of the first *Black Papers* and the new educational radicalisms, social democratic conceptions of education acquired an almost monopolistic dominance. In this sense, education provides an important exception to the conventional leftish account of Labour's fortunes from 1945 to 1965 — a descent from epic heights to bathos.

Finally, of course, post-war changes shifted the actual terrain of Labour's policies., Labour's initial programme of "secondary schooling for all" was pre-empted by the Butler Act of 1944. The major issue thereafter became the *forms* of secondary schooling, a battle fought out first within the party itself. It was in these conflicts and in the crystallisation of Labour party solutions that the teachers and the sociologists were so important.

II The Sociology of Education

In this part we shall examine the emergence of the sociology of education, its institutional location, and its characteristic intellectual paradigms. But at the same time we wish to stress that the sociology of education was a *developing* tradition of inquiry, with shifts of emphasis and method as well as limits and continuities. In this internal history, it is possible to distinguish two main phases, with a shift in the early 1960s. An awareness of this shift has structured our account. Though in both phases the intellectual paradigm was broadly "functionalist", the early functionalisms took a classically institutional form, dealt with problems at a "macro" level, and drew heavily on quantitative techniques. Latterly, sociologists drew on a functionalism of "norms" and "value systems" to explain more microscopic or local features of the educational system and its relation to "class". At the same time methods became more "qualitative". We have sought to sketch the main external determinations of this change.

But we are also concerned with the relation of the sociology of education to social democracy and to Labour Party policy. At almost every level, including the actual careers of individuals as both sociologists and advisers to Labour, the relation was, as we shall show, peculiarly close. Ideologically, too, there were both convergences and shared presuppositions and influences. The Fabian tradition, for instance, was a constituent in the actual formation of the sociology of education. Even so, the sociologists did make their own specific contribution to the post-war pattern, and it is this that persuades us to view the whole constellation Labour Party/ Sociologists of Education as a coalition and not, simply, as a unity. Sociologists were not simply party advisers — the academic wing of the party. Often they were further from this role than the inter-war Labour intellectuals. They were also academics of a particular kind, appearing as the "experts" of the region, winning a wider currency and authority for their work outside the party. Their ideas came to be dominant within the educational apparatus. So far as the party was concerned it was through their work that further objectives were added to the inheritance of "secondary schools for all" and Labour's post-1944 goals were given precision. Although the fit with "revisionism" was very close indeed, the contribution was nonetheless specific.

In what follows we deal first with sociology and the sociologists, then with their influence within the educational system and on Labour Party policy.

Developments

The sociology of education had its roots in the "political arithmetic" tradition of

159

empiricist sociology, which had concerned itself directly with questions of poverty and social inequality. It was during the 1930s, following the establishment of a Department of Social Biology at the London School of Economics, that systematic efforts were made to investigate the part played by education in maintaining and perpetuating the class structure, and in promoting social mobility. It was in this context that the findings of mental testing, usually cited in support of a selective system, were turned to an opposite use. In 1935, Gray and Moshinsky, in their key article, "Ability and Opportunity in English Education", combined psychological and sociological techniques in a survey of the relationship between ability and attainment. They concluded that there was a "large reservoir of unutilised ability" (1936 p.364).

The institutionalisation of this fact-finding project at the LSE, and its subsequent development after the 1944 Education Act, marked the birth of the sociology of education as a legitimate academic discipline. In terms of the problems that were initially addressed, the emergent sociology of education was greatly influenced by its antecedents in Fabian socialism and its links with government educational policy: on the one hand a concern with equal opportunities, and on the other a concern with the problems generated by the gradual transition to a peace-time economy. In the case of the latter there was an imperative to increase productivity to meet the demands of the internal economy and also to re-establish links with external markets. At a time of full employment, the response to these "needs" involved two strategies: firstly, increasing the individual productivity of the labour force, and secondly, efficient utilisation of technological skills and developments. Crucially, the success of this strategy was seen to be largely dependent on increasing the supply of highly skilled technologists, and in this respect the education system was seen to be inadequate. Thus the primary focus of sociological research, particularly that sponsored by official and semi-official government agencies, was upon those handicaps which prevented a perfect relationship between measured ability, educational opportunity, and performance.

The sociology of education of the Halsey, Floud and Anderson era was directly concerned with the relationship between education, the economy and the social system. As Floud expresses it, they were "fascinated by the spectacle of educational institutions struggling to respond to the new purposes of an advanced industrial economy" (Floud 1961 p.60). From this perspective — broadly structural functionalism — society is viewed as a system of interrelated parts each of which performs some function for the others and thus for the society as a whole. So, in these terms, it makes sense to talk about the "needs" of the economy, the "functions" of the educational system, and so on.

Characteristically demographic in approach, the sociology of education attempted to analyse the influence on educational attainment of components such as the child's age and sex, the size of the family, and the parents' education and reading habits. They identified and documented the under-representation of working-class children in selective secondary and higher education; the gap in the attainments of children from different social class backgrounds; and the widening of this gap as children progressed through the education system. As Halsey and Floud pointed out: "Widespread social amelioration since World War II has not removed persistent class inequalities in

160

the distribution of ability and attainment" (1961 p.7). An unselected reserve of educable talent was being wasted. Thus working-class failure in education was viewed as a wastage of "society's talent".

Parallel with this work were the investigations by other agencies into the validity of the selection mechanism itself. In 1957 research reports from the National Foundation for Educational Research and the British Psychological Association disputed the reliability of the eleven-plus as a predictor of educational capacity. These findings fuelled growing middle-class dissatisfaction with the selection process and the eleven-plus. Previously, they had been able to purchase a secondary education, but the abolition of fees, and the operation of the eleven-plus, prevented this. This position was exacerbated by the uneven grammar-school entrance rates in different authorities — varying from 10% to 45% of the total intake.

The impact both of the educational sociologists' findings and of the general discontent in relation to selective education was not confined to the Labour Party. The myth of "parity" between the different schools had been exploded, and by the early 1960s concern was again being expressed about the shortage of scientists and technologists, a concern which received added emphasis in the light of Britain's developing economic problems. In 1961 the Conservative Education Minister, Eccles, asked the Central Advisory Council to report on the "average and below average pupil" (Newsom CAC 1963). Macmillan also commissioned a special report on higher education, to consider how the system could be brought up to date (Robbins 1963). The Nuffield Foundation sponsored the first curriculum development projects concerning themselves particularly with science teaching, and in 1963 the Schools Council on Curriculum and Examinations was established.

Thus, by the early 1960s the nature of the educational debate had already shifted fundamentally. Sir Edward Boyle, Eccles' successor, made the point:

> After 1963 it was hardly controversial to say that you had massive evidence of the number of boys and girls who were being allowed to write themselves off below their true level of ability. I think 1963 was a watershed here, Newsom and Robbins both coming out in that year. It was those reports that really cemented the work that educational sociologists had done in the previous years. (Kogan 1974 p.91).

There were however further shifts in the early 1960s which provided a new context for the developing sociology of education. The dominant assumptions underlying the ideology of affluence were systematically attacked on both theoretical and empirical levels. The rediscovery of poverty, growing industrial militancy and the appearance on the political arena of a series of social problems, previously submerged, contributed to a "rediscovery" of class. Within sociology this "rediscovery" focused on the community. Whilst it was accepted that working-class material standards had improved, it was argued that they still constituted distinct social groupings. Throughout sociology — from the Affluent Worker monographs to the poverty investigations — a re-engagement with the reality of class was initiated.

·Within the sociology of education this shift was apparent in a move away from the "macro" concerns of the orthodoxy, to small-scale studies of educability — a move away from the "needs " of post-capitalist society to the "definitions" of the local community. This is epitomised, for example, in the work of Jackson and Marsden (1966) and the earlier work of Halsey and Floud (1961). Both studies are directly concerned with the relationship between working-class children and the grammar schools, but their methodological approaches to the problem are fundamentally distinct. Similarly, this shift in approach and emphasis paralleled a change in the structural position of the sociology of education. Like the other social sciences it was expanding with the institutional growth of higher education. Specifically, it was increasingly incorporated into teacher training colleges and university education departments, and this also had significant implications for the nature of the "problems" to which research was addressed.

Thus the changing theoretical frameworks and institutional basis meant that by the 1960s investigation no longer focused on the material handicaps traditionally underlying educational inequality. Research now attempted to identify social factors impinging on the intellectual development of individuals, and also explored the social and cultural circumstances affecting working-class pupils' attainment at a given level of ability. The research attitude, that is the theoretical paradigm employed, had important implications for the way in which class was viewed. As one sociologist put it:

> Given the kind of educational system and the kind of relationship between school and home which exists . . . differential educability is linked to social class background. But social class is just a shorthand way of referring to a complex of factors which correlate with occupation. It describes the distribution or incidence of a phenomenon but does not explain its occurence in any causal sense. (Sugarman 1966 p.287).

So the task was to explain the occurrence in a meaningful way, once more sociologists drew on the functionalist paradigm, but less overtly and crudely, assimilating the sophistications of the small-scale studies conducted by the social anthropologists.

From this perspective social behaviour is structured by norms, enforced by implicit or explicit sanctions which organise, in a regular and predictable fashion, the social life of individuals and the relationships they enter into. Thus, the analysis focuses on rules of conduct as mechanisms of social control, on the constellation of rules that govern particular forms of social grouping, for example kinship; and on the effects which these norms have for the structure of social relationships in given areas of social life. The "meaningful" fabric which constitutes social life was therefore found, not in culture, but in institutions considered as regulative social relationships. This largely descriptive approach to social phenomena is given a certain dynamic by the use of the concept of function — the "adequate causal mechanism". Institutions are seen as functioning parts of a social whole, such as the community, which serve to maintain it in a more or less stable condition. The logic of the approach then becomes circular, because in so far as these institutions continue to contribute to the maintenance of the social system, that is, if the system "works", then they are seen as functional for it. This approach, by definition, leads to a focus on the mechanisms of control that serve to ensure conformity to the prescribed normative order.

In practice this approach leads to a concentration on "normative" facts ("treat social facts as things") so social structure refers to relations between actual, empirically given, social phenomena. These relationships are either given in the facts as directly observed, or arrived at by simple abstraction from the facts. Thus social structure, when used in a functional analysis, refers to no more than the actual organisation of a social system — "you too could see it if you took the time"

To give a short example of how this approach is used, and how it actually obscures that which needs to be explained, we can look at those parts of J. Klein's survey *Samples from English Culture,* dealing with education and mental activity. Traditional working-class communities, for example the mining community studied by Henriques *et al* (1956) are seen to be inward-looking, with a social structure based largely on ascribed roles. These workers have short term rather than long-term goals, they do not discuss these rationally, and insist on a high degree of conformity. Klein describes this mental state as "cognitive poverty" — an intellectual stagnation precipitated by the conformist pressures of this type of community.

Apart from the obvious criticism that the level of educational experience is not considered in the original study, or by Klein, the implicit suggestion is that "cognitive poverty" arises inevitably from the conditions of working-class life. As she makes clear:

> Even the most sympathetic writers on working-class ways of life remark on what appears as a stubborn determination not to develop — and not to allow others to develop — attitudes or behaviour that would make for a richer and more interior life. (1965 p.7)

But this does not explain anything. It gives us a necessarily determinist picture: 'That's the way workers are in traditional communities'. The question still to be answered is *'Why* are they that way?'

To return to the main argument, the starting point of research was that schools and education were "good" things. Thus it was assumed that the factors inhibiting the educational development of the working-class child were external to the school. So it was necessary to go outside the school and analyse the pupils' social environment. To understand his attitudes to education and his behaviour in the school it was necessary to understand the values he received from his home and local community. An implicit acceptance of the present social and economic structure of society led to a simple comparison of the cultures of those who succeed in school and those who do not. Thus, to our surprise, we are told that the working-class have certain deficiencies, vis-a-vis their middle-class counterparts — in linguistic competences, in values and so on. Even when the impact of the school experiences was examined, their effect was seen to reside in compounding these cultural deficiences through, for example, streaming.

The academic sociology of education developed initially as a response to post-war economic 'problems' as perceived within the apparatus of the State. It was also shaped by the meritocratic ideologies present in the Fabian end of Labour Party traditions. For sociology this dual problematic had important consequences for its understanding of the relationship between the education system and working-class children. The initial demonstration of an untapped pool of ability identified certain statistical correlations associated with working-class failure, but provided no explanatory power. Importantly, class was understood not as a dynamic relationship, but as a number of variables correlated with income. Thus the search was on for the adequate causal mechanism, and in line with developments in sociology generally, the cause of failure was located in the attitudes, values, and language of the local working-class community. Subsequently, these findings were articulated more clearly in theories about a "culture of poverty" or the "cycle of deprivation". Working-class failure in education was precipitated by the deficiences in their cultural and linguistic backgrounds and, logically, policy should aim to compensate for these deficiencies.

Impacts

The impact of these findings needs to be assessed at two levels: in relation to policies about the internal organisation and activities of the school, and in relation to Labour Party policy. In the first case it broke the stranglehold of psychology on school organisation and on progressive teaching methods. As Simon (1974) demonstrates, the development of intelligence testing and its related selection procedures generated the introduction of internal streaming, and subsequently legitimated the tri-partite system. Sociologists criticised these practices, by pointing out the unreliability of the selection mechanisms, then by questioning the whole basis of differentiation, and finally by demonstrating their "self-fulfilling" quality. So for J.W.B. Douglas, the selection and streaming reinforced, and was largely based on, the cultural/material deficiences of the working-class child (1964).

Secondly, child-centred teaching had been advocated in government reports since the 1930s, alongside proposals for classifying children by intelligence levels. Both concepts were related to a psychological understanding of man as a creature with innate, determinate capacities. Intelligence level was, however, pivotal, and set limits on the capacities and potentialities that could be drawn out by a child-centred approach. Thus, intelligence determined structure and organisation, and within these confines a child-centred approach could be utilised. The compatibility of these views is demonstrated by the joint appendix to the Hadow Report (1933) written by Sir Cyril Burt, "the father of intelligence testing", and Susan Isaacs, one of the most influential progressives. Sociology, then, by undermining the concept of intelligence, removed the theoretical linchpin which legitimated the organisational structure, and consequently released progressivism as a method from its constraining and determining influence.

Thus, sociologists were able to demonstrate that it was the school's reinforcement of working-class deficiencies, rather than innate incapacity, which contributed to working class failure. Consequently, the structural and internal organisation of schooling should be reorganised to compensate for these deficiencies, rather than compound them. The political force of this argument was augmented by government reports in the later 1950s and early 1960s, which not only recognised the need for more highly-trained technologists, but also argued that a higher level of attainment was necessary for even those of average ability. They were able to do this by pointing to the decrease in absolute number of unskilled jobs and a rise in the level of skills demanded by the occupations which had emerged as a direct consequence of technological developments. Previously, reports of this nature, such as the Norwood Report, had presupposed a belief in three broad categories of children whose intellectual capacity and potential were largely predetermined. However, by the time of the Newsom Report we find that this assumption has been undermined and that:

> intellectual talent is not a fixed quantity with which we have to work but a variable that can be modified by social policy and educational approaches. (1963 p.6.)

That is to say:

> The evidence of research increasingly suggests that linguistic inadequacy, disadvantage in

164

social and physical background and poor attainment in school are closely associated. Because the forms of speech which are all they ever require for daily use in their homes and the neighbourhoods in which they live are restricted, some boys and girls may never acquire the basic means of learning and their intellectual potential is therefore masked. (1963 p.15)

Therefore, the Newsom Report, with its sociological definition of capacity, is able to argue that the "average and below average pupils are sufficiently educable to supply the additional talent", and thereby meet the needs of the labour market. This was seen to require more flexible and "relevant" education programmes, the raising of the school leaving age and the provision of adequate staffing and facilities.

From an original limited concern with selection and social mobility, attention was now given to education as a preparation for life — particularly economic life. So the theoretical position developing within sociology was mediated by government reports and translated into policy prescriptions for the schools.

In looking at the impact of the educational sociologists on Labour Party policy, it is important to recognise the implications of the sociologists' structural position. We have already identified the link between Fabianism and the work of the LSE, and it is widely acknowledged that most orthodox educational sociologists had some degree of commitment to comprehensive reform and the Labour Party. However, the relationship differs significantly from that of the pre-war Labour intellectuals whose work was organically connected both theoretically and practically, to the politics of the Labour movement. Indeed, this point is recognised by Crosland when he argues:

Educational research, in any case a very new tool, can give new facts, illuminate the range of choice, show how better to achieve a given objective, but it cannot say what the objective ought to be. For this must depend . . . on judgements which have a value component and a social dimension. (Crosland 1974 p.207)

The emergence of a specialist, academic sociology of education, carried with it commitments to objective professional work, implying a definite division between institutional research and political activity. The consequences of this for the work produced are significant. Importantly, by working within an institutionally and professionally delimited field of knowledge, which specifies key problems and approaches, the work is distanced from the direct political/moral/philosophical discussions which characterised the work of people like Tawney and Webb. Furthermore, the technical concerns and professional expertise required by writing within sociology, the need for an "objective" and fair treatment of the material and subject, generates political ambiguities, but at the same time gains legitimacy as being "scientific".

Labour's alliance with the sociology of education in the post-war period — its use of the technical expertise and the findings — directly influenced the direction and implementation of its educational policy. Kogan, in his interviews with Crosland and Boyle (Kogan 1974), points to the growth of a new educational establishment in the late 1950s and 1960s made up of social scientists and the like, drawing on the work of professional experts such as Vaizey and Halsey. Furthermore, this process was accelerated with Labour's return to office. Crosland tells how, when in office, he effectively exploited the ideas of sociologists like Halsey and Burgess and constituted an informal consultative body made up of similar "experts" such as Young and Donnison. Indeed, Crosland attributes the successful undermining of the eleven-plus to such "experts":

It wasn't the Department, in fact, that cracked the Eleven Plus doctrine, but it was mainly such outsiders as Vaizey, Floud, Halsey and the rest. (Kogan 1974 p.186)

More importantly, the framework of assumptions within which the sociologists worked was compatible with, and complemented, Labour's post-war revisionism. Both accepted the framework of Welfare State capitalism and its hierarchical occupational structure, which was seen, somehow, to reflect directly the technical requirements of the production process. Having accepted this stratification as given, the question posed for political policy is *access* to positions in the hierarchy. Equality of opportunity, in this perspective, is understood as equalising chances in the lottery of job allocation. But now the basis of differentiation in education, the IQ test, has been undermined and shown to be largely a function of the environment. Therefore education takes on a new role: we must allow, as Crosland says, "the beneficial influence of education to compensate for the deficiencies of upbringing and early circumstance" (Crosland 1974 p.199).

From these assumptions flows the argument for comprehensive and other policy initiatives. If we consider Crosland's major speech in 1966 on the necessity for comprehensives, we find that he argues that the research of the sociology of education, and the government reports, prove that working-class children, for various reasons, are unable to exploit their educational opportunities effectively. Therefore, policy must necessarily be aimed at ameliorating those factors inhibiting the "equal" chances of the working-class child. Yet the abolition of fees and the provision of "secondary education for all" have not, as educational sociologists have con-clusively and "scientifically" demonstrated, improved the relationship between working-class ability and attainment. Research has also demonstrated that the eleven-plus is unreliable as a predictor of capacity, and furthermore, that the tri-partite division in education perpetuates anachronistic class privileges and divisions which are no longer relevant to a modern post-industrial society. Finally, the demands of the economy in terms of the average level of skill required necessitate the provision of a more effective, and efficient, education for the "average and below average ability" pupil. Thus, he concludes that the tri-partite system is "educationally and socially unjust, inefficient, wasteful and divisive." (Crosland 1974 p.165).

These arguments and assumptions, widely held in the Labour Party, represent and epitomise a shift in the way Labour understands inequality and social change. From the pre-war emphasis on wide-scale redistributive policies, we now have an emphasis on a technical/organisational problem in a relatively discrete social policy area. This fracturing characterised Labour's response to the "social problems" con-fronting the political system. These discrete areas reflected, and in part generated, the intellectual fields occupied by organised professional interests. Within sociology, for example, the various sub-disciplines relating to social policy worked within intellectual fields which specified quite narrow empirical problems. Working with specific metho-dologies and addressing particular "technical" problems, evidence and recommendations were advanced, "objectively", to inform the process of political decision-making. Thus, the "problem" of poverty was divorced from that of ownership, the "problem" of working-class educability was divorced from that of real, ongoing, class relationships, and so on.

The sociology of education not only provided the "legitimate" rationale for

Labour's comprehensive programme, but also, crucially, helped to generate the political consensus on education characteristic of the 1960s. In responding to the economic, political, and social "problems" of the period, the characteristic assumptions and pallia-tives of the ideological alliance precipitated the era of educational expansion.

III Teachers and Teacher Professionalism

Before attempting to locate the specific contribution of teachers to the ideological coalition we are describing, we feel it is necessary to say something about their class location. Apart from rejecting the simplistic thesis that class is a familial characteristic passed on from one generation to another, we would also argue against the thesis that teachers, because they are wage-earners, are unambiguously members of the working-class. (Teachers' Action Collective 1975). Whilst it may be useful to see them, alongside the family, as playing a crucial role in the production of labour-power, in the production of value which later appears on the market, we would argue that it is an error then to assume a direct correspondence between the school and the factory. Fundamentally, the school is not a factory, characterised by the appropriation of surplus value and by capitalist relations in the classical sense, and furthermore teachers are not proletarians, they are "unproductive" labourers.

Similarly, the reduction of teachers to the unambiguous status of "workers" neglects the particular determinations of what Poulantzas (1975) describes as the political and ideological levels. Centrally, the whole tendency of teacher organisation has been to define themselves as professionals, experts, and so on; to reinforce the fact that in terms of the work they do they are firmly distinguished from manual labour. Their class location is not simply given by their economic position as wage earners, but is also defined both ideologically and politically, and their place on the mental-manual labour divide in this context is crucial. Thus, it is an error to characterise "professionalism" as a "wrongheaded and subjective term which is used to place teachers into a classless limbo" (Lawn 1975). Rather, teachers and their organisations have emphasised (with fatal continuity) their *professional* status, the mental-manual labour divide, their distance from parentdom, and so on, so that teaching has been *ideologically constructed* to emphasise differences from the working class.

The ideology of professionalism has been used by the teaching organisations to either defend their middle class status, or to assimilate themselves into that class. Trapped between the developing power of monopoly capital and the advances of the working class, professionalism can be understood as a petit-bourgeois strategy for advancing and defending a relatively privileged position. For the teachers it has manifested itself as an occupational strategy aimed at creating a unified and self-governing profession.

Reviewing the achievements of the NUT in its centenary year, Sir Ronald Gould, the retiring General Secretary, felt able to comment that with two exceptions the original aims of the union had been largely met. The exceptions he noted were the failure to secure adequate salaries for all members, as well as the failure to secure control over entry to the profession and over teacher registration. One of the aims which he assumed as being long secured, a pre-requisite for the pursuit of the others, was the right of teachers to be free from "obnoxious interference". In the light of recent events, Callaghan's speech in particular, Gould's assumption seems unwarranted. The Callaghan speech signals a direct confrontation with the practice of teachers as well as a challenge to the autonomy which they exercise in the control over their own affairs, both inside and outside the classroom. Though this confrontation has been experienced differently by the various sections of the teaching force, their responses have operated on one base-level assumption. This assumption, common to the different teaching organisations, is that of the professional nature of teaching — albeit unrecognised in any formal structure — as a counter to suggestions of outside interference or direction.

Professionalism and Educational Reform

The struggle for professional status has characterised the teaching organisations since their emergence as a force on the political landscape during the educational debates of the late nineteenth century. Their initial interventions in the debate on the Revised Code were dismissed, characteristically, by Robert Lowe, in the following terms: "teachers desiring to criticise the Code were as impertinent as chickens wishing to decide the kind of sauce in which they would be served" (Coates 1972 p.8). This cynical response emphasised the lack of status and effective power of the National Union of Elementary Teachers. Its very title reflected the internal divisions among teachers. Separate organisations represented teachers in the private and secondary schools, and in their case there was a real determination to defend their status and relative privilege against the expanding body of elementary school teachers. Furthermore, within the ranks of the elementary teachers sectionalism was rife. The division between certified and unqualified teachers produced, not only two distinct organisations, but continual conflict over "dilution" issues. Even when this was resolved by the NUT's acceptance of uncertified members, the issue of equal pay for women precipitated another split with the formation of the National Association of Schoolmasters.

Out of this alignment and re-alignment of forces a relatively coherent policy on professionalism emerged. For the elementary teachers the notion of professional self-government, with teacher control over professional standards and a register of qualified teachers, was seen as a means of equalising conditions within teaching and thereby raising the status of the elementary sectors. Thus, the aim of a single profession and the unification of the schools into one system was central to the development of their occupational strategy. While the grammar-school teachers argued for keeping the primary and secondary system distinct, elementary teachers and those in the higher grade schools called for the integration of the two, with the right of automatic transfer from one stage to another as a means of extending overall educational provision. It was in this educational context that the first calls for "equality of opportunity" were heard from outside — the TUC making such a call as early as 1897, demanding that secondary education be placed within the reach of every worker's child.

The co-existence of these demands, one articulated from within the education system by the unions and the other politically expressed by the Labour Party, was a key feature of educational politics in the inter-war period. But whereas the Labour Party's educational policy was part of a broader social and political strategy, of which education was an integral and important part, the unions' policy was essentially an educational one with its own discrete rationale.

The major practical aim of the teachers' organisations and the Labour Party during this period was the expansion of secondary education, with the "ultimate" objective of "secondary education for all". The contentious area was the nature of the provision to be implemented by the proposed expansion. The teaching organisations broadly supported "multi-lateral" or "multi-bias" proposals, where one school could cater for a whole range of abilities in the same building or on the same site, albeit internally divided into academic and non-academic sections. The Assistant Masters' Association expressed support for this scheme as early as 1925, and the NUT was similarly in favour. The "multi-bias" proposals, as well as potentially offering the equalisation of working conditions, also offered the possibility of extended job opportunities for women, hence the support of groups like the Association of Assistant Mistresses. Similarly, the division between the Higher Grade schools and the secondaries could also be overcome with the implementation of a system of "common schools"; thus within the NUT the teachers in the Higher Grade Schools were particularly vociferous in their support for the proposals.

It is important not to exaggerate the distinction between professional and political interests. Indeed, one of the characteristics of these years was the general drift of teachers towards electoral support for Labour — underpinned by the party's opposition to cuts and economies, and by its commitment to reform the education system. This trend, particularly in the early 1920s, provoked consternation in Government circles, and alarm amongst Conservative teachers. Speaking of this drift, one ex-NUT President was moved to argue that there "will be a danger not only to the teachers themselves but to the State generally" (Simon 1974 p.120). This concern with the political orientation of teachers as a group prompted, among other things, Special Branch surveillance of the activities of the Teachers' Labour League. A group of Tory MPs even tabled a "Seditious Teachings Bill" directed at preventing the diffusion of anarchistic ideas among the young, on pain of imprisonment.

Within the Labour Party it was only the Teachers' Labour League which consistently raised the "content" of education as a matter for political debate. Their "proscription" by the party in 1927 signalled Labour's evacuation of that area. For the party, therefore, the intermediate level between the scale of provision and what went on in the classroom, namely the level of the curriculum, remained uncontested. The subsequently re-constituted teachers' interest group, the National Association of Labour Teachers', concentrated almost exclusively on the organisational form that "secondary education for all' should take.

While the teachers' unions stressed the educational and professional benefits of multi-lateralism, the NALT, as the main spearhead of Labour's educational policy, was eager to pursue the "common school" as a means of mitigating the divisive social effects of the existing system. However, in implementing the 1944 Education Act the new Labour Minister of Education did so on the basis of the Norwood Report (1943), which had recommended the tri-partite system. Controversy raged — on the one hand the Minister emphasised the "parity" of the separate schools, that is their financial and organisational equality, and on the other hand, successive NALT Conference resolutions were passed rejecting the tri-partite system and calling for the rapid development of comprehensive schemes. The end result was that during Labour's period of

169

office only thirteen comprehensives were established, with eight more granted to the LCC on an interim basis.

It was during the period of opposition in the 1950s that the Labour Party became firmly committed to comprehensivisation and the abolition of the eleven-plus. Those revisionist changes in the party, and the findings of the educational sociologists and psychologists, discussed above, saw the "right" and "centre" of the party, under Gaitskell, unite around the call for comprehensivisation.

However, while it is obvious that NALT teachers enjoyed membership of the NUT it is clear that the over-riding rationale employed by the teachers' organisations in support of "secondary education for all", was of securing equalised conditions, as well as furthering their longer-term professional and educational aims.

Teacher Autonomy and Progressivism

In this section we wish to examine those longer-term professional and educational aims which occupied a central place in the teachers' support for education reform. Crucially, we want to look at the development of teacher autonomy over, and control of, the curriculum. The demand for professional status was closely related to the struggle for autonomy. More importantly, it was the teachers' control of this area, coupled with the development of "relevance" and "progressivism", which provided the missing centre of social democratic policies in the 1960s, that is, the content of the curriculum. However, it is important not only to analyse these developments at the policy level, but also to consider the immediate school context in which they operate.

Control of the secondary school curriculum was relinquished by the Board of Education in 1917, when effective control passed to the examination boards. These institutions ensured that the secondary school curriculum was appropriate for university preparation and, since the boards determined syllabuses their control might have been indirect but it was absolutely effective. Likewise in the elementary schools, the concern was, after 1907, not only to instil good conduct and discipline but more specifically to win the maximum number of "free" places at the grammar school, which was now required to offer a quarter of its places, free, to children from the public elementary schools.

The winning of free places as a primary concern of elementary schools led to the internal organisation of the school being subordinated to this aim. In this respect streaming represented the "pragmatic" solution, though the increasing numbers of children qualifying for scarce places resulted in the introduction of more sophisticated selection mechanisms, particularly intelligence testing. Thus, whilst in the inter-war years no "formal" prescriptions existed about what had to be taught, a very real set of determinations operated on the teaching situation through the elementary and secondary stages. The public recognition of teacher "autonomy" in this respect came from Lord Percy in 1927:

> If government, whether local or national, began to prescribe to the teacher a certain method of teaching, or even attempt to influence such matters, we run the risk of all those evils that we have seen in various forms, both in the Prussia of the past and in the Russia of today. (Bernbaum 1967 p.90)

The curriculum was to remain, in Sir William Pile's words, a "Secret Garden", into which politicans entered at their peril, since any incursion could be represented as totalitarian in nature and intent.

For teachers, in the inter-war period, one of the main sources of dissatisfaction with the "educational" practices of the unreformed system was the concern to secure greater freedom within the curriculum. The all-pervasive influence of the examination boards, and the effects on the elementary and secondary schools of streaming and selection, provided ready arguments for a move towards institutional arrangements whereby the direction of the examination boards could be circumvented. Furthermore, in those areas of the schools least affected by the external determinations — the lower streams of the elementary schools — experimental curricular reforms demonstrated the viability of alternative modes of teaching. As the teaching force expanded, pupil-teacher ratios decreased. Coupled with the introduction of "progressive" methods, via the training colleges and the Inspectorate, the elementary school curriculum began to develop in a child-centred, inquiry-based direction. However, this movement was not universal; reports as recent as Plowden (1967) still called on teachers to adopt such an approach. The pressures to enter more and more pupils for the selection exams, and the demand for more educational qualifications, inhibited the spread of these methods.

Thus, within the education system the struggle for comprehensivisation was one directed not only at the formal organisation of schooling, but also at the external control exercised over the curriculum both by the selection procedures, and by the examination boards. The NUT, for example, called in 1946 for the abolition of external examinations. In the post-war period the proliferation of external examining bodies intensified the problem and it was not until the Beloe Report in 1960 that the teachers gained control of their own examination system — the CSE. This was followed by another success in 1963 when, after considerable controversy and argument, the teachers gained control of the Schools Council on Examinations and Curriculum. This Council, as one of its working papers makes clear, has no direct power to influence the curriculum:

> The Council's intention in all its development work is not to impose a new curriculum, but to reinforce the freedom of the head in making his own decisions by extending the range of courses and materials from which he can choose. (Schools Council 1971 p.5)

So, whilst the Council is concerned to promote and initiate curriculum developments, its constitution and position act to reinforce and enhance teacher autonomy in the classroom.

These developments in the education infrastructure were paralleled by the organisational changes being promoted at the policy and political levels. Particularly in the 1960s, the introduction of comprehensivisation and other reforms opened up areas and spaces within the schools requiring a new content, and it was this area which the teachers controlled.

However, this "control" is not an abstract quality, but a freedom which operates in a specific context — the school. Obviously, activity within the school is structured by powerful external determinants, but it also contains within it social and cultural processes of considerable complexity. One of the most important of these is the characteristic resistance of a large number of working-class children to the overt

171

aims of schooling. (Hargreaves 1967, Lacey 1970, Willis 1977, Hammersley 1976).
This resistance cannot be simply explained by the working-class "deficiency"
model, which assumes that if the child fails or succeeds, then it is something external
to him which is responsible — be it cultural values from the home and the community
or a simple structural determination, such as status achievement or deprivation.
Even where research is carried out in the school, it is the institutional practices
of streaming, for example, which are seen as wholly responsible for his success or
failure. Hargreaves (1967), for example, argues that the peer group reinforces and is
predicated on failure. Failure, and the concomitant rejection of the school's
values, provides the organisational focus of the group, status in the group being
accorded with the degree of rejection. The implication being, seemingly, that
there was some original "fall from grace".

Within these frameworks, no understanding can be developed of the ways in
which these children create a culture in response to the institutional practices
and organisation of the school. An analysis which reduces this culture to inherited
values or a simplistic acceptance or inversion of the "official" message of the
school basically rejects the role and nature of subjective experience.

Fundamentally, the actions of the pupils in the school must be viewed as
intentional, logical and geared to doing or getting things done. In this sense, subjective experience provides and informs the active, day-to-day process of the creation
of frameworks of meaning, which, in the case of the "anti-school" culture, undermine the teachers' expectations and the school's objectives, and provide the pupils
with attitudes, practices and evaluations whereby they make sense of their own
situations. Similarly, it would be dangerous to see the "achievers" as simple vacuums
for the overt messages of the school. Here too, though with important differences,
cultural meanings are created through subjective experience. The school's objects
and the teachers' expectations achieve a particular resonance, but in many areas,
ambivalence and even opposition are generated. The configuration of peer groups
in the social landscape of the school provides meanings and affiliations of considerable complexity.

Apart from this overlapping and social interpenetration amongst the pupils
themselves, it must be remembered that the home, neighbourhood, class, etc.,
provide a reservoir of accumulated meanings and cultural practices which are used,
changed and appropriated by the children in creating their own practices and
meanings, to come to terms with and, in certain cases, subvert, the official organisation and ideology of the school. In this sense the cultures of the pupils' social
groups can be seen to draw upon, and be situated within, the wider context of working-class culture.

It would be wrong to suggest that these children have total autonomy and freedom in developing their cultural responses to the schools. The process of cultural
response occurs strictly on the terms and parameters delimited by the structure —
'It is a 'stony desert', which they have to make habitable by their own efforts'. Thus,
a hidden curriculum comes into play — other people organise their life, they are
streamed by 'ability', it is legitimate for teachers to make demands on them and so
on. Paradoxically, the creation of meaningful frameworks, within these parameters,
implies an accomodation to these forces. It submerges the potential oppositional

172

stance of cultural responses — not inevitably, but practically.

Again, as Paul Willis has attempted to demonstrate in his study of working-class adolescents: "it is not so much that the creation of subjective meanings and its related actions reproduce the existing social relations of production, so much as that in their outcomes these things maintain — indeed are — the fabric of the present structure" (Willis 1976 p.8). Thus, the "success" of the "habitation" created by the anti-school culture, the informal group culture, leads into and prepares the way for the culture of the shop-floor.

These processes — manifestations of class struggle at the level of the classroom — are "hidden" to the educational policy makers. They are unable to conceptualise class as a relationship, rather it is a complex of variables which impinge on the school from outside. The policy thrust is to accomodate the variables, through resource-based learning, a relevant curriculum, school assessment schemes, remedial departments and so on. Thus areas are opened up within the school which can be colonised and invested with meaning. The "achievers", however, must tread the line between the arid instrumentalism of commitment to exams, and the pull towards, and partial adoption of, cultural meanings visible on the social landscape. It would be too simplistic to infer that these were the only cultural options, but what we want to indicate are the unintended consequences of reform — their use and appropriation by the pupils. That is to say, while the schools reproduce the social relations of production, "behind their backs", they also reproduce historically specific forms of resistance.

It is within this school context that the policy prescriptions outlined in government reports, Schools' Council documents, and so on, have to be translated, via the teachers, into actual classroom practice. In this context, there have been three basic developments feeding into the curricular work of the school — the science curriculum work of the early 1960s, the prescriptions about "relevant" working-class education outlined in government reports, and the curriculum work of the Schools Council. However, the relationship between the curriculum projects and proposals generated by "researchers" and their reception in actual classroom practice is complex.

This curriculum work has been framed within certain assumptions about the teachers' pedagogic stance and relationship with his pupils. Importantly, this work has been designed for use in a "child-centred" approach, where the older, traditional mode of education as the performance of hard labour has been replaced by a "community of interest" between teacher and taught. These pedagogic assumptions say more about the distance from the school of the researchers, than they do about the actual classroom situation.

Progressivism as an ideology has a history distinct from the more utilitarian concerns of professionalism. Its roots in romanticism can be traced back to the Rousseau of *Emile*, or even further. However, its articulation as a pedagogic style and approach is much more firmly rooted in the period of compulsory State education. Its initial reception and development in the educational infrastructure during the 1930s was constrained and channelled via its subordination to the central concept of intelligence. Its prescriptions, and its acceptance in the training colleges, partly fuelled the teachers' demands for autonomy in the classroom. Without that autonomy, the flexibility demanded by this approach was sharply limited by the external determinants on classroom practice and organisation.

In the post-war period, with the attack on the concept of intelligence and the divisive structures of school organisation, progressivism was increasingly presented, via the training colleges, the "specialists", and so on, as *the* desirable mode of teaching. Indeed, government reports recognised and argued that the external determinants were preventing the more widespread adoption of these methods. Crowther made the point in 1959:

> the most promising part of the educational system for experiments in new methods of teaching relatively difficult things will be in the middle streams of the modern schools — but only if they are left free from the cramping effects of a large-scale external examination. (1959 p.94)

Thus, the policy arguments about the forms of secondary education were informed by an implicit assumption about the new modes of teaching this changed organisation would require. This aspect, however, was separated off as a professional concern, and was only developed and extended by the research and training industry which emerged in the wake of institutional reforms. This approach, which acquired its own hegemony in the regions of the training colleges and research institutions, particularly in the 1960s, corresponded with the real power and space of teacher autonomy and was directly related to the relatively spontaneous ideology of romanticism, common to students and teachers.

However, if we look in particular at the work of the Schools Council, the major institution in this field, we find complex mediations between the findings of research and their implementation in the classroom. The first point to note is the distance of research from the classroom. If we look at the document *Projects,* issued in June 1971, we find that of the 111 projects discussed 76 were situated in universities, 11 in colleges of education, and two in schools. Furthermore, as Jenkins and Shipman point out:

> The Schools Council lacks the infrastructure, the advisory staff, and the local support to go far beyond projects that develop ideas, methods and materials . . . and leave behind publications and evaluations. The consequent take up remains largely in the hands of the teachers themselves. (1976 p.53)

This position is reinforced by the central principle enshrined in the Schools Council, via the voting power of the teaching unions, of teacher autonomy — its proposals have to be designed on a voluntaristic basis. The contradictions in this stance have been outlined by M.F.D. Young (1972), who points out that whilst it is legitimate for the unions to have a policy on exams, they would be infringing autonomy if policy decisions were made on the curriculum of the school. This individualistic notion of autonomy turns out, in practice, as the right *not* to do something. Curriculum developments are received, and then rejected or accepted. This involves the teacher responding, not initiating. So for example, faced with RSLA pupils, he must choose between resource-based learning, integrated studies, and so on. Yet the choice is made within the parameters of the particular projects, and the parameters of his, and his pupils', past experience.

The levels between the research bodies and the school are occupied by a complicated web of institutions — from the local "advisers" to the teachers' centres; from the subject bodies' publications to the local examining board committees. Even within the school, complex hierarchies operate; from the curriculum innovations of the Deputy Head, to the innovations of the remedial teacher. It is within this context that we have to see the *practice* of progressivism, which may be far removed from the theoretically coherent accounts developed in the original research.

At this point it is important to stress the distinction between "progressivism" and "professionalism", neither of which is simply reducible to the other, even though they share roots in petit-bourgeois ideology. Professionalism, as such, is not concerned with the method or content of teaching *per se,* its central concern is with the economic status of teachers. Similarly, progressivism is an educational and ideological approach to the technical and pedagogical problems of teaching which is not concerned with the occupational position and status of the teacher as such. Both ideologies, as they are expressed in the educational apparatus, have institutional supports and generators — in the training colleges, in the unions, in the research institutes, and so on. It is through these bodies that they exert a powerful influence on the conduct of teachers and on what happens in the classroom. At the same time, it is important to note the disjunction between the level of practice and ideology. The incorporation of progressivism into classroom practice, as an approach and a method of control, takes place within the determinants of the class struggle in the classroom.

We have argued that the occupational strategy of the teachers' organisations was implicitly tied up with the rationalisation and equalisation of the educational system. Furthermore, we have argued that around this assertion of professionalism — institutionally supported by a separate form of education — has been constructed a teachers' educational policy and ideologies. Importantly, the struggle for autonomy has been closely linked with the development of the ideology of progressivism. Thus, the teachers' ability to respond to the "needs" of their pupils was enhanced by their control over their own exams and the curriculum. This flexibility, though more apparent than real, has had important consequences for the internal development of the schools. While it was possible for the Labour Party to avoid the question of content, the teachers were obliged to translate policy prescriptions into actual classroom practice.

IV   Educational Expansion in the 1960s

In the preceding discussion we have tried to identify certain key elements and institutions which, both ideologically and materially, legitimated the educational expansion and "consensus" of the 1960s. Crucially, the convergence between these elements, both institutionally and politically, provided a framework of basic assumptions within which educational "problems" were understood and policy prescriptions formulated. The political dominance of this framework was assured with Labour's return to office in 1964. In this section, via a brief outline of Labour's policies, we want to extract the fundamental assumptions underlying those policies and subsequently, by looking at a key text, to see how those assumptions were articulated or submerged within the ideology.

On return to power Labour was committed to the abolition of the eleven-plus; the introduction of comprehensive reorganisation; the expansion of further and higher education; a massive increase in teacher training to reduce class sizes to 30; and the raising of the school leaving age. This was the "new" Labour dedicated to the eradication of the archaic hangovers which frustrated Britain's technological development.

The new government was there to lead, and to protect and advance the national interest. Nowhere was this more evident than in education; it introduced sweeping reforms and embarked on massive expansion plans. For the first time expenditure on education was to outstrip that on defence. Labour's commitment to make British capitalism work, and its meritocratic impulse, had increasingly identified education as the lever for social change, as against the redistributive policies of the pre-war period.

The 1960s was also characterised by educational consensus, as well as expansion. Apart from its general acceptance of the meritocratic argument, the Tory Party's policy on comprehensive education changed dramatically. Conservative spokesmen at both national and local levels increasingly recognised that the principle of early selection was no·longer viable, educationally or electorally. A grudging acceptance of the "good" comprehensive school crept into their speeches in the early 1960s, and by 1967 the approach of the 1958 White Paper *Secondary Education for All: A New Drive,* which had aimed at the vigorous development of secondary modern schools towards "parity of esteem" with grammar schools, became Heath's "it has never been a Conservative principle that in order to achieve (selection or grouping by ability) children have to be segregated in different institutions" (Jenkins 1973 p.131).

The parties still disagreed over the pace and details of comprehensive reorganisation, particularly in its effects on the status of independent and direct-grant grammar schools, but on most educational issues there was consensus. Even in 1970, a year after the publication of the first *Black Paper,* both Manifestos were fundamentally similar — more resources for nursery and primary education, raising the school leaving age to sixteen, expansion of further and higher education; — the only difference was Labour's commitment to legislate for compulsory comprehensive reorganisation and the Conservative pledge that local authorities would have the right to determine their own form of secondary schooling.

In summarising the practical policies of the Labour Party in power during the 1960s we can note that it postponed RSLA until 1972. It endorsed the Robbins Report (1963) and transformed the Colleges of Advanced Technology into universities. It issued a White Paper in 1966 establishing the binary system in higher education, whereby universities retained their independence and other sectors remained under the control of LEA's. Similarly, it created the new polytechnics and the Council for National Academic Awards, and expanded teacher training. As regards comprehensivisation it issued Circular 10/65, which initiated the phase of reorganisation, and set up inquiries into the status of public and direct-grant grammar schools. When Labour came to power there were 189 comprehensives in 39 authorities. By the time it was defeated in 1970 the number of comprehensives had risen to 1,300 educating 35% of children (though some existed alongside selective schools).

Finally, the development of pre-school education was encouraged, particularly after the publication of the Plowden Report in 1967. This Report also had implications for the schools, through its endorsement of progressive teaching methods and its suggested policy of positive discrimination. Its basic idea, the Educational Priority Area, indicated that policy should intervene in social inequalities. It designated areas where positive discrimination, in the form of better school facilities, more teachers, greater resources, etc., should be implemented. The Government responded with a £16m. programme.

The policies pursued by Labour in office can be seen as a response to certain "problems" impinging on the educational apparatus. Their status as "problems" is delivered by their effects on the "national interest". That is to say, there is an economic problem about the manpower requirements of the economy, and at the same time, a political and social problem about equal opportunities and the "realisation of individual potentialities". These problems are articulated as a concern with working-class failure in education.

Centrally, this "failure" is seen as socially determined — by the "cycle of deprivation" or the "culture of poverty" — and is considered amenable to social policy and educational approaches. Underpinning this assumption is a view of class which sees it as a combination of cultural and material deficiencies — the response is to compensate for the deficiencies, via the schools and social policy. However, the present educational structure is seen as irrelevant and in certain instances damaging — through streaming, selection, etc., — so it must be modernised, both in terms of relevancy and organisation. Crucially, the response to working-class failure is to change the structure of education and to provide more of it.

Thus, if working-class failure in education can be overcome through more resources, better teachers, a relevant curriculum, etc., and if at the same time a more educated labour force is a crucial determinant of our economic success, it is not only logical to call for more "investment" in education, but that redirection of resources becomes a moral and economic imperative. This logical process is underpinned by a view of education as self-evidently a "good" thing, a view which constantly displays itself as naive optimism:

> The Government believe that better educational provision can by compensating for the effects of social deprivation and the depressing physical environment in which many children grow up, make an important contribution to over-coming family poverty. Better education is the key to improved employment opportunities for young people in these districts and to enabling them to cope with the social stresses of a rapidly changing society. (Department of Education and Science 1967)

Now, when the explicit link between education and the economy is made, in terms of "investment", it necessarily opens up the content of education, to see "if it's doing its job". At the same time, report after report had stressed the need for a "relevant" education for the "average and below average" pupil, both to realise his individual potential and to dredge the "pool of ability". Also these reports, and political developments, created institutional areas within the schools requiring a new content, for example the "social" education side of the comprehensives, the CSE's, etc., However, these areas are not amenable to policy prescriptions, but fall within the expertise of the teaching profession.

Whilst curriculum innovation and research can be organised and disseminated, and "good practice" encouraged by the Inspectorate, in the final analysis what is taught in the classroom is, theoretically at least, the teacher's autonomous domain. A domain jealously guarded by the teachers' organisations, and extended by their control of the Schools Council and CSE's. Even the external examining bodies were under attack in this period. For example, the Labour Secretary of State, Edward

Short, in October 1969 referred to them as "a millstone round the necks of the schools" and hoped that before long people in education would apply themselves "to ridding our secondary schools of the tyranny of the examination" (Locke 1974 p.8).

Teacher autonomy was rarely questioned in the 1960s. Throughout the reports and policy documents it is assumed that given adequate facilities and training *teachers can do the job* — what happens in the school is their domain of expertise. Recommendations can be made and structures changed, but it is the teachers who *control* the implementation of these changes at the "chalk-face".

During this period the most influential body which articulated the relationship between the political problems about education and the changes necessary within education, via its reports, was the Minister of Education's Central Advisory Council, established under the 1944 Act. During the 1950s and 1960s the Council issued a series of influential reports which provided the rationale for major policy initiatives, such as RSLA, and provided guidelines enabling the schools to develop their internal responses to these changes. It was this body, according to Crosland, which documented "the good and the bad of the system and, in particular, legitimised the radical sociology of the 1950s and 1960s". (Kogan 1974 p.174). Fundamentally, these reports displayed those central assumptions which characterised the basic elements of the ideological convergence that was taking place during this period. We now wish to look at these assumptions as they are articulated in one particular report — the Newsom Report — the central importance of which has been indicated in an earlier section.

The Newsom Report, *Half Our Future,* was commissioned in 1961 to advise the Minister on the education of pupils aged 13 to 16 of average and less than average ability. The report itself adopts a problem-solving stance, though the problems to which it is addressed are never clearly spelt out. However, two central concerns do stand out. Primarily, "our children", as the report describes them, are seen to be bored, apathetic and rebellious in school, and this is seen to be a "bad" thing and damaging to the individual's personal potential. (It should be noted in this context that the late 1950s and the early 1960s witnessed a visible increase in delinquency rates, with their associated moral panics — the Teds, the Mods etc.) Furthermore, the demands of a rapidly expanding technological economy are seen to be creating the need, not only for skilled workers, but also for a much higher general level of skill in the average worker. Thus:

> the future pattern of employment in this country will require a much larger pool of talent than is at present available; . . . and at least a substantial proportion of the "average" and "below average" pupils are sufficiently educable to supply that additional talent. The need is not only for more skilled workers to fill existing jobs but also for a generally better educated and intelligently adaptable labour force to meet new demands. (1963 p.5)

Importantly, the solution to these problems is seen to reside in the schools,particularly as ability and attainment are now thought to be amenable to the initiatives and activities of social policy. The greatest barrier to "our children" in the schools is seen to lie in their inability to participate and communicate effectively, due to linguistic inadequacy and the schools' lack of relevance to their real needs:

> There is a gulf between those who have and the many who have not, sufficient command

178

of words to be able to listen and discuss rationally; to express ideas and feelings clearly; and even to have any ideas at all . . . . This is a matter as important to economic life as it is to personal living; industrial relations as well as marriages come to grief on failures in communications. (1963 p.15)

Thus a longer period in schools which have adequate resources, coupled with curricular and internal organisational changes, is necessary if "our children" are going to be able to develop their potential.

The writers of the report are not naive, in that they recognise that for most of "our children" the world of work will not offer them great opportunities for personal expression and realisation:

In any immediately foreseeable future large number of boys and girls who leave school will enter jobs which make as limited demands on them as Arthur Seaton's[2]: can their time in school help them to find more nourishment for the rest of their personal lives than loony-coloured phantasies? (1963 p.27)

To this question, they answer with an unqualified "yes". The schools must provide, not only instruction in the three Rs, but experiences which "will help them to develop their full capacities for thought and taste and feeling". So, on one level, the schools will provide curricular relevance, through work-experience, craft training, domestic science, etc., yet on another level, they must also provide a social education which will help "our children":

to develop a sense of responsibility for their work and towards other people, and to begin to arrive at some code of moral and social behaviour which is self-imposed. It is important that they should have some understanding of the physical world and of the human society in which they are growing up. (1963 p.27)

We can see, then, that the report is concerned with the social and economic role of the working class. Though class is submerged in euphemisms such as "socially deprived", "disadvantaged", etc., the report acknowledges that "five out of six are likely to be children of manual workers, skilled or unskilled". Throughout, the report displays a consuming concern with control — to stop the pupils being bored and rebellious, education must be relevant, to stop workers having "loony-coloured phantasies" in dead-end,repetitive jobs, they must have outside cultural/social interests which compensate for job deprivations, and so on. Though couched in the language of equal opportunities, its policy prescriptions reinforce status and economic hierarchies. Indeed, its very title *Half Our Future,* reifies those educationally created categories which differentiate between "those who work with their heads" and "those with their hands". It is the future work situation which is the determining factor — it is the natural and unproblematic needs of the labour market which structure the suggested educational reforms.

To achieve these objectives the report argues that we need to invest more money in education and that the teachers who deal with "our children" need a more appropriate training coupled with an improved financial and social status. Not surprisingly, these teachers, during their training, "should have some introduction to sociological study . . . in order that they may put their own job into social perspective and be better prepared to understand the difficulties of pupils in certain types of areas" (1963 p.103). The value of this perspective was no doubt underlined by the nature

179

of the evidence supplied to the committee by people such as Jean Floud, Brian Jackson and Basil Bernstein. Throughout the report there is an implicit reliance on the professional expertise of teachers. Whilst it is legitimate to suggest both improvements in training and curricular materials, the ability of the teachers to carry out the work suggested is never questioned.

So the assumptions — that education is a "good" thing, that we need to "invest" more, that the teachers can do the "job" with the right materials, that intelligence is amenable to policy initiatives, and so on — provide the ideological framework of the report. Contradictions are neatly resolved, or do not surface. Opposed class interests are collapsed into an inability to communicate. So:

> Given the opportunities we have no doubt that they ("our children) will rise to the challenge which a rapidly developing economy offers no less to them than to their abler brothers and sisters. But there is no time to waste. Half our future is in their hands. We must see that it is in good hands. (1963 p.xiv).

V Critique

From time to time through this essay we have noted assumptions that have underpinned the prescriptions of "experts" and politicians. These assumptions have been surprisingly constant within the social democratic tradition. We wish, in this section, to recapitulate the more deep-rooted presuppositions and to establish a critique of them. We shall argue that social democratic ideology attempts to reconcile contradictory goals, poses objectives that cannot be realised by the means that are proposed, and fails in its political purposes — the mobilisation of popular support. This analysis of "theoretical" or intrinsic inadequacies will be followed, in Section VI, by a practical demonstration of the current weakness of social-democratic positions. For the "education crisis" is in large part a crisis *of* social democracy, in which the ideological initiative has passed to rivals.

Recapitulation: The Dual Repertoire

Social-democratic ideology is a *complex formation*. Much of this complexity arises, as we have seen, from the heterogeneity of its supports in a particular social coalition and political alliance. But the ideology has been complex in another sense: it has revolved around a persistent *duality of ideas* which, we will argue, has been rooted less in any direct social basis than in the external and internal relations of the Labour Party as an organisation. This duality is by no means limited to the educational region of Labour's ideology — it spans the whole range of its political discourse — but is particularly evident there.

Labour's educational rhetoric has always moved, as we noted at the start, between two poles. These poles may (in a convenient and familiar shorthand) be dubbed those of "equality" and "equality of opportunity". The demand for "equality" has been essentially social and cultural in nature, a demand for "community", for the equalisation of conditions, for the forging of a "common culture". Equality has been valued because it is a source of cohesion; inequality opposed because of its divisiveness. Such notions have their ultimate point of reference in a social organicism shared with more conservative philosophies and they have been carried in

180

England typically in the culture-and-society tradition. "Equality of opportunity", by contrast, is best understood as an economic goal, based on the conception of education as a "good" which ought to be more fairly shared, the use and consumption of which has pertinent economic effects. The ultimate point of reference for this series of notions has been an essentially liberal conception of society as a market, within which individuals compete. The point, according to this "philosophy", is to enable them to compete more fairly.

For both positions, then, "class" is a problem. But it is a problem in different ways. For egalitarians it is a problem because it creates social conflict, envy and domination. For "Fabians" (we use the term in the most general sense) it represents a range of artificial restrictions on the acquisition of skills or the employment of talent. For both positions, likewise, education is a very important means to reformation, but is somewhat differently envisaged. Egalitarians stress acculturation and the absorption of democratic values; Fabians stress skills, especially "useful" ones. In matters of "scaffolding" too, there are differences of emphasis between those who see limited resources as the only bar to universal provision (the egalitarian position) and those who see selection as necessary, while hoping it can be made more flexible and fair. In general egalitarians view education as a "right" co-extensive with citizenship or "humanity", in general Fabians view its distribution as ultimately, a matter of utility. The two poles may, in summary, be presented as follows:

Egalitarians	*Fabians*
"equality"	"equality of opportunity"
social/cultural goals	economic goals
class as division	class as inhibition
education as attitudes	education as skill
rights	utility
social order or "community"	market or "efficiency"

It is possible to cite relatively pure examples of both positions, especially in the early history of the repertoire. As we have seen, Tawney, in his general moral stance, if not always in his detailed proposals, personified educational egalitarianism. Sidney Webb personified Fabian "capacity-catching" and a unity (of a rather modern kind) of "national efficiency" and meritocratic arguments. The distinction is also inherent in more recent debates. Defenders of "community schooling" or of de-streamed comprehensives, for example, may be counted egalitarians (Jackson 1970, Midwinter 1972); defenders of streaming or, in another sphere, of the binary system and the "new polytechnics", may be deemed out-and-out Fabians (e.g. Robinson 1968). Much more typically, however, and especially among the politicians, the two strands have been combined and even conflated. To Crosland, for instance, comprehensives are necessary to remove the waste of talent revealed by Robbins and Crowther *and* "to increase the sense of social cohesion in contemporary British society" (1974 p. 206). But Sir Harold Wilson supplies us, as usual, with the classic instance of Labour's dualism, speaking to the party faithful in the run-up to the 1964 election:

we cannot afford to force segregation on our children at the 11+ stage. As socialists, as democrats, we oppose this system of educational apartheid, because we believe in equality of opportunity. But that is not all. We simply cannot as a nation afford to neglect the educational development of a single boy or girl. We cannot afford to cut off three quarters or more of our children from virtually any chance of higher education. The Russians do not, the Germans do not, and the Japanese do not, and we cannot afford to either.

The movement of the argument is typical: first the "gut" appeal to the party's egalitarianism (*"segregation"*, *"our* children", "educational *apartheid"*); then the invocation of WHERE WE STAND "as socialists" (and in case this is a bit too strong for all present, as "democrats" too); finally, the slide, through "equality of opportunity" with its fundamental ambiguity, into the most obvious of "national efficiency" arguments.

The interest in the analysis of this repertoire lies, then, more in its internal *relations* than in the disappearance of whole components. One such change has already been noted: the shift to dominance of "equality of opportunity" after the War, together with a more markedly economic or technocratic inflection within this complex itself. But even at the height of Labour's enthusiasm for "modernisation" the egalitarian rhetoric (as the quotes from Crosland and Wilson show) was not abandoned.

Politically, indeed, the co-existence of the elements has been of crucial importance. The party's egalitarianism has "spoken" to rank-and-file socialists who constitute its most active workers and, more residually perhaps, to working-class parents. Its retention has much to do with the party's need for a popular base and its reliance on trade unionism. Labour's Fabianism, on the other hand, reflects quite directly the party's structural and historical commitment to managing and reforming a capitalist society. This involves securing, through appropriate social and educational policies, a really progressive capitalist adaptation. The chance or reality of office and the inescapable exigencies of governing within the structures of an untransformed capitalist State have rendered this part of the repertoire dominant. In this way, social democratic ideology in education is very much an expression not of working-class educational "demands" (itself a wholly problematic concept), nor of a pure capital logic or interest (an even more problematic idea), but of the particular place of the Labour Party in British society and politics.

Critique I: The Elements Are Contradictory

It is a commonplace of social philosophy that the two kinds of equality represent different positions and point to contradictory outcomes. In *Equality*, Tawney identified equality of opportunity as a fundamentally bourgeois creed, born in the struggles with the *ancien régime*, particularly over legal privileges. His dismissal of its relevance to more popular needs stands as a classic and ought to be quoted:

Slavery did not become tolerable because some slaves were manumitted and became slave-owners in their turn; nor, even if it were possible for the units composing a society to be periodically reshuffled, would that make it a matter of indifference that some among them at any moment should be condemned to frustration while others were cosseted. What matters to a nation is not merely the composition and origins of its different groups, but their opportunities and circumstances. It is the powers and advantages which different classes in practice enjoy, not the social antecedents of the varying individuals by whom they happen, from time to time, to be acquired. Till such powers and advantages have been equalized in fact, not merely in form, by the extension of communal provision and collective control, the equality established by the removal of restrictions on property and enterprise resembles that produced by turning an elephant loose in a crowd. It offers everyone, except the beast and his rider, equal opportunities of being trampled to death. Caste is deposed, but class succeeds to the vacant throne. (1964, p. 111)

An an invocation of an historical transition, and for the moral security of its humanism, this is superb. But long after the publication of *Equality* in 1931 (and despite frequent official recapitulations of Tawney's truths), Labour Party leadership has continued to combine "bourgeois" attacks on "privilege" with the more "socialist" conceptions which, rightly, Tawney saw as incompatible with them. Whatever the slips and slides of language, there is a real, substantial and irreducible difference between the two conceptions. Equality challenges (however futilely in practice) the distribution of "powers" and "advantages" which divide classes, while "equality of opportunity", though it may be pressed toward equality in practice, is concerned merely with the occupancy of class places.

Politically, Labour's ideological mix was quite successful. In retrospect, however, it is easy to see that this success rested on historically specific conditions, Some of the relevant contingencies were quite apparent, acknowledged within the ideology itself. It was overtly part of social-democratic ideology, part of the bargain struck with "the people", that a faster rate of "economic growth" was necessary in order to pay, as the saying went, for "more hospitals and schools". In other words the strategy of educational expansion and of "equalising" social policies in general was dependent upon economic success, the success, that is, of a basically capitalist economy. Yet, as we have already noted, by the mid-1960s the inverse relation was also assumed. The expansion and equalisation of education would make a tremendous contribution to economic success. It would cure the "waste of talent" and remove "the scarcity of skills". At the same time it would secure something that was important for its own sake — a greater social justice. We may recall, once more, Crosland's formulations of 1966:

But there is also . . . a wider social waste involved. If ever there was a country which needed to make the most of its resources, it is Britain in the second half of the twentieth century; and the chief resource of a crowded island is its people. Moreover the proportion of relatively inexpert and unskilled jobs to be done declines from year to year. To believe in these circumstances as though there was a fixed 25 per cent of top ability at eleven not only flies in the face of the evidence which I have quoted; it amounts to feckless prodigality. (1974 p.200)

Before examining these assumptions more closely, we ought to note the absolute centrality of Crosland's argument about "skill". The notion that late capitalism required, generally and not merely for its elites, a wider diffusion of "skill", and that the education system could supply it, was completely taken for granted. Moreover this assumption held together all the main elements in the repertoire. First, it provided a thoroughly hard-headed and vulgar-materialist justification for equalising policies — ending or mitigating selection, comprehensivisation and even the EPAs. Without this, the charge that such policies were "doctrinaire" and even "socialist" was liable to stick. Secondly, it reconciled the inevitable tension between the characteristic humanist/ideology of educational practitioners — the importance of doing your best for the personal development of each individual child — and the world of work afterwards. For educators were informed (whatever their more direct experience might suggest) that there would always be plenty of up-skilled and interesting jobs for their pupils to enter. Thirdly, since the form of the relation of school to production was left extremely vague, teachers could conscientiously fill the empty spaces with stimulating and relevant activities, reassured by a sense of their usefulness, even though their pupils might appear inexplicably uninterested in what was on offer. Finally, the education — growth combination fitted perfectly the kind of alliance which the Labour leadership in this phase sought to build: workers, especially those in the newer technologies, petit-bourgeois professionals like the teachers, and the more progressive, modernising sections of management and national capital.

In fact, as events have shown, educational expansion which is egalitarian in form and more or less indiscriminate in content is by no means self-evidently beneficial to capital. Labour's recent *volte-face* marks a recognition of this. It is now easy to criticise the older view, but it is much more difficult to establish some alternative conception of this important set of relations. What is involved is not merely the substantiation of a critique of social democracy, but the development of a whole theory about the post-war movement of capital and its relation to educational expansion. We offer here a few pertinent points.

First, the 1960s argument was based on a limited, reductive and largely unexamined concept — "skill". As Ted Benton (1974) has noted in an excellent critique of social democracy, the 1960s saw a heavy emphasis on "technical development" and, in effect, upon a technological determinism. Just as the general economic problem was analysed in terms of the need for progress in technique, so occupational roles were narrowed to "skill" or "technical knowledge". While we doubt whether in the 1960s the "technological ideology" was as pervasive within education as Benton argues (it seems to us a good deal stronger in the 1970s), its effect was undoubtedly to mystify the whole relation of school to production and to hide altogether, at this moment of analysis, the relation of school to the social relations of production. As Benton argues, drawing on Althusser, the reduction to "skill" neglected "the crucial ideological training for the place that the student is to occupy in the structure of power and authority relations which is woven into the occupational structure" (1974 p.25). If we are to think the school-production relation more complexly, it is probable that the category "skill" will have to be abandoned altogether in favour of more precise categories: technical knowledge, ideology and control. The everyday inventiveness of "awkward" children in a classroom is, after all, quite as much a "skill" as the ability to read.

What is true of learning "skills" is true also of their exercise. "Skilled", "unskilled" and "semi-skilled" are among the least precise categories of industrial sociology. Again other concepts are necessary that stress the extent of the workers' or capitalists' control of the labour process or the extent to which the conception and execution of tasks are divorced. Using Marx's categories, Harry Braverman (1974) has argued, with great power, that post-war capitalism in the USA has seen a tendential process of de-skilling, an increasing dependence of labour on managerial control and a more complete division, even within the "mental" side of labour, of conception and execution. The logic of such

184

a process is systematically to lower the educational requirements of the mass of occupations, including many white-collar jobs. More detailed studies will probably reveal
an altogether more complex and uneven picture — skills recomposed as well as destroyed
— yet the general tendency which Braverman describes seems at present altogether more
plausible than the sociological orthodoxies of which he disposes.

We may conclude that the assumption of an unproblematic complementarity between
educational expansion (in its 1960s forms) and economic growth was almost certainly
incorrect. It seems quite as likely that the 1960s was a period of the marked autonomy
of the educational system. The ultimate determinations from the movements of capital
and from the forms of class struggle remain to be examined. But it is clear that they
worked in altogether more mediated and subterranean ways than the determination
through the need for and evocation of "skills". In the early 1970s, by contrast, a
strenuous work began of returning to a closer conformity between the educational
system and the necessities of production.

Critique II: The Objectives Cannot be Realised

We insist here on the utopianism of the social-democratic position, especially of its
egalitarianism. This is best considered through the notions of "class" which inform
equalising strategies and party rhetoric. Without these conceptions, "equality" cannot be thought at all.

For social democracy, class *is in*equality. It is inequality, especially of culture and of
social condition. Its economic content is reducible to income or, at best, the reductive
view of "occupation". But the economic criteria are usually limited to the sphere of
circulation.

Class, then, is an essentially distributive term. It follows that one can have more or
less of it and that it is meaningful to speak, with Crosland, of "the *distribution* of
wealth, power, and *class status*" or even of " a *more* classless society" (1974, p.107,
our emphasis). It follows that class is removable. In some versions indeed it dissolves at
the sociologist's touch, in a scatter of variables, emerging only in social work euphemisms
like "deprivation", "social handicap" or "disadvantage". In the more culturalist
versions, educational solutions may suffice. In the post-war social policy mainstream,
concerted attacks on cultural and material deprivations (which always assume the in-
feriority of the "sufferer") are envisaged, the strategy implying the possibility of an
ultimate success or at least "a more classless society". Sometimes, "class" is not merely
removable, but actually archaic and residual, a passive reminder from the past.

As in the case of "equality" there are several, sometimes contradictory, conceptions
here. No full anatomy can be attempted. We merely note, speculatively, four main
tendencies: the more technical, sociological conceptions we have already described; the
liberal attack on privilege ("class" as it is used in the public-school debate for instance);
the anti-industrial (and hence anti-class) organicism of the culture-and-society tradition;
and barely visible under all this, the relatively spontaneous, grass-roots egalitarianism
of working-class culture, especially of the culture of work. All these traditions, except
perhaps the last, while acknowledging "class" as important, emasculate it severely, or
render it rather ephemeral. Thus when "divisions" repeatedly re-appear (even after
their end has been celebrated), explanations seem quite inadequate. In the absence of
anything better, stress is sometimes laid on amazingly persistent national traits. As

185

Crosland put it (1974, p.44) "British Society -— slow-moving, rigid and class-ridden has proved much harder to change than was supposed". In the same way, it is hard to explain, within the built-in optimism of the social-democratic framework, why compensatory policies fail to remove the inequalities which are diagnosed. As Marx said of the French social democrats of the mid-ninteenth-century: "No party exaggerates the means at its disposal more than the democratic party; no party deludes itself more frivolously about the situation" (1973 p.176).

It is always open for social reformers to plead for another trial. But it is possible that in modern Britain this particular repertoire is exhausted. It has moved all the way from "secondary schools for all" to Priority Areas and 'Action Research', the latter a kind of agitational community politics actually displaced, in an extraordinary manner, into the State apparatus itself! As the current fate of Community Development Projects suggests, action research represents the outer limit of social policy solutions — the point where they start to change into something else, *and have therefore to be stopped.*

In fact British socialists have repeatedly rejected or ignored some of the categories which might really illuminate their dilemmas. Both Tawney's socialism and Crosland's revisionism, the latter quite explicitly, were constructed as answers to (a kind of) Marxism. Crosland's work is full of attacks on "Marxists" and the "New Left". But what if class in capitalist society is neither residual, nor passive, nor removable but an ever-present source of transformations? What if classes are intrinsic to the production of material life itself? What if they are systematically and daily reproduced as part of the organic workings of the society along with their concomitant inequalities? What, in short, if class is rooted in social relatións of production, a category which is quite invisible in social democratic ideology? From the stand-point of such a conception of the social formation the futility of social policy can be fully grasped. It can deal with no more than occasional symptoms which must constantly re-appear and must serve to hide what lies beneath them. More absurd still must be the attempt to "equalise" through an education which is supposed also to serve to reproduce relations within capitalist production.

Critique III: The Policies Must Fail

Initially, so we have argued, Labour's commitment to educational expansion was attuned to organised working-class demands and, to some extent, to parental aspirations. Latterly, expansion was argued for, among other things, as responding to the interests and "needs" of ordinary parents and children. Yet there has been little sign since 1944 of large-scale popular support for comprehensivisation or any other aspect of Labour policy. Parents have usually been indifferent; their children have actually resisted the effects of policy, as the school counter-cultures and opposition to RSLA suggests.

If we recall the argument at the beginning of this essay this apparent paradox need not surprise us. Nor need we invoke some notion of the natural apathy of working-class parents to an education of any kind. The fact is that the Labour Party has never sought to educate the popular classes from within, but has sought access to the state to educate them from there. But this state is not the neutral "machinery" which Social Democracy takes it to be: it systematically transforms the political demands

186

that are made on it on behalf of subordinate classes. What is claimed "as of right", returns in unrecognisable forms. Of this process education is the best example. In a general sense, pressure for the extension of social rights and for greater "equality" has fuelled the long-term growth of the state system. But in practice this process has been inflected and given its content by specific features of the state in the educational region. The key features have been the structural separation of the schools from other kinds of learning and their tendency to monopolise the whole notion of education; the professionalisation of the teachers and their pursuit of sectional interest within the apparatus; and, above all, the structural necessity for educational policy-makers and administrators to take account of capital's interests. So it happens that, as in production so in school, a nature-imposed necessity — to learn — is experienced as something quite alien. School becomes, moreover the site of class struggle. The divisions of parent, teacher and child, barely disguised antagonisms, are intrinsic to the apparatus itself. The general tendency of Labour's policy in concert with the teachers, moreover, has been to exalt the "experts" of the region over the mere parent and to devalue the common sense of the parental culture. The social reforming tendency in the party's ideology does this in an absolutely insulting way, scarcely compensated for by a romantic opposition (Bernstein 1973, Rosen 1973). At the same time progressivism has rendered schooling more and more esoteric. In this way, Labour's whole educating stance, not only vacating the ground of agitation, but actually sponsoring new forms of oppression, has opened up massive opportunities for a demagogic, anti-bureaucratic, anti-statist Toryism.

VI The Crisis

In the preceding sections we have offered an account and critique of the salient features of social democratic educational ideology in the 1960s. In doing this we have sought to point out the inherent theoretical weakness of the social democratic perspective, and its ramifications in educational policy. In this section we therefore wish to address ourselves to the nature and form of the current "crisis", in the light of the analysis already offered. When we speak of a crisis we are referring to more than the individual experiences of those in education, to which we alluded in the introduction, though this subjective dimension is important. The crisis of the educational sector is bound up with the overall crisis of the economy and the State. But while we recognise that the specific form of the educational crisis has its determinations in the general crisis, we must insist that the educational crisis is *also* a regional one. It is a crisis which is not simply reducible to financial retrenchment or the breakdown of a consensus, but which must be examined in terms of its own social base and the coalition which gave rise to it.

Social Democracy and its Enemies

Recently the assumptions which underpinned Labour's educational programme have been increasingly attacked, from both inside and outside the Party. Our awareness of this has been greater during the least year because of the increased intensity of that critique, and Callaghan's speech has formally signalled a sort of "open season" on educational issues — intended to further the overall policy shift already in motion. But Callaghan's sentiments were not original for Labour politicians, even if his tone was.

187

During 1969, for example, suggestions that tighter controls on teachers might be forthcoming were made to curb an increasingly militant teaching force. Edward Short addressing the 1969 NAS Conference, referred to the adoption by teachers of trade union modes of struggle, and pointed out that this could involve unpalatable consequences for them:

> Do we really want a rule book which will lay down the minutiae of how the teacher is to do his job? Let me assure you that you are within weeks of considerable pressure to introduce one. . . once begun the process might be difficult to halt and impossible to reverse. (Burke 1971 p.49)

Later in the same year Harold Wilson pointed out the curiously exposed nature of teachers' work and the vulnerability of their situation — an implied warning that should "professional" standards be eschewed in favour of traditional methods of wages struggle, then public opinion could easily be mobilised against them.

Callaghan's speech shows how far the Labour leadership has moved from the "velvet glove" approach. Instead of the advice and "persuasion" offered to teachers in the late 1960s, the choice is now for a much more robust challenge. Though this shift does have an immediate political character, in making a pre-emptive move to wrest the initiative away from the Tories, the underlying change is contingent on a series of other developments. These are essentially concerned with the systematic challenge to the assumptions of the previous educational programme — a challenge which has developed since 1969.

We can see that the assumptions which gave rise to the Newsom Report, discussed earlier, have been found wanting, and therefore the institutional forms which they gave rise to have come under attack. Thus, from viewing the schools as *the* means of solving a problem, namely working-class failure and its attendant economic and cultural consequences, the emphasis is now one which charges the schools with failing to do this, despite the resources which have been invested.

Concretely the shift has been marked by a series of educational "events" which have been identified against a background of dissensus. Through the period of the Tory government, and the industrial struggles which marked it, but also during the late 1960s, the Right came to identify education as an important causal factor in the "moral crisis" of the period. The *Black Paper* of 1969 was able to identify the subversive effects of egalitarianism in the ruptures of 1968/69, while the associated moral panics of the period around the issue of "youth" all served to reduce the causal base to the institutional framework of education. It is in this context that educational events have been publicly defined.

The allegations of a decline in reading standards in ILEA schools between 1968 and 1971 touched an exposed nerve — because of the emotive connotations of reading as perhaps *the* raison d'être of schooling. Thus when Start and Wells had their findings published by the National Foundation for Educational Research in 1972, Thatcher was able to exploit the ensuing controversy by setting up the Bullock Report (1975) into the whole question of literacy, its assessment and control. More recently, in the wake of Bullock's findings, the focus on schools has been accentuated by the events at William Tyndale and by the reception accorded Bennett's report on teaching methods (1976). Continued failure of working-class children, and the apparent lack of impact of the compensatory programme, have all validated the charges that the

188

internal organisation of the school, and specifically the teachers, are at fault.

The culpability of schools, in facilitating educational failure rather than success, has been a central theme in the *Black Papers* since 1969. Their equation of progressivism as a method with anarchism and moral disintegration as consequences, has been coupled to a general critique of declining standards in higher education, this latter phenomenon being reduced to the nature of the post-Robbins expansion. In the 1975 *Black Paper,* marked by the emergence of Boyson as co-editor, this analysis was given a programmatic political dimension. A much more populist line was espoused, parental involvement in the work of schools becoming a basic tenet of the programme. Legitimacy for the *Black Paper* positions was no longer sought solely through explicit and rather academic discussions of the political and philosophical issues, but rather through criteria of parental approval for the work schools were seen to be doing. Thus popular definitions of the purpose of education and of the most appropriate teaching methods, were invoked against the alleged orthodoxy of progressivism, as practised by teachers owing responsibility to no one outside the school. The call was therefore for "public accountability".

One aspect of the Right's offensive was the re-emergence of the 'nature/nurture' debate, having been fostered in the pages of the *Black Papers* by Cyril Burt, and further promoted by Eysenck, Jensen and others in the educational area. Significantly, this element has not entered into popular conservatism, though it does provide an alternative explanation for the failure of social democratic education policies. Its reappearance in the USA was precisely in this context.

While the political Right had been developing its own ideological initiative, a critique of a different order had acquired a currency within the sociology of education. The emergence of the "New Sociology" (Young 1971), with its emphasis on epistemological questions, and its rejection of positivistic assumptions which underpinned much previous work in the sociology of education, challenged the hegemony of those assumptions which were so important in the social democratic/sociology of education coalition. Instead of providing the "scientific" and theoretical rationale for the specific forms of expansion adopted, such as comprehensivisation, the new sociology argued that such policy shifts did not fundamentally alter the previous situation. The performance of working-class children had not improved dramatically, and the reasons for this lack of success should be sought in the specific political location of schooling. The implication was, therefore, that remedial action could not simply be enacted by policy prescription. Consequently the logical continuity between sociological research findings and overall policy development, so central to the main thrust of social democratic expansion in education, was lost. The new sociology, itself, had no clear policy implications; if anything it pointed to variants of de-schooling.

The subsequent emergence of Marxist and neo-Marxist critiques of this position, and of social democratic perspectives, have in turn further removed sociology from the persisting assumptions of social democracy, and from any immediate political articulation with the Labour Party. While the expansion of the 1960s was seen as offering qualitative change through quantitative provision, the evidence emerging in the 1970s was that this qualitative change had not in fact occurred. The conclusion seemed inescapable that "equality of opportunity", even if accepted in principle, could not be secured by institutional arrangements, universal access or compensatory programmes.

The Significance of Bullock

The disintegration of the sociology/social policy coalition can be concretely identified in the official policy formation process. The Bullock Report, (1975) a report as symptomatic of the 1970s as Newsom was of the 1960s, was concerned with the fundamental issues of language development and educational achievement. It relied on the old repertoire of compensatory theory so generative in the Plowden Report. Conceptual innovation was, however, replaced by a much harder set of policy proposals for the implementation of the old theory. The suggested programme of intervention assumed that the causal chain of educational failure could be traced back to the pre-linguistic stage of child development, specifically to the ante-natal social environment of "the home". The appropriate remedial action was seen to take the form of systematic intervention in the home environments of the target population, that is, the homes of unskilled manual workers in the Educational Priority Areas. The purpose of this intervention was to restructure the early linguistic environment of those infants who were "at risk" Such a programme would have required a considerable expansion in the number of visitors and counsellors, and would have amounted to the *reductio ad absurdum* of a "compensatory education for the foetus".

Despite the revival of genetic explanations of inequality, Bullock maintained its commitment to compensatory education, but at the same time it explored the contemporary educational determinations of failure. In this respect teachers were identified as the crucial variable, whose skill in teaching could offer the possibility of longer-term success for children otherwise handicapped by environmental factors. The report noted that because of the predominance of progressive teaching methods, and the inexperience of many young teachers, considerable confusion existed about the most effective teaching methods. This situation could best be resolved through the development of teaching schemes, at the level of the school, but the report also proposed the desirability for regular, national, monitoring of standards of attainment in schools. The assumption, so apparent in these proposals, was that the competence of teachers could no longer be automatically relied on. Teaching was basically too important to be left to the teachers.

In this last respect the report is a signal one, providing legitimate strategies for intervention within the home and within the school. It is therefore surprising that the reception accorded to Bullock, by both the national and professional press, failed to seize on the longer-term implications of the report's recommendations. The main discussion revolved around the contentious issue of whether standards had fallen, while the expansionist aspects of the recommendations were generally welcomed — especially by the NUT. However, it was clear from Prentice's remarks in accepting the report that in the context of financial retrenchment the major proposals were inoperable because of the prohibitive costs involved (£100m. according to the NUT). Although the analysis of teacher failure and the proposals for assessment and monitoring were to prove perfectly suited to a situation where efficient control of public spending had become a major issue, at the time of publication they were referred to the Assessment of Performance Unit at the DES, the significance of which was only later to emerge. Callaghan's critique, two years later, was clearly informed by Bullock's analysis and internal DES responses to the "public panics" around Tyndale and other *causes célèbres*.

In giving concrete expression to efforts directed at restricting teacher autonomy, Callaghan was able indirectly to invoke Bullock to lend legitimacy to his proposals. This is not to suggest that this was the purpose or the intention of its authors, but their work made available the detail for a political campaign. The report was appropriated selectively, rather as Robert Lowe once appropriated the report of the New-castle Commission in support of the Revised Code of 1862.

The DES and the "Great Debate"

We have now seen how the hegemony of the Labour Party, teachers and educationalists collapsed in the 1970s. The economic crisis undercut its first premise that an expansive capitalism would supply the means. At the same time an extraordinarily successful and (in its own terms) accurate Tory critique, forced Labour's leadership to shift its ground. It became obvious, too, that social democratic solutions had almost reached their necessary limits, or now involved, as in the case of Bullock's proposals, a quite disproportionate expenditure. Within the sociology of education, the dominance of what had once been a "radical" tradition was ended by still "Newer" sociologies, and by a revived Marxism, always social democracy's hidden antagonist.

The collapse of these orthodoxies posed acute political problems for the Labour Government, whose general political position was in any case quite perilous. What was to replace the old hegemony? Some new inflection had to be given to the social democratic ideology; some new combination of elements or some drastic simplification. Similarly there was a need for new (or refurbished) agencies of control, to steer the whole system onto a new tack. The key solutions were, in fact, a reassertion of control from the DES and the ideological work of the Williams—Callaghan "Great Debate".

In a general sense the events of the 1960s had seen the DES taking a back seat to the teachers when it came to taking specific initiatives *within* schools. For example when the Curriculum Studies Group was established in 1962 by the Ministry of Education, to examine the question of curriculum organisation and reform, it was strenuously opposed by the teachers' organisations. The major result was the abandonment of the CSG and the establishment of the Schools Council. The subsequent development of CSE courses from 1965 onwards, and the implementation of the Mode 3 (teacher assessed) schemes in 1970, were further pointers to the shift away from external controls, towards regulation originating within schools. The final stage of this development was seen in the reception of the 16-plus examination proposals, which if accepted would have given almost total control of the curriculum to the teachers. The response to this proposal tended to crystallize the various concerns about teacher autonomy, and the extent to which teachers should be in control, as opposed to being merely the functionaries at the "chalk face".

In the "Yellow Book" of 1976, prepared by the DES on Callaghan's instructions, teacher control is the major issue, especially the domination of teachers' interests on the Schools Council. The success of the Schools Council in its development of curriculum projects, and its initiation of reform through non-statutory means, has syste-

191

matically eroded the influence of external agencies — the DES and the Examining Boards. Moves to re-establish external control have been fuelled by the Auld Report into William Tyndale. This report precisely addressed the problem of teacher autonomy, arguing that without clear guidelines the Inspectorate is ineffective and cannot fulfill its function of maintaining "proper standards" in schools. These proposals have already been taken up in London, where there has also been a considerable increase in the size of the Inspectorate's establishment. Thus the role of the DES and the Inspectorate has been systematically highlighted as a centre of "sanity" and arbiter of standards, checking the excesses of the teachers.

Callaghan's intervention into the debate was, as we mentioned earlier, a carefully managed media "event". Having assumed Boyson's populist mantle for the occasion, he was able to set the "legitimate" concerns of the parents against the actual organisation of the school and its relative inaccessability to them. The proposals for a "core curriculum", a necessary precondition for any national comparison of "standards", were presented as equalising conditions, serving the interests of both parents and children, and in the process the political and economic strategy of the state. It is clear that in initiating the "Great Debate" on educational issues, the Prime Minister was also concerned with the wider cultivation of political consent. However, in the Regional Conferences subsequently announced, the initial implication that the debate might be an exercise in participatory democracy was reinterpreted somewhat — only 200 guests and the press being invited. Likewise, the conference agendas, concerned as they were with the curriculum, assessment, teacher training and the relationship between schooling and life, addressed issues which have been developed as *of* concern to parents, but which do not necessitate parental involvement to resolve them.[3] It is implicitly assumed that the "interests" of parents are represented through the rational organisation, by the State, of the school/work transition, and the matching of the appropriate skills to the requirements of the labour market.

The main ideological shifts contained in the "Great Debate" are the retention and further stress, now in more precise forms, of the education-equals-growth arguments; the attempt to cover the major weakness over parental involvement and the almost total disappearance of the Labour Party's egalitarianism. Callaghan's targets — the teachers and their autonomy — have proved incapable of making any coherent response, beyond economic struggle and calls for opposition to any formalisation of central control of curriculum. The National Association of Schoolmasters has even colluded with calls for greater accountability, in order to establish its members' professional competences, if only in opposition to the alleged dillettantism of the typical NUT member. Similarly, the generally conservative stance of the NAS/UWT against progressive methods, and their hostility to any radical educational content, has facilitated an expedient alliance between them and the Labour Party's new strategy. This weakness in the teachers' organisations is exemplified by the Schools Council's ready acceptance of the need to reform its own structure, in the light of the Callaghan critique.

The "Great Debate" has revealed the *metaphorical character* of education. Education, the universal, unifying experience, has become the vehicle, par excellence, for the exploration of wider social questions. The relationship of education to the economy, the relationship of the individual's development to the "national interest", captures other themes which are currently part of the political discourse. The bidding for

192

consent, the forging of a new hegemony on the basis of a corporate capitalism, can be seen through the educational debate. Central to both are themes of discipline, and the subordination of the individual to the collective interest. The collective interest is now defined, however, less in Labour's old terms of a "more equal society", but more in terms of the survival of a capitalist economy.

1. It is acknowledged that we do not supply an adequate explanation in fully Marxist terms of the post-war expansion of the educational system. This is an important absence to which further work will be addressed. We would note that our object here is primarily a study of educational ideologies, not the educational expansion as such. So far as the larger process is concerned, we reject simplistic explanations of the type, for instance, which reduce the phenomena in question to the effects of a one-dimensional tendency in the economic base. eg. de-skilling.
2. The Sillitoe reference comes from the introduction to Chapter 4 of the Report which is introduced with the following quotation from *Saturday Night and Sunday Morning:* "If your machine was working well . . . you went off into pipe-dreams for the rest of day. . . You lived in a compatible world of pictures which passed through your mind like a magic lantern often in vivid and glorious loony-colour." (p.27)
3. The involvement of parents in school government is being considered, among other things, by the Taylor Committee, which is due to present its report to the Secretary of State during the latter part of 1977. This will be rather too late to give parents a voice in "the Great Debate".

Bibliography

Althusser, L. 1971 "Ideology and Ideological State Apparatuses" in *Lenin & Philosophy* (New Left Books)

Anderson, P.1964 "Origins of the Present Crisis", *New Left Review, 23*

Barker, R. 1972 *Education and Politics 1900-51 A Study of the Labour Party* (OUP)

Bennett, N. 1976 *Teaching Styles and Pupil Progress* (Open Books)

Benton, T. 1974 'Education and Politics' in D. Holly (ed.), *Education or Domination* (Arrow)

Bernbaum, G. 1967 *Social Change and the Schools, 1918-1944* (RKP)

Bernstein, B. 1973 *Class, Codes and Control* (Paladin)

Board of Education, 1943 *Report of the Departmental Committee on Curriculum and Examinations in Secondary Schools* (Norwood) (HMSO)

Board of Education, 1933 *Report of the Consultative Committee on Infant and Nursery Schools* (Hadow) (HMSO)

Burke, V. 1971 *Teachers in Turmoil* (Penguin)

Braverman, H. 1974 *Labor & Monopoly Capital* (Monthly Review Press)

Central Advisory Council for Education, 1963 Newsom Report: *Half our Future* (HMSO)

Central Advisory Council for Education, 1967 Plowden Report: *Children and Their Primary Schools* (HMSO)

Coates, D. 1975 *The Labour Party and the Struggle for Socialism* (CUP)

Coates, D. 1972 *Teachers Unions and Interest Group Politics:* A Study in Behaviour of Organised Teachers in England and Wales (CUP)

Cox, C.B. & Dyson, A.E. (eds.) 1969 *Fight for Education: A Black Paper* (Critical Quarterly Society) 1969 *Black Paper II: Crisis in Education* (Critical Quarterly Society) 1970 *Black Paper III: Goodbye Mr Short* (Critical Quarterly Society)

Cox, C.B. & Boyson, R (eds.) 1975 *Black Paper 1975 (Dent)*

Crosland, C.A.R. 1956 *The Future of Socialism* (Cape) 1962 *The Conservative Enemy (Cape)* 1974 *Socialism Now and Other Essays* (Cape)

Department of Education & Science Circular 11/67, School Building Programme: *School Building in Education Priority Areas* (HMSO)

Department of Education & Science 1975, Bullock Report: *A Language for Life* (HMSO)

Douglas, J.W.B. 1964 *The Home and the School* (MacGibbon and Kee)

Floud, J. 1961 "Sociology and Education" *Sociological Review Monograph*

Gramsci, A. 1971 *Prison Notebooks* (Lawrence & Wishart)

Gray, T.L. & Moshinsky P. 1938 "Ability and Opportunity in English Education" in L. Hogan, *et al., Political Arithmetic* (Allen & Unwin)

Hall, S. *et. al.* 1975 Mugging & Law'n' Order (CCCS Stencilled Paper, Birmingham)

Halsey, A.H., Floud J. & Anderson C.1961 *Education, Economy and Society* (Collier-Macmillan and Free Press)

Hammersley, M. and Woods, P. 1976 *The Process of Schooling* (Open University, RKP)

Hargreaves, D.H. 1967 *Social Relations in a Secondary School* RKP

Henriques, P., Dennis N. and Slaughter C. 1956 *Coal is Our Life* (Eyre and Spottiswoode)

Howell, D. 1976 *British Social Democracy* (Croom Helm)

Jackson, B. 1964 *Streaming: An Education System in Miniature* (RKP)

Jackson, B. and Marsden D. 1966 *Education and the Working Class* (Pelican)

Jencks, C. 1975 *Inequality* (Peregrine)

Jenkins, D. and Shipman, M.D. 1976 *Curriculum: An Introduction* (Open Books)

Jenkins S. 1973 "Conservatives and Comprehensives" in Bell, R. *et. al. Education in Great Britain and Ireland* (Open University and RKP)

Johnson, R. 1976 "Really Useful Knowledge", *Radical Education 7 and 8*

Klein, J. 1965 *Samples from English Culture* (RKP)

Kogan, M. 1974 *The Politics of Education* (Penguin)

Lacey, C. 1970 *Hightown Grammar* (Manchester U.P.)

Lawn, M. 1974 "Educational Worker" *(Radical Education 2)*

Lister, I. 1974 *Deschooling: A Reader* (CUP)

Locke, M. 1974 *Power and Politics in the School System* (RKP)

Marx, K. 1973 *Surveys from Exile* (Pelican)

McKibbin, R. 1974 *The Evolution of the Labour Party* (OUP)

Midwinter, E. 1972 *Priority Education* (Penguin)

Miliband, R. 1972 *Parliamentary Socialism* (Merlin Press)

Ministry of Education : Secondary Schools Examination Council (Beloe Committee) 1960 *Secondary School Examinations Other Than the GCE.* (HMSO)

Nairn, T. 1964 "The Nature of the Labour Party" *New Left Review 27 and 28*

Pelling, H. 1965 *The Origins of the Labour Party* (Penguin)

Poulantzas,N. 1975 *Classes in Contemporary Capitalism* (New Left Books)

Robbins, Lord (Chairman) 1963 *Higher Education: Report of the Prime Minister's Committee on Higher Education* (HMSO)

Robinson, E. 1968 *The New Polytechnics* (Penguin)

Rosen, H. 1972 *Language and Class: A Critical Look at the Theories of Basil Bernstein* (Falling Wall Press)

Schools Council 1971 *Choosing a Curriculum for the Young School Leaver* (Evans/Methuen)

Simon, B. 1974 *The Two Nations and the Educational Structure 1780-1870* (Lawrence and Wishart)

Simon, B. 1974 *Education and the Labour movement 1870-1920* (Lawrence and Wishart)

Simon, B. 1974 *The Politics of Educational Reform 1920-40* (Lawrence and Wishart)

Stedman Jones, G. 1974 "Working-Class Culture and Working-Class Politics in London 1870-1900: Notes on the Remaking of a Working Class", *Journal of Social History*

Sugarman, B. 1966 "Social Class and Values as Related to Achievement and Conduct in Schools", *Sociological Review 14 No. 3*

Tawney, R. H. 1922 *Secondary Schools for All* (Allen and Unwin)

Tawney, R.H. 1964 *The Acquisitive Society* (Fontana)

Tawney, R.H. 1964 *Equality* (Allen and Unwin)

Teachers Action Collective 1975 *Teachers and the Economy*

Thompson, E.P. 1960 "Homage to Tom Maguire" in A. Briggs and J. Saville (eds.)
  Essays in Labour History (Macmillan)

Thompson, P. 1967 *Socialist Liberals and Labour: the Struggle for London 1885-1914* (RKP)

Thompson, P. 1976 *The Edwardians: The Remaking of British Society* (Weidenfeld and Nicolson)

Williams R. 1961 *Culture and Society 1780-1950* (Pelican)

Willis, P. 1977 *Learning to Labour: How Working-Class Kids Get Working-Class Jobs* (Saxon
  House, forthcoming)

Willis, P. 1976 *The Main Reality: Transition from School to Work* (CCCS Stencilled Paper,
  Birmingham)

Young, M.F.D. 1972 "On the Politics of Educational Knowledge: Some Preliminary
  Considerations with Particular Reference to the Schools Council", *Economy and
  Society*

Young, M.F.D. 1971 *Knowledge and Control : New Directions for the Sociology of Education*
  (Collier-Macmillan)

Part III
Subjectivity
and Individuality

Ideology, Subjectivity and the Artistic Text

Steve Burniston, Chris Weedon

Introduction

This article began as an attempt to pose the problem of the relationship between art, literature, and ideology. This attempt was related to our projects, which were concerned with developing a theoretical account of the literary text. We had become increasingly convinced of the impossibility, at present, of this project. On the one hand, it is impossible to theorize the literary text in isolation from much larger theoretical operations. On the other hand, the existing larger theories themselves do not seem to provide an adequate basis for the theorization of artistic practice in general and this would be a prerequisite of our attempt to theorize the literary text. The article became the first part of an attempt to explore this general dilemma.

In Section One, Marxist approaches to the question of art, literature, and its relation to ideology, are examined. A critique is offered of the inadequacies of these theories in their own terms. These are seen as a consequence of the inadequacies of Marxist theories of subjectivity. Accordingly in the second section we present an exposition of the key concepts of the Lacanian theory of subjectivity. This is an account of the subject which shares some of the basic features of Althusserian theory, and which Althusser often refers to and has written about at length (Althusser 1971, p.189). It is also of importance for Julia Kristeva's theory of art in the social formation, which is the other main focus of our second section.

We characterize Kristeva's work as an attempt to provide Marxism with a theory of subjectivity, which, however, suffers from a considerable lack of precision at vital points; a vagueness as to the exact nature of its own project. We consider this vagueness to be centred around the problem of the relations between Althusserian Marxism and Lacanian psychoanalysis. In Kristeva's work the reconciliation of these two discourses is presented as a *fait accompli*. We cannot accept such a solution and in the third section of this article, we attempt to sketch the nature and dimensions of this problem. We argue that it is no less than the problem of the theory of the social formation, since only such a theory can provide us with a theoretical account of the relation between Althusser's and Lacan's work. The attempt to develop a theory of ideology and its relation to artistic practice and the artistic text depends, in our view, on a solution to this problem.

These questions are explored at much greater length in an earlier draft of Section

Three, which will be available from the Centre as a Stencilled Paper entitled "Marxism, Psychoanalysis and the Theory of the Social Formation".

Section One: Marxist Approaches to the Problem

The problematic nature of the relationship between art, literature and ideology is central to any attempt at theorizing the role of art and literature in the social formation. The ways in which Marxist aesthetics have approached the problem to date, have in each case depended upon the initial status accorded to ideology. It has been seen variously as a form of false consciousness, imposed upon the individual from above by the dominant class, as a consequence of a limited view of the whole, resulting from the individual's class position as a perceiving subject within the social formation, and — taking it to its furthest limits to date — as the result of the ideological nature of the perceiving subject *per se,* who is brought into being through his or her insertion into ideological signifying practices, which form the substance of lived experience, within ideological state apparatuses.

Apart from the more explicitly economistic forms of aesthetic theory, those of Plekhanov, Mehring and to some extent Trotsky, in which art is seen as an automatically produced ephiphenomenon of the economically determined movement of history, Marxist theorists have attempted to distinguish art and literature from ideology as such, and to assign them some sort of more or less effective role in the class struggle. This required the recognition of an effective status for the *ideological* class struggle, which can be found in Lenin's writings as early as 1905,[1] but it also requires an adequate theorization of the relationship between the ideological, political and economic levels, which we would argue is yet to be achieved.

Central to the question of the nature of the ideological class struggle is the status of the subject in signifying practice. By "subject" is meant the "ego" or "I" as situated in language, or signifying practice in general, which refers to practices within the social formation, inasmuch as they can be analysed in terms of the psychic conditions of that formation. This point cannot be explained fully here, but it will be raised again in Section Three. Generally the subject assumes one of two forms: either that of the constitutive subject, creating history under determinate historical conditions, as theorized by Marx in *The German Ideology* and later by Lukács in *History and Class Consciousness,* and his aesthetic works, or the subject as agent or bearer of socio-economic historical processes, as seen in varying forms in Plekhanov and Althusser. The theory of the constitutive subject is less problematic in the problems it raises, since the subject is of necessity transcendent (i.e. eternally fixed in the subject-object relationship), and the "individual" at all times equals the individual subject. Thus the subject-object relationship is fixed in reality and in language. The non-constitutive subject is theorized in Althusser's essay "Ideology and Ideological State Apparatuses" (Althusser 1971). Here the individual is assigned the role of bearer or agent of ideological practices, which he or she experiences as interpellated subjectivity, i.e. subjectivity imposed on the individual, through ideology, in which the individual is addressed as subject. This however raises the problem of the role of what Althusser calls "ideology in general" (1971 p.164), by which individuals are "always-already subjects" (ibid). This theoretical lacuna not only poses the question of the formation of the human individual as an "always-already" subject, but also the role of language in this process. An understanding of this is essential to a fully worked out theorization of the relationship between art, literature and ideology.

Whereas in idealist aesthetics,[2] art and literature are seen as realms beyond politics and class, in which one is able to transcend the limits of everyday experience and reach eternal human values and truths, Marxist theory has attempted to locate art and literature firmly within the social framework and undermine the empirical process, whereby all that is necessary for a full understanding of a work of art or literature is a perceptive reading of the work, either in its own terms or as a direct reflection of the author's own life. In practice, however, much of the Marxist aesthetic theory and even more so socialist cultural policy has been coloured by the presuppositions of idealist aesthetics. This is found not so much in their aspiring to politically neutral, eternal values, but in their assertion that art and literature can give a full and as such *non-ideological* picture of the social formation and the motors of social change seen as inherent within it, by incorporating the most progressive political and social forces. Such aesthetic theory, for example that of Lukács, relies on a theory of the linear progressive movement of history, in which a particular class is seen as the creative subject of history and is assigned the role of bringing about socio-historical progress. In the realm of aesthetics, the individual "creator", given in idealist theory, for example in romanticism, is replaced by the notion of the collective creator, i.e. the social class of which the artist is agent. However this too is tinged with an idealism, which has no place in a fully materialist aesthetic, since it suggests that the "world vision" of that class which is the motor of history at any particular period, as expressed by the creative artist, is non-ideological, and thus accords some sort of absolute, transcendent quality to art. Because this theorization is founded on the notion of the social formation as an expressive totality, signification, i.e. communication by means of signs, whether linguistic or otherwise, is reduced to a process of expression, where the sign is the unproblematic unity of referent, signifier (sound or graphic image) and signified (concept). It has taken a new approach to the problem of knowledge in terms of the relationship between science, ideology and art, coupled with a model of the social formation which attempts to assign relative autonomy to art and literature (though this is in itself problematic) to divest Marxist aesthetics more thoroughly of these idealist traits. This approach is of course found in Althusser's theorization of science and ideology, which in the case of aesthetics has been developed more fully by Pierre Macherey.

Ideology in Macherey's Aesthetic Theory

Macherey adopts Althusser's theorization of ideology as his starting point, a theory in which the role of ideology is to dispel apparent contradictions in lived experience by offering a false but seemingly adequate resolution to a real debate. An ideology is always a closed system, contained by its own limits, which presuppose its existence and which it cannot itself recognise. In order to stay within these limits, an ideological system must remain silent on questions which go beyond its boundaries, and in order to make sense of an ideology, within the wider context of the social formation, it is necessary to step outside of it and give form to what it fails to express. Since any social formation simultaneously holds several conflicting ideologies, apart from

201

the one which can be recognised as dominant, conflicting ideologies, which have their bases in various substrata, groups and fractions within society, and since these various ideological strands are, according to Althusser, seen in their effects in social practices, the interrogation of one ideological system from the standpoint of another, while not leading to true knowledge (which only science can deliver) can establish the limitations of the ideology in question. Thus the status of "truth" accorded to ideologies by individuals whose experience is structured by them in terms of it, can be undermined. Althusser and Macherey suggest that art and literature offer a unique medium for exposing the ideological (in the sense of incomplete and untrue) nature of the interpretation of lived experience provided for individuals by the ideological systems into which they are inserted as subjects. Thus Althusser writes:

> the peculiarity of art is to "make us see" (*nous donner à voir*), "make us perceive", "make us feel" something which alludes to reality . . . What art makes us see and therefore gives us in the form of "seeing", "perceiving", "feeling" (which is not the form of knowing), is the ideology in which it bathes, from which it detaches itself as art, and to which it alludes . . . when we speak of ideology we should know that ideology slides into all human activity, that it is identical with the lived experience of human existence itself; that is why the form in which we are "made to see" ideology in great novels has as its content the "lived" experience of individuals. (1971 p.204)

Macherey takes as his object literary, as opposed to general artistic production. More specifically, he concentrates on literary criticism to which he attempts to give some sort of scientific foundation, in the Althusserian sense of scientific practice. He places aesthetic theory firmly within the realm of general theoretical activity suggesting that it is closely allied to political theory and cites Lenin and his work on Tolstoy in relation to the political situation in Russia in 1905 as exemplary of the tying together of the two forms of theory (Macherey 1966 p.126). However the precondition for establishing the relation between literary aesthetics and other theoretical practices is an understanding of the relationship between literature and historical reality, which involves a theorization of the working of ideology in literature.

Macherey's theory, in common with all Marxist aesthetics, presupposes a necessary relationship of some kind between the text and the historical period. The first problem of analysis, which Macherey conveniently suggests does not belong to aesthetics or literary criticism, is to construct this historical period, by which he means, to demonstrate its historical unity and its dominant, convergent tendencies. The period to which a literary text is related does not necessarily correspond to the creative life of the author. The link with history cannot be reduced to the spontaneous or simultaneous. There may well be a time lag between the work and its period or the author may attach himself to secondary tendencies of his epoch or to surviving tendencies from the past. The work does however draw distinctive traits from its period and characterises it by *evoking* the contradictions which are specific to it. However since the relationship is not one of simple reflection, or the expression of an expressive totality, the coherence of the historical period and that of the literary text must at all times be held distinct.

Whereas the historical period produces a series of ideologies determined by global relations of forces, the work of literature, written from, but not reducible to, a specific class perspective, draws upon one or two ideological strands to which it attempts to give the status of truth. Thus the picture given by a work of literature depends upon the particular authorial class perspective and this is inadequate in itself and does not produce knowledge. To obtain knowledge it would be necessary to hold on to all ideological strands at once, from a transcendent position beyond lived experience, experienced subjectively, an impossible position for which the only temporal, knowledge-giving substitutes are scientific practices. Thus literature does not give a full historical analysis but a "point of view", which is partial but not *a priori* false.

The author's task is to bring to life the contradictions inherent in the historical structure by telling their story. It is the fictive element which gives the work its literary value, which is not measured in terms of whether its overt political perspective is reactionary or progressive but by how far it is *non-reducible* to this ideological position. Thus in the case of Tolstoy, the author grasps the characteristics of his age with a certain bias and with all the inadequacies inherent in his viewpoint. Tolstoy, though born a count, a member of the feudal aristocracy, allied himself with the class perspective of the peasantry. He portrayed his time as one of upheaval but was unable to disengage the emergent order which was taking command of the situation. He was sensitive to the consequences of the development of capitalism, which put into question the existence of both count and peasant, and yet he was incapable of characterising the power of the bourgeoisie or of understanding the formation of the bourgeois order. Hence the development of material forces remains completely obscured in his work. The fragmentation which determines the series of partial relations which Tolstoy's work evokes, gives rise to a particular ideology through which he attempts to reintegrate the account. Thus the ideology or doctrine of the literary work is initially located in the class perspective of the author, but it is not the author's creation, rather it is constituted independently of him by a particular class or class fraction with which the author aligns himself. This class perspective mediates his relationship to the historical reality of his period and forms the first term in the process of mediation which takes place between historical reality and literature, the other term being "literary style". For the sake of clarity, it should be noted again that "historical reality" as used by Macherey refers to the period as constructed by a theoretical science of history. The defining quality of "great art" is that it is not equal to and cannot be reduced to the ideological system which it contains, whereas mediocre or bad art is merely ideological and therefore strikes the reader as *déjà-vu*, dull and uninteresting. Macherey writes that:

> What produces the literary text is fundamentally the operation of one or more ideological contradictions to the point where those contradictions cannot be resolved within ideology. It is in the last analysis the operation within ideology of contradictory and intrinsically irreconcilable class positions. (Macherey, *Littérature,* 14, p.138)

The individual author's role in the production of this effect is neither determining nor neutral.

> He is a material agent, situated in a definite intermediate position within contradictions that by definition he cannot master, resulting from a specific social division of labour characteristic of the ideological superstructures of bourgeois society which he individualises. (ibid, p.44)

The irreconcilable class positions present in the ideological contradictions can only be formulated materially in the literary text. Thus they are realised in a form which simultaneously represents their imaginary solution, or rather which displaces them by substituting imaginary and soluble contradictions within the ideology of religion, politics, ethics, aesthetics or psychology, transposed onto a fictive plane. The imaginary solution of imaginary contradictions in literature is what is termed "literary style" by Macherey, who is here drawing on the work of René Balibar,[3] and it is literary language which is the key to this process. To quote Macherey and Balibar:

> (The dialectic of literary style) is able to produce the effect, the illusion of the imaginary reconciliation of irreconcilable terms by displacing the whole ensemble of ideological contradictions onto the terrain of one of them, or of one of their aspects, that of linguistic conflict. (ibid. p.44)

Thus all forms of signifying practice, which make up the texture of lived experience, are reformulated in terms of language alone, and this necessitates a full theorization of the nature of language.

Macherey deals with language, by which he means language in the sense of discourse, from the outside, as it were, taking it as a socially given signifying system. He treats it as a system into which individuals are inserted as subjects, simply by being addressed as such through the structure of the language used. This structure is always founded on an ideological rather than "true", transcendent subject-object relationship. Macherey does not touch on the problem of how individuals come to be in a position to respond to language in this way. However, once this function of language vis-à-vis the individual is established, if not, needless to say, theoretically founded, Macherey turns his attention to the social nature of language, in the sense of its relation to the class struggle. He stresses the essentially non-neutral nature of language (always understood here in the sense of discourse, rather than the Saussurean notion of a system of linguistic signs, each composed of a signifier (sound image) and a signified (concept), he suggests as a starting point that literature develops from a "national" language in a determinate fashion. By "national" or "common" language he means French or English etc., understood as a language which has developed (exactly how is not specified) as the historical result of specific class struggles and which is linked with bourgeois democracy and bourgeois sovereignty. He suggests that the assumption that there is a unified common language is in fact empirical and ideological, since language consists of the contradictions between differing practices within it. At this point Macherey draws upon Althusser's identification of the educational system as the key ideological state apparatus of advanced capitalism, engaged in the reproduction of the relations of production (Althusser 1971 p.39). Macherey suggests that while a policy of education for all, which includes literacy, suggests that the national language is common to all, its real divisive nature is institutionalised in the hierarchical structure of education, which admits different social groups to different levels of literacy. Language, which forms the basis of literary practice, is thus never innocent. Linguistic practices because of their contradictory character cannot be used as simple raw materials:

> every use is an intervention, a choice of positions, a taking of sides within the contradiction and so an active contribution to its development. (ibid. p.39)

The resolution of real contradictions on the imaginary plane of language works through an identification between *linguistically* constituted ideological subjects.

This mechanism, which is asserted rather than theorized in Macherey's work, rests primarily on incomplete elements taken from Lacanian psychoanalytic theory of the constitution of the subject in the symbolic realm, i.e. in language. Apart from ideological recognition being reduced to a functional element of ideological practice, the whole foundation and working of the symbolic realm of language is not raised as a problem. Macherey's immediate source in this theory of literature is Althusser's partial appropriation of elements of Lacan in his theory of "ideology in general", which according to Althusser underpins the ideological practices which constitute lived experience. This theory, set out systematically in Althusser's essay "Ideology and Ideological State Apparatuses" (1971), attributes a necessary and immutable structure and functioning to ideology in all social formations. Ideology in any specific social formation, according to Althusser, always exists as an apparatus and in its practice or practices, which themselves exist in the material actions of the subject.

In literature, the practices of subjects in real ideological apparatuses, religion, politics etc., are transposed onto a fictive plane, where an attempt is made to resolve the contradictions between them, which result from various class interests, by subsuming them under a dominant ideological perspective. In order to appropriate the ideology of the text, it is necessary that the reader be transformed from a real individual into an ideological subject. This is accomplished via a mechanism of identification. Literature, Macherey suggests, is constantly producing subjects in its characters and in the author himself in his relation to the text. These subjects address the reader as a subject, calling upon him or her to identify with their position in the text, and thus confer on the reader as an individual, a subjectivity which is apparently real but actually illusory. This process is what Althusser calls the "ideological recognition function" (1971 p.161).

As St Paul admirably put it, it is in the logos, meaning in ideology, that we "live, move and have our being". It follows that for you and me the category of the subject is a primary "obviousness" (obviousnesses are always primary): it is clear that you and I are subjects (free, ethical etc. . . .) Like all obviousnesses including those that make a word "name a thing" or "have a meaning" (therefore including the obvious "transparency" of language), the obviousness that you and I are subjects, and that that does not cause any problems, is an ideological effect, the elementary ideological effect. (ibid.)

It is through this ideological function of recognition that the text is able to transform the reader into an ideological subject, thus enabling him or her to become the apparently "free" bearer of the ideology in the text. However, in the case of great art and literature, the process is by no means simple and uniform. Those contradictions in the work which cannot be resolved within its ideological perspective, leave open the way to ideological *mis*-recognition on the part of the reader, in which case s/he will see through the ideology and will be unable to identify fully as a subject with the subject in the work.

Macherey suggests that the lack of simple interior unity in a great work of literature can be registered in the manifold interpretations to which any one work is open. Through holding the various interpretations in mind at once, the apparently unified centre of the work — its obvious meaning — becomes displaced by conflicting meanings. It is here, Macherey suggests, that the truth of the work lies, not reflecting historical contradictions as such, but evoking them by allowing one to grasp the relations between the contradictions and in this process the outer limits of the ideologies

205

present within the text. Thus while literature cannot provide knowledge in the Althusserian sense of scientific knowledge, it gives a particularly acute perception of lived experience, which is not the same as ideology, though it is structured by it. Thus the literary process involves the undermining of the immediate, obvious, ideologically determined response which the ideological perspective of the text offers the reader.

Thus what emerges is a theory of literature as an evocation in fictive form of the kind of structural contradictions which are present in historical reality. The main ideological perspective present in the work attempts to resolve these contradictions by suggesting that they are part of the very nature of things, of an eternal order in which everything has its place. The actual structure and content of the work, as seen in relation to the readers' responses, suggest that this is not so. A recognition on the part of the reader of the contradictions inherent in the work, does not require the idealist notion of "sensitivity of spirit", but relies on the technique of what Althusser calls "symptomatic reading", i.e. reading for absences.[4] This process however is most completely and successfully carried out by the materialist literary critic who undertakes a scientific work of transformation of his object, the literary text, by examining at once all possible responses to it, in the light of an understanding of the period to which the text relates.

Macherey's Theory and Alternative Marxist Approaches (Lukács, Goldmann and Adorno)

It is clear that in Macherey's literary aesthetic the text must, in the last analysis, be related back to a particular ideological perspective which is that of a class or class fraction. This is seen in conflict with other ideologies which are embodied in the practices of characters and set against the way the author is attempting to make the reader see them. However the notion of literature being tied to a specific authorial class allegiance is a long-standing one in Marxist aesthetics. An attempt will now be made to broaden the discussion out into a consideration of other Marxist theories in order to offer mutual criticism and comparison, which should, in some points, take us beyond the theoretical position reached by Macherey.

In Lukács' and Goldmann's theory, the literary text is written from a class perspective or "world vision", which is the result of the author's class allegiance. However their theorization of the relation of the text to this class perspective is essentially different from that of Macherey. Taking a base/superstructure model of the social formation, and giving it the particular form of an expressive totality, Lukács theorised literature as the structured expression of a unified class world vision. Given that the literature in question is "great", this world vision would of necessity be that of the historically specific ascendent class, and therefore it would be able to transcend ideology. The mode of reflection of the social formation at work here is not a simple mirror image, but rather the expression of the typical features of a particular class position and class world vision, to which, unlike in Macherey, the work is in the last instant reducible. Thus for Lukács if a literary work is not totalising, i.e. does not correspond to a historically specific dominant class perspective, then it falls into the realm of ideology, from which it is otherwise detached. Thus literature which depicts society as destructive and purely negative (Kafka is a favourite example) and does not contain elements for a potential resolution within it, is seen by Lukács as mere descriptive reflection of partiality or "bad" art. This point relates back to Lukács' theory of the class subject as the creator of history under determinate conditions, since in description, as opposed to narrative, the individual appears as a reified object rather than as a subject of society, and society does not appear as the product and source of action. For Lukács and Goldmann it is the totalizing quality of the great work of art that takes it out of the realm of ideology, since its typicality makes it hold true beyond the immediate context of the work itself. It has a unity which is not that of apparent, everyday, lived experience, but which is a microcosmic expression of the essential unity of the social totality.

It is clear that there is a radically different theorization from that of Macherey and Althusser at work here, which is directly related to their different theorizations of the social formation. In the expressive totality, the various features of the social formation are, as Goldmann puts it, "structurally homologous" (Goldmann 1964), the unifying factor being the "world vision" or potential consciousness of a social class of which art alone can be the full expression. Here ideology becomes equated with a partial reflection — or perception — of reality, in terms of its underlying structure, rather like an incomplete jigsaw puzzle, and is not a functionally necessary instance of the social formation as in Althusser and Macherey. In its cruder form, as in Lukács' work on bourgeois critical and socialist realism (Lukács 1963) or Goldmann on the *nouveau roman* (Goldmann 1964), this theory of art as an expression of the social totality becomes prey to economic reflectionism, in which the artistic and literary superstructure is seen as a mirror reflection of the economic infrastructure. In Lukács' case, this has dire consequences for his theory of form.

With respect to the social formation, Macherey is much closer to Adorno, who identifies it as an essentially contradictory, as opposed to expressive, totality. Adorno stresses that unless a concept of totality incorporates what it is not, i.e. what it is defined against, then it can only be ideological. For instance (and this is a crucial link with Macherey), the values of a particular class taken in isolation can only be ideological. Since Adorno holds art to be irreducible to ideology, it follows that it cannot be theorized as the expression of a particular class world vision. On the contrary, Adorno sees great art as giving form to historical contradiction, as in Macherey. However Adorno places his emphasis firmly on form, which Macherey fails to consider, at the expense of ideological content. With regard to form, Adorno accepts a simple, reflective model of the relationship between art and the economic level, without the Lukácsian mediation of the economically constituted, historically ascendent social class, whereas Macherey goes no further in his theorization than to specify the relative autonomy of the ideological and therefore artistic and literary levels.

Drawings on Lukács' concept of reification as the distinguishing feature of late capitalist society, Adorno attempts to develop the implications of the extension of the division of labour into the sphere of private life, which has drawn it into the service of commodity production. He sees this process as having undermined any theory of a unified or organic subject, which informed Lukácsian as well as bourgeois, idealist aesthetics. In this context art can only serve as a challenge to reified society, a challenge addressed to the individual subject whose security, in his or her manipulated existence, it should undermine. The form which this challenge takes is determined by art's refusal to stand for anything else, i.e. to mirror reality in a coherent way as the expression of a unified social totality. If it were to do so, it would become prey to commodity consumption. Instead of this, social contradictions become the dialectic of aesthetic form. Thus for example the fragmentation of individual subjectivity through reification under advanced capitalism is signalled by Schoenberg's and Stravinsky's musical forms, which replace forms generated by conceptions of the unified, bourgeois individual, as expressed for example in Beethoven's violin concerto! Thus, in Adorno's system, art offers a radical critique of the status quo, because in giving form to contradictions, it challenges the false harmony, based on an ideological closure, which Adorno identifies as the foundation of domination in society.

Form and Practice: Lukács, Brecht and Benjamin

The question of form, so firmly placed in the forefront by Adorno, is central to aesthetic theory. As we have seen, Macherey subsumes the problem beneath the concept of literary style, which when it is successful produces great art. To a certain extent this is a result of his object, since first and foremost he is attempting to provide a scientific theory for scientific, literary-critical practice. It also results from his attempt to break decisively with Lukácsian aesthetics, in which the work of art is in fact created by the author as a class subject. However, Macherey's treatment of the role of the author as a material agent (Macherey 1966 p.134), who is neither determining nor neutral, while making him or her a relatively autonomous agent, free of Plekhanov's direct determination by the economic, does not tell us much about the specific nature of literary practice and what determines it other than the author's ideological class allegiance. Moreover it completely leaves out of consideration the question of committed revolutionary art as a form of practice within the ideological class struggle, which reintroduces the notion of subjective practice even if this be ideological, a perspective which becomes central in the aesthetics of Brecht and Benjamin.

Lukács attempted to deal fully with the question of the form and effectivity of art and literature. However because of his insistence on the world vision of the historically ascendent class as the only possible foundation for great art, he was forced to reject all art which could not be so classified. Drawing on what he identified as the peak of bourgeois literature, he attempted to extract and universalize the historically specific form of nineteenth-century realism and rejected all other contemporary and post-realist forms of art as "modernist". Thus he stabilized the formal elements of the work of art, making the variable feature the class perspective from within which a novel was written. This formalism was tied in with his theory of the ideological function and effectivity of art.

The ideological effect of great art and literature in Lukács' aesthetics is based on the notion of "catharsis", a transformation of the reader's consciousness which would resolve the contradictions between the everyday appearance of reality and the forces moulding it, and thus emancipate the individual from the determinist constraints imposed upon him by the dominant ideology. In order to bring this about, the work of literature must of necessity be totalizing, i.e. it must embody the *typical* features of a particular class position and class world vision. This is achieved through the formal elements of a typical hero/ine and a narrative. Thus in the novel, the individual hero/ine must bear the traits of his or her class position as the typical class subject of history, and she or he must be placed in a situation which contains within it evidence of the progressive forces shaping society, which her or his fate should reveal. The catharsis takes place, Lukács suggests, through the reader's identification with the typical hero/ine. Thus what the author must do is, in effect, find the archimedean point in the midst of social contradictions and analyse them.

Brecht rejected outright the Lukácsian notion of art as a cathartic, expressive totality, and the formalism of Lukács' aesthetics which had led him to reject all modern developments in artistic techniques. He also rejected the claim that empathy alone, even with a typical hero, could bring about an understanding of the true nature of social relations. He adopted instead a dialectical practice in which empathy with the characters in a play, i.e. implicit acquiescence in their understanding of their own situation, is interrupted in mid-stream by artistic techniques which break down the "natural" flow of conscious reception and call it into question, allowing the audience to see the *obvious* old familiar reality in a new light. This involved a revolutionizing of artistic techniques, a breaking down of classical genres and an introducing of new forms.

Brecht was concerned to reveal specific historically situated contradictions, through content carefully structured in its formal presentation to reveal contradictions whose meaning should become clear and easily appropriable by the audience. Thus in Brecht's plays, the characters' own understanding of their situation is called into question and the audience is forced to go beyond this level of consciousness and to penetrate the workings of ideology. For Brecht, art was essentially practice not only for the authors and/or actors, but also for the audience or reader. He broke definitively with traditional notions of the "great" work of art, favouring collective authorship and constant revision of plays, including traditional works, in the light of discussion with audiences. Thus art should be both an enjoyable experience and a concerted political attack on the taken-for-granted rationalization of lived experience provided by the dominant ideology.

Brecht's radical rejection of the category of "great" art and of the high cultural tradition as an object for reverential enjoyment rather than adaption to the present political struggle was complemented by Benjamin's theory of the new status and therefore new potential of art as set out in "The Work of Art in the Age of Mechanical Reproduction" (Benjamin 1973). Benjamin argued that "authentic, great art" before the age of mechanical reproduction was located in cult and ritual, as the unique creation of one individual, whose very uniqueness gave it a certain "aura". At this time reproduction counted as mere forgery and thus the potential audience and effectivity of the art work was severely limited, enhancing its elitist, cult status. With the coming of mechanical reproduction, however, reproductions which were no longer considered to be forgeries became widely available, meeting their audience halfway with, for example, the gramophone record bringing the concert hall into the sitting room. Thus the semblance of autonomy of the work of art has been undermined and it must be relocated firmly in the production relations of its time and, more specifically, within the relations of literary production. The consequence of this process has been the overt politicization of art. To quote Benjamin:

> The instant the criterion of authenticity ceases to be applicable to artistic production, the total function of art is reversed. Instead of being based on ritual, it begins to be based on another practice, politics. (Benjamin 1971 p.226)

Thus Benjamin argues that the attainment of technical progress in literature eventually changes the function it can exercise as art. This implies a change in the intellectual means of production, and the status of the author as producer. The cult status of the artist as a creative genius and of the artefact as his unique creation is replaced by the artist as producer in a specific social and ideological context, using the tools of language and style specific to that period, to produce something the measure of whose greatness vis-à-vis all other cultural products can be located in the skill and originality with which the author(s) manipulate(s) language and style to undermine accepted understandings of the world.

Positions and Problems in the Marxist Tradition

Brecht and Benjamin saw artistic practice as a direct form of political practice, in which a conscious, collective effort is made to bring about the ideological effect of transforming a given interpretation of lived experience. For this to be possible, a direct engagement of the audience is necessary, in which they are pushed to a point from which things can and logically *must* be seen differently. In contrast to Brecht, Macherey and Adorno do not see art as a conscious political practice. Rather they suggest that the subversive process of undermining ideologically determined interpretations of the world is always inherent in great literature, irrespective of the intentions of the author(s) in setting the work up in a particular way. For Macherey the key to understanding the ideological process at work in a text is a symptomatic reading. The irrelevance of whether art is committed specifically to socialism as opposed to religion or whatever other ideology, comes in part from the fact that Macherey's theory of literature encompasses the literary tradition in general. This does not bring in the question of committed art as part of the current struggle, since this must of necessity be tied directly to the present conjuncture, and seen in terms of scientific analysis is itself ideological. There is however an unresolved and problematic dualism between literature in general and literature as an integral part of the ideological class struggle, a dualism which hides all the problems of consciously committed art, art and propaganda, mass art etc. Brecht resolves the question by rejecting the notion of the high cultural tradition and demanding that all art be relevant to today.

Any attempt to bring together a theory which is first and foremost one of scientific literary criticism, and a theory of artistic practice, which by extension involves a theory of consumption (the reception of art and literature) is in itself problematic, since it calls into question the problem of subjective practice, which the Althusserian system manages to elide. Macherey succeeds in eliding the question of how, and under what sort of determinations "man makes his own history",[5] by subsuming the dimension of signifying practice under a mechanism of ideologically determined subjectivity given in ideological practices within ideological state apparatuses. Thus the level of signifying practice disappears from view, and artistic practice in the Brechtian sense is no longer included within the object of a scientific analytical theory. We would argue, however, that both aspects of theory, a scientific theory of the working of ideology in art, and a theory for political practice, which could assign art and literature a role in the ideological class struggle, are necessary to Marxist aesthetics. This duality of theory can only be possible where the level of signifying practice is included within the theory, i.e. where there is a theorization of the status and role of the subject and of subjective intentionality; a theory of she and he who are acting, and she and he who are acted upon. Whereas the centrality of this theory to political practice is apparent, since it alone can provide strategies for action, we would argue that it is also a necessary complement to Macherey's analytical theory of literature and ideology, which, as it stands, can only theorize the role of language and the constitution of the subject in language descriptively, as the result of a mechanism, whose content is determined by the class struggle.

Lukács developed his aesthetic theory from the perspective of political practice. His theory of the subject and of "signifying practice" (Lukács does not use this term) is simplified by the way in which his theoretical model is set up. Thus the subject is the transcendent, *typical, class* subject, who creates history. Lukács' theory of the subject is the *explicit* foundation of his aesthetic theory, which Brecht attacks with such vigour. Brecht's own artistic theory and technique is *not* theoretically founded as regards the status of the subject. Whereas Brecht is working with an implicit model of false or ideological consciousness, which is contained within the framework of a fixed, transcendent subject, this is not placed within a model of the social formation as an expressive totality, with the class as the constituting subject. On the contrary, the subject remains unspecified and untheorized. This leaves his theory and techniques open to appropriation by an aesthetic based on a new theory of the subject and signifying practice.

As we have seen, Macherey departs radically from the Lukácsian model, replacing the absolute, transcendent subject by the ideological subject, which is constituted in the functional mechanism of ideological recognition, which is in fact misrecognition. For Macherey, following Althusser, there is no such thing as non-ideological recognition by the subject, since ideology can only be transcended in science, where the subject has no role. Thus, whereas for Lukács, signification is an unproblematic process of identification between the referend, signifier, and signified on the basis of the transcendent subject, for Macherey the whole process of signification is rendered ideological, *not* via a questioning of the *nature of signification itself* but through the ideological status accorded to the subject. The subject is the result of an empirical process of recognition and as such has no role in scientific discourse. However it is not enough to assert that all recognition is, *per se,* ideological. This axiom needs to be underpinned by a scientific theorization of the constitution in language of that subject of which the individual is bearer.

The science/ideology divide in Althusserian theory, according to which an individual's experience of subjectivity is located in the realm of ideology, as a result of that process of misrecognition which makes possible those ideological practices (within ISAs) which form the substance of everyday life, elides the general concept of signifying practice. Signifying practice, which is founded on the subject/object divide, must include scientific discourse within it. It is by attempting to make the

211

veiled subject of scientific discourse self-conscious, that one might begin to re-
theorize the science/ideology divide and call into question, from the perspective of
signifying practice, the nature of the subject and its constitution in language. It is
this which forms the basis of Julia Kristeva's theoretical project, with which we shall
be dealing in Section Two of this article.

Section Two: The Subject and Signifying Practice: Lacan and Kristeva

The object of Julia Kristeva's work is to provide Marxism with a psychoanalytically
based theory of the subject and of signifying practice, which will be able to account
for what she calls the marginal discourses, marginal to the symbolic order of meaning, foremost among which are art and literature. Her central support in this project is
the psychoanalytical theory of the constitution of the subject in language as developed by Lacan, and it is at this point that we must begin, before we can consider
Kristeva's project, and its relation to Marxism, in more detail.

Lacan's Theory of the Constitution of the Subject in Language

In this section we present only an introduction to Lacan in simplified terms; this is
an attempt at a *reading* and a *systematization* of Lacanian psychoanalysis.

Lacan presents his work as a return to Freud, an extraction of the scientific concepts of Freud's work from the confusing mass of definitions and redefinitions. His
own style of writing is often ambiguous and many of his crucial sentences are open
to several possible interpretations. At one level this ambiguity is a function of Lacan's
method, since there is no final signified in his work, and each concept in his discourse
has its specificity in the character and multiplicity of its relation to the other concepts. (There is a problem here of how to characterize Lacan's work in terms of
"scientificity" which will be taken further in Section Three.) Within the limits of this
article, it is only possible to give a brief introduction to the concepts of Lacanian
psychoanalysis and to move on to the role of language in more detail. Lacan's concepts are of necessity introduced individually here and it should be noted that their
order of exposition bears only a distant relation to the order in which they are conceived of as operative in the psychic development of the human infant. It should also
be remembered that earlier psychic states can coexist in the psyche with later developments and play an important part in the formation of neurotic symptoms in adults.

a. The Pre-Oedipal

The pre-oedipal is both a system of concepts and the moment in the psychic development of the individual which these concepts construct. The distinction between the
Oedipal/post-Oedipal and the pre-Oedipal made here, is useful for the purposes of
exposition and argument only. It is not a distinction which would be made in the
same way in actual analysis, where the pre-Oedipal shades into the Oedipal, and
where symptoms associated with both moments may coexist and interfere with each
other.

The concepts of the pre-Oedipal: (i) The fragmented body

The human infant is seen as being concerned, at first, with the exploration of sensory perception and its main characteristic is its auto-eroticism. At this stage the infant has no organisation of data into those associated with its own body and those associated with exteriority. It has no sense of its physical separateness or of its physical unity. This is the moment which will be referred to retroactively, after the "mirror phase", by the phantasy of the "body in fragments".

(ii) The Mirror Phase; the I and the Ego

The mirror phase is the moment when the infant realises the distinction between its own body and the outside; the "other". The infant sees its reflection in a mirror and identifies with it.

> We have to understand the mirror phase *as an identification* in the full sense which analysis gives to the term; namely the transformation which takes place in the subject when he assumes an image . . . (Lacan 1968 p.72)

The image which the infant assumes through identification appears to the infant

> in a contrasting size that fixes it and a symmetry that inverts it, which are in conflict with the turbulence of the motions which the subject, the infant, feels animating him (ibid p.73)

The image with which the infant identifies, which Lacan says can be described as the "Ideal-I", is positioned in the world *exterior* to the infant. Thus the mirror phase announces the alienation which is at the heart of identification, since in order for identification to take place there must be two Is, a perceiving I and a perceived I. For an understanding of the mirror phase it is important to distinguish the *I* from the *ego* and the *subject*.

> [In the mirror phase] the *I* is precipitated in a primordial form before it is objectified in the dialectic of the identification with the other, and before language restores to it, in the universal, its functions as subject . . . this form [the I] situates the instance of the *ego*, before its social determination, in a fictional direction . . . (ibid. p.72-3)

Thus the I is the (primordial) precondition for the constitution of the ego, which results from the entry of the I into an identification with an object in the other. (the non-infant). The *subject,* to which we shall return later, is a concept proper to another part of the theory, i.e. the Symbolic, and it is only in language that the ego is constituted as a subject.

(iii) The Imaginary and Misrecognition

The process of identification described by Lacan as the mirror phase inaugurates the "Imaginary" relation in which the "imaginary" derives from the mirror-image. In social relations the ego replaces the I as the "subject" (used in a general sense) of the imaginary relation to the object. This relation may be said to rest upon a misrecognition (*méconnaissance*) in which the individual misrecognises as itself the perfect (unified, powerful) image which appears in the mirror and with which it identifies as being everything the individual *imagines* it will be. It is in the mirror phase that the basic structure of misrecognition, which is the foundation of all imaginary relations, is constituted, a point which becomes important in Althusser's appropriation of Lacan's concepts.

213

(iv) The Mother-Child Relation; oral, anal and genital relationships

Following the mirror phase, the first form of identification with an object outside of the infant, is the infant's identification with its mother. This relation determines the attitude of the infant to the zones of its own body, according to the significance which they are given within the relationship. (Thus Freud points to the unwillingness of infants to defecate except in the presence of someone whom they know well. He suggests that the giving up of faeces by the child is a sacrifice which can only be justified by the attention which it claims from the object of identification.) The fact that the genital aspect of the infant's relationship to its mother cannot be developed, brings the pre-Oedipal phase to an end.

(v) The Beginnings of Language in the Child; anxiety

The anxiety associated with the conditions of existence of the ego is exacerbated within the mother-child relationship by the periodic and, to the child, inexplicable absences of the mother. Freud saw the beginnings of language in the child as an attempt to master this anxiety. For example in the *fort/da* game with the cotton-reel, cited by Freud, the child's action of drawing the cotton-reel to it and throwing it away again, to the accompaniment of the words *da* (here) and *fort* (gone) enabled the child to symbolise a control over the presence and absence of objects, and by extension, over the movement of the primary object, the mother.

b, The Oedipus Complex

The "Oedipus Complex" is the term given to the stage or moment when the intervention of the 'Father' necessitates the child's abandonment of its exclusive relation with the mother and its entry into the structures of human sociality. The child is assigned a position in language and in the family and masculine or feminine sexuality. The repression of those elements of the psychic life of the child which do not conform to this positioning constitutes the unconscious.

The Castration Complex

The infant's attempt to include genital functions among those which can be expressive of the identification between child and mother is unsuccessful because the infant is faced with a rival, the "Father", against whom it is powerless. The term "Father" is not intended to designate the real parent of the child, although the real male parent may occupy this position in the structure. However, in this case, he does so only as the representation of all Fathers or of the ultimate Father (in Christian cultures, God the Father). The Father is essentially that authority which can intervene in and *delimit* the mother-child relation.

In view of this authority which stands above the mother-child identification, the child is faced with the possibility of an absence, not temporary, like that of the mother, but absolute. The mother, who has been the repository of all identity for the child, the basis of the child's conception of itself, is seen now as a mere testimony, empty in itself, to the self-constituting, self-sufficient presence, the Father. The opening of this fundamental lack, or gap, in identity inspires in the infant the fear of castration. At this fundamental level, the gender of the child does not affect the fear, although it does affect the specific forms taken by the fear — the complex

— and its resolution. Thus it is the genital function which is subject to the prohibition which introduces conclusively the authority of the Father, and the threat posed to the child, by the existence and authority of the Father, expresses itself for the child as the threat to the genitals. Before we go on to examine the consequences of the concept of the Oedipus complex for Lacan's theory, we must turn our attention to Lacan's most complex concepts — those which relate to language.

The Role of Language

"Language" in post-Saussurean linguistics means the formal structure which underlies and makes possible individual acts of speech. It is a system of rules which is not accessible to the consciousness of the ordinary language user, but which can only be elicited through systematic linguistic analysis. The two crucial Saussurian concepts for our present purposes are the *sign* and the concept of language as merely a system of differences in which there are no positive terms.

For Saussure the sign is the union of signifier and signified. The signifier is the word image (whether acoustic or graphic) and the signified is the concept with which it is associated. The sign as a whole receives its meaning not by virtue of its reference to some object in the real world, but by its specific differentiation from the entire body of other signs or "lexicon". A sign has meaning because it occupies a particular place in the lexicon. This is part of what is meant by language being only a system of differences.

The Saussurean notion of the sign is criticised either explicitly or implicitly in the theoretical work of Derrida, Kristeva and Lacan. The basis of their objection can be expressed in the following way. In the union of the signifier (word image) and signified (concept) it is impossible to assign any irreducible status to the concept (the signified). If the signifier can be unified with a mental concept, it is only by virtue of the fact that other signifiers enable the mind to formulate stable concepts. Rather than a unity of signifier and signified, we have a constant relay of signifiers. The signified (concept) as pure signified is never reached. For example the signifier "dog" would, according to this theory, only be intelligible in relation to the further signifiers "canine", and "quadruped" and more generally "animal" or "pet". Language is thus a vast system of tautology in which the pure concept (signified) is *never* isolatable.

The child can only use language fully by submitting to this conventional system which Lacan terms the *Symbolic Order.* It can only begin to use language in a coherent way by taking up a position in this system of conventions. That is, the child must identify itself with certain terms — "boy" or "girl", "son" or "daughter" — terms which themselves receive their significance by their relation to a *central signifier.*

Desire

In order to clarify the nature of this central signifier, we must first examine more closely the reaction of the infant to the threat of castration. The infant can only resolve the situation by, on the one hand submitting to the paternal authority, and on the other hand, identifying with that authority. This process is seen as ending differently according to the gender of the infant, a point which will be clarified later. It is clear that this identification of the infant with the Father cannot be of the same type as that enjoyed in the mother-child relationship. It is based not on a relation of immediate identification, but on one of *supposed eventual identity*; that is to take the case of the male child, he submits to the Father's Law so that he should not lose his genital — so that he may someday himself occupy the place of the Father. An important difference between the pre-Oedipal and the post-Oedipal identification is that the former is disturbed by the child's anxiety and its aggressivity — two legacies of the mirror phase — while the latter is disturbed by the child's aggressivity towards the Paternal authority, and by its *guilt* because of this aggressivity towards the authority with which it wishes to identify.

As we have intimated, the submission of the infant to the Paternal authority *includes* its becoming subject to the rules of language. This *entry into the Symbolic, which is finally constitutive of the subject,* has the effect of making it impossible for the subject to express its desire. This desire, which can be seen as the urge to achieve identity with the Other, the Father, is both alienated and insatiable. It is alienated because the subject can only express its desire by means of the system — language — which precisely embodies its submission to and distance from the Father. The position of the subject in language, as determined by the Paternal Law, renders certain positions in discourse impossible for the subject. Thus for example, a subject being positioned as "son" may wish to express its desire for the Father by acting the part of "wife" — (this is a way of expressing the position of the patient in Freud's "Wolf-man" analysis (Gardiner, 1973). The subject in this case has to *repress* any appearance of this transgressive desire in its discourse, which would constitute a transgression of the Symbolic Law which states that the proper destiny of the "son" is not to become "wife" and "mother" but "husband" and "Father".

Desire is insatiable because it is desire not of a real person but of a Symbolic position — the position which is powerful, self-constituting, source of the law, arbiter of the possibilities of the expression of desire. The desired object, like the signified, constantly recedes, being only the idea of an ultimate, transcendent guarantee of identity. With this view of desire in mind, we can return to the question of the central signifier which supports the symbolic order.

The Phallus

The phallic signifier is the signifier of desire. It is not identifiable with the real penis, but, as a signifier, it is part of the *Symbolic* system. It is here that the role of the real penis becomes crucial in the differential entry of the two sexes into the Symbolic. (The following account is implicit, rather than explicit in Lacan's work.) In the situation with which the child is faced at the moment of the intervention of the Father in the pre-Oedipal relation, the paternal authority is inseparable from maleness. The penis, the distinguishing mark of maleness and thus of the possibility of direct identification with the Father (if only *in prospect*), thus becomes the crux of the complex.

In the Symbolic system this appears as the phallic signifier — not just the signifier of a particular male organ, but the signifier of a potential power, in its possessor. The concept "Father" in the Symbolic system is that position which can wield the phallus; it must be remembered that the position "Father" is a Symbolic position also. The phallus is the signifier of desire and because the place of the Father as the arbiter of the expression of desire is the same as his place as wielder of the phallus, the control of desire (the phallus) is proper to him.

In language, the Name of the Father (which in some cases, e.g. Judaism, it is considered blasphemous to pronounce), is the name of the possessor, par excellence, of the phallus. It can now be seen how the phallus is able to act as a central signifier in relation to which positions in language become meaningful to the infant struggling to resolve the Oedipus complex. To clarify this we can enumerate the familial positions which are constituted in the Symbolic in relation to the phallus.

Familial Positions and their Relation to the Phallus in the Structure of the Symbolic
The *Father* is the possessor of the phallus, source of the law. The *son* has a more complex relation to the phallic signifier: on the one hand he represents the phallus, as it were, at one remove, for the mother; on the other, he has the prospect of possessing the phallus as future holder of the paternal position. The *husband* is a position which must be distinguished from that of the father. In his position as husband, the male partner represents, like the son, the possession of the phallus at one remove for the mother-wife.

This will become clearer if we examine the position of the female terms in relation to the phallus. From the castration complex it is clear that the control of access to the female (the mother) is a property of the controller of the phallus. The desire for identification with the father arises out of the pre-Oedipal desire for identification with the mother. The only way to possess the mother is to become the father. Desire for the maternal identification stands, as it were, behind the entire symbolic order, and this fact, threatening as it is to that order, cannot be included or expressed in its structure. The power of the father stands as a power independent in itself of all desire, since it controls desire. In actuality, then, the male adult parent cannot fill the symbolic position of the father, he can only stand as a reference to this authority which justifies his identification with the mother/wife. At the level of this identification, he reverts to the position of husband/son. There is a fundamental ambiguity of position here.

For the *daughter,* the Oedipus complex can only be resolved by the admission that the subject will never enjoy direct possession of the phallus. However there remains open to the daughter a role which is not symbolic, but *pre-symbolic,* that of the mother, the ultimate object of desire. It can be seen that the symbolic order is constantly troubled at the level of family positionality by the very basis on which it is reared — the maternal relation. However the daughter can only fulfil a maternal position in as much as that position does enter, in however ambiguous a fashion, into the symbolic order. As the mother, the female is the object of the desire of her son; as wife/mother, she is the object of this desire which reappears as the desire of the husband. As the object of desire she possesses, or rather *includes* phallic power (the power of the wielder of the phallus) in as much as she has power over the men for whom she is desirable. In this way, as wife and mother, she has the phallus at one remove and as daughter, she has the prospect of filling the maternal position.

Repression, the Unconscious and the Subject
As we have noted, the resolution of the Oedipus complex is only possible by the repression of tendencies, inappropriate to the individual's positioning in the symbolic order. This body of repressed tendencies constitutes the unconscious. It is

that position of concrete, transindividual speech which fails to be at the disposal of the subject for him/her to re-establish the continuity of his conscious speech. (Roussel, NLR 51)

For our present purposes, within the limits of this article, it would be impossible to go further into the Lacanian concept of the unconscious, since this necessitates a return to advanced linguistic concepts, inappropriate here, together with a much more detailed examination of Lacan's whole theoretical system.

As we have seen, the notion of the *subject* is appropriate to the individual in as much as it has become subject to, and taken up a position in, the paternally defined symbolic order, i.e. in as much as it can use language coherently on the basis of its relation to the central signifier, the phallus. Strictly speaking, it is only of the subject that we can use the pronouns he and she in any sense other than biological,, since it is only with the full entry into subjectivity that sexual identity becomes a fixed attribute of the individual. The subject, furthermore, is constantly troubled by the "return of the repressed"; the effects of repression appear in the subject's discourse as the "Freudian slip", physically as "hysterical symptoms" (e.g. the wolf-man's chronic constipation) and in dreams.

The Importance of Lacan for Kristeva's Theory of the Subject and Language

As we indicated at the beginning of this section, Lacan's theory of the constitution of the subject in language, i.e. in the Symbolic Order, via the various psychic moments outlined above, is the basis for Kristeva's theory of the subject and of signifying practice, which attempts to theorize fully the nature of artistic and literary discourse and thus dispel the absences which were inescapable in the Marxist aesthetics which we have examined so far, via a *retheorization* of language and the Saussurean notion of "signification" in terms of signifying practice. Any understanding of Kristeva's theory demands a willingness on the part of the reader to come to terms with her unfamiliar and, as such, difficult terminology. In the section which follows, we shall attempt to examine the two key moments in Kristeva's theory. These are first the concept of the "subject in process" which replaces the transcendental ego, which Kristeva terms the *thetic subject,* which is fixed in language, and which is the result of the *process of misrecognition* in Lacan's theory. Secondly, Kristeva's redefinition of signification which becomes one strand within signifying practice as a whole, which Kristeva calls *signifiance. Signifiance* includes what Kristeva terms the *symbolic* realm, Lacan's Symbolic Order, which is the level with which Saussurean linguistics deals, and the semiotic realm, which corresponds to the unconscious in Lacan and which has its site in what Kristeva terms the *semiotic chora.* Having thus located the origin of Kristeva's concepts in Lacanian psychoanalytic theory, we can proceed to look at Kristeva's own theory in detail.

The Theory of the Subject and of Poetic Language in the Work of Julia Kristeva

As was mentioned at the beginning of this section, the object of Kristeva's work is to provide Marxism with a psycho-analytically based theory of subjectivity, able to deal with marginal discourses, particularly that of poetry. It is specifically in relation to a reading of Mallarmé and Lautréamont that she undertakes this project.

Kristeva sets out to theorize the nature of the "always-already" given subjectivity which constitutes Althusser's concept of "ideology in general". This project

218

requires a retheorization of the social formation which Kristeva does not undertake in any fully systematic way. Rather she takes over the Althusserian model of the social formation, as if it were unproblematic to do so, and she attempts to show how the mode of socio-economic production and the mode of sign production belong intrinsically together. Thus she attempts to create a space for a revolutionary change in the status of the subject, which would be an intrinsic part of any structural change in the mode and relations of production, and which is of central importance for the feminist struggle, since it challenges the norms of what is often referred to as *civil society*, including the family structure.

Kristeva's starting point is the predication of the whole tradition of Western thought on the concept of the unified, transcendental, self-present subject, which is the basis of rationalism and which underpins Saussurean linguistics. It achieves its clearest expression vis-à-vis the philosophy of language in the phenomenology of Husserl. (By transcendental is meant a subject which is fixed in, and is one of the bases of, the subject-object relation.) In this tradition the subject-object division, which is the prerequisite for the use of language, is given both philosophically and in the syntactical structure of language as a system, which operates through the structure of a subject and a predicate, which is seen both in relation to and as distinct from the subject. There is a correlation between the signified object and the transcendental subject, through the mediation of the signifier, which must itself be transcendent. In Kristeva's theory, the subject is constituted in language through predication, i.e. through the subject-object relation as given in syntax. Kristeva calls this rethinking of the apparently transcendent subject, the "thetic subject", and locates it firmly in what she calls the symbolic realm, which is the established linguistic and social order, the realm of signification. The symbolic is the realm which establishes the limits and unity of signification through the linking of signifier and signified in the sign. It is the sum of the laws of human sociality, the realm of all discourse, of the law and its judgements, etc. and it functions through the subject-object relationship of predicative syntax. However Kristeva suggests that signifying practice is not limited to this thetic or symbolic realm, which following Lacanian theory is founded on a repression necessary for the establishment of a transcendent signifier, the phallus, which is the key support of the structure of language.

In fact Kristeva suggests that in signification the sign elides the real on behalf of the transcendent signifier and, as a consequence, meaning is constituted for the consciousness of the "transcendent" subject at the price of the repression of the drives, which are what underpins the symbolic order, i.e. the psyche. Following from this, Kristeva suggests that there are signifying practices which cannot be reduced to the symbolic order and as such pose a threat to it and therefore have been pushed to the periphery of discourse. Foremost among them are poetic language, art, religion and magic. Of these Kristeva chooses to concentrate on poetic language. She writes of poetic language that in as much as it functions with and communicates meaning, it also shares the features of symbolic signification, but is not limited to the symbolic realm.

> We might also say that while the thetic predicative operation and its correlatives (signified object and transcendental ego) are valid for the signifying economy of poetical language, they are only one of its limitations: a constitutive one, certainly, but not an all-encompassing one.

> In such a way it is in fact possible to study the sense and signification of poetical language (by revealing either its structures or its functioning, according to the particular method used) but after all, this kind of study would be equivalent to reducing poetical language to the phenomenological horizon and thus overlooking what is in the poetical process which falls outside the realm of the signified and the transcendental ego and makes of that which we call "literature" something other than knowledge: the very place where the social code is destroyed and renewed. (Kristeva 1975 p.11)

Kristeva's reference to the phenomenological horizon is a reference to the subject/object/meaning problematic of the phenomenologists, e.g. Husserl. The phenomenological horizon refers to that which is contained within the symbolic realm of fixed meaning. That which falls outside this horizon, outside the symbolic realm, and which the constitution of the symbolic realm represses, is called the *semiotic* order by Kristeva. It is the other order which is constantly threatening the symbolic and which *together with it* constitutes signifying practice, which Kristeva calls *signifiance.* These two modalities of *signifiance,* the symbolic and the semiotic are always present in language as a social practice, variously combined according to the type of discourse and signifying practice.

Drawing on Lacan's theory of the constitution of the subject in language, Kristeva describes the semiotic as what can be hypothetically posited as logically preceding the imposition of the symbolic order on the individual via the mirror phase and the acquisition of language. It is the already-given arrangement of the drives and so-called primary processes which displace and condense energies in the form of facilitations or pathways (*Bahnungen* in Freud) and their return to the symbolic system proper in the form of rhythms, intonations and lexical, syntactical and theoretical transformations. This arrangement of drives, which underpins language and the symbolic order, is termed the *semiotic chora* by Kristeva. It is the site of what she calls *negativity,* the process of semiotic generation whereby the drives constantly challenge and transform the subject in the symbolic order. The semiotic order is heterogeneous to meaning, i.e. external to it, meaning being contained within the symbolic order. It is however always either with a view to meaning or in a relation of negation or excess with regard to it. Kristeva stresses that in poetic language, which *is* socially communicable, this semiotic heterogeneity that theory can posit is *inseparable* from the symbolic function of signifiance.

Kristeva states that the semiotic chora is revealed genetically in the infant's first attempts at expression in prelinguistic rhythms and intonations which reoccur in psychotic discourse. She quotes these two areas of research (pre-mirror stage children and psychotic discourse) as aiming to describe the semiotic processes in question (rhythms, intonations) and their dependency relative to the instinctual body, which can be observed in the muscular contractions and in the libidinal or sublimated cathexes (interests, investments, intentions in Freudian theory), which accompany vocalizations. In poetic language, for instance that of Artaud, Kristeva suggests that the net of drives can be read across the drive bases of the non-semantic phonemes in his work.

As we have noted, both modes of *signifiance,* the symbolic and the semiotic, are present in signifying practice. However Kristeva suggests that in poetic language, the semiotic is not only a constraint, like the symbolic, but tends to take over as *the* major constraint, to the detriment of the thetic and predicative constraints of the judging consciousness of the subject. Thus rhythmical constraints not only play a structuring role in all poetic language, which can transgress grammatical rules, often neglecting the thetic meaning, but even cause non-recoverable syntactical elipses. Nonetheless:

> The symbolic function persists as an internal limitation of this bi-polar economy because a multiple and sometimes imperceptible signified is communicated. (Kristeva 1975 p.14)

The semiotic order is, as we have suggested, logically prior to the symbolic, and the constitution of the symbolic order is based on a break with the semiotic, which, following Lacanian theory, takes place in the development of the child via the mirror phase and the resolution of the castration complex. The semiotic order is pre-linguistic, pre-symbolic and *cannot therefore rest on any concept of a fixed subject which is constituted in the symbolic realm and of which it is the central support.* The semiotic realm is the precondition for the constitution of the subject in language, in the symbolic order. It is the site of what Kristeva, following Hegel, calls negativity, a constant process of expulsion (the counterpart to repression) which is constantly being repressed by the (re)constitution of the subject in the symbolic realm. It is the site of what Kristeva calls the "subject in process" of which the constantly repeated fixing of the transcendental subject in signifying practice is but a moment. Thus we have a model where signifying practice (*signifiance*) is determined by both the symbolic and the semiotic orders. The subject in signifying practice, as in Lacan's theory of the subject, is being constantly reformulated in the struggle between the two orders and reinserted into the symbolic as a fixed moment (a stasis) in the subject in process, which involves both orders. Thus Kristeva is able to present a theorization of how the ideological subject, on which Macherey, drawing on Althusser's ISAs essay, bases his theory of literature, is actually constituted in language. It is clear that for Kristeva, the symbolic order of ideology and ideological signification, which rests on the subject-object relationship, is part of *signifiance,* which includes the semiotic realm. However, for Althusser and Macherey the existence of what Kristeva terms the symbolic order of signification, which they implicitly cover by their term "ideological practice", located in ideological state apparatuses, is taken to be a *sufficient* account of ideology. We would argue, following Kristeva, that the dimension of the subject and signifying practice cannot be theoretically subsumed in a general term, such as ideological practice, but is essential to any theory of ideology and the social formation. Kristeva attempts to show, in the light of Freud and Lacan, that what determines the symbolic order cannot *simply* be located at the level of the class struggle and language as an unproblematically given system, determined by class, but must take account of the constitution of the subject. She tries to show too that signifying practice, which she defines as

> that through which the mode of production signifies its stabilization and its self expenditure — the conditions of its renewal (Kristeva 1976 p.64)

cannot be wholly reduced to symbolic signification within ideological state apparatuses. However the problem which arises at this point is that of identifying

> the intrinsic belonging of a mode of sign production to the mode of production of the socio-economic ensemble (ibid).

221

Earlier on, we mentioned that the semiotic chora consists of an "already given arrangement" of the drives, and it is at this point that Kristeva attempts to relate the semiotic realm to the social formation and ultimately to historical materialism and political practice. Kristeva writes of the arrangement of the drives in the semiotic chora of the infant:

> Discrete quantities of energy traverse the body, later to be a subject and in the course of his or her becoming, arrange themselves according to the constraints imposed upon this ever semiotizing body by the *familial and social structure* (Kristeva 1973-4 p.21; our emphasis).

She suggests that the way in which the drives are arranged prior to the acquisition of language is determined from the ouside by the family and social set-up and the way in which this acts upon the child's relation with its mother. In this way the child is constantly being prepared for a full entry into the symbolic: into language and self consciousness, through the resolution of the castration complex which causes the primal repression and the formation of the unconscious. Once the child has entered into self-consciousness and language as a subject, its position there needs to be constantly reaffirmed since, as we have noted, it is under constant attack from the semiotic chora. Social relations (the relations of production as maintained by the State and the legal system) and the relations of reproduction within the family structure, which are predicated on the repression of the drives and maintenance of the Symbolic Order, hold in place a certain type of relation between unity (the transcendent subject, the Symbolic Order, language, ideology, scientific discourse etc.) and process (the semiotic chora).

According to Kristeva it is in the speaking subject that the two realms, the semiotic and the Symbolic, come together, and that the socio-economic mode of production meets the mode of production of the subject in signifying practice. Hence there are two levels of contradiction, articulated together; that between the forces and relations of production and the contradiction of the process of *signifiance,* which finds its expression in

> the unsociable elements in the relations of reproduction (experience of sexual difference, incest, death drive, pleasure process) (Kristeva 1976 p.68).

Kristeva suggests that

> modern anthropology has succeeded in including kinship relations as an internal part of the 'economic and social formation' by insisting on the simultaneously economic and political role these relations play.

It is however equally important to include the part played by semiotically motivated signifying practices within any conceptualisation of an economic and social formation.

> It is these signifying practices that can reveal the economic and social formation that shelters them as a *provisional articulation,* constantly exceeded and threatened by the permanent contradiction proper to the process of signifiance — a contradiction between Symbolic and semiotic inherent in any speaking being from the moment it speaks to another by means of signs (Kristeva 1976 p.68; our emphasis).

It is this contradiction, inherent in *signifiance,* which according to Kristeva, makes every agent of structure an element of potential mutation. Thus from the level of

222

the subject, who is precariously installed within the Symbolic Order, which is upheld by socio-economic and familial forces, it is possible to challenge the unity of the social formation. Kristeva suggests that this challenge at the level of signifying practice could not but find itself aligned with political experiences and social movements that contest the existing relations of production. She writes that it is now possible to subject the unity of the social formation to analysis and concede to it a role which is structuring and yet ephemeral. Potentially this role could be based on the pleasure process, rather than its repression, and this would lead to a relativization of the function of the State and family and a new position for women within the Symbolic Order.

In this conception of the social formation, which includes the "signifying economy of sociality", certain signifying practices more than others would correspond to the dynamic as opposed to the stabilizing elements in the social formation. As we have seen, art and literature are foremost among the dynamic signifying practices, since they are constrained to a greater degree by the semiotic than other discourses, and are thus in a position to challenge the unity of the subject and its support in language and the socio-economic formation. Art and literature are those realms in which the semiotic component of *signifiance* breaks down to various degrees the Symbolic Order, which is constituted by and gives support to the laws and conventions of the social formation, and is the site of ideology and its "rational" explanation of lived experience. Thus Kristeva suggests that art can do more than merely allude to ideology as in Althusser and Macherey's theory; it can undermine the structures which give support to ideology itself.

Kristeva's attempt to introduce a theory of subjectivity into a Marxist theory of the social formation relies on two substantial factors. These are first an acceptance of the "scientificity" of Lacanian psychoanalytic theory, and secondly an acceptance of the intrinsic unity of the socio-economic mode of production and the mode of production of *signifiance,* understood as a unity of the symbolic and semiotic. Kristeva justifies this reformulation of the social formation by pointing to "the rapid and brutal truncation of the Hegelian dialectic" which she sees as forming the basis of "Marxist" attempts to trace discourse back to the economic mode of production *alone.* She suggests that

> This falls short of the Hegelian attempt to think through the efficacy of a signifying system on a subject, a society and a history (Kristeva 1976 p.64).

Kristeva locates this truncation of Hegel in Feuerbach rather than in Marx and suggests that there is a lack of a theory of subjectivity in Marxism, which should not, and indeed cannot be filled by Feuerbachian theory. It is to this theoretical lacuna that her theory of the subject and signifying practice is addressed.

Conclusion

Thus in bringing Section Two of this article to a conclusion, we are faced with all the problems to which any attempt at reformulating the social formation in terms of an intrinsic unity of the socio-economic mode of production and the mode of production of signifying practice, as theorised by Kristeva, gives rise. What is lacking in Kristeva's theory is a sustained and serious attempt to think the relation between these two concepts (economic mode of production and mode of production of signifying practice) which are drawn from very different discourses. We have pointed to the need for a theory of subjectivity for an understanding of the ideological instance in general, and art and literature in particular. However, in her attempt to resolve the dilemma of the role of the subject, Kristeva brings together two discourses (Althusserian Marxism and Lacanian psychoanalysis) without coming to terms with the fundamental, epistemological dimensions of such a move. It is with raising these problems that Section Three of this article will be concerned.

Section Three: The Problem of the Theory of the Social Formation

In the first two sections of this paper, we have tried to pose the problems which arise within the theoretical positions which we are considering, and we have related these different positions to each other. This necessarily involves taking up a position outside the individual theories considered.

If we are to have grounds for examining the theories of Macherey, Lacan and Kristeva and their relation, those grounds can only be argued fully by going beyond the level of critical exposition. An examination of either Macherey's or Kristeva's theory of art and ideology in isolation would of course be possible. But both these theories present themselves as a means of approaching the artistic (specifically, the literary) text. If we are to attempt to place the artistic text politically and theoretically, we must come to terms with the fact that these theories offer alternative and mutually exclusive approaches to that task. We wish to retain both theories in their inadequacies and their usefulness, and to proceed on this basis to an analysis of the wider implications of their coexistence.

The present section has two aims. First, it aims to provide some introduction to and commentary on our larger project. Secondly, it aims to justify what would otherwise be an arbitrary and unfounded juxtaposition of the two theories of art and ideology, and a mere statement of the importance of their interrelation. This will unfortunately involve us in assertions concerning theoretical matters of a more general kind, which cannot be fully supported in the space available.

Our immediate problem is that of theorizing the inadequacy and the usefulness of Macherey's and Kristeva's theories of art and ideology. But we can hardly fail to be aware that entailed in both are implicit theories of the social formation. In Macherey's case, the theory of the social formation on which the work depends, is, as we have seen, an Althusserian one. In the case of Kristeva, the problem is more complex: a theory of the social formation is assumed rather than made explicit in her work; she claims to "follow" Althusser, and at the same time criticises Marxism in a radical sense.

Kristeva's work in general displays the tendency to unceremoniously couple concepts from very different sources — the phenomenology of Husserl, the psychoanalysis of Melanie Klein and Lacan, the Marxism of Althusser. We would argue that this theoretical method cannot give rise to a satisfactory science of the social formation in the sense in which we intend that phrase.

In this connection we may note the reluctance of the entire *Tel Quel* group to claim for themselves any scientific status (cf Roland Barthes' refusal, in *S/Z* [Barthes, 1970]) to present his five codes of the narrative as scientific concepts; they remain only reading strategies. We would suggest that the difficulty and elusiveness of the Lacanian style also relate to this question. The prevailing tendency among these writers is to dismiss the whole problem of science; for them the attempt to constitute a science is itself an ideological attempt. It represents the illusion that discourse can enter into the real, given object and discover its essence. By contrast, Kristeva, Barthes, and, one might argue, Lacan, are concerned to celebrate the impossibility of escape from the prison-house of language. Their writings are conceived as strategies for the constant restating of that impossibility — the least ideological act that discourse can be made to perform being the realization of its own arbitrariness. (In the case of Lacan, the discourse in question being importantly that of individual subjects.)

Our problem was the alternative theorizations of the social formation entailed in our two theories of art and ideology. We can now say that we do not consider that Kristeva's work presents a viable alternative theorization of the social formation; despite the suggestive and seminal quality of her remarks on this point. We take the two main theoretical supports of Kristeva's work to be Lacanian psychoanalysis and Althusserian Marxism. Accordingly, it is to the problem of the relation between these two theories, rather than to that of the relation between Althusser's and Kristeva's works, that we address ourselves.

We assume that the works of Althusser and Lacan represent the most sophisticated formulations of their respective theoretical traditions. In this way we are able to characterize the relation between these two theories as the relation between Marxism and psychoanalysis in general.

We approach the task of analysing the relation of these two theories along two closely related routes. We must develop a position which is outside that of either tradition; and to do this we must construct the epistemological component and the theoretical component of such a position. The separation between these two components is made for purposes of clarity in exposition; no statements are being made about their interrelations within the science which they constitute.

Epistemologically, we begin by assuming that no science can make any claim to being, in an absolute sense, "true". We argue that the question of "truth" is a philosophical question, a question without an answer. This position, which owes something to the work of Derrida, finds its most explicit formulation in Althusser's work. Here philosophy is seen as intervening on behalf of scientific practice to draw the dividing line between science and ideologies. The later work argues that this philosophical practice represents the class struggle in the realm of theory. The science of historical materialism creates its own epistemological criteria by which to justify its own scientific status and detach itself from ideologies.

Starting from this position, we must attempt to develop the concept of a science which can be seen as determined to some extent by its relation to the social formation within which it is an element. At the same time we must attempt to go beyond the point of claiming that a discourse is scientific inasmuch as it enters the class struggle on the side of the progressive elements. We would argue that one important aspect of science is not its having an expressive relation to a real world but its having the justification of an extension of control over the given; that is, as a discourse having an operative relation to the structured constraints which, while being unknowable in any absolute sense, must be taken into account as a precondition of successful action.

Given this provisional characterization of science, two consequences follow. On the one hand, the developments of particular sciences can be accounted for in terms of their interrelations and conflicts on the particular level of the social formation proper to theoretical discourses, as well as in terms of its effectivity elsewhere in the social formation.[6]

On the other hand, the fact that a successful science involves an extension of control over the given, means that a successful science of the social formation must inevitably be a progressive political force. This assumes that progressive political struggle involves the extension of conscious rational control over the social formation's workings and developments.

In this sense we can add a political criterion to our epistemological tenets. This allows us to begin the analysis of the statuses of and relations between Marxism and psychoanalysis, since these two disciplines manifestly claim political as well as theoretical significance. This epistemological position is an extension of and departure from that taken by Althusser in *Lenin and Philosophy* (1971).

Theoretically, our starting-point is the simultaneous awareness of the concepts of both historical materialism and of psychoanalysis. In the light of this, the two systems of concepts comment upon each other, and the assets and liabilities of each can be assessed. We can say no more of this complex process than that an act of distanciation and synthesis begins to make possible the development of new concepts.[7] It must be one of the first tasks of the new theory to provide an adequate account of the confrontation between historical materialism and psychoanalysis.

The logical starting point of this new theory is the reconceptualization of the specificity of the human social formation. We can begin by placing the whole realm of the "cultural" or "social" in its relation to the "natural"; that is, we would wish to end the radical separation between the "human" or "social" sciences (the very confusion of terms here is symptomatic) and the "physical" or "natural" sciences.

At this early stage we must be content to state that the theory envisaged is one which would characterize the defining function of the social formation as "the maintenance of its subjects". This maintenance is necessary in two senses: the social formation must maintain its subjects inasmuch as their subjectivity demands as a support the mass of individual human animals, which must be fed, clothed, sheltered, and reproduce itself. Equally the social formation must by definition maintain its subjects as *subjects,* in a state of psychic subjection and organization. The social formation is seen as being, at its most general, both an economic and a psychic structure.

Consequently, we can move on to the task of theorizing the confrontation between historical materialism and psychoanalysis. One of the first aims of our theory is to account for its own origins. In undertaking this task, one of the first necessities must be the conceptualization of the social formation within which the development of the new theory has taken place. We would argue that the social formation characterized by the dominance of the capitalist mode of production involves a basic contradiction. In carrying out the task of maintaining its subjects in an economic sense, the formation necessitates, due to the peculiarities of the capitalist economic mode, calling into question the mode of psychic subjection and organization of its subjects.

In pre-capitalist formations the Law which Lacan identifies at the level of the family forms the basis of political institutions. The subject finds its subjectivity affirmed by all the institutions with which it is in contact. By contrast, the institutions which reflect the abstract, impersonal necessities of the expansion of capital have only a distant, and often an antagonistic relation to the structures of subjectivity. The expression of these structures is relegated to the subordinate places of religious, familial and "community" associations.

It is in terms of a social formation determined by this contradiction between the economic and the subjective that we would situate political practice, or as we have called it earlier, "signifying practice". Specifically, we might mention artistic practice, agreeing with Kristeva's basic contention that it represents an attempt to come to terms with a weakening of, or crisis in, subjectivity. The same process might be seen as the basis of the possibility of a feminist consciousness and the struggle against sexism. It is in terms of these struggles, as well as of the struggles of the working class, that we would begin to account for theoretical developments.

Marxism and psychoanalysis may be seen as the representations of these practices at the level of theory. Accordingly they might both be seen as sciences in our sense of the term; and since they share this status there is a possibility of their being in a relation of confrontation. Our analysis of that confrontation involves the hypothesis that, to put it crudely, Marxism and psychoanalysis both claim to explain the same phenomena. Because of this, a situation arises wherein one of these theories attempts to engulf the other by raiding its concepts and installing them in a subordinate position within its own system of concepts. We would argue that this is the interpretation which is to be made of Althusser's treatment of psychoanalysis in "Freud and Lacan" and the second part of the essay "Ideology and Ideological State Apparatuses" entitled "On Ideology" (Althusser 1971). This interpretation would not of course depend on Althusser's telling us that this is what he intends to do, nor would it expect any such announcement. There is an even more complex analysis to be made of the origins of this theoretical confrontation in the failures, impasses and rivalries of the various forms of political struggle.

We may now claim to have sketched the elements of a position which is distinct from those of either Marxism or psychoanalysis. This new theory of the social formation would assign a basic determinacy to the psychic, as well as the economic, as historical materialism does not. The theory of subjectivity which would be a component of the new theory would differ from psychoanalysis, not only because of the radical differences in the modes of thinking social formations as between the two systems (one need only think of Freud's writings on civilization and its mythical origins to realize this). It would differ radically also in its mode of thinking the psychic life of the individual. Kristeva's theory of subjectivity (Kristeva 1974) constitutes the beginnings of such a theory.

These arguments and invocations of arguments can do no more than serve as a beginning and as an introduction to a much longer debate. They represent our progress so far in the task of formulating a mode of analysis of the artistic text, and

227

of its relation to ideology. One need hardly point out the far-reaching consequences of this project. What began as an attempt to think the specificities of art and ideology, and their relationship, necessarily leads us (or so it seems to us) into an attempt to build and maintain an entirely new epistemological and theoretical position. If our enterprise seems scandalous, nothing could be better testimony to the scandalous nature of those artistic texts which challenge us to analyse them.

While we could hardly have hoped to solve the problem of the relations between art and ideology, in the absence of any finished conceptualization of either, we do hope to have begun to point to the solution. (We accept the impossibility of a fully theorized approach to any artistic text now and for some time.) For the present we must be content that our argument brings much closer the moment when we shall be able to think fully the inadequacies and the usefulness of the theories of Macherey and Kristeva concerning the relation of art and ideology. Not least, we hope to have demonstrated the centrality of this problem of the artistic for the future development both of theory and of political practice. Our theoretical project has a view to the theorization, unification and facilitation of the political struggles which it thinks of as its progenitors.

Notes

1. See Lenin, *Party Literature and Party Organisation,* 1905.
2. For example those of Kant, German classical theory and romanticism.
3. The reference is to *Les Français fictifs: le rapport des styles littéraires au français national* Hachette 1974.
4. A symptomatic reading is a reading which constructs the problematic including the *absence* of problems and concepts in a text, i.e. the unconsciousness of the text, on the model of the Freudian analyst's reading of his patient's utterances. See L. Althusser, *For Marx* Allen Lane, London 1970.
5. See K. Marx, *The German Ideology Part One* Lawrence and Wishart, London 1970.
6. We are assuming here a social formation including a level of theoretical production, although this is a question which must remain unresolved as yet.
7. It is important in approaching this question to bear in mind the point made by Althusser (1970 p.27): "The whole process takes place in the dialectical crisis of the mutation of a theoretical structure in which the 'subject' plays not the part it believes it is playing, but the part which is assigned to it by the mechanism of the process."

Bibliography

L. Althusser, *Lenin and Philosophy* NLB, London 1971.

L. Althusser, *Reading Capital* NLB, London 1970.

R. Barthes, *S/Z* Cape, London 1970.

W. Benjamin, *Illuminations* Fontana, London 1973.

M. Gardiner, *The Wolf-man and Sigmund Freud* Penguin 1973.

L. Goldmann, *Pour une sociologie du roman* Gallimard 1964.

J. Kristeva, *The Speaking Subject and Poetical Language* 1975: a paper presented to the inter-disciplinary seminar on *Identity in Anthropology* organised by Jean-Marie Benoist under the direction of Claude Lévi-Strauss, Professor at the Collège de France: The English version was delivered as a lecture in the University of Cambridge.

J. Kristeva, "Signifying Practice and Mode of Production" *Edinburgh 76 Magazine* no. 1 1976.

J. Kristeva, *The Subject in Signifying Practice:* paper presented at Columbia University seminar on the theory of literature, 1973-4.

J. Kristeva, *La Revolution du Language poetique* Seuil 1974.

J. Lacan, *The Mirror Phase* NLR 51.

G. Lukács, *The Meaning of Contemporary Realism* Merlin, London 1963.

P. Macherey, *Pour une théorie de la production littéraire* Maspero, Paris 1966.

P. Macherey and E. Balibar, "Sur la littérature comme forme idéologique: quelques hypothèses marxistes" *Littérature* no 14.

J. Roussel, *An Introduction to Lacan* NLR 51.

F. de Saussure, *A Course in General Linguistics* Fontana 1974.

Notes on Marx
and the
Problem of Individuality

Victor Molina

Introduction

The conceptualization of ideology has recently been related, mainly by the important formulations made by Althusser, to the problematic of individuality.

This problem is polemical in itself, and has a history of its own. It has always
been the field of a "humanism" strange to Marxism, theoretically and politically.
A related problem, that of subjectivity, has been a crucial weapon for arguing for
a relationship between Marxism and, for instance, psychoanalysis, a combination
which also poses theoretical and political problems. In relation to both problems
we have the existence of attempts to relate Marxism to the traditional "human"
disciplines: anthropology, psychoanalysis itself, etc.

If one goes into the details of this situation, one can see that these problems
relate necessarily to a discussion about the basic principles of Marxism. If these
proposals involve *theoretical concessions,* and we think they do, then the problem
is not merely an academic one, because what is present is a "bargaining over
principles".

This paper is an effort to examine some of the theoretical problems which arise
when the problem of ideology is related to "individuality" (and also to "subjectivity"). These problems concern Marxist theory *as such.* In this sense the paper
is not one on a theme like "ideology and individuality", but implies a unilateral
emphasis on the problem of individuality as such.

First, we examine the treatment of individuality as it exists in Marx's own
theory. We argue for the validity of two essential theses about "individuality", with
the conclusion that there is no such "theory of the individual" in Marx.

Second, we examine some aspects of the problem of a Marxist "humanism", and
here we argue for the validity of the thesis of an anti-humanism in Marx.

Finally, we look briefly at the particular concern about "individuality" which is
present in Althusser's formulations on ideology.

Marx on Individuality

Individuals under Definite Social Relations

The theoretical status of the category of "individual" is clearly formulated by Marx
when he resumes the "guiding thread" for his studies:

> In the social production of their life, men *enter* into definite relations that are indispensable, and independent of their will, relations of production . . . The sum total of these relations of production constitutes the economic structure of society, the real foundation, on which rises a legal and political superstructure and to which correspond definite forms of social consciousness. (Marx, *1859 Preface* p.503)

This thesis, which is the base for Marx's theoretical work, was formulated in *The German Ideology*. His central argument is there based on a conception about "men" in terms of *men in their given social connection,* in contra-distinction to Feuerbach who "stops at the abstraction 'men'". From now on, Marx's theoretical interest will be precisely the nature of this given "social connection", based on the social process of production.

There is always the temptation to see in the above formulation the starting-point of a conceptualization about the *concrete individual.* But, on the contrary, it is precisely there where Marx separates himself from the "concrete individual" as an analytical object. We must bear in mind that all the references by Marx about concrete individuals refer only to the existence of some obvious *premises*:

> The premises from which we begin are not arbitrary ones, not dogmas, but real premises . . . they are the real individuals, their activity and the material conditions under which they live . . . The first premise of all human history is of course, the existence of *living* human individuals. (Marx, *The German Ideology* p.19)

But this implies that

> we must begin by stating the *first premise* of all human existence and, therefore, of all history, the premise, namely, that men must be in a position to live in order to "make history". But life involves before everything else eating and drinking, a habitation, clothing and many other things. The *first historical act* is thus the production of the means to satisfy these needs, the production of material life itself. (*The German Ideology* p.30)

Briefly, *The German Ideology* shows precisely that Marx's conceptualization is not one about the premise of "living individuals" but one about this "historical act". He is explicitly trying to argue for a materialist conception of history which is founded in the particular existence of social *relations*:

> Thus it is quite obvious from the start that there exists a *materialistic connection of men,* which is determined by their needs and their mode of production, and which is as old as men themselves. This connection is ever taking on new forms, and thus presents a "history" independently of the existence of any political or religious nonsense which would specially hold men together. (*The German Ideology* p.32)

It is Marx's conception of history, which "depends on our ability to expound the real process of production" (*The German Ideology p.41*), which posits from the start the conceptual formula by which to theoretically think the "individual": *definite individuals under definite relations of production* (and other social relations). In other words, what we confront are individuals *within* that "ensemble of social relations" which is, from the *Theses on Feuerbach,* signalled as the theoretical object of Marx's theory. This means that what we find in Marx is by no means the development of a theory of "individual" but a theoretical account of social relations. The category of "individual" is from this time on completely subordinated to the theorization about these relations, in particular to that of the relations of production. And this priority is not a methodological one (like the current "sociological" abstraction) but it is based in the specificity of the social relations themselves.

It is because Marx is confronting an analysis of *relations,* which are constituted as a complex "ensemble" of relations, that there is the need to reject the category of "man" as a concept by which to think society. This category cannot be more than an *initially "unitary" concept* (Gramsci) by which the dialectic of *real* relations cannot be thought, except in terms of that idealist "relation of man to himself" criticized by Marx (and which is the idealist base of the humanist notion of "alienation").

These formulations have decisive importance, because for Marx the social relations are not relations between "individuals":

> These relations are not relations between individual and individual, but between worker and capitalist, between farmer and landlord, etc. (*The Poverty of Philosophy* p.87)

In fact, for Marx the concept of "society", and its relation with the category of "individual", is a very strict one:

> Society does not consist of individuals, but expresses the *sum of interrelations,* the relations *within* which these individuals stand. As if someone were to say: seen from the perspective of society, there are no slaves and no citizens: both are human beings. Rather, they are that outside society. To be a slave, to be a citizen, are social characteristics, relations between human beings A and B. Human being A, as such, is not a slave. He is a slave in and through society. (*Grundrisse* p.265)

Society exists for the individuals as the sum of the relations in which they stand. The individuals exist *within* these relations only as determined by the social determinations provided by the relations as such. To be a "wage-labourer" is not an original determination for an individual A but it is a determination proper to the *relation* in which he is opposed to an individual B, who carries the determination of being a "capitalist". These determinations exist only in the relation itself.

What is more imporant, these individuals exist as such individuals (as "human beings") only *outside society,* outside the social determination. In fact, Marx is always making a clear separation between a conceptualization of individuals as *personifications* and the same individuals as *individuals.* This separation is what distinguishes Marx's theoretical treatment of the individual and a proper "theory of the individual" in general.

In *The German Ideology* this distinction appears as one between a *personal* individual and a *class* individual. Marx speaks about a "division within the life of each individual, insofar as it is *personal* and insofar as it is *determined* by some branch of labour and the conditions pertaining to it" (*The German Ideology* p.66). There this distinction corresponds to a difference between the individual *as a person* and *what is accidental to him* (a form of intercourse, i.e., the social relations).

In the *Grundrisse* this distinction is related to the difference between *personal* relations (personal dependency relations) and *objective* relations (objective dependency relations).

Finally, in *Capital* this distinction takes its definitive formulation in the difference between individuals taken "only in so far as they are the *personifications* of economic categories" (Marx, *Capital I,* p.21) and the individuals taken "as individuals" (Marx, *Capital I,* p.160). This is the reason why the thesis on personification expresses precisely the theoretical status of the category of "individual" in Marxist theory.

232

Thus in Marx's theory of capitalist relations of production the individual is an individual entirely determined by society, the individual is already *posited* in the relations which constitute the social totality. These social relations, which are *objective* relations, are the only source of determinations for the individual in Marx's theory.

This particular existence of the individual corresponds to the nature of capitalist relations. In fact, in the categories representing the capitalist relations of production is already implied a separation between a *social existence* and a *natural existence.* This is what is behind the double character of the commodity, for instance, and in concepts such as money and capital. What is more, the functioning of capitalist relations of production implies the permanent extinction (within the capitalist process of production) of the "natural" individuality of its elements. Capitalist relations imply a specific *indifference* towards the "natural" particularity and individuality of its elements. Not only does commodity exchange imply this, but so also does the "abstract" character of labour, the concept of money, and also the concept of capital.

In fact, in the functioning of the relations of production is implied a particular existence of individuality (in general). In other words, inherent in the nature of social relations is a particular relation to individuality.

It is in this sense that exchange relations, for instance, imply for Marx the existence of "individuals who are indifferent to one another" (*Grundrisse* p.156). This "mutual indifference" concerns a very precise thing: in the exchange relation the subjects are

> as equals, at the same time also indifferent to one another; whatever other individual distinction there may be does not concern them; *they are indifferent to all their other individual peculiarities.* (*Grundrisse* p.242)

Of course, in the exchange relations, this indifference is related to the "equality" which is presupposed in this relation (it is a relation of equivalents), which is not the case for the more specific relations of production (for instance, capital/wage-labour) in which

> individuals relate to one another no longer merely as exchangers or as buyers and sellers, but in specific relations, no longer all of the same character. (*Grundrisse* p.247)

But this indifference "to all their other individual peculiarities" is also true for all capitalist relations, in the sense of an indifference to "natural" peculiarities, i.e., to peculiarities (differences) not coming from the determinations of the social relation itself. We shall see, for instance, that the concept of personification is based precisely on this indifference.

What has misled some interpretations of this problematic is the fact that in the exchange relation the "mutual indifference" expresses not only an indifference to "natural" peculiarities but also an indifference to "social" peculiarities (differences) arising, in this case, from the relations of production:

> A worker who buys commodities for 3s. appears to the seller in the same function, in the same equality — in the form of 3s. — as the King who does the same. All distinction between them is extinguished. (*Grundrisse* p.246)

It is the extinction and refutation of "more developed, contradictory forms" inherent in the exchange relation, taken in its simple character, that is behind the particular fetishism which arises from this relation, a fetishism based on that "infantile abstraction" of some economists criticized by Marx (see for instance *Grundrisse* pp.249-50). In this sense, in the exchange relation we find an extinction of all the "social" difference posited by contradictory social relations, in which "the extremes which stand opposite one another are *specifically* different" (*Grundrisse* p.266) — for instance, capital/wage-labour.

The double character of that "indifference" (to natural and to social determinations) has led to a misinterpretation of the "mutual indifference" as a mere phenomenal form or "ideological form of an individual dis-connection" assumed for what is in reality a relation of individual "mutual inter-dependence" (see, for instance, Hall 1974 p.134). For Marx, however, the category "indifference" does not correspond to a category of "independence": both relate to different problems. When Marx says that "the reciprocal and all-sided *dependence* of *individuals who are indifferent to one another* forms their social connection" (*Grundrisse* p.157), he is not making an opposition between "dependence" and "indifference", but grasping the specificity of an *objective* dependence (characterized by "indifferent individuals") in distinction to a *personal* dependence (in which there is, of course, no indifference to personal particularities). That is why Marx describes capitalist relations as characterized by a "personal independence founded on objective dependence" and why he speaks of "connection of mutually indifferent persons".

In fact, the "mutual indifference" inherent in the exchange relation relates mainly to the objective character of capitalist relations as "external" with respect to individuals, and concerns the negation of all "peculiarity" which does not arise from the relations themselves. In this sense, we must not forget that exchange value, in the argument of the *Grundrisse*, is a *generality*.

> Activity, *regardless* of its individual manifestation, and the product of activity, *regardless* of its particular make-up, are always exchange — value, and exchange value is a *generality* in which *all individuality and peculiarity are negated and* extinguished. (*Grundrisse* p.157)

But the concept of abstract labour implies this "generality" and "indifference" too:

> labour is not this or another labour, but labour pure and simple, abstract labour: absolutely indifferent to its particular *specificity,* but capable of all specificities . . . the worker himself is absolutely indifferent to the specificity of his labour; it has no interest for him as such but only in as much as it is in fact *labour* and, as such, a use value for capital. (*Grundrisse* p.296)

Finally, even the concept of capital implies this character:

> capital *as such* is indifferent to every particularity of its substance, and it exists not only as the totality of the same but also as the abstraction from all its particularities . . . capital can come into relation with every *specific* labour; the particular one it confronts at a given time is an accidental matter.

Briefly, this "mutual indifference" concerns the fact that capitalist relations of production and exchange "presuppose the dissolution of all fixed *personal* (historic) relations of dependence in production" (*Grundrisse* p.156). For instance, "in the money relation, in the developed system of exchange . . . the ties of personal dependence, of distinction of blood, education, etc. are in fact exploded, ripped up"

(*Grundrisse* p.163). What occurs is a dissolution of the relations of dependence into a *general form,* into the form of relations which are external to and autonomous of individuals.

It is because of this objective character of the relations of production that in Marx's theory the individuals are related *only* to their social bonds. The individual appears only in his "economic (social) character" in distinction to his "personal (natural) character" as individual.

The result of this complex argument is a very precise one: the individual (in Marx's theory) is exclusively *determined* by society, it exists *only with* the social determinations coming from relations of production. There is a theoretical absence of any "natural" (non-social) determination for the individual. This explains why it is impossible to consider Marx's theory as one about concrete individuals, whose concreteness implies precisely something more than its "social" determinations.

In fact, Marx's conceptualization is one about *relations* and not about the *subjects* which stand in these relations. This is because, as Marx states, "in general, relations can be established as existing only by being *thought,* as distinct from the subjects which are in these relations with each other".

In this respect, the theoretical fate of the individual is similar to that of the commodity, which suffers a complete "abstraction" of its natural existence (as a particular commodity) and is considered in Marx's analysis purely in respect to its *economic* existence (as value). And we must remember that Marx's theory is not a theory of commodity.

Returning to our individual, we must consider that, of course, he is a complex of "social" and "natural" determinations; but Marx's thesis of an individual "already posited by society" implies a very precise dialectic: that of the capitalist society where "personal relations flow purely out of relations of production and exchange" (*Grundrisse* p.165). In this sense, social relations (society) are not a mere "social framework" with respect to individuals, but they stand as the very structural "ensemble" which *constitutes* individuality itself. Individuality is precisely a *product* of the ensemble of social relations.

When Marx formulates the starting-point for the analysis of material production as being that of "individuals producing in society", he opposes this category to that of the "isolated individual" of the Robinsonades who appears as an individual without *social* connectedness (1857 Introduction, *Grundrisse* p.83). In capitalist society the individual appears as "independent" because "detached from *natural* bonds". But what the notion of "isolated individual" also does not grasp is that this detachment *from* natural bonds is simultaneously a complete attachment *to* objective social bonds. In fact, only in capitalist society

> do the various forms of social connectedness *confront* the individual as a mere means towards his private purposes, as *external* necessity. But the epoch which produces this standpoint, that of the isolated individual, is also precisely that of the hitherto most developed social (from this standpoint, general) relations. The human being is in the most literal sense a political animal, *not merely a gregarious animal,* but an animal which can *individuate* itself *only in the midst of society.* (1857 Introduction, *Grundrisse* p.84)

This strong and rich conception of an individuation *through* the social determination condenses all the previous theses. Also this argument proves wrong any conception which presents the individual as an *a priori* with respect to society or as its starting-point. It shows as wrong any formulation of an individuation *against* society (Marcuse). It also makes necessarily wrong any circular statement in which the individual is product-creator of society, such as Schaff's: "the individual is always social — that is, he is a product of society which he creates" (*Socialist Humanism* p.145). With respect to this last formula, it must be noted that it is an impossible thesis because it implies a *simultaneity* (of processes) which is difficult to sustain theoretically, and because it confuses in one simple formula a thesis belonging to a theory of individuality (individual as a product) with one belonging to a theory of history (society as a creation of the individual), both of which need a completely different argumentation (the second being a theoretical absurdity). Finally, any thesis which interprets Marx's Thesis VI on Feuerbach in terms of a thesis about individuality ("the individual as the entirety of social relations" — Schaff, *Socialist Humanism* p.144) is obviously completely wrong too.

Individuals as "Personifications"

The preceding line of argument, coming mainly from the *Grundrisse,* is completely in accordance with the treatment of the category of "individual" in *Capital.* What is more, it is in *Capital* that Marx formulates with outstanding clarity the strict meaning of his conceptualization of the individual, by means of the thesis on "personification":

> here individuals are dealt with only in so far as they are the *personifications of economic categories, embodiments* of particular class-relations and class-interests. My standpoint, from which the evolution of the economic formation of society is viewed as a process of natural history, can less than any other make the individual responsible for *relations whose creature he socially remains,* however much he may subjectively raise himself above them. (*Capital I* p.20)

To avoid problems of translation we can quote a more recent account of this thesis:

> individuals are dealt with here only in so far as they are the *personifications of economic categories,* the *bearers* (*Träger*) of particular class-relations and interests. (*Capital I* Penguin p.92)

All the theoretical work in *Capital* presupposes this thesis. Whatever opinion we may have about the Althusserian thesis of individuals as mere "supports of functions", one thing cannot be denied: that *Capital* is an analysis of capitalist *relations* of production; in which the *only* existence of individuals is as "bearers and agents of *these* relations" (*Capital III* p.209).

Even more, we may agree or disagree with Marx but, again, it cannot be denied that he is very clear when he continuously states, without ambiguity, that he is dealing with *agents* of production, i.e., with "bearers of the various *functions* in the production process" (*Capital III* p.822).

The theoretical implications of this thesis are very important, and they are a natural consequence of the character of Marx's theory of capitalism, in which

> The principal agents of this mode of production itself, the capitalist and the wage-labourer, are as such merely *embodiments, personifications* of capital and wage-labour; definite *social characteristics stamped upon individuals* by the process of social production; the products of these definite social production relations. (*Capital III* p.880)

236

In fact, what Marx is saying is that he is dealing with individuals only in terms of their "social characteristics", but these *social* characteristics are not determinations of the individuals as such, they constitute an *economic character* which is merely *"stamped upon" individuals.* This is the reason why the individuals are precisely personifications of *economic categories* (categories belonging to an "economic" theory but *not* to a theory of the individual). In other words, Marx's analysis is one concerning the objectivity of these "social relations of production" and *not* one concerning the objectivity of individuals. It is an analysis of a *purely social reality* (*Capital I* p.54), that of social relations in its "pure form", and this reality is not a reality *of* individuals but it is a reality within which they *stand.*

In this sense, for the individuals, this economic character is only "the indicator of their social function or social relation towards one another" (*Grundrisse* p.241). When Marx speaks of capitalist and wage-labourer as personifications of capital and wage-labour, he is precisely speaking about "the character which capitalist and worker have as the extremes of a single relation of production" (*Grundrisse* p.297).

Capital contains a particular repetition of this thesis:

> in the course of our investigation we shall find, in general, that the characters who appear on the economic stage are but the personifications of the economic relations that exist between them". (*Capital I* p.89)

Individuals appear only as *"economic* dramatis personae" (*Capital I* p.147), confronting one another as buyer/seller, capitalist/wage-labourer, etc., that is, in accordance with definite *economic* determinations, belonging to definite social relations, and expressed in *economic* categories. Thus it is not surprising to see that the capitalist is *"merely* capital personified and functions in the process of production *solely* as the agent of capital" (*Capital III* p.819) or that, if the process of reproduction includes production and circulation as functions of capital, then "therefore it includes the necessity of having *representatives* of these functions", i.e., agents of production and agents of circulation (*Capital II* p.130).

All this implies without doubt that the determination of "capitalist", for instance, is attached to an individual only when he is representing a definite *function* in the production processes. To be a capitalist is not a definition of an individual *as such,* it is not an "internal" determination carried by the individual, but it is a category corresponding to a function he is accomplishing — just that. The fact that his individuality is affected by this is a different problem.

Because in *Capital* we are dealing with a social character "stamped upon individuals", an interesting problem arises. As in the case of the means of production (which as such are not capital), the treatment of individuals stands in *Capital* on the same theoretical basis in which the treatment of "things" stands:

> It is not a question here of definitions, which things [or individuals, VM] must be made to fit. We are dealing here with definite *functions* which must be expressed in definite categories. (*Capital II* p.230)

If the implications of this thesis are taken seriously, and they are very clear in *Capital,* it seems that any opposition or misunderstanding of the thesis of "personification" implies the danger of a particular "fetishism" about the problematic of individuality. In fact, because Marx's theory is one concerning social relations of production, the problematic of the specificity and objectivity of these *relations* stands in the same form for individuals as for so-called "things". In other words, the problem of the distinction between a *social* and a *natural* existence, between an *economic* and a *material* (natural) character etc., which is so crucial for Marx, is also a distinction which is present in Marx's conceptual treatment of individuals.

This is why he always made a distinction, for instance, between a *personal* and a *class* individual (*German Ideology*), between *personal* and *objective* relations (*Grundrisse*), between *social characters* and *individual human nature as such* (*Contribution*) etc., and between *individuals as personifications* and *individuals as individuals* (*Capital*). If these distinctions are not made we have again the same confusion between what is a "social, economic character impressed on things in the process of social production" and what is a "natural character stemming from the material nature of those things" (*Capital II* p.229), a confusion which is characteristic of the fetishist treatment of the concept of capital (confusion capital/means of production), or the concept of value (confusion value/use values), etc.

Here we cannot go further into this problem, but it seems that the whole argument of Marx tends to conclude that when facing the reality of the individuals, we are facing a reality similar to that of commodities as "sensuous things which are at the same time suprasensible or social" (*Capital I* Penguin p.165). This would be the reason why in the same way as we do not find in Marx a theory of the commodity as such, so we do not find a theory of individuality as such. In *Capital* we find only that economic character *impressed on* individuals and nothing more.

Of course, individuals are not things. They are for Marx "conscious representatives". When an individual functions as a capitalist he obviously functions as "capital *personified* and endowed *with consciousness and a will*" (*Capital I* p.151). The relations of production are, also, obviously "social conditions of production *within* which the individual is *active*" (*Grundrisse* p.172). But the fact of this consciousness, will and activity of the individual does not affect the nature of the relations of production (nor its theory). What is important for Marx, on the contrary, is the fact of this "personification" (and this activity of the individual within social conditions of production), which indicates the real situation of the individual with respect to the social relations (and with respect to Marx's theory). Our individual is not a thing, but this difference refers only to the problem of the process by which the social relations are *impressed on* or *stamped upon* the individuals. The effects of this impression on individuality as such (individuals as individuals) implies a *production* of a specific individuality by these effects, an implication which is not present in things. In other words, it concerns the problem of that "individuation in the midst of society" signalled by Marx, and also concerns the problem of how "personal relations flow out of relations of production and exchange". But this problematic is not Marx's own.

When treating the problem of the creation of surplus-value, while remaining theoretically in the sphere of circulation, Marx asks himself if the difficulty in resolving this problem might not come from his thesis on "personification":

> Let us therefore keep within the bounds of exchange where sellers are also buyers, and buyers, sellers. Our difficulty may perhaps have arisen from treating the actors *as personifications* instead of *as individuals*. (*Capital I* p.160)

238

And then he proves that this is not the case. But what he was asking was precisely if the cause of the appearance of a surplus-value did not perhaps arise from a purely individual superiority of one individual over another (in this case, greater cleverness), i.e., from a difference of *natural* (individual) origin, rather than from the character of the social relation itself (in this case, the exchange relation) personified in the actors. He proves, then, that his persistence in treating individuals as "personifications" is not only a correct one but a necessary one for the analysis of capitalist relations as such, explaining later the creation of surplus-value from the nature of the relation of production.

But what is important for us is that he explicitly formulates a clear distinction between a theoretical treatment of individuals *as personifications* (as bearers of economic categories) and a treatment of individuals *as individuals* (according to individual differences which do not arise from the economic relation itself). The question and its answer correspond clearly to a difference between what is the problem of the status of the category of "individual" in Marx's theory and what would be the problem of a theory of individuality *as such*, the latter problem not being present in Marx.

All this relates to the fact that the concept of personification, the only one by which Marx thinks individuality in *Capital,* expresses the existence of that *indifference* with regard to any determination not arising from the social relations themselves, by which Marx characterized individual relationships in the *Grundrisse.* Individuals exist within the social relations only as bearers of the determinations which arise from the ensemble of these relations. This, in turn, implies that individuals in Marx's theory are always posited in this indifference towards the *natural* existence of their individuality.

This is not surprising if one takes account of the specific objectivity of the relations of production as *external* with respect to individuals. The externality and autonomy of these relations, their existence as functions expressed in economic categories, represents for Marx a particular *accidental* character of the relations (and of the determinations which they constitute) with respect to the individuals.

For Marx, the concept of capital contains the capitalist, but this occurs with a complete indifference to what concrete individual is implied in this determination. Criticizing the utopian socialist thesis that "we need capital but not the capitalist", Marx specifies:

> But capital in its being-for-itself is the capitalist. Of course, socialists sometimes say, we need capital, but not the *capitalist.* Then capital appears as a pure thing, not as a relation of production which, reflected in itself, is precisely the capitalist. I may well separate capital from a given individual capitalist, and it can be transferred to another. But, *in losing capital, he loses the quality of being a capitalist. Thus capital is indeed separable from an individual capitalist,* but not from *the* capitalist, who, as such confronts *the* worker. Thus also the individual worker can cease to be the being-for-itself of labour; he may inherit or steal money, etc. But then he ceases to be a *worker.* As a worker he is nothing more than labour in its being-for-itself. (*Grundrisse* p.304)

In fact, Marx specifies that the economic character of the wage-labourer is to be "carrier of labour as such", of abstract labour (creator of value), and in these terms he exists as a wage-labourer *in opposition to the capitalist,* i.e., in a definite *relation*

239

of production (as one of its extremes). This determination exists only in the relation itself and is accidental to every specific individual except to that which is already posited in this relation.

This is contained in the "abstract" and "total" character (*Grundrisse*) of capital and labour in capitalist relations. It is implied that

> labour is of course in each single case a specific labour, but capital can come into relation with every *specific* labour; it confronts the *totality* of all labours, and the particular one it confronts at a given time is an accidental matter. (*Grundrisse* p.297)

This *accidentality* explains why the treatment of individuals does not go beyond their conceptualization as "personifications": the specific individuality is irrelevant for the social relation as such. The determinations, functions, of capitalist relations imply, as we have seen, at the same time an *indifference to* and a *capability of* all specificities. It is within those limits that the problem of individuals exists for Marx.

The same occurs with other categories. Marx, for instance, liked to emphasize the case of money. Being also a social generality, money

> does not at all presuppose an individual relation to its owner; possession of it is not the development of any particular essential aspect of his individuality; but rather possession of what lacks individuality, since this social (relation) exists at the same time as a sensuous, external object which can be mechanically seized, and lost in the same manner. Its *relation to the individual* thus appears as a purely *accidental* one. (*Grundrisse* p.222)

As a generality, in money, we find, again, that "all individuality and peculiarity are negated and extinguished" (*Grundrisse* p.157). Money does not presuppose a specific individuality but, on the contrary, causes *effects* on the individuality which possesses it: "the individual carries his social power . . . in his pocket". It is interesting to note that this problem is curiously related with that Shakespearian "equation of the incompatible" (*Grundrisse* p.163) which Marx celebrated in the *Manuscripts* of 1844:

> The extent of the power of money is the extent of my power. Money's properties are my properties and essential powers — the properties and powers of its possessor. Thus, what I *am* and *am capable of* is by no means determined by my individuality. I *am* ugly, but I can buy for myself the most *beautiful* women. Therefore I am not *ugly,* for the effect of *ugliness* — its deterrent power — is nullified by money . . . Does not my money, therefore, transform all my incapacities into their contrary? *(1844 Manuscripts p.167)*

Of course, this digression is made only as a curious comparison, without a "humanist" intention or interpretation.

Notes on Humanism

Anti-Humanism

What we have signalled is the presence in Marx of different theses concerning individuality. The main consideration is that these theses do not constitute a theory of individuality in the strict sense, which in turn implies also that the "individual" is *not* Marx's analytical object (neither the starting-point nor the theoretical point of arrival). In these theses we find a different thing: they stand only as theoretical *principles* by which to think individuality. The formulation of a problematic about individuality can arise only from the existing knowledge of capitalist social relations.

These theses lead us to a very precise conclusion: the "individuals" who are present in Marx's theoretical discourse must be thought, as Luporini does, only as *"naked* individuals". By this we only mean something already said: the individuals appear dispossessed of every determination except those coming from the social relations. As Luporini states:

> The expression "naked individuals" is present in Marx every time he adopts the word "men" after he has destroyed the ideological myth of the "essence of men". This expression has not for him a value by itself, but as a function of social relations, in the first place of the "relations of production"; only in this *function* has it a scientific value. And it is only by starting from it that we can begin to reconstruct what is the concrete human individual in a non-ideological way. (*Dialectica Marxista* p.63)

This theoretical fact is clearly formulated in the Althusserian thesis about individuals (in Marx's theory) as *supports* of social relations:

> The structure of the relations of production determines the *place* and *functions* occupied and adopted by the agents of production, who are never anything more than the occupants of these places, insofar as they are the "supports" (*Träger*) of these functions. (*Reading Capital* p.180)

Controversial as this thesis may be, we think it is the only one which expresses the real status of the category of individual in Marx's theory.

But now we have a different problem. With respect to a Marxist conceptualization of "individuality", it seems that all we have is, again in Luporini's words:

> In no way the *solution* of the problem of the individual . . . but only the *starting-point* for formulating the problem. (*Dialectica Marxista* p.64)

In fact, within the actual discussion, it is not only the character of Marx's theoretical treatment of individuals that is in question, but a much wider problem concerning the pertinence of a Marxist problematic of individuality itself (the theoretical validity of its formulation and its development). At the centre of this polemic is a heavily criticised thesis: that of Althusser about Marxism being, theoretically, an *anti-humanism*. Every argument sustained within this debate becomes clear when it comes to take a position in relation to this important thesis, which has not always been understood in the correct way.

Althusser's main formulation is as follows:

> Strictly in respect to theory, therefore, one can and must speak openly of *Marx's theoretical anti-humanism,* and see in this *theoretical anti-humanism* the absolute (negative) precondition of the (positive) knowledge of the human world itself, and of its practical transformation. It is impossible to *know* anything about men except on the absolute precondition that the philosophical (theoretical) myth of man is reduced to ashes. So any thought that appeals to Marx for any kind of restoration of a theoretical anthropology or humanism is no more than ashes, *theoretically.* (*For Marx* pp.229-30)

This thesis is a conclusion of Althusser's conception of the character of the *break* which is at the base of the theoretical foundation of Marxist science, and which is a break, in the first place, with the theoretical humanism of Feuerbach. In this sense, Marxist theory is clearly founded from the very beginning in opposition to an anthropological philosophy.

241

But it is at this point that the problem begins. Leaving aside the apologetic argument in favour of an anthropological *foundation* of Marxist theory (the usual "humanism"), we find some formulations which recognise a positive and a negative aspect in this thesis. We will take their discussion only because they point directly to our problem about the pertinence of a problematic about individuality within Marxism.

For instance, Luporini expresses his own reservations about Althusser's thesis:

> I think that the *epistemological break* of which Althusser speaks, and which Riazanov had already anticipated, is a fact whose recognition or rejection determines any attitude one can have about theoretical marxism. But it is necessary to state that it is a problem of foundations, a displacement of foundations from a "philosophical" terrain towards a scientific terrain. But I think there is no need to extract from that, conclusions against the so-called Marxist (or communist, if you like) "humanism", as Althusser does, because I think that in this liquidating operation are confused two completely different problems: the first, precisely that of the *foundations*; the second, that of a problematic of the human animal (or if you like of its destiny) in the Marxist field. What is evident is that this problematic cannot remain a simple repetition, expansion or accentuation of some themes from the "young Marx", but must be based, from the start, on the scientific basis of Marxism and on the other scientific foundations that can be added to it. We can say that *humanism* and *philosophy* have been expelled from their place of "foundation", but this is no reason for giving to their subject a certificate of death. ("Introduction à l'*Idéologie allemande*" p.31)

Luporini is arguing that what we find in Marx is not a denial of a "humanist" problematic but a scientific transmutation of it. He thinks, for instance, that in the VIth Thesis on Feuerbach we have an *elliptical* proposition, against Althusser's interpretation of it as a mere *signal*. For him, this thesis proves that "the scientificity of Marx's text consists properly in the fact of thinking the structures as a function of the individuals and vice versa". His conclusion is that this "gives rise again to the problem of *humanism*" (p.34). The base for this problematic would be the recognition that "the human individuals are situated in the social relations" (p.34) but, at the same time, they interiorize them.

A more extreme argument comes from Lucien Sève. For him the "anti-humanist" thesis is correct only in the sense that it expresses Marx's rejection of any *speculative* humanism, but it is wrong in its rejection of any possibility for a marxist *scientific* anthropology:

> The relationship between mature Marxism and the philosophical humanism still present in the works of the young Marx is often reduced — incorrectly — to a "break", whereas the real relationship is not only one of break with the speculative character of his humanism but also of a scientific transmutation of its content. (*Marxism and the Theory of Human Personality* p.25)

It is interesting to see what this *transmutation* means, because it is there that the consequences of this thesis arise, with respect to our problem of "individuality":

> His (Marx's) break with the speculative illusions which hold sway here is in fact a *necessary theoretical detour*. It is taken with the aim of eventually working out a scientific concept of man and so of getting back to the concrete individuals and returning scientifically to the problem of humanism. (p.28)

242

Here the problematic of "individuals" is one forming a very particular unity with a "concept of man" and with a "problem of humanism". What appeared to be only a problem about the construction of a theory of individuality, and a defence against the Althusserian excesses, is a more complex argument.

It seems to be necessary to return to Althusser, because his "anti-humanism" is more constructive than it may seem. His thesis is, in the strict sense, a very precise one:

> A knowledge of the ensemble of the social relations is only possible on condition that we do completely without the *theoretical services* of the concept of man. (*For Marx* p.243)

In fact, with respect to the Marxist scientific problematic, the thesis on the "anti-humanism of Marx" is, above all, one about the theoretical pertinence of some specific categories. In particular, this thesis implies a rejection of the concept of man as a Marxist category; it refers explicitly to:

> the elimination of the concept of man as a central concept by the Marxist theory of social formations and of history. (Althusser, *Essays in Self Criticism* p.200)

In other words, the Althusserian 'anti-humanist' rejection is one concerning the "theoretical purpose (*prétentions*) of a humanist conception to explain the society and history" (*Self Criticism* p.201).

This is a very precise problem, which must not be confused with that of a construction of a theory of individuality.

Paradoxically, there is nothing in Althusser's work which can be interpreted as a *closing* of a problematic of "individuality". What we have is only the formulation of some rigorous principles by which to posit this problematic, but this *rigour* must not be confused with a closing of this problem. Criticizing the validity of the problem of the "role of the individual in history", he states that there is, indeed, another problem:

> a true problem, one which arises by right in the theory of history: the problem of the concept of *the historical forms of existence of individuality. Capital* gives us the principles necessary for the posing of this problem. It defines for the capitalist mode of production the different forms of individuality required and produced by that mode according to functions, of which, the individuals are "supports" (*Träger*) in the division of labour, in the different " "levels" of the structure (*Reading Capital* p.112).

This implies the recognition that

> of course, there exists in man something more than the simply economic and the simply political. There exists the biological, there exists the psychic, etc. But there exists also (and necessarily by virtue of the type of efficacy of the social structure on the human individuals) the effects of the social structure on the human individuals. Schaff's mistake with respect to this, is to discover in an imaginary theory of individuality what is nothing more than the *absent (unconnus) effects* of the social structure on the human individual. It is necessary to construct a theory of individuality, of the forms of existence of individuality, starting from the existent structures of the existent mode of production: this is the only way to grasp what constitutes the *effects* of the existent structures on the actual individuality. (Althusser, *Polemica Sobre Marxismo y Humanismo* p.197)

Briefly, "the *individual* is also the object of science" (Althusser, *Lenin and Philosophy* p.205).

243

Of course, in Althusser we do not find a development of this problematic, he does not go beyond these formulations. But these formulations are very precise and do not exclude a *theoretical* problematic of individuality. The thesis of a "theoretical anti-humanism", which is more precisely one of an *a-humanism* (*Reading Capital* p.119), is a thesis on the nature of Marx's historical materialism and must be confronted as such. It is not an "anti-individuality" thesis, as is implicitly stated, for instance, by Sève.

One can see the theoretical difficulties that the formulations by Sève raise, when one finds in them a direct return to the old humanist formula about history as the "realisation of man". Of course, he offers also a "humanist" version of *Capital:* "while all this deals with economic categories it is at the same time about human individuals" (p.33).

But there is something more. Theoretical projects such as Sève's concern not only an interpretation of Marxist theory but they are directed specifically towards a Marxist intervention in the field of the so-called "human sciences". In the case of Sève, his formulations are made as an effort to construct a "theory of personality", this time on a Marxist basis, within the field of psychology. In this sense, the effort is based on the recognition that "Marxism, as dialectical and more specifically as historical materialism, is the basis of scientific anthropology, the corner stone of all the sciences of man" (p.54).

This proposition is not far from that of Althusser. From the very beginning Althusser posited as one of the consequences of the development of Marxist theory that of "the transformation of domains in which a Marxist theoretical practice does not yet really exist." (*For Marx* p.169). But for Althusser this intervention-transformation implies a strict starting-point: the exact knowledge and interpretation of the character of Marx's existing theory, and it is this knowledge which is behind his thesis on "anti-humanism". The problem of the "human sciences" is related also to an understanding that there is a particular situation in which some "philosophies serve as an ideological substitute for a theoretical base which the human sciences lack" (*Philosophie Spontanée* p.38), in particular philosophies of the "human essence" of man. And this implies that there is no need to see Marxist theory as a new "philosophy" for the human sciences; there is always the danger of again providing an "ideological substitute". We think that this is a real problem with regard to the polemic: "scientific humanism" versus "theoretical anti-humanism", and not the one about the rejection/defence of a problematic (such as "individuality").

The practical answer is provided by Althusser himself, when discussing the problem of a marxist theory of art:

> now I believe that the only way we can hope to reach a real knowledge of art, to go deeper into the specificity of the work of art, to know the mechanisms which produce the "aesthetic effect", is precisely to spend a long time and pay the greatest attention to the *"basic principles of Marxism"* and not be in a hurry to "move on to something else", for if we move on too quickly to "something else" we shall arrive not at a *knowledge* of art, but at an *ideology* of art. (*Lenin and Philosophy* p.208)

We are not arguing about the anti-humanist thesis as such. We only wanted to say that this thesis does *not* imply a rejection of a problematic of "individuality"

244

but, being a rigorous thesis about historical materialism and directly concerning the theoretical validity of the concept of man, it exists, on the contrary, as a theoretical principle by which to posit any problematic about "individuality". In this sense it stands in the same terrain as the "scientific humanism" thesis in respect of "individuality". It is not "extremely harmful" (Sève) for a problematic of "individuality", but only for a "humanist" development of it.

What is harmful for a discussion of this problem is the confusion of the arguments about the possibility for a "science of individuality" with those about the "humanist" nature of Marxist theory and with those of a "marxist intervention in the human sciences". They are different problems. To think "individuality" (scientifically) we do not need to start with a concept of man: this is all the *anti-*humanism we have.

"Socialist" Humanism?

It seems necessary to remember some features of the classic "humanist" position and its relation with Marxism. We are referring here specifically to the so called "Socialist humanism" which, despite its several systematic tendencies, can be recognised as a very specific "problematic". We will see, starting from some of its main principles, that the humanist position (presented as a Marxist position) shows a particular *humanist logic* in action, to which every theoretical question is referred and answered. And it is the activity of this "logic" which characterises "humanism" as a particular Ideology. We will take just four aspects of this problem.

1. The best known fact about the humanist position is its thesis on the nature of Marxist theory. Its main effort is to prove that at the centre of Marxist theory there is a philosophy of man, i.e. that the theoretical foundations of Marx's own theory reside in an anthropological philosophy. The basic concepts would be those of man, man's essence, alienation, etc. The whole of historical materialism is *reorganised* around these categories. Thus history is seen as the self-realisation of man, society is the "creation of man", social relations are "human" or even "existential" relations, and so on.

It is enough to remember some formulations:

> We can say that the anthropology of the young Marx is the clue to his economy, and in the same way, of all his later creation. (Schaff, *Marxismo* p.40)

> The route to Marx's sociology started from the problem of the human individual. (*ibid.* p.85)

> His *examination* of the economy will be realised specifically having in mind the *question* if the economy realised the GATTUNGSWESEN (universelles Wesen) of man. (Marcuse, *Marx y el Trabajo Alienado* p.11)

Or in a very suggestive way,

> the Marxist interpretation of history can be called an anthropological interpretation of history if you want to avoid the ambiguities of the terms "materialist" and "economic". (Fromm, *Marx y Su Concepto* p.8)

> Man is the theme of history and the key to understanding its laws. (*ibid.*)

But the humanist position is not just a *wrong* interpretation of Marx's theory. In other words, it is not just a bad account of the specificity of Marxist theory but in-

245

volves a real *negation* of this specificity. And it is this characteristic which is at the centre of the theoretical and practical (political) *purpose* of any humanist thesis.

To defend an anthropological foundation for Marx's theory is to negate the *scientificity* of Marxist theory which is its specific theoretical and political feature. Not only has Marxism its foundation in a *science* (historical materialism); not only *is* Marx's theory a science; but also the Marxist political practice has its foundations in a scientific "concrete analysis of concrete situations" (Lenin), as the theoretical duty of Marxist-Leninist political organizations (as the premise of even the simplest political slogan). It is the understanding of this scientificity which is resumed in the thesis of a theoretical *anti*-humanism of Marx, which is clearly formulated not only in the work of Althusser, but also in Engels and Lenin.

As we have said, there is something more. The anthropological argument is clearly related to a thesis about a theoretical and political *continuity* between Marx and Utopian Socialism. This continuity is particularly important for the "humanist" position because in it is implied a continuity with "humanism" itself; it would be not only a theoretical but also a political continuity of the humanist ideology as such.
With ambiguity:

> Marx's scientific socialism, which radically transformed the preexistent *form* of socialism, but *not its starting-point* which continued to be the human individual and its affairs . . . (Schaff, *Marxismo* p.66)

or without ambiguity:

> man was the first and main preoccupation of Marx (who) never broke the spiritual links with Utopian Socialism. (Rubel, *Socialist Humanism* p.214)

Briefly, there is neither a *break* with the theoretical starting-point (Schaff), nor a break with the theoretical (the real meaning of Rubel's thesis) links with Utopian Socialism, which for them was "humanist". It is because there is no break with a *previous* Socialism that it is possible to reorganize Marxist theory according to the *aprioristic* logic of Socialist humanism.

It is interesting to note that so-called "Socialist humanism" involves a particular contemporary *combination,* despite some arguments to the contrary (see Mezraros), of that philosophically "true" Socialism and that Utopian Socialism which were criticized by Marx and Engels in *The Communist Manifesto.* Not only do we find precisely that "emasculation" of the "French socialist and communist literature" (this time it is the *Marxist-Leninist* literature) based on a rhetoric about "alienation" and representing the interests of "man in general", etc. (Marx, pp.130-2), but also we find that for the humanists (see Marcuse, Fromm, Goldmann) the proletariat "offers to them the spectaclè of a class without any historical initiative or any independent political movement", etc. (p.134).

That is why, among other things, the specificity of marxist theory is reduced merely to that of a *critical* theory:

> Marx's philosophy is a philosophy of protest. (Fromm, *Marx y su Concepto* p.8)

> Historical materialism appears, *in the first instance,* as a denunciation of the materialism inherent in bourgeois society, and the materialist principle, in this sense, functions as a *critical instrument of denunciation* directed against the society which enslaves men. (Marcuse, *Marx y el Trabajo Alienado* p.150)

And, for Marcuse, this *critical* nature of Marxist theory is based in other features whose recognition involves a complete misunderstanding of Marx's theory itself: for instance, that in Marx there is a "restoration of the category of *use value* at the centre of the economic analysis" (p.50), a thesis which is impossible to sustain if one reads *Capital*.

Thus, when we speak of "Humanism" we are arguing for something more than the usefulness of such concepts as alienation, man, human essence, etc. We are, in fact, defending the protocols of an idealist interpretation of history and of class struggle.

2. This particular concern of the humanists with the arguments of Utopian Socialism, with which Marx is identified, also shows the way to what is a *methodological axis* of Socialist Humanism. For them, Marxist theory involves the formulation of a *theoretical* equilibrium in opposition to a *real* (existing in reality) disequilibrium. This equilibrium exists in the "Utopia" (see Rubel), or in the idea of a society organised according to "human nature" (the communist society). That is why history is the self-realisation of man. The historical movement as an antagonistic process of class struggle disappears. It is replaced by a movement made by men (a category that is necessarily *unitary,* i.e. in equilibrium) searching for the (future) realisation of an "ideal" (the reality of a still non-realised human essence): the *a priori* equilibrium of the concept searching for an *a posteriori* equilibrium of the real. That is why this "ideal" (human essence) can serve, as in Marcuse, as a critical category: the present can be criticised by the future. We all know this kind of argument.

The theoretical procedure is clear. The possibility of an idealist interpretation of history has a theoretical base:

> The individuals, who are *no longer subject to the division of labour,* have been conceived by the philosophers as an ideal, under the name "Man". They have conceived the whole process which we have outlined as the evolutionary process of "Man", so that at every historical stage "Man" was substituted for the individuals and shown as the motive force of history. The whole process was thus conceived as a process of the self-estrangement of "Man", and this was essentially due to the fact that the *average individual of the later stage was always foisted onto the earlier stage,* and the consciousness of a later age on the individuals of an earlier. (*The German Ideology* p.76)

In the humanist argument this *later stage* is the communist society (as a Utopia), by means of which history is theoretically conceived as the continuous (but never attained) realisation of man (in which man is the man of communist society, i.e. realised human essence).

This simplified version of idealism leads us to an interesting problem. The arguments concerning the realisation of a "human essence" and of "Utopia" imply a particular process of *eternalisation* of an "ideal" historical moment. Methodologically, we are confronting the same mistake made by Political Economy and heavily criticised by Marx.

In fact, in the humanist argument we find that social relations attributable to communist society are conceived as *natural* relations, in the same way as Political Economy conceived the relations of production in capitalism:

> When the economists say that *present-day relations* — the relations of bourgeois production — are natural, they imply that these are the relations in which wealth is created and produc-

247

tive forces developed *in conformity with the laws of Nature. These relations therefore are themselves natural laws* independent of the influence of time. They are eternal laws which always must govern society. *Thus there has been history but there no longer is any.* There has been history, since the institutions of feudalism existed, and in these institutions of feudalism we find quite different relations of production from those of bourgeois society, which the economists try to pass off as natural and as such, eternal. (Marx, *The Poverty of Philosophy* p.105)

When the humanist thesis presents the "communist society" as an Utopia, according to some "human nature", we have the same theoretical operation. What is presented as natural and "eternal" is, of course, no longer those "present-day relations" (as in the case of Political Economy) but the alleged "future" communist relations, this time in conformity with the laws of human "nature". The only difference is that in Political Economy we find *eternalisation* towards the future (towards the consolidation of the existing order: bourgeois society), whereas in the humanist case we find a real *eternalisation towards the past* (from the ideal consolidation of the order already obtained in the "Utopia"). In fact, we have again the presence of the *later stage* in the analysis (which can now be an "evaluation") of the past and present reality alike, for instance, capitalism.

Because in this case what is "eternalised" is a future communist society, we are confronted with an inversion of the problem of history. For Political Economy, as Marx remarked, "there has been history, but there is no longer any". The humanist argument, on the contrary, is that there has been *no* history, that the real history of man will start only with communism. But these theses are the same: if there has not been any history it is because there have been feudal, capitalist etc., institutions, and we find in them "quite different relations" from those attributed to "human nature".

We also find here the humanist need for a replacement of scientific analysis for a *critical evaluation* (critical concepts in Marcuse, etc.) in which there is a confrontation between an "ideal" category and an existing reality, this category involving not a representation of reality but the Utopian equilibrium (the unity expressed by the concepts "Man", "Human Nature", etc.). What we have here is the ever present *doctrinarism* in which, as in the case of Proudhon, "the contradiction exists solely between his fixed ideas and the real movement" *(Marx, Poverty of Philosophy* p.161). The humanist fixed idea has several "unitary faces": Man, human essence, communism (as an *ideal*), etc. And the contradiction which humanism discovers (between its ideas and reality) is also one with several faces: self-realisation, self-alienation, etc.

It must be noted that what is fulfilled by the humanist argument is, perhaps, a real problem. The proletarian revolution is, in fact, one which "cannot draw its poetry from the past, but only from the future" (Marx, *The Eighteenth Brumaire* p.400). In this sense, what Socialist Humanism offers to us can be seen as a positive "poetry of the future" useful for convincing the opponents and the undecided, i.e. useful for winning an ideological struggle. This is the curious argument pronounced by humanists such as Lefèbvre (who explicitly denotes the "ideological" importance of the concept "alienation"), Schaff, Goldmann, etc.

In this sense, Schaff is very clear:

the intensified interest in the philosophy of man must be placed in the contexts of the new forms and meanings of ideological struggles. Marxists are now increasingly concerned with the philosophy of man . . . also because they are interested in the ideological struggle. For the philosophy of man has recently become not only the subject but also an instrument of this struggle. (*Socialist Humanism* p.148)

Ideological struggle is for him an "argument against the system of values opposed to our views" in which "we must set forth our own system of values". These values, of course, are "humanist" values.

Humanist ideology, being theoretically a "philosophy of man", lays claim to its practico-social function as ideology which will be a programmatic function in a socialist movement. But the theoretical price is a very particular one: a *rejection* of Marxist concepts, and even a correction of Marx himself. Analysing this aspect we come near to the specificity of humanist ideology itself: a non-proletarian ideology and an anti-Marxist theory.

3. There is, in the humanist argument, a true *rejection* of Marx's theory. It takes different forms: sometimes it is a matter of emphasis, at other times an explicit correction of Marx's mistakes. We are going to examine one of these forms, as an example of the theoretical "operations" which are found behind the humanist discourse.

One of the preferred theses of humanism concerns a position about the revolutionary conditions of the proletariat. Its argument is based on a particular conception of (a) an economic law of the absolute pauperisation of the proletariat, and (b) a theory of alienation.

a. For them (see Fromm, Goldmann, Marcuse, Rubel) the revolutionary character of the proletariat derives from a capitalist law entailing the progressive pauperisation of the proletariat and "its necessary evolution toward an awareness of its own revolutionary role" (Goldmann p.43).

In the first place, there is nothing in Marx to justify such a law. Marx's thesis is about a "relative" pauperisation of the proletariat under capitalism. To speak about an absolute pauperisation, as a law, means that we are referring to something clearly *incompatible* with Marx's analysis.

Secondly, this means that we are taking a criterion that is totally incompatible with Marx's own: *poverty* as a passive "human condition", based on what is nothing more than a "standard of living" (the distribution of use values). In this sense, we are within the same theoretical limits of Utopian Socialism: "only from the point of view of being the most suffering class does the proletariat exist for them" (*The Communist Manifesto* p.134)

b. The revolutionary character of the proletariat also resides for them in its being the support of a condition of alienation, which is again a "human condition". In this respect:

Marx supposed that the alienation of labour, existing through all history, reaches its summit in capitalist society, and that the working class is the most alienated. (Fromm, *Marx y su Concepto* p.60)

Marx believed that the working class would lead in the transformation of society because it was at once the most dehumanised and alienated class, and potentially the most powerful, since the functioning of society depended upon it. (Schaff, *Socialist Humanism* p.ix)

249

The humanist thesis resumes both arguments:

Marx's conception of the revolution was based on the existence of a pauperised and de-humanised class. (Marcuse, *La Sociedad* p.40)

This argument is the result of a humanist assimilation of Marx's theory. Both theses imply a distortion of Marx's own formulations. Once this assimilation is made, nothing is easier than to prove that Marx was mistaken, and to propose the "humanist" solution. In fact:

History has made just one correction of Marx's concept of alienation; Marx believed that the working class was the most alienated class, that is why emancipation from this alienation necessarily started from the liberation of the working class. Marx did not foresee that alienation would be transformed into the situation of the majority, especially that sector which manipulates symbols, and men more than machines. The employer, the seller, are now more alienated than the qualified manual worker. (Fromm, *Marx y su Concepto* p.67)

In this respect, Marx was wrong "in his romantic idealisation of the working class, the result of a purely theoretical attitude and not of the observation of the human reality of such a class" (Fromm, *Psicoanàlisis* p.76).

The proletariat which was to validate the equation of Socialism and Humanism pertained to a past stage in the development of industrial society. Socialist theory, no matter how true, can neither prescribe nor predict the future agents of a historical transformation. (Marcuse, *Socialist Humanism* p.117)

Socialist action in industrial societies of the West can no longer be founded on the premise of the increasing pauperisation of the proletariat and its *necessary* transformation into a revolutionary force. The workers are no longer *necessarily* driven by increasing pauperisation to choose the path of Socialism as Marxist theorists of the nineteenth century believed. (Goldmann, *Socialist Humanism* p.45)

This humanist distortion of Marx is completed by an analysis of modern capitalism in which it is treated as "opulent society", "industrial society" etc. What is implied in this concept is that modern capitalism is a society which "has superseded the conditions of classical Capitalism" (Marcuse, *La Sociedad* p.45). And what has been superseded is, curiously, capitalist economic exploitation itself:

in the economically most developed country, the United States, the economic exploitation of the masses has disappeared. (Fromm, *Psicoanalisis* p.89)

In the industrial societies, economic exploitation of the proletariat remains, but attenuated. (Gabel, *Sociologie* p.25)

In the Occident we have arrived at the situation where the boundaries which separate the social classes have begun to disappear. (Gabel, *Imagen* p.72)

Of course, the humanist use of the concept of economic "exploitation" has nothing to do with Marx's concept which is based on the theory of surplus-value. Here it is just a category related to "living standards": but it has a humanist usefulness because it serves to transform the problem into one concerning the sphere of "consumption". Exploitation and alienation no longer appear as attributes of the sphere of production. Rather, in their humanist guise, they become features of the sphere of consumption, and the proletariat is consequently dissolved into an undetermined group of consumers.

Paradoxically, the young Marx is also superseded, because:

the form of alienation typical to the actual stage of industrial societies is no longer economic alienation. (Gabel, *Sociologie* p.25)

He (Marx) did not foresee the development of capitalism to the point where the working
class would prosper materially and share in the capitalist spirit while *all of society* would
become alienated to an extreme degree. He never became aware of that *affluent alienation*
which can be as dehumanising as *impoverished alienation.* (Fromm, *Socialist Humanism* p.ix)

And we can continue ad infinitum. Our only interest is to show a particular case
of distortion of Marx's theory when it is assimilated to the humanist logic. And in
this case the consequences are severe. What is at stake is not just an academic problem but is precisely one which is central to political discussion about the proletarian revolution.

4. Finally, we can locate the *class* character of the humanist ideology. If we take
seriously the mechanics of the humanist logic, the result of which is the distortion
of Marxist theory — dissolution of its theoretical and political principles, etc. — we
can see that we are confronting, at best, a non-Marxist position. But, we see also
that humanism involves, in one way or another, the realisation of a non-proletarian
class interest. This character is explicitly exposed by Goldmann in formulating that
the final objective the proletarian revolution is, without ambiguity:

an integration of the major values *inherited from middle-class* humanism (universality,
individual freedom, equality, the dignity of the human person, freedom of expression) so
as to endow them, for the first time in the history of humanity, with a quality of authen-
ticity, instead of the purely formal status that they had previously been granted in capitalist
society. (*Socialist Humanism* p.40)

Socialist society was expected to restore and further develop the *values of Western Humanism,* since it would not only strip them of their merely formal character by suppressing all
exploitation and class distinctions, but also bind them organically to a community both
truly human and fully conscious of those trans-individual values which would be liberated
at last from the heavy handicaps that poverty and exploitation had imposed in the pre-
capitalist periods of history (p.50).

In this sense, the objective of the proletarian revolution would be to give a practical
existence to middle-class values. The revolution would be an act of practical *realisation* of values, the realisation of petit-bourgeois ideology. Emancipation of the proletariat means, above all, the emancipation of some *trans-individual values* organised
as *humanism.* It is, explicitly, the practical realisation of Humanism itself.

In the humanist conceptualisation (which is an explicitation of values) we find the
foundation (which is a philosophical one) of a determined organisation of society.
And what is important is that these humanist values are the values (theoretical expression of class interests) of the petit-bourgeoisie. Humanism is, in this sense, the
theoretical expression of the interests of the petit-bourgeoisie when pretending to
control, lead, or evaluate the proletarian movement.

We can say also that, at its best, and with respect to marxist political practice,
the "humanist" position expresses theoretically the conceptual limits within which
the petit-bourgeoisie, as such, can *live* both Marxist theory and revolutionary practice. It shows the way in which the revolutionary movement can be lived from a
petit-bourgeois position. In other words, it shows the way of the petit-bourgeois
intervention in the proletarian struggle. But nothing more.

251

"Scientific" Humanism?

The above formulations come from what is now seen as a "speculative" humanism, which of course it is. But starting from the first mentioned thesis by Luporini and Sève — as a direct reaction against the Althusserian "anti-humanism" thesis — it is possible to pose again the problem of a Marxist humanism. The new formulation tends to be one arguing for an alleged *scientific humanism.* As we have seen, for them there is in Marx not only a rejection of every speculative humanism, but, at the same time, there is a *transmutation of the content* of the old philosophical humanism. For them the problem does not concern "humanism" as such, but only its character, which can be "philosophical" (when it is posited as the foundation of Marx's theory) or "scientific" (when it is *based* on Marx's theory). Can there exist a scientific humanism without posing again the old damaging problematic? Up to the present there is no proof for this possibility.

Let us take Sève. For him, we confront in Marx at the same time both a "materialist reversal of the whole conception of man *and* history" (p.27). In Marx we have again a theory, which is now scientific, of the "human essence". Without ambiguities:

> If humanism, in the theoretical sense, means that history is seen as a *process of the realisation of man,* then one may undoubtedly say that marxism is a *humanism which has become scientific.* (p.29)

The "scientific" status of the humanism comes from the fact that now it is not based on a *reduction* of the materialist concepts into "humanist" categories but from a *correspondence* between the concepts of historical materialism and the categories about "human" instances (individual, man, etc.). In this sense, Marxism is the "scheme of man which coincides with the science of history" (p.30).

But this "correspondence" leads Sève to the same old humanist theoretical circle and then to eclecticism: for him the individual is "bound up in his essence with the *social relations* which produce him at the same time *as he produces them*" (p.30). In fact we have the same old thesis of an individual as product/ producer of social relations, which implies a "humanist" conception of history. The notion of social relations as being *produced* by the individuals cannot but be taken as a "humanist" argument, and precisely not a *scientific* one. In Marx there is no place for this "production"; even in his economic theory, the social relations are never produced but always *re-produced* by a complex process which excludes, theoretically, the individual as such.

If there is (for Sève) an *immediate connection* between humanism and the science of history, it is because in reality there is an *immediate* connection between men (or individuals) and the social relations. One of these immediate connections is, for instance, that "between the superstructures and ideologies, on the one hand, and men, on the other" (p.32). The theoretical (and political) danger of this *immediacy* can be seen clearly when Sève states his own conclusion: "The consciousness of the individuals *cannot* therefore pass beyond the *limits,* nor escape the problems — and solutions — characteristic of their class" (p.32). This thesis is in complete contradiction to Marx's, in which we find an example of the importance of considering theoretically the "accidental" character of the social relations with respect to the individuals. For Marx this impossibility of passing beyond the limits posited by social relations exists only for the class but not for the individuals as such, and this formulation has precisely its greatest validity with respect to the nature of ideologies.

What is more, this last problem has its greatest importance when it comes to the time of *concrete analysis,* which is precisely *not* the time of the theoretically "concrete" individual. Lenin, in the middle of the very concrete processes of 1917, needed to formulate the anti-humanist principle that a Marxist "must reckon with objective facts, with the masses and classes, and *not with individuals* (and so on)" (II p.42). It is precisely the need for a materialist understanding of the *objective* distinction, not only between the different classes, but also between class ideologies, and then, also, between political trends, which makes important, among other things, a Marxist theoretical *non-immediacy* between individual and social relations. This is, for instance, the argument which interested Lenin when he argued that "every Marxist knows that classes are distinct, even though individuals may move freely from one class to another; similarly, *trends* in political life are distinct in spite of the fact that individuals may change freely from one trend to another, and in spite of all attempts and efforts to *amalgamate* trends" (II p.54).

Briefly, we can say that the "humanist" character of the argument for a "scientific humanism" in Marx (against the anti-humanism thesis) comes not from the old and direct reductionism of Marxist concepts to ' humanist" categories, but from a more subtle thesis which poses the theoretical problem of a *"connection* between the conception of historical materialism and that of the structure of human individuality" (which in general, can be a valid theoretical problematic in itself) as a paradoxical *necessity for the "coherence" of the marxist theory* (Sève p.33). The concept of man, for instance, is now not at the *centre* of Marx's theory, but it is a concept (one of the concepts) on which the *coherence* of Marx's theory depends. But if we go into the detail, this coherence is nothing more than a "humanist" coherence. And indeed it is a very distorted coherence, in which the concept of man, produces, as usual, theoretical miracles. If history is "the history of man" then it is not surprising to find that "each social formation produces in the long run the men whom it needs, including the men whom it needs in order to transform it by revolutionary action" (p.33). The "social formation" is seen as a *subject* having the *need* to produce the men "whom it needs". Returning to the above Leninist thesis, it is the "effort to *amalgamate* trends", which this time are theoretical trends, which is the ever-present problem of any "humanism" and the danger for Marxist theory.

It is this search for a theoretical *coherence* for Marxist theory which curiously unifies this new form of scientific "humanism" with another contemporary amalgam: that implicit in the problematic concerning "subjectivity". We are not denying the theoretical rights for this analytical purpose as such, but we think that when this problem is posited in relation to a need for the development of a "Marxism of the Subject", things become problematic. For instance, in the article by John Ellis in *WPCS* 9 we witness again an effort directed towards the construction of a "science of human nature" (Ellis p.205) which this time would permit a theoretical account of what is conceived as the *"subjective moment* of the social process".

The thesis goes directly against the alleged mistake of thinking "the external aspects *without* the internal aspects" (for instance, with respect to the aspects of the capitalist process of reproduction) or against thinking "the objective *without* the subjective". This theoretical need for coherence is resolved by the amalgam of Marxism and psychoanalysis.

After this discovery of a new eclecticism (on the one hand . . . and on the other . . .) which for Lenin is always a replacement of dialectics, it is easy to relate the theoretical problem to a political one:

> It is *vital* for Marxism to take into account this *process of the unconscious* whose effects are heard and felt in the conscious. If not, the psychology at work in propaganda and political action remains mechanistic, a simplistic causality. (Ellis p.214)

In even clearer terms, there is a "fundamental lack in mainstream Marxist politics", and this is a *lack of psychology in politics* (p.216).

Leaving aside the political implications of this statement — partly because it is based on a misunderstanding of Mao's references to the "subjective" (which are far from calling for psychoanalysis) — we have theoretically the same humanist correspondence between social relations and man. The only difference is that now the moment of man is the moment of the "unconscious". What in Sève was just the "structure of human individuality" is now a precise thing: the unconscious.

This is the reason why this argument is seen as "'surpassing the traditional division of Marxism between humanism and anti-humanism" (p.205). Precisely because the "humanist" sphere is now posited *outside* Marxism itself, in psychology, or more precisely, in psychoanalysis. What is conceived from many Marxist positions (but dominated by the "humanist" argument) as an intervention of Marxism in psychology is here its reverse: an intervention of psychology in Marxism. This position is far more complicated because there is no need to prove Marxism is correct, in developing the problem of individuality as "subjectivity". Ellis never asks himself, for instance, if what he sees as a lack of psychology in (Marxist) politics is related to something which is perhaps more important and decisive (theoretically and politically) for a Marxist: *a lack of (Marxist) politics in psychology itself*.

Ellis does not need to argue in this polemic about humanism precisely because he is not concerned with the problem of thinking what are the "theoretical principles" of Marx's theory and of Marxism in general. But what if these principles imply the theoretical absence of a "subjectivity" problematic? We think, evaluating the character and development of Marxist theory, that they do imply that. If this is correct then any amalgam is nothing more, but also nothing less, than a "theoretical disorder" in which the loser is always Marx and the revolutionary movement.

Considerations on Ideology

If we now turn to Althusser for a moment, we see that at the centre of his propositions on ideology (see *For Marx* and *Lenin and Philosophy*) there is a very specific thesis:

> Ideology represents the imaginary relationship of individuals to their real conditions of existence. (*Lenin and Philosophy* p.153)

This thesis implies a complete break with a conceptualization of ideology in terms of "false consciousness". In fact, for Althusser ideology does not concern a representation (true/false) of reality, but a representation of the *(imaginary) relationship of individuals* to reality (relations of production and the relations which derive from them). In other words,

> what is represented in ideology is therefore not the system of the real relations which govern the existence of individuals, but the imaginary relation of those individuals to the real relations in which they live. (*Lenin and Philosophy* p.155)

It is in this sense that what is represented in ideology is a "relation of the second degree" (*For Marx* p.240). This character of ideology also implies that its existence concerns the field of so-called "human experience" (as *individual* experience). Ideology relates to men's *lived relations* to their conditions of existence, i.e., to the way in which the individuals *live* their conditions of existence. Furthermore it can be said that

> when we speak of ideology we should know that ideology slides into all human activity, that it is identical with the "lived" experience of human existence itself. (*Lenin and Philosophy* p.204)

That is why, for instance, the idea of "justice" is an "ideological" notion: because is a notion *under* and *in* which men can *live* their relations to their conditions of existence *and to their struggles* (see *Philosophie Spontanée* p.57). Also this is the reason why a situation of poverty, as in Bertolazzi's *El Nost Milan,* can be *lived* in the arguments of the moral and religious consciousness (see *For Marx* p.140). In this sense, ideology not only involves a representation *of* individual relations to the social relations, but it is, at the same time, a representation *given to* individuals.

In fact, ideology is addressed to individuals. The practico-social function of ideology is precisely to *constitute* concrete individuals as *subjects,* i.e., to transform the individuals into subjects. This transformation-constitution is accomplished by means of the particular mechanism of "interpellation" based on the existence and functioning of the "category of the *subject*" which for Althusser is at the centre of *all* ideology. Briefly, "the existence of ideology and the hailing or interpellation *of individuals* as subjects are one and the same thing" (*Lenin and Philosophy* p.163).

The nature of ideology (concerning individual *lived* relations) and its practico-social function (constituting individuals as subjects) are based on the particular *materiality* of ideology: ideology exists in material ideological apparatuses, in its "rituals" and practices. It is by functioning "in the practical rituals of the most elementary everyday life" (*Lenin and Philosophy* p.162) that the subjects recognize themselves as such, i.e., it is by their participation in the practices of an ideological apparatus (and there is no practice except *by* and *in* an ideology and its apparatus) that concrete individuals are constituted as subjects. In this sense, for the individuals, ideology is clearly not a mere system of representations (ideas) but a complete material system (based on a specific ideological apparatus) which has a particular effect: that of constituting them as subjects.

It must be noted that here, as in Marx's theory, the individuals are only the *supports* of these *lived* social relations that constitute ideology, the supports of this process of constitution of subjects.

In this very descriptive account of Althusser's propositions we can see, at least, that we are confronting a specific reality: that of *"individuals who live in ideology"* (*Lenin and Philosophy* p.156) and their social existence as subjects.

Paradoxically (with the alleged "theoreticism" of Althusser), this problematic is much less concerned with an "epistemological" problem than most other positions. In fact, Althusser's theses are very far from a problematic concerning an "epistemological causality" for the existence of ideology. His theoretical effort directly concerns the specificity of ideology in terms of its social *effectivity* within a social formation. And it is interesting to note that this effectivity is one which is accomplished *at the level of individuality*.

In this sense, we must remember that the problematic of ideology is for Althusser a part of his theoretical programme of explaining the mechanisms behind the "society effect" which constitutes the complex *body* of a society as a structured social whole:

> The mechanism of the production of this "society effect" is only complete when all the effects of the mechanism have been expounded, down to the point where they are produced in the form of the very effects that constitute the concrete conscious or unconscious *relation of the individuals to the society* as a society, i.e., down to the effects of the fetishism of ideology (or "forms of *social* consciousness" — *Preface* to *A Contribution . . .*), in which men consciously or unconsciously *live* their lives, their projects, their actions, their attitudes and their functions, as *social*. (*Reading Capital* p.66)

It is this separation from an "epistemological" conceptualization, which no theory based on the "false consciousness" problematic can achieve (such as for instance, the "phenomenal forms" problematic), which is at the centre of the theoretical *aperture* which Althusser's theses imply, an aperture which in turn seems to be closely linked to the unexpected appearance of a problematic of "individuality" in relation to ideology.

In fact, the thesis that "what is represented in ideology is not the system of the real relations which govern the existence of individuals" is, at the same time, a thesis about ideology as being *itself* a system of (imaginary) relations *which govern the existence of individuals.* In this sense, with the recognition of the specificity of the ideological as a level of social reality, formulations about ideology as comprising "social-imaginary relations" (Poulantzas) and constituting itself an "area of ideological social relations" (Hirst) are faultless.

So, the "ideological relations" — by means of their specific nature — form part of the entire totality of relations within which individuals stand. But the individuals, as *concrete* individuals, stand as "supports" or as "bearers" of these relations, in the same way as for the relations of production. In other words, the "ideological relations", as specific social determinations, are part of that "synthesis of multiple determinations" that make the individual a *concrete* individual. The ideological determination operates through the class struggle and through the ideological apparatuses and their material practices in which this struggle is exercised. In this sense, the ideological class struggle is a fight for an effectivity at the level of individuality.

The problematic suggested by Althusser's formulations has many aspects to be developed and to be resolved: the "imaginary" character of ideology, the problem of the "Subject" and of the "subjects", etc. But with respect to the problem of "subjects" it must be noted that it concerns a process of constitution of "social" subjects. As Hirst points out (p.401), Althusser's treatment of this problem is based on a rejec-

256

tion of the notions of a *collective* and of a *constitutive* subject. It can also be said that it does not refer directly to a problem of "subjectivity" in its psychological (internal, subjective, etc.) dynamic. This last position has sometimes been interpreted as a *timidity,* because in Althusser we cannot find a "reconciliation of the discoveries of Marx and Freud" (Ellis p.210). But this is precisely because his theoretical problem is one concerning ideology and not a dubious "Marxism of the subject".

As a final and general point, it is useful to agree with Althusser and his advice "to spend a long time and pay the greatest attention to the *basic principles of Marxism* and not to be in a hurry "to move on to something else". (*Lenin and Philosophy* p.208). One of these principles, with crucial importance for the problematic of individuality (which this time also concerns a theoretical account of ideology) is the one embodied in the *anti-humanist* thesis. Resuming all our propositions, and paraphrasing Marx, it can be said that if we cannot explain "individuality" (and its related problems) upon the "anti-humanism" supposition, we cannot explain it at all.

Bibliography

L. Althusser *et al. Polemica sobre Marxismo v Humanismo* (Siglo XXI) Mexico, 1968
L. Althusser *For Marx* (Penguin) 1969
L. Althusser *Reading Capital* (NLB) 1970
L. Althusser *Lenin and Philosophy* (NLB) 1971
L. Althusser *Philosophie et philosophie spontanée des savants* (Maspero) 1974
L. Althusser *Essays in Self-Criticism* (NLB) 1976
J. Ellis "Ideology and Subjectivity" *WPCS* 9, 1976
E. Fromm (ed.) *Socialist Humanism* (Anchor) 1966
E. Fromm *Psicoanalisis de la Sociedad Contemporanea* (FCE) Mexico, 1964
E. Fromm *Marx y Su Concepto del Hombre* (FCE) Mexico, 1966
J. Gabel *Sociologie de l'alienation* (PUF) 1970
J. Gabel "La Crisis del Marxismo y de la Psicologia" in *La Nueva Imagen del Hombre* (Alonso) Bs.As.
   1971
L. Goldmann "Socialism and Humanism" in Fromm (ed.) *Socialist Humanism*
S. Hall "Marx's Notes on Method: A 'Reading' of the 1857 Introduction" *WPCS 6,*
   1974
P. Hirst "Althusser's Theory of Ideology" *Economy and Society* Vol.5 No.4, November 1976
V. Lenin *Selected Works* (Vols I-III) (Progress) 1975
C. Luporini "Introduction à l'*Idéologie allemande*", *L'Homme et la Société* 7, 1968
C. Luporini *Dialectica Marxista e Historicismo* (Pasado y Presente) Argentina, 1969
H. Marcuse *Marx y el Trabajo Alienado* (Perez) Bs. As. 1969
H. Marcuse *La Sociedad Industrial y el Marxismo* (Quintaria) Bs. As. 1969
H. Marcuse "Socialist Humanism" in Fromm (ed.) *Socialist Humanism*
K. Marx—F. Engels *Selected Works* (Vols. I—III) (Lawrence and Wishart) 1973
K. Marx *Economic and Philosophical Manuscripts* (Lawrence and Wishart) 1973
K. Marx—F. Engels *The German Ideology* in *Selected Works*
K. Marx *The Poverty of Philosophy* (Progress Publishers) 1973
K. Marx—F. Engels *The Communist Manifesto* in *Selected Works*
K. Marx *The Eighteenth Brumaire of Louis Bonaparte* in *Selected Works*
K. Marx *Introduction to a Contribution to the Critique of Political Economy* in *Selected Works*
K. Marx *Grundrisse* (Penguin) 1973
K. Marx *Capital I* (Lawrence and Wishart) 1974

K. Marx *Capital I* (Penguin) 1976
K. Marx *Capital II* (Lawrence and Wishart) 1974
K. Marx *Capital III* (Lawrence and Wishart) 1972
M. Rubel "Reflections on Utopia and Revolution" in Fromm (ed.) *Socialist Humanism*
A. Schaff "Marxism and the Philosophy of Man" in Fromm (ed.) *Socialist Humanism*
A. Schaff *Marxismo e Individuo Humano* (Grijalbo) Mexico, 1967
L. Seve *Marxism and the Theory of Human Personality* (Lawrence and Wishart) 1975

Index

WORKING PAPERS IN CULTURAL STUDIES

Owing to continual cost fluctuations there is no way that we can organise a system of annual subscriptions. However, standing orders can be arranged with the Centre to ensure that subscribers receive each issue, with the invoice included. Please write to Judy Jefferson at the Centre for Contemporary Cultural Studies if you are interested in placing a standing order.

A few back copies of WPCS 5 and 9 are still available. WPCS 7/8 has been reprinted by Hutchinsons as an Open University set book.

A series of Occasional Papers is also available:

CCCS STENCILLED OCCASIONAL PAPERS
AT MARCH 1977

1.	Stuart Hall: A 'Reading' of Marx's 1857 *Introduction* to *The Grundrisse*	25p
2.	Adrian Mellor: Theories of Social Stratification	25p
3.	Richard Johnson: The Blue Books and Education, 1816-1896	25p
4.	Stuart Hall: External Influences on Broadcasting	25p
5.	Stuart Hall: The 'Structured Communication' of Events	25p
6.	Roland Barthes: Introduction of Structural Analysis of the Narrative	25p
7.	Stuart Hall: Encoding and Decoding in the TV Discourse	25p
8.	Dave Morley: Industrial Conflict and Mass Media	20p
9.	Dave Morley: Reconceptualising the Media Audience	25p
10.	Marina Heck: The Ideological Dimension of Media Messages	20p
11.	Stuart Hall: Deviancy, Politics and the Media	25p
12.	Bryn Jones: The Politics of Popular Culture	20p
13.	Paul Willis: Symbolism and Practice: The Social Meaning of Pop Music	25p
14.	Clarke and Jefferson: Politics of Popular Culture: Cultures and Subcultures	20p
16.	Stuart Hall: The Hippies — an American 'Moment'	25p
17.	Jefferson and Clarke: "Down These Mean Streets" — the Meaning of Mugging	20p
18.	Clarke and Jefferson: Working Class Youth Cultures	20p
19.	Paul Willis: Performance and Meaning: Women in Sport	25p
20.	Dick Hebdidge: The Style of the Mods	20p
21.	Dick Hebdidge: The Kray Twins: Study of a System of Closure	25p
22.	Tony Jefferson: The Teds: a Political Resurrection	20p
23.	John Clarke: The Skinheads and the Study of Youth Culture	20p
24.	Dick Hebdidge: Reggae Rastas & Rudies: Style and the Subversion of Form	25p
25.	Dick Hebdidge: Sub-cultural Conflict and Criminal Performance in Fulham	25p
26.	Richard Johnson: Peculiarities of the English Route	25p
27.	Paul Willis: Transition from School to Work Bibliography	15p
28.	Brian Roberts: Parent & Youth Cultures	20p
29.	Chas Critcher: Football Since the War: Study in Social Change & Popular Culture	25p

Now Available

CCS Pamphlet No.1

Forthcoming

Allon White: Exposition & Critique of Julia Kristeva
State Group: Poulantzas' Theory of the State.

Bibliography

1. *Coaching for Improved Work Performance*, Ferdinand Fournies, 2003

2. *Coaching Skills Workshop*, Intel Corporation, 2001

3. *The Leadership Challenge*, Kouzes and Posner, Jossey-Bass, 2007

4. *Performance Management*, Robert Bacal, McGraw-Hill, 2005

5. *The Role of Supervisor*, Nick Leforce, Los Rios Community College District, 2004

6. *Constructive Confrontation*, Intel University, 2003

7. *Expert OJT Workshop: SMART Job Aids*, Jeff Nelson, 2003

8. *The 21st Century Supervisor: Nine Essential Skills for Frontline Leaders*, Humphrey & Stokes, Jossey-Bass, 2000

Author Bios

Dennis Wade (dennis@ppldev.com) has been involved in private and public employee development for over 20 years in the greater Sacramento area. His experience in Human Resources Development, Information Technology, and Intel Corporation management prepared him to work with Robert Mondavi, Affymetrix, CalPERS, Caltrans, UC Davis Health System, RagingWire and other Northern California organizations in the areas of team development, customer service, management/leadership, and structured on-the-job training.

A graduate of UC Davis, he also has a master's degree in Human Resources and Organization Development from the University of San Francisco. He is certified in Bob Mager's Criterion Referenced Instruction, William Bridges' Transitions, Jeffrey Nelson's Expert OJT, and Achieve Global's Leadership for Results.

Dennis firmly believes that training is not the only answer to employee development. It is a major component in a systematic approach that includes employee integration, coaching, OJT, feedback, and connection to specific organizational objectives.

He lives in the Sacramento area with his wife of 35 years.

Tyler Wade (tyler@ppldev.com) spent nine years in the "win-lose" world of California politics before moving on to the positive, collaborative, "win-win" world of workplace learning and performance.

His greatest thrill as a people developer is the "Aha! Moment"—that moment of clarity when some additional understanding, wisdom, or recognition brings learning home.

Tyler has a master's degree in Public Policy from Pepperdine University.

He lives in the Sacramento area with his wife and two sons.